TEARS IN THE DARKNESS

The Story of

the Bataan Death March

and Its Aftermath

TEARS IN THE DARKNESS

MICHAEL NORMAN

and ELIZABETH M. NORMAN

Farrar, Straus and Giroux • New York

Farrar, Straus and Giroux

18 West 18th Street, New York 10011

Copyright © 2009 by Michael Norman and Elizabeth M. Norman

Map copyright © 2009 by Jeffrey L. Ward

All rights reserved

Distributed in Canada by Douglas & McIntyre Ltd.

Printed in the United States of America

First edition, 2009

Grateful acknowledgment is made for permission to reprint lyrics from "Red Sails in the Sunset," written by Jimmy Kennedy and Hugh Williams. Used by permission of Shapiro, Bernstein & Co., Inc. All Rights Reserved. International Copyright Secured.

Library of Congress Cataloging-in-Publication Data

Norman, Michael, 1947 Oct. 2–

    Tears in the darkness : the story of the Bataan Death March and its aftermath / Michael Norman and Elizabeth M. Norman.— 1st ed.

      p. cm.

    Includes bibliographical references and index.

    ISBN-13: 978-0-374-27260-9 (hardcover : alk. paper)

    ISBN-10: 0-374-27260-3 (hardcover : alk. paper)

    1. Bataan Death March, Philippines, 1942.   2. World War, 1939–1945—Prisoners and prisons, Japanese.   3. Prisoners of war—United States—History—20th century.   4. Prisoners of war— Philippines—History—20th century.   5. Prisoners of war—Great Britain—History—20th century. 6. Prisoners of war—Netherlands—History—20th century.   I. Norman, Elizabeth M.   II. Title.

D805.P6 N67 2009

940.54'7252095991—dc22

2008047163

Designed by Abby Kagan

www.fsgbooks.com

1   3   5   7   9   10   8   6   4   2

FOR

JOSHUA

AND

BENJAMIN

I am very calm. Let the months come, and the years, they'll

take nothing more from me, they *can* take nothing more from me.

—Erich Maria Remarque,

All Quiet on the Western Front

CONTENTS

CONTENTS

Camp O'Donnell

Capas

Cabanatuan

LUZON ISLAND
MANILA, BATAAN, AND ENVIRONS

Zambales Mountains

Mt. Arayat

San Miguel

CLARK FIELD   Angeles

San Fernando

Baliuag

Calumpit

Dinalupihan

Olangapo

Subic Bay

Hermosa

Orani

Samal

BATAAN PENINSULA   *Mt. Natib*

Abucay

Bataan Peak

Balanga   Pilar

Morong

Orion

Pantingan River

Manila Bay

Bagac

Mariveles Mountain

Limay

Lamao

Quinauan Point   Mariveles   Cabcaben

Manila

NICHOLS FIELD

Cavite

Laguna de Bay

Corregidor Island

South China Sea

To Tayabas Road

0 Miles   10   20

0 Kilometers   20

N

© 2009 Jeffrey L. Ward

THE TITLE of this book comes from a literal translation of the ideograph, or kanji, for the Japanese word *anrui* (on-RUE-ee).

The word and the image it conveys are meant to explain the kind of pain and sorrow that, literally, cannot be seen. Among English idioms, the metaphor that best expresses this is "a broken heart."

It is true that some men—men of greed, ambition, or raw animus— love war, but most, the overwhelming number who are forced to bear arms, come home from the killing fields and prison camps with *anrui*, "tears in the darkness."

THE DRAWINGS that appear throughout the book are taken from the sketchbooks of Ben Steele and were made during his six decades as an artist and teacher in Billings, Montana.

TEARS IN THE DARKNESS

GHOSTS

THEY WERE STATIONED far from home when the fighting started—seven thousand miles across the Pacific from San Francisco in a large archipelago that stretches north and south for a thousand miles between Formosa and the Dutch East Indies in the warm tropical waters of the South China Sea.

Compared to some of its neighbors, the Philippines, an American possession since 1898, was a bit of a backwater. None of Singapore's sparkle or the hustle of Hong Kong, but the guidebooks of the day called the place "paradise," and the books were right. Manila was beautiful, palms leaning gently over the seawall along the bay, the night filled with the sweet scent of kamias.

Besides its charms, paradise had the best deep-water port in the southwest Pacific, and in 1941 that port, that strategic transit point, made the Philippines valuable to the Japanese and American generals and admirals who were furiously preparing for war, a war in the Pacific almost everyone in uniform believed was at hand.

On December 8, eight hours after it attacked the American Pacific Fleet at Pearl Harbor, Japan sent its bombers and fighters against American air, infantry, and naval bases in the Philippines. Two weeks later, 43,000 Japanese troops invaded the islands.

Waiting for them was a large force of American and Filipino defenders, more than 130,000 men, untried and ill trained, most of them. The Japanese pushed them back and back again until they were forced to retreat to a small thumb of land on the west coast of Manila Bay, the peninsula of Bataan.

There, in jungle wastes and tangled woodlands, they dug trench lines and bunkers, an army of Americans and Filipinos preparing to fight for their lives, the first major land battle for America in World War II.

Starting in January 1942, the Japanese took the peninsula under siege and left the Americans and Filipinos cut off from all help and supplies. The two sides fought for ninety-nine days, the Japanese taking horrendous casualties, the Americans and Filipinos falling back under the Japanese assaults from one "final" defense line to another. At last, on April 9, sick and starving, without an air force to protect them or a navy to relieve them, the men of Bataan surrendered.

More than 76,000 Americans and Filipinos under American command laid down their arms—the single largest defeat in American military history. The sick, starving, and bedraggled prisoners of war were rounded up by their Japanese captors and made to walk sixty-six miles to a railhead for the trip to prison camp, a baneful walk under a broiling sun that turned into one of most notorious treks in the annals of war, the Bataan Death March.

It is impossible, so the locals say, to walk the ground where this story takes place, the jungles and woodlands and savannas of the Philippines, without feeling the presence, the lingering tenancy, of the men who once fought there—Americans, Filipinos, Japanese. Perhaps that is why at night, Bataanese villagers in their nipa huts often think they hear history stumbling along in the darkness outside their doors.

Some nights it is voices they hear, voices begging for food and water, voices pleading for their lives. Other nights it is the sound of shuffling feet, thousands of feet heavy with fear and fatigue, dragging north through the dust mile after mile up the Old National Road.

All of this is memory, of course, the memory of the old ones who lived along the route, or their children and children's children who tell and retell the stories of Bataan as if they were reciting from sacred texts.

As the events of 1941-1942 passed into the hands of historians, both the battle for Bataan and the death march became symbols, the former as a modern Thermopylae, a stirring last stand, and the latter as a crucible of courage, the courage to continue on a walk to the grave.

In some sense these conceits were true, but when the dross of propaganda and myth is skimmed from the surface of history, what's left, in this case, is an example of the miscarried morality and Punic politics that underlie every appeal to arms—the bad leadership, the empty promises, the kind of cruelty that crushes men's souls. Proof too that the instant the first shot is fired, the so-called rules of war, *guerre de règle*, give way to *guerre à outrance*, war without clemency or quarter.

So much suffering leaves any piece of ground spectral. Little wonder, then, the locals along the road hear voices, and the survivors of that battle and march, old men now, keep the company of ghosts.

BEN STEELE came of age as a cowboy, or an echo of a cowboy, which in his time, the early decades of the twentieth century, was probably the same thing. He grew up in a pine-log house by a crystal spring in the shadow of the Bull Mountains on Montana's eastern plain. By the time he was eight he could ride, rope, and shoot. He herded cattle, he drove horses, he tended sheep. Alone at night on the open range he slept in a circle of rope to keep the snakes out of his bedroll. In 1940, just before his twenty-third birthday, he joined the Army Air Corps and was shipped to the Philippines to fight the Japanese. After ninety-nine days of battle he became a prisoner of war and spent three years behind barbed wire and watchtowers. Every day he was starved or beaten by his keepers: "the Bug," "Mickey Mouse," "the Killer." He never forgot those faces. They insinuated themselves in his psyche, permanent residents now, along with wild mustangs, sheepherders, ambling cowboys, and antelope gamboling through the sage. This is all in his sketchbooks.

THE SKETCHBOOKS are stacked on shelves and in closets, black buckram and hardbound, most of them. They date from his first days in art school, more than thirty volumes of trials and exercises—sixty-one years of sketching and painting every day, searching for the perfect line, the exact color, the proper balance and emphasis, proportion and perspective. At ninety years plus, a lifetime of trying, as artists say of their work, to "get the thing right."

On occasion he works from models in a studio or tramps out to the prairie to sketch a scene. He likes to draw horses. He hasn't been on a horse in nearly twenty-five years, but his respect and affection for the animals run deep, back to the blizzards of his boyhood when his horse would lead him through a blinding whiteout back to the safety and warmth of the pine-log house at Hawk Creek.

By and large, however, the leaves of his sketchbooks hold his ghosts:

page after page of prisoners of war and the Imperial *hohei* who guarded them, the men who held Ben Steele captive for one thousand two hundred and forty-four days.[1]

He cannot say why after six decades he still sketches the faces that followed him home from the camps, the faces of old comrades in prison rags, and the faces of the Japanese soldiers who herded them from place to place and kept them penned behind barbed wire.

These ghosts pop up everywhere in his sketchbooks, sometimes like rogues in a gallery but as often as not singly in quick profile or thumbnail, sometimes on the same page with bucking mustangs and cow ponies or, like interlopers, peering in from the edges of landscapes, intruding on the cottonwoods and sage.

In the early sketchbooks, the ones he filled after the war while attending college and during his first decade as a professor of art, the drawings of his keepers and his comrades tend to be imitative, realistic, the faces filled with the meanness and misery of war, as if the artist's aim was to document his experience.

After a certain point, however—ten years postbattle, perhaps fifteen—the drawings become simpler, less emotive. No longer are the faces rendered with the kind of shading and crosshatching that create tone and mood. Most are simple line drawings in pen-and-ink, quirky enough to qualify as caricature. In his later work the prisoners look more hapless than hopeless, hoboes in bedraggled dress, and the guards appear more often than not as comic grotesques, a little lunatic or just plain goofy.

This is "perspective and proportion" of a different sort, and it has nothing to do with either the geometry or the grammar of art. Ben Steele, brown eyes aglint, almost always wears a smile, like a man who knows he finally "got the thing right."

ONE

HE ENLISTED on the advice of his mother, Bess.

In the late summer of 1940, Ben Steele was working as a camp tender at a large sheep outfit east of town. It was hard, sometimes filthy work, but the freedom of it made him happy—on his own every day, riding a horse or driving a rig between the far-flung camps of the sheepherders, delivering mail and supplies, sleeping in the open, wrapped in an oilcloth, staring up at a big sky dark with bright stars.

One weekend that summer Ben Steele's mother and father drove out from Billings to visit. His mother had an idea. He'd been a ranch hand most of his life, she said. He was twenty-two now, grown up. Maybe it was time to consider something else. She'd heard on the radio that President Franklin D. Roosevelt had just signed a law creating the first peacetime military draft. The inaugural call-up, she said, was scheduled for late October.[1]

"You know, I've been thinking," she went on. "You really ought to get in before they draft you. Maybe if you do, you could, you know, do what you want in the army?"

He wasn't sure he wanted to wear a uniform, but since he usually took his mother's advice to heart, he tucked her suggestion away, and a while later, over a smoky campfire perhaps or riding the green hills and valleys, he remembered something; the boys he knew from Billings who had enlisted in the army were usually sent west for training to the golden valleys of California.

He thought, "Going to California—that sounds good. A little adventure." And on a nice warm day in mid-September, he borrowed a car, went into town, ambled over to the Stapleton Building on Twenty-eighth Street and into the recruiting station there, where he found a sergeant sitting at a desk.

"I want to go into the army," he announced.

"Well now," the recruiter said, looking up at the lean ranch hand standing in front of him, "we have the Army and we have the Army Air Corps, which one you want?"

Ben Steele knew nothing about soldiering, but some years earlier a couple of fellows up at the Billings Municipal Airport got themselves a Ford Tri-Motor (a propeller under each wing and one on the nose) and for a dollar a head started taking people for a ride. It wasn't much of a ride—the plane took off from atop the rimrocks, circled the Yellowstone Valley below, and a few minutes later landed to pick up another load of wide-eyed locals. But that short hop stirred something in Ben Steele.

"The Air Corps?" he said. "That sounds real good. Give me that!"

A few weeks later, on October 9, 1940, a month shy of his twenty-third birthday, Ben Steele stood in a line of enlistees at the United States Courthouse in Missoula, Montana, raised his right hand, and repeated one of the republic's oldest oaths: "I do solemnly swear that I will support and defend the Constitution of the United States against all enemies, foreign or domestic . . . So help me God."

LIKE EVERYONE ELSE, like every American who read the newspapers, listened to the radio, went to the movies, and watched newsreels, Private Ben Steele of the United States Army Air Corps was convinced his enemies would be German. Japan was a threat, all right—that fall, in fact, America cut its shipments of scrap steel and iron to Japan—but Germany, threatening all Europe, was the menace of the moment.[2]

The Germans had invaded Poland, Denmark, Norway, Belgium, the Netherlands, and France. By the time Ben Steele arrived at the induction station in Missoula in the fall of 1940, the German Luftwaffe had been bombing Great Britain for three months.

Reading about all this in the *Billings Gazette* or listening to it on KGHL radio, the most popular station in that part of the West, most Montanans wanted no part of the trouble overseas. Like the rest of America, they were focused on finding jobs and recovering from the Great Depression, not crossing swords with the saber-rattling Germans. In a national opinion poll conducted the week Ben Steele enlisted, 83 percent of the those surveyed said they did not want to send American troops overseas.[3]

Young men looking for a job or a little adventure don't pay much attention to opinion polls. The army was offering a paycheck, plus "three hots and a cot" and perhaps a chance to travel. Since they had no feel for the killing and dying in Europe, no sense at all of facing Panzer tanks and Stuka dive-bombers, the ranch hands, soda jerks, delivery boys, and railroad workers on their way to training camp with Ben Steele were full of brio and eager for action.

"If war's gonna come, I wanna be in it," Ben Steele thought. "Hell, I want to be over there where it's happening."

Saturday, October 4, 1941, San Francisco
Blue sky, bright sun, seventy-two degrees, a good day to set sail for paradise.

On a pier off the Embarcadero, the men of the 19th Bombardment Group, United States Army Air Corps, waited in long queues to board the United States Army transport *General Willard A. Holbrook*, a lumbering troopship used to ferry men and matériel to American bases overseas. In the ranks on the wharf, moving slowly toward the gangway, was Benjamin Charles Steele, serial number 190-18-989, a newly minted private. He had been in uniform nearly a year now, and he liked the life of a soldier. The army had given him just what he wanted, a chance to cross the mountains and see the Golden Land.

California wasn't as golden as he'd imagined, but he liked it well enough. Training camp was a dusty tent city on the dry brown flats at March Field near Riverside. The boys from the cities and suburbs thought these accommodations "kinda primitive," but the men who had been ranch-raised looked around and saw luxury: tents with wooden floors and gas stoves, hot showers nearby, latrines that weren't buzzing with flies, and a mess hall that served seconds if a man wasn't sated.

Air Corps basic training was short, just six weeks, long enough for men who would be working as airplane mechanics, gunners, ground crews, and supernumeraries. They attended classes on military courtesy and discipline. They reviewed army rules and regulations. They endured hours of close-order drill and the ritual of forced marches.

These little walks, as Ben Steele thought of them, were too much for many of the men. After one eight-mile hike the road was lined with recruits doubled over, gasping for breath and grousing about their training. Ben Steele had never heard such bellyaching.

"Holy Christ!" he said, to no one in particular. "Eight miles is nothing. Back home I'd walk that far before breakfast."

"Oh yeah?" one of the malcontents came back. "Where the hell did you come from?"

"I'm from Montana," Ben Steele said.

THE ARMY sent him to New Mexico after basic training and assigned him to the 7th Matériel Squadron, 19th Bombardment Group, Kirtland Field, Albuquerque. As soon as he was settled, he made inquiries about buying a horse.

A local stockman wanted fifty bucks for an old plug named Blaze. Not much of a horse, nothing like the spirited animals he was used to, but he missed riding, so he went to a finance company, borrowed the money (agreeing to pay five dollars a week against the balance), and made a deal with a nearby rancher to pasture his mount. His father shipped him a saddle, and every weekend Ben Steele rode out among the cactus and scrub grass. It was hot, sandy country but he didn't care— he was on a horse, and a horse reminded him of home.

The Air Corps made him a dispatcher, tracking flights, and after a month or two of this work he got it in his head that he wanted to be a pilot. Never much of a student, he found a math professor at the University of New Mexico to tutor him privately in the algebra and geometry that he would need to pass the exam to become a cadet. He studied for several months and was about to take the test when word came down that the 19th Bombardment Group was being sent overseas.

"You can't ship me out," he told his commanding officer. "I'm fixing to take the cadet exam."

"Oh yeah, we can," the squadron commander said. "The whole outfit's goin'."

October 3, 1941
Dearest Mother and Family,
Thought would drop you a few more lines before departing the U.S.
Am sailing tomorrow afternoon . . . We don't know for sure how long we
will have to stay in foreign service but hope it isn't too long, but it may be

*alright . . . Will write you every chance I get so you will know about where
I am at . . . Just heard we were going to the Philippines, but that is just a
rumor not certain. Can't believe a thing you hear around here . . . Don't
worry about anything, because everything is O.K. Will write as soon as I
can make connections. It is possible we will stop at some port along the way,
and if we do will send you a line.*

Lots of Love to you all
Bud.

AMERICA REMEMBERS the attacks on its bases in the Pacific in 1941 as
acts of treachery, but to label them "sneak" attacks is more propaganda
than plain truth. For more than twenty years, a standing committee of
admirals and generals in Washington had been planning against just such
an attack. They looked at Japan as America's chief antagonist in the Pacific, and they knew well the value of surprise and Japan's history of success with this tactic. The military planners were sure that when war came,
it would begin "with a sudden, surprise attack." They did not know exactly where or precisely when, but they were convinced that the Philippines, just eighteen hundred air miles from Japan and sitting directly
between it and the oil- and mineral-rich Indonesian archipelago in
the southwest Pacific, would top Japan's list of targets. So in the early
fall of 1941, with war consuming Europe and with the Japanese Army
on the march in Asia, American war planners—more in an attempt to
deter an attack than defend against it—began to rush cannon, tanks, airplanes, and men to the Philippine Islands. The men of the 19th Bombardment Group, United States Army Air Corps, were part of that
consignment.[4]

The *Holbrook* set sail on the evening tide that October 4. In the ship's
galley cooks had prepared a greasy ragout of pork, and as the men passed
through the mess line, stewards slopped the dinner on their trays. Later that
night the wind picked up, the waves began to swell and the *Holbrook* began
to pitch and roll, and it wasn't long before all that greasy pork began to
reappear. Soon the crappers were clogged and the sinks were overflowing.

October 10, 1941
Dearest Mother and Family,
*Have been sitting out on the deck this morning watching flying fish. They
are about six inches long and sail through the air like a bird . . . The water*

has been sort of rough all the way . . . The ship is bobbing up and down and from one side to the other till I can't even sit still. Am sitting here on the deck and writing on my knee. Hope you can read this.

AFTER HAWAII, the sailing was easy, flat water most of the way and light tropical breezes. Most men spent mornings topside, watching the water or staring at the horizon, absorbed by the vast vista of the sea. Some played cards on the hatch covers or spread out their towels and baked in the afternoon sun. In the evenings Quentin Pershing Devore of eastern Colorado came topside to listen to his Hallicrafter shortwave radio. One evening a dark-haired fellow with a friendly face eased over and sat down next to him.

"I'm Ben Steele," he said, holding out his hand.

"I'm Pershing Devore."

"What do you get on that thing?" the fellow asked.

"I get the news, sometimes I get music," Devore said.

Devore too had grown up outdoors, working the land and livestock in the rye- and wheat-farming country of Yuma County, a day's drive or so from the Nebraska border. He considered himself "a plain boy with no frills," and that's how this fellow from Billings struck him, too, "real plain."

"Where did you get that name, Pershing?" Ben Steele asked.

"Well, my name is Quentin Pershing Devore, but they call me Pershing."

"That's too complicated," Ben Steele said. "I'm just going to call you Q.P."[5]

October 18, 1941
Dearest Mother, Dad + Family,
Met a new friend. He likes hunting and fishing about as well as I do. We get together and talk over old times. It sort of makes me feel at home . . .

They talked for hours, about farming and ranching and cattle and sheep, about the "hard-up" life on a Colorado farm and the hardscrabble days on a Montana homestead. Ben Steele often turned the conversation to horses—cow ponies, broncs and quarter horses, chestnuts, Appaloosas and bays.

Q.P. thought, "This guy is crazy about horses."

They talked about war as well. Their convoy was flanked by destroyer escorts, and at night the ship was blacked out, a shadow on the sea.

A week and a half out of Hawaii, their company commander called them together. They were going to the Philippines "to fight a war," he said.

Thursday, October 23, 1941, Pier 7, Manila, Philippines
Assembled on deck, the thirteen hundred soldiers of the 19th Bombardment Group were preparing to greet paradise. Down the pier a line of trucks was waiting to take them north to their billets at Clark Field, a lattice of sand-and-turf runways laid out on a hot, dry plain fifty miles northwest of Manila. As the young Americans made their way down the gangways and ladders to the queue of open trucks, they were wide-eyed with wonder and delight.

October 24, 1941
Was sure glad to get off the boat after being on it for so long. We were as dirty as a bunch of hogs when we landed.

It is sure interesting around here . . . The natives are as thick as bees . . . and live in little bamboo shacks . . . Drive little horses about the size of a good sized dog, hitched to a little cart. Some have oxen [carabao] hitched to old wooden wheeled carts, sure is interesting to watch them . . . They are always trying to sell us something. They are running from one barracks to the other trying to get a job making our beds, and shining our shoes . . . Would hate to think I was so lazy I couldn't make my own bed. We have to have mosquito nets over our beds at night so we can sleep. The mosquitoes here are like humming birds . . .

Don't worry about me because I never felt better in my life, and am having a swell time. So please <u>don't worry</u>. This will be one of the greatest experiences of my life.

FOR DECADES the Philippines had been a backwater post, a collecting pool for those on the way up, young officers eager to get their tickets punched for promotion, and those on the way out—the deadwood, the drunks, the disappointed who had been passed over for rank and were now holed up in a quiet billet, waiting to put in their papers and take a last parade.

It was a gorgeous backwater. Manila was known as "the Pearl of the

Orient," and parts of the city, especially the precincts where Americans and Europeans lived and worked, looked like arboretums. Along the boulevards, the trees were trimmed and ringed with pink hydrangeas, and white butterfly orchids grew in the coconut husks.

The duty was easy too, inspections and formations for the most part, then at noon, the workday ended and the enlisted men would head for the beaches and ball fields and brothels of the nearest barrio where they would "shack up" with their "brown-skinned squaws," their Filipina concubines. Life had its annoyances, of course—the soaking summer monsoons, the suffocating heat of the hot season, the incessant insects, the choking dust—but for less than a dollar, a trooper could buy enough Ginebra gin and San Miguel beer to drink himself senseless.

The officers lived like aristocracy. They played polo, tennis, and golf, then made for their private preserve, Manila's fabled Army and Navy Club, a three-acre toft and croft along the east shore of Manila Bay that looked like a beaux arts mansion set on a waterfront green of palms, flame trees, and bougainvillea. The club hosted dinners and soirees, women and their escorts dancing under the stars and toasting one another over centerpieces of yellow trumpet flowers and white Cadena de Amor. First, and above all, however, the Army and Navy Club was a men's club, and the men of the Philippine garrison and Asiatic Fleet liked to drink.

Almost every officer in the islands bellied up to the club's long polished bar—pilots, tankers, artillerymen, chasseurs, submariners, marines—but none more frequently than the gentlemen of the 31st Infantry, the only "all-American" army regiment in the islands.

> We are boys from the Thirty-first
> We are not so very meek
> We never wash behind our ears
> And seldom wash our feet.
> Oh we're below the scum of the earth
> And we're always looking for booze
> Now we're the boys from the Thirty-first
> And who in the hell are youse![6]

That was garrison life.

Then—it seemed to happen so fast—those unhurried mornings, sul-

try afternoons, and sybaritic nights were interrupted by an irritating interloper: the Japanese.

Nippon had been on the march in Asia. In 1931 the Imperial Army occupied Manchuria; in 1937 that same army, reinforced, moved south to invade northern China; in 1940 Japan pushed into lower Asia and stationed troops in upper Indochina. To the Roosevelt administration, the Japanese now appeared ready to move against the Dutch East Indies, islands and archipelagoes rich with tin, rubber, oil. Convinced that America would soon be fighting in Europe, the president wanted to avoid a two-front war, and he decided to impose economic sanctions on Japan, hoping to get them to pull back, perhaps even declare a cease-fire in China. He withheld the carrot, then in the early winter of 1940 he started to show them the stick.

America's military planners began marshaling reinforcements for the Philippines. They knew they could never make the islands a redoubt—Japan, with millions of men under arms, could easily overwhelm any garrison—but, as the thinking went, the new defenses, especially a new long-range B-17 bomber, might deter the Japanese, make them reconsider the cost of attacking the Philippines. If not, then the presence of reinforcements might at least make them pause long enough for the garrison to ready itself to receive the blow.

In the late spring 1941, the wives and children of American servicemen were ordered to evacuate the islands and sail for home. In July the president recalled General Douglas MacArthur from retirement (he had been serving as a military adviser to the Philippine Commonwealth government since 1935) and named him commander of United States Army Forces in the Far East. The same month the Commonwealth government mobilized the tens of thousands of reservists that made up the Philippine Army. In September, American troop ships and freighters began to arrive regularly at Pier 7. By the end of November, the U.S. Army garrison had been increased to nearly 31,000 troops (19,000 Americans, 12,000 Philippine Scouts), triple its original strength. Almost immediately thereafter MacArthur ordered beach defenses dug and manned by the Philippine Army at the most likely landing spots on the main island of Luzon.

November 9, 1941
Dearest Mother, Dad and Family:
. . . Well I suppose you have been reading the head lines about the U.S. and Japan, but don't get excited. Can just see you running around worrying yourself sick. Of course we don't hear much about it. I think we are safe. We get some of the news and there is a lot we don't get.

The workday was longer now as men and machinery moved north and south from the piers and warehouses of Manila. Days carried the din of hammering and sawing, nights the rumble and whine of trucks on the roads. The polo fields were often empty, the tennis courts quiet. Some evenings the bar girls at Cavite's Dreamland Cabaret ("Call us ballerinas, please!" the taxi dancers insisted) toured the dance floor alone or in one another's arms.

And yet there was still an air of assurance in the islands, a sense that the latest alarm or clarion call would pass without incident and paradise would soon be paradise again. Intelligence reports about Japanese troop movements arrived daily at headquarters, but the majority of officers under MacArthur's command had convinced themselves "it would be absolutely impossible for the Japanese to attack the Philippine Islands successfully!" Japan, they reasoned "had everything to lose by going to war and nothing to gain."[7]

So they went about preparing for war with little sense of urgency or imminence. And this strange stupor, this "weakness," as Colonel Ernest B. Miller, a tank commander from Brainard Minnesota, saw it, led to "things left undone," so many things that even in the end, "with the black clouds of war directly overhead, it was well nigh impossible to quicken the tempo" of the work.[8]

And why should they? General MacArthur had told his officers that intelligence reports on "the existing alignment and movement of Japanese troops" had convinced him that if Japan, in fact, attacked, it would not do so until the spring of 1942, April at the earliest. Many of his subordinates disagreed, but there was no arguing with the general. The enemy, he insisted, wasn't coming till spring.[9]

Japan wasn't much of an enemy either, or so the Americans believed. For more than a century whites in Asia had looked on the tawny "locals" as less than human. They thought the Japanese "monkey men"—short, slight, bucktoothed, "slant-eyed sons of bitches" who "couldn't see straight," even through their horn-rimmed glasses, because, as everyone knew, "their eyeballs didn't open up to the proper diameter." An enemy who could not see straight could not shoot straight, could not keep his planes on course or drop his bombs on target. The war wouldn't last three weeks, they told one another. "We'll knock the living shit out of them."[10]

Even at General MacArthur's headquarters, where war planning should have sent up a din, "men went about their work as usual." On the evening of December 5, for example, MacArthur's clerk, Paul Rogers, settled himself in a seat at the Manila Symphony and enjoyed a program of Mozart.[11]

And it didn't take long for the young enlistees and reservists fresh from the States to assume that same attitude of indifference. To be sure, there were a few who went against the tide, officers who'd come to the islands "to soldier," as they put it, professionals who now bridled at being part of "a military force afflicted" with "siesta-itis," but their complaints were lost in the laughter around the bar and the sighs coming out of the seraglios.[12]

Monday, December 8, 1941 (December 7 across the International Dateline),
Manila, Philippines

Frank Hewlett, a United Press wire service reporter, got the cable from a colleague in Hawaii around 2:00 a.m. local time. Stunned and looking for official confirmation, Hewlett quickly called the office of Admiral Thomas C. Hart, commander of the Asiatic Fleet. At Fleet Headquarters in Manila, a duty officer answered the phone. Hewlett read him the cable: "Flash! Pearl Harbor under aerial attack."

What did he mean, under attack? The man at Fleet HQ thought Hewlett was goading him. He was tired and in no mood for another "Jap joke."

"Tell your Pearl Harbor correspondent to go back to bed and sleep it off," he told Hewlett, then hung up.[13]

At the same time, across Manila Bay at the Cavite Naval Base, Seaman Second Class Frank Bigelow, a tall, lean message clerk from Pleasant Lake, North Dakota, stumbled aboard the submarine tender USS *Canopus* tied up at a wharf. Bigelow had been out drinking and "catting around" with the local amourettes at one of many brothels in nearby Cavite City. Now, "about half drunk," he crawled up into his bunk and was just about to drift off when another sailor came running into the compartment.[14]

"They're bombing Pearl Harbor!" the man shouted. "They're bombing Pearl Harbor!"

Bigelow didn't believe him and turned his face to the bulkhead to sleep.

The first public word of the attack came over KZRH commercial radio sometime after 2:30 a.m. A short while later, MacArthur and Admiral Hart alerted their commands, but the officers, for the most part, did not tell the men in the ranks until they awoke for breakfast.

North of Cavite and Manila, some fifty miles up the dusty main highway, was Fort Stotsenberg, an army base adjacent to Clark Field. At the nurses' quarters near the fort hospital, the women had just settled themselves down in the mess to their fruit, eggs, rolls, and coffee when someone reached up and switched on a radio and the familiar staccato of announcer Don Bell started to issue from the box.

"Hey, listen to that!" one of the women said. "They're having a war in Hawaii. And here we are in the Philippines, and we're going to be left out of it."[15]

Less than two miles away, on a road just east of Clark Field, Corporal Zoeth Skinner of Portland, Oregon, part of a five-man crew in a half-track, a kind of tank without a top, was parked in the sun at the side of the highway. The tank battalions had a complement of half-tracks to cover their flanks and scout their points, and for several days the battalions had been on "maneuvers" near the field. In fact they had been deployed to protect the airplanes, but the crews thought they were on another pointless exercise. Then their platoon commander rolled up on a motorcycle.

"Hey, fellas!" He was excited. "The war's started. They've bombed Pearl Harbor!"

Then he roared off.

"Aw, that's just part of the maneuvers," one of the men said.[16]

West of the road, across acres of bamboo and sugarcane, sat airplane hangars and barracks for the ground crews at Clark Field, among them the men of the 19th Bombardment Group. At morning chow an officer had climbed up on a chair and announced: "We've been attacked by the Japanese at Pearl Harbor, but there is no word yet on the extent of the damage."

Maybe "it wasn't all that bad," Ben Steele thought. Then, throughout the morning each new report brought a few more details: battleships had been hit, sunk, or badly disabled; casualties were rumored to be high; there was talk that the country's formidable Pacific Fleet had been hard hit, perhaps crippled.

The men at Clark Field could "hardly believe" what they were hearing. They had not expected war to "start so soon" or the enemy to sally that far from home.

It just didn't seem real. Shocking, perhaps, but not real, a war without pain or pounding fear, far away, five thousand miles to the east. So the men at Clark Field went to work. The flight crews reported to the flight line, the armorers to the armory, the pilots to their planes. And they waited. They waited and watched the sky. Seven o'clock, seven thirty, still nothing.

They were also waiting for word to strike back. Air Corps commanders in the Philippines knew from intelligence reports that Japanese Army and Navy bombers would likely come at them from Japanese bases on Formosa, five hundred miles due north. And Major General Lewis H. Brereton, the commander of the Far East Air Force, and his staff had been prepared since November 27 (the day Washington warned all commanders in the Pacific that it believed Japan was ready to go to war) to bomb the Formosan airfields or the harbor at Takao, the likely place the Japanese would gather an invasion force.

To his staff, Brereton was "a square-rigged, stout-hulled believer in action." Earlier that morning, after he had learned of the attack on Pearl Harbor, he had rushed to MacArthur's headquarters at One Calle Victoria in Manila and asked permission to arm and launch the nineteen new B-17 bombers of the 19th Bombardment Group standing by at Clark Field.[17]

MacArthur's chief of staff, Major General Richard Sutherland, told Brereton to wait for MacArthur's approval. Brereton went back to Air Corps headquarters at Nielson Field and sat. And sat. At seven fifteen he could sit no more and returned to headquarters. Again Sutherland told the Air Corps commander, wait.

AT CLARK FIELD, Ben Steele and his Air Corps comrades wanted to hit the Japanese on Formosa before the Japanese came at them. Most of all they wanted to get their bombers and fighters off the ground, where they were the most exposed and vulnerable.

Word had come down that the Air Corps planes at Hickam Field in Hawaii had been parked wingtip to wingtip, an easy target for Japanese bombardiers. Enraged by the folly at Hickam, the Air Corps chief in Washington, Major General Henry H. Arnold, had called General Brereton in the Philippines and warned him not to make the same mistake at Clark.

Sometime between 8:00 and 9:00 a.m., Major David R. Gibbs, the acting bomb-group commander at Clark, was handed an alert: enemy planes had been spotted over Lingayen Gulf northwest of Clark Field, headed toward Manila. Fearing Clark might be their target, Gibbs immediately ordered the squadrons of bombers into the air, but without bombs. MacArthur still had not given his permission to arm the planes for an attack on Formosa, so the bomber pilots were told to cruise high overhead.

At last, around 11:00 a.m., MacArthur authorized a reconnaissance flight over Formosa to be followed by bombing missions later that afternoon, and the bombers from Clark were immediately recalled to arm them for the mission. The squadrons of pursuit fighters that had been flying protective cover over Manila and other parts of Luzon that morning were also brought down to refuel. By 11:30 most American warplanes in the Philippines were on the ground, being serviced and readied to take off again.

After the crews and pilots at Clark Field finished this work, they went to lunch in shifts. Some of the aircraft were properly protected behind revetments, others dispersed, but many, too many, were parked in neat rows in the open on their ready lines, noses to the runway. From above they looked like toys on a large lawn, silver toys perfectly outlined against the greensward of Luzon's wide central plain.[18]

December 8, 1941, 11:00 a.m., 19,000 feet somewhere over the South China Sea
in the cockpit of an Imperial Navy A6M2 Zero fighter
It was not a lonely impulse of delight that had sent Saburō Sakai aloft to make tumult in the clouds. It was duty, a sense of obligation born of both politics and myth.

The myth begins in heaven before the world was the world. Looking down one day, the celestial kami (gods) created a new domain: the Eight Great Islands at the Center Of The World, a misty land of emerald hills and jade valleys known to moderns as Dai Nippon, great Japan.

The rest of the earth, so the Shinto myth goes, was mere matter, seafoam and mud, but Nippon, the issue of the gods, was sacred soil, superior to all other lands, the aegis of Amaterasu, the goddess of the sun.

Amaterasu sent her grandson, Ninigi no Mikoto, to consolidate her domain, then she named her great-great-grandson, Jimmu Tenno, to rule there. By heavenly charge he became "emperor," the first of Amaterasu's earthly line. Grateful for the appointment, Jimmu Tenno made his "illustrious" foremother a promise: he and his semidivine seed would extend the rule of heaven "to embrace" the entire earth. *Hakko-ichi-u,* "the world under one roof," they called it, the plan of a people blessed by heaven and ruled by the descendants of the goddess of the sun.[19]

The myth of Amaterasu instilled in the Japanese an unfaltering feeling of uniqueness, *Yamato-damashi,* "the spirit of being Japanese." The feeling, more powerful than any sense of self, stirred every Nipponjin, especially Japan's fighting men, men like Petty Officer First Class Saburō Sakai.

The twenty-five-year-old Imperial Navy fighter pilot, flying south with a squadron of Mitsubishi Zeros on the late morning of December 8, 1941, marveled at his luck. It was a perfect day for an attack, bright sun, clear sky.[20]

Just before 11:30 a.m., Sakai looked down and saw "the Philippine

Islands hove into view, a deep green against the rich blue of the ocean." Then "the coastline slipped beneath" him, "beautiful and peaceful."[21]

It was the opening hours of what the Japanese would call "the Greater East Asian War" or "the Great Pacific War." The Japanese had marshaled four armies and fleets to strike American, British, and Dutch targets in the central and southwest Pacific, as far south and west as Malaya and as far east as Hawaii—a battle zone shaped like an immense fan some four thousand miles long and seven thousand miles wide with Tokyo as its pivot. The fan covered a large slice of the globe, all the way from Burma west to Hawaii, six major meridians of time into the heart of the vast Pacific.

Saburō Sakai, stick in his right hand, throttle in his left, was part of this great effort, the effort to bring the world under one roof and, myth and religion aside, to take the territory and resources Japan claimed were hers by right and necessity. A holy war and a fight for survival rolled into one and draped with a cloak called honor.

The atavists in the army, and there were many of them, liked to use history and an old injury to advance their agendas and aims. They looked back a century, to July 8, 1853, when the ambitious Commodore Matthew C. Perry sailed into Edo (Tokyo) harbor with four black-hulled warships and orders from the president of the United States to open Japan, a closed and feudal society, to the West. Those black ships and Perry's implied threats shamed the Japanese, and to recover their honor and preserve their independence, they moved quickly to make themselves modern.

In the four decades that followed, they cast aside the feudal shogunate, the moribund military autocracy that had governed Japan since the twelfth century, and replaced it with a constitutional monarchy. Then, with help from the French, British, and Prussians, they created a modern, Western-style army and navy. They also set up new industries, built transportation networks, and established a national system of public schools. But in their rush to strengthen their emerald domain and safeguard their precious sovereignty, the parvenus who were racing to embrace the present also held hard to the past, for at heart they were traditionalists, aristocrats, many of them, who did not want Japan to lose its soul—that deep sense of divine origin and the ancient impulse to loyalty and sacrifice that they believed held their society together. They borrowed from the West, these reformers of the Meiji Restoration, as that great change came to be called, borrowed some of the West's social science and many of its machines and fashions, but their aim always was to keep Japan Japanese. "Eastern ethics, Western science," was the adage of the day, though Eastern ethics apparently included the West's inclination for empire and the notion that a strong arm was needed to acquire it.

After the turn of the twentieth century, Japan found itself in conflict with Russia over concessions in Korea, just across the Sea of Japan and strategically important to the Japanese. Most military observers of the day predicted that the Russians would swiftly overwhelm the force Japan sent against them, "The Eagles had . . . already fixed their talons on the carcass," wrote one British officer. Nippon, however, struck fast, and its troops, as fierce as any the West had ever seen, defeated the mighty Russians at Port Arthur.[22]

In just fifty years Japan had transformed itself from a feudal overlordship into a modern military and industrial state, and now it was ready to share in the swag and booty of empire, to grab territory and force concessions in China and domains south, just as the Europeans had been doing in the Pacific since Magellan's famous sorties in the first decades of the sixteenth century.[23]

Japanese diplomats, pressed to defend their country's aggression, claimed necessity. Japan had suffered a series of recessions, and by 1929, the year of widespread financial collapse, the economy was faltering. Ultranationalists in government, aided by right-wing army officers, pressed for a military solution. And by 1937, the army had provoked so many military "incidents" on the Asian mainland that they got what they wanted—a full-scale war. By the end of 1938 the Japanese had more than a million troops fighting in China.

Alarmed, America began an economic war of nerves with the Japanese. Using embargoes of vital materials such as scrap iron, machine parts, and aircraft, America hoped to force Japan to pull back from China. When nothing worked, President Roosevelt in July 1941 froze all Japanese assets in the United States, in effect creating an embargo of the commodity Japan needed most—crude oil. And since America was Japan's chief source of oil, the boycott left the Imperial Army and Navy in a crisis.

The Japanese decided to take what they needed, and what they needed was in the hands of the British and the Dutch. War planners in

Tokyo knew well that by striking the East Indies they would provoke Europe's ally, the United States, into a fight. They also knew that they could not defeat the industry-rich Americans; the United States with its vast resources and its capacity to manufacture whatever war matériel it needed would eventually wear them down. Japan's only chance was to win as much as they could as quickly as they could, then sue for peace and the status quo. Keep the Americans off balance for six months, seize the mineral-rich colonies in the southwest Pacific, then set up a ring of defenses to protect their gains.

SURPRISE WAS ESSENTIAL. Surprise had helped Hideyoshi in Korea in 1592 and had carried the day against the Russians at Port Arthur in 1904. Officers of the Imperial Japanese Army and Navy also knew well the words of the Kendo master Miyamoto Musashi: "You win in battles with timing . . . the timing of cunning . . . a timing which the enemy does not expect." Surprise leaves an enemy low, outwitted, taciturn. America "will be utterly crushed with one blow," an Imperial Navy admiral told the commanders of the Pearl Harbor task force at a briefing before the battle. "It is planned to shift the balance of power and thereby confuse the enemy at the outset and deprive him of his fighting spirit."[24]

But a surprise attack, a modern coup de main, demanded careful planning, constant practice, strict secrecy, a willingness to sacrifice, and a lot of luck.[25]

The Japanese have seven gods of good fortune, and on December 8, 1941, these seven kami were with them. The attack on Hawaii left much of the Pacific Fleet burning or at the bottom of Pearl Harbor. The surprise sorties against the other targets in the Pacific were stunning victories as well. Still, of all the units on the attack that day, the force with the most luck was the 11th Air Fleet, Saburō Sakai and his fellow pilots in the fighters and bombers that had soared into the air from bases on Formosa to bomb Clark Field in the Philippines.

The battle plan had originally called for the Formosa squadrons to take off at 2:30 a.m., which would have put them over the target just after first light, roughly the same moment that the Pearl Harbor attack force, some five thousand miles to the east, was diving on Honolulu's airfields and on the battleships of the American Pacific Fleet. But a rare and very unseasonal "thick pea-soup fog" rolled in from the Straits of Formosa that morning. And standing on the tarmac in their flight suits,

Saburō Sakai and his comrades could not see more than five yards in front of them.

Through the fog came a voice from the loudspeakers on the control tower: "Takeoff is delayed indefinitely," and with that announcement, every pilot instantly understood that the element of surprise had been lost, for surely the Americans at Clark Field and at the other U.S. bases in the Philippines would have heard of the attack at Pearl Harbor and would be prepared for them, or perhaps the enemy was on its way to attack Formosa and the Japanese airfields there.[26]

Sakai and his fellow pilots, cupping their hands to their ears and listening for the sounds of American bombers overhead, waited for the fog to lift. Five o'clock, six o'clock, seven o'clock. At last the fog gave way to mist, mist to blue sky, and by eight forty-five, all squadrons were headed south.

The attack was now six hours behind schedule and Sakai was sure "after the long delay . . . [the enemy] would be awaiting us in great strength."

Just after noon the formation of fifty-three bombers and forty-five Zeros came roaring in from the South China Sea and the Zambales mountains. Below them, on the plains of Pampanga Province, was Clark Field, the main air base of the United States Army Forces in the Far East, General Douglas MacArthur's army in the Philippines. When Sakai looked down, he saw "some sixty enemy bombers and fighters neatly parked along the airfield runways . . . squatted there like sitting ducks."[27]

The Japanese airman was astonished. Why, he wondered, weren't the Americans in the air, "waiting for us?"

The bombers made their passes first. To Sakai, whose squadron of fighters was circling above, protecting the bombers, the attack on Clark Field looked "perfect." He watched from his cockpit as "long strings of bombs tumbled from the bays" of the bombers "and dropped toward the targets." When they hit, "the entire air base seemed to [rise] into the air with the explosions. Pieces of airplanes, hangars, and other ground installations scattered wildly. Great fires erupted and smoke boiled upward."[28]

Now the Zeros took their turn. They "circled down to 13,000 feet . . . still without enemy opposition." Then, with his two wingmen in tow, Sakai nosed over, "pushed the stick forward and dove at a steep angle for the ground." He picked out two American B-17s sitting on the runway unscathed by the explosions and "poured a fusillade of bullets into the big bombers."

Later, safely back on Formosa, the Japanese pilots were elated. "Now," said one, "we have dealt a spectacular blow!" But, overall, they were surprised by their success and "bewildered" by their luck. They told their debriefing officers that they had "found the enemy's planes lined up on the target fields as if in peacetime." It was almost "as if the enemy did not know that war had started."[29]

THE AMERICAN PILOTS and ground crews were eating their lunch when they heard the drone of planes overhead. Some of them rushed outside and looked up.

A few, veteran pilots mostly, knew immediately it was the enemy, but many on the ground, the uninitiated and unknowing, mistook the formations for "friendlies." The planes, flying in giant V formations, were perfect in their spacing, their precision, their unerring course, "beautiful," some men thought, and stirring against the vault of powder blue.[30]

Then they began to see something strange, something that seemed to be floating beneath the giant Vs: small strips of silver glinting in the sun like tiny pieces of tin foil, "sparkles," Ben Steele thought. And all at once, they knew—bombs. Suddenly the air raid klaxon began its urgent warnings: *Eah— Eah— Eah—*

"Japanese!" Ben Steele heard someone yell. "Take cover!"

At roughly 12:15 p.m., the first of some forty-two tons of incendiary and fragmentation bombs started to fall toward the field. Some of the men simply stood there and stared, transfixed by the Vs and the silver sparkles falling from the sky.[31]

Then the base erupted. A line of explosions advanced across the field, then another line, and another. Each bomb held roughly a hundred pounds of explosive in its warhead, enough TNT to bring down a building, blow up an airplane, blast a hole in a runway twelve feet wide, and turn a flesh-and-blood human being into a spray of red. The men on the south side of the field watched the explosions approach—five hundred yards, three hundred, one hundred . . . a burst of blinding white, a sharp, painful *crack!* followed by an enormous rip, a tearing of the air, then, finally, a deep shudder in the ground, the earth set atremble.

A bomb blast is lethal science, fluid mechanics meant to maim. First, the shock wave, a surge of air that hits a man like a wall of wind, hits him so hard his cerebrum starts to shake concussively in his skull, swelling at first, then hemorrhaging, rivulets of blood running from his nose and ears, vomit from his mouth. An instant after the shock wave passes, the atmosphere turns hot and dense, high pressure sucking the low pressure from every recess around it, from a man's lungs and ears and eye sockets, leaving him gasping for breath and fighting the feeling his pupils are being pulled from their sockets. Finally, fluid mechanics turns to terminal ballistics as the blast blows apart the bomb's casing, sending hundreds of jagged fragments—pieces of white-hot shrapnel, some no bigger than a pebble, others as big as a brick—slicing into anything in their path.

Q. P. Devore was hit right away.

He had spent the morning sorting armory supplies and at mess call had met his friend Ben Steele for lunch. He ate quickly that afternoon; the fellas in the control tower had invited him up for a look, so he climbed the stairs to the cupola on top of the first hangar to chew the fat with the operations boys and take in the view. All at once a voice came over an intercom: "Enemy bombers overhead." Devore laughed. Another false alarm. "Hey fellas, I'm going to step out on the stairs for a look," he said, and he began to descend from the cupola, down the stairs that hugged the outside of the hangar. When he heard the drone of engines, he stopped and looked up. He was halfway down the stairs when he heard the loudest noise he'd ever heard, and just like that, his world went blank.

When he came to, he was on the ground, lying among a litter of empty gasoline drums at the bottom of the stairs. His body ached, his head was thick and heavy. And he kept hearing a voice, faint at first, as if it were far away.

"Help . . . help."

As his head cleared, the voice grew louder.

"Help me! Please! Somebody help me!"

Devore rolled over and saw a man he knew, a lieutenant from his unit. He blinked and looked again. The man was wobbling, struggling to stand, to get up on the one leg he had left.

A truck stopped nearby and the driver rushed over to the two men. "Let's get this officer to the hospital at Stotsenberg," he said, and Devore helped him load the lieutenant in the pickup, then jumped in the back.

At Stotsenberg hospital the wounded from Clark Field were everywhere, filling the wards, the halls, the concrete porch in back. When Q. P. Devore arrived with the mangled lieutenant, orderlies were putting men on blankets on the front lawn, and a nurse pressed Devore into service as a litter bearer, unloading truckloads of hobbled, bleeding, unconscious men. He hefted and hauled, stretcher after stretcher, until a nurse stopped him and said, "Hey, what's the story with you?"

"I'm okay," Devore said.

"Really? Take a look."

His coveralls were soaked with blood and riddled with tiny holes. "Oh," he thought, "I didn't even feel it."

Now and then a nurse, doctor, or patient would wander over to a window or the front door and look toward Clark Field, less than two miles away. The base was burning—airplanes, hangars, huts, barracks, trucks, and fuel tanks, even the fields of cogon grass were ablaze—and giant twisters of black and gray smoke and clouds of ocher dust were rising high over the runways. Soon the sky, the great blue dome above the central plain, was dark with carbon and ash.

Then they heard gunfire from that direction, the stabbing *tchat-tchat-tchat* of machine guns and airplane cannon. The Japanese Zeros had come down from the clouds to rake and strafe what the bombers had left.

The attack was over in less than an hour, but all afternoon and into the evening, trucks and cars carted the casualties up the road to Stotsenberg.

The injured, when they could talk, described brimstone scenes and stygian slaughter: bombs falling in trenches, dismembering and decapitating those caught cowering there; orange fireballs of gasoline and oil rimmed with a cockscomb of thick black smoke; pilots trying to take off, shot in their seats or trapped in their flaming cockpits; an airfield that looked like an airplane junkyard, the runways and aprons littered with pieces of wings, tails, and fuselage, and the riddled wrecks of bombers and fighters still smoking. Finally, amid all, derelict corpses and other detritus of war—an arm, a leg, a helmet with holes in it.

When the Zeros came down to finish the attack, they came in low, often just thirty feet off the ground, flying through the smoke and fire left by the bombs, shooting their rounds and tracers into planes and buildings, emplacements and men. Some of the wounded swore they could see the faces of the Japanese pilots and shot at them with their rifles and sidearms, sometimes sighting on the big red circles on the Zero's fuselage and wings, those "goddamn red meatballs" and "big fried eggs," the *hinomaru* of Amaterasu, "the circle of the sun."[32]

In the operating room at Stotsenberg the wounded were taken four and five at a time, laid out on wooden doors set on crates and boxes. Helen Cassiani, a surgical nurse from Bridgewater, Massachusetts, had "never seen such carnage."

"Oh Lord!" she said to herself, "this is a madhouse."

In truth it was more like a knacker's yard, with stretchers of flayed flesh and splintered bone "all over the lawn, the porch, the hallways, anywhere you looked." Outside was better than inside, where the smell of suffering—the stench of blackened flesh and the reek of green bile and vomit—collected in the still air of the corridors and wards. Most of all, the overpowering smell of blood, sweet with a hint of musk, so much that it made Cassie, as they called Helen, think of her family's chicken farm and the way the barn smelled on days when the birds were being slaughtered.[33]

Some of the wounded shrieked and howled, but overall the scene was strangely quiet. Cassie noticed that most of the wounded were "shuddering from the deathly cold that comes from shock" or were so numb with morphine they kept their pain to themselves. Now and then a man with a crushed or dangling limb would summon a nurse to come close, and he would whisper a question: Was he going to lose his hand, his foot, his arm, his leg? Don't worry, Cassie would tell them; the doctor would do what he could. In the end, of course, the doctor would amputate. There was no time, no equipment, no way to reconnect what had been torn loose and left hanging or rebuild what had been blasted into shards of bone and bloody bits of flesh. So they would shoot up the man with more morphine and clamp off the wound's arteries and veins, and a surgeon would take a scalpel and pare down the muscle, pare it down to the bone, then the room would fill with the sound of sawing.[34]

Q. P. Devore had been lucky. The shrapnel had bounced off a rib instead of slicing into him. His legs had been peppered with fragments too, but looking at the litters queued up for surgery, he considered himself almost unscathed. Medics cleaned his wounds and gave him new coveralls and, in the afternoon, sent him back to Clark Field.

He was tired and sore when he wandered into the barracks, and there, waiting for him, was his good friend Ben Steele. Each man had prepared himself for the death of the other. And now, sitting side by side in a barracks full of bullet holes, bullet holes even in the blankets, each counted himself twice lucky, once for his own sweet life, once for the life of his friend.

"And what happened to you?" Q.P. asked.

"After lunch I went on back to the hangar area," Ben said. "Bunch of us were walkin' about fifty yards from a trench when we hear this high drone, and we look up. They dropped so damn many bombs the sides of the trenches were caving in, you know? Then the fighters came in, just coming in right out of the smoke. Hell, I was shooting at them with my forty-five. Really, right at point-blank range."[35]

The conversation carried them outside, over to the wreckage of the hangar and control tower stairs where Q.P. had been hit. Ben told Q.P. that after the attack he had run to the tower to look for him, but all he found was a jumble of gasoline drums under the stairs, and—he reached into his pocket—this wristwatch, which he held out to show him.

Q.P. looked, looked again.

"Hey, that's mine!" he said. "That's my watch. I didn't even know I'd lost it."

The two stood there, looking around them. The base was a wasteland of debris and burning junk. Gone were most of the barracks, offices, hangars, repair shops, fuel and ammo dumps, chow halls, and the base communications shack. In the gray half-light of evening, the two runways had so many craters that the field looked like a moonscape. Seventeen of the nineteen B-17 bombers and most of the American pursuit planes had been destroyed or heavily damaged. MacArthur's Far East Air Force was now a line of wrecks smoldering in the sun.

"They really demolished this place," Ben Steele said. "They got everything."

The graves registration unit was still busy past sundown collecting the dead. More than 250 men had been wounded and some 100 killed, roughly 10 percent of the force manning the base.[36]

Many had fought well—pilots taxiing down the runway under fire, antiaircraft crews staying at their guns as fighter planes bore down on them, soldiers rushing into burning buildings to save buddies or retrieve valuable gear—but surprise strikes deep. And a large number of men, green privates bewildered by the bombs and veteran corporals and sergeants who had left their courage in a warm bed or in a bottle, were finished. At dark they simply abandoned their posts and fled into the woods and hills and barrios.[37]

The barracks were almost empty, just Ben Steele, Q.P., and a few others. Where the hell had everyone gone? they wondered. One of the officers said that sentries along the shoreline had spotted "troop transports" up north in the South China Sea, "an invasion force." Invasion? How were they going to stop an invasion now, without an air force? Another man was sure he could hear the sound of tanks in the distance, but whose tanks?

Q.P. was in rough shape. He told Ben he was so sore he could barely stand. Most of all, his nerves were shot; he was sure the barracks would be hit again and he wanted to get out of there.

"That bombing put the fear of God in me," Q.P. whispered to his friend. "I'm afraid."

Ben Steele helped his buddy outside and across the airfield and into the relative safety of the woods. He bedded him down on a rush of cogon grass, and for two nights he ferried food to him and kept him company until he was ready to fall asleep.

GOING TO GROUND

BEN STEELE was five years old the first time he fell off a horse.
Happened over at the Gilberts', neighbors a few hills away
who raised racers. Grover Gilbert had put him on a retired plug
named Old Pardner. "You just grab ahold of the horn and hang on,
Bud," Gilbert said, but as soon as that horse stepped onto the hardpan
oval it took off, pitching the child into the bunchgrass and dirt. He was
too young to remember the spill, but he heard about it often enough.

His father had been a cowboy, among the last to ride the open range,
so it was only natural that the Old Man would take the measure of his
oldest son by the boy's ability to keep his seat.

At their ranch at Hawk Creek, the Old Man put him on a frisky cow
pony, a mare named Squaw. In the afternoons—he was six or seven years
old now—father and son would saddle up, cross a meadow, and climb
into the hills.

Their second, maybe third time out, Squaw caught a hoof on broken ground, and Bud went flying.

The Old Man stopped his horse, looked down, shook his head.

"Horse stumbles and you fall off? You're a helluva of cowboy!"

Then he dismounted, brushed the boy off, and hoisted him back into
the saddle.

For a while Ben Steele was about half afraid of that animal, but he
never spoke of his fear lest the Old Man leave him home and ride the
hills without him.

TWO

December 8, 1941, 11:00 a.m., Takao Harbor, Formosa,
aboard the troopship Yae Maru

LIEUTENANT RYOTARO NISHIMURA, commander of the Fifth Company, 2nd Battalion, 9th Infantry Regiment, 14th Army Group, was belowdecks with his men staging for the invasion of the Philippines when he heard the news over the ship's loudspeakers: "Today, December 8, before dawn, the Imperial Army and Navy entered into a state of war with American and British forces."

So the hour was at hand. Soon now he would sail with the 14th Army, one of four Japanese armies to sally forth that December fortnight— 200,000 troops on their way to drive the British, Dutch, and Americans from the archipelagoes and island groups of the southwest Pacific.

Reflecting on this, Ryotaro Nishimura's first thoughts were the same as those of all Japanese soldiers. He thought of death.

"I will do whatever I am ordered," he told himself.

Then, like every man-at-arms approaching a battle, he turned back for a moment to glance at the life he was so ready to leave, his life at home in Fushimi: the willows on Nishihama Street in front of his father's store, the barge boats plying the canals, the flowers in the rushes along the Uji River.[1]

AT SEA, clear sky, calm waters. The men of the Fifth Company, 2nd Battalion, 9th Infantry were on deck, sitting in a semicircle around their commander. They were anxious, these young conscripts, Kyoto boys, the sons of farmers and shopkeepers, most of them. They knew that two weeks hence, December 22, they would be going into battle. And they would be led in this great and dangerous task by a new commander, a young lieutenant they had met only a fortnight before.

Ryotaro Nishimura was standing in front of them now, speaking just loud enough to be heard, almost a whisper above the wind.

He did not want to raise his voice. In his early years in the army he had served as a training officer, and he had learned a little something of how men thought and what men felt. As the invasion force approached its staging area, Ryotaro Nishimura knew that the boys gathered around him on desk were homesick and afraid.

He had called the company together, he told them, so they could look north, toward Japan.

"This is your farewell, farewell to your home country, to your family." So look toward Japan, he said, and say good-bye. "Once you head into battle, you must cut your feeling for your family and town or you will not be able to fight."

A subaltern practicing basic psychology on his men, trying to harden their hearts before the bitter work of battle, part of the catechism of any army. But this particular young lieutenant's allocution was also uniquely Japanese, for it invoked the ancient code of the warrior, the old Ōtomo pledge. *Kaerimi wa seji! Kaerimi wa seji!*

> Never will I look back!
> Never will I look back!

"If you have regrets, some worry about your family or home or countryside," Nishimura continued, "then, as the saying goes, *ushiro gami o hikareru*"—your head will be pulled back—"and you cannot concentrate on the things that are to come, the things you have to face. Cut everything now so that you can move forward."

The men listened respectfully to their new company commander, listened as they would listen to a father, their "army father," and they knew he was right—regret was as lethal as an enemy bullet or bayonet—but they could not stop themselves from thinking of home, and neither could the man lecturing them.

He thought of his family: his mother, younger brother, and father and their home on Kasho Machi by the Hori River in the busy Kyoto suburb of Fushimi.

As a boy he had loved the bustle of the place, the noisy commerce of the streets, the *chin-chin* of the trolley bells, the *gatakoto-gatakoto-gatakoto* of the locomotives on the tracks.

At a local college of commerce, Ryotaro Nishimura had prepared himself to enter the family lumber business. Then in 1932, around his twentieth birthday, the government sent him a draft notice. His mother thought him too weak for the army, but his father, who revered the Throne and believed Japan a nation with a divine destiny, was proud his oldest son had been called to serve the emperor.

Commissioned an officer, he was assigned to the reserves near his home, then in 1936 he was called to full-time duty, fought in China the following year, rotated home, and in the fall of 1941 was ordered to report to the 9th Infantry. By the second week in December he was on his way with his men aboard a ship in the South China Sea, part of a flotilla staging for an invasion of the Philippine Islands.

On the early morning of December 22, eighty-five transports carrying 36,000 troops from the 14th Army's invasion force dropped anchor in the waters of Lingayen Gulf off the main Philippine island of Luzon, preparing for a predawn attack. On the *Yae Maru*, Ryotaro Nishimura

went among his men checking their equipment and quizzing them on the order of battle.[2]

He had worked hard to "get familiar" with his troops, to treat them with "affection" and "consideration," sleeping in the same hold, eating the same food, by turns encouraging and calming them. He knew well that combat was close work (is there anything more intimate than dying in the arms of a comrade?), work driven by love, not hate or fear. He also knew that men never follow a bully (they'd been bullied enough in training), so he spared them the tub-thumping lectures on the evils of the West, loyalty to the emperor, their duty to give up their lives.

"Do not die for no purpose," he urged them. "Think well before doing things. Don't hurry to die."

On the morning of the invasion he woke his men at three o'clock and huddled with them at breakfast: miso soup and an egg over a thick porridge of barley and white rice. Japanese soup always reminded the men of home, but on this morning the troops complained the miso had a "strange" flavor, and Ryotaro Nishimura knew that the men had awakened with the metallic taste of fear in their mouths.

He tried to keep his mind on the moment (there was much to think about—the objective, the weather, the terrain), but as he ate his porridge and soup his thoughts began to drift.

"Even in a little war," he thought, "we have only one life as a human being. And even in a little battle we are worried about that life, our one important precious life to be lost. Now we are in a big war with a big enemy, a war very different from the war we fought before in China. This enemy is a very difficult enemy to attack." Naturally, the men were worried about their lives. "I am worried too, worried about my own life, my one precious life to be lost in battle."

And then the call came to assemble on deck. The men silently shouldered their packs and queued up at the ladders to go topside. They were breathing heavily, sighing, and shifting about.

On deck, waiting for the landing boats to return from shore to pick up his battalion, Ryotaro Nishimura looked at his watch—the boats were late. This was not good. They had wanted to land in the dark to shroud their movements, but now he could see the first approach of dawn, the slow gray awakening of day he had watched so often at home above Mount Momoyama.

By the time the landing boats returned, the sun was well above the horizon. The tillermen reported that the swift currents and rough seas had carried the first battalion south of its assigned beach to a spot near Bauang, where troops of the Philippine Army's 12th Infantry Regiment were waiting with machine guns. Casualties had been heavy. Now Nishimura's battalion was being taken out of reserve and sent into the fight. The lieutenant would get his orders on the beach, he was told.

So they would be landing under fire after all. Ryotaro Nishimura looked at the lines of soldiers waiting on deck. The men would do fine, he thought. They had been trained to fight hard. Then he caught sight of his battalion commander weaving his way toward him through the lines of men. The colonel put his hand on the lieutenant's shoulder.

"I will pray for the safe landing of your company," he said.

The wind was up and the sea was full of swells, some ten feet high. The landing boats were rising and falling and banging against the hull, and the men climbing down the side of the ship on nets and rope ladders felt awkward and clumsy, the weight of their packs and ammunition and heavy equipment throwing them off balance in the pitch and roll.

Now the boats were heading toward shore, the wind blowing them south toward the beach at Santiago. Ryotaro Nishimura noticed debris in the water ahead of them, round metal casings floating off the bow. Mines!

At almost the same moment, he could hear the *ping* and *snap* of bullets passing overhead, then came the *sh-h-h* and *whump* of mortars or perhaps small artillery shells landing around them.

As the boat approached the heavy surf it started to founder, and the company sergeant jumped over the side and ordered the men into the water.

They were bobbing about now in their life belts, beginning to separate, and the lieutenant threw the sergeant a rope from the boat. He was a good man, this sergeant, a very clever man, and he told the men in the water to grab the rope, and then he began to tow them to shore, through the roiling surf toward the beach and the sandy bluffs and earthen redoubts where the enemy was waiting.

ONCE ASHORE and driving toward their objectives, the invaders knew they would be outnumbered but they did not feel overmatched. They had air and naval power, and the enemy did not. More tanks, too. Most of all, they were sure they had better troops. The Japanese estimated that 130,000 Filipinos and Americans would be dug in against them at various places on Luzon and the other islands, but they believed that an Imperial Army force less than half that size would be more than enough to carry the campaign.[3]

[Pre-invasion Report] The Americans have the makings of excellent soldiers, but due to the torrid zone, there is a tendency to physical and mental laxness and subsequent lack of eagerness.[4]

And they were right. According to a U.S. Army report, "the average enlistee" in 1941 "was a youth of less than average education, to whom the security of pay, low as it was, and the routines of Army life appealed more than the competitive struggles of civilian life." They resented their officers, the army's remote upper class, and saw their sergeants as crude overseers promoted more for their mindless forbearance, their time in uniform, than their merit. They thought the training rote and stupid, drill for "nitwits": marching in formation, scrubbing barracks floors, shining shoes, standing frequent inspections. Instead of *esprit de corps*—a "moral force," Ardant du Picq said, that wins battles—the average soldier in the Army of the United States had *esprit étroit*, narrowing self-interest. "Don't stick your neck out," he would tell his buddies, then reach for another beer.[5]

In their pre-invasion reports, the Japanese thought even less of the Filipinos: "Their military ability is lower than the Americans'."[6]

In 1934 when the U.S. Congress voted to grant the Philippines full independence (effective in 1946) and created a Commonwealth government, the first president, Manuel Quezon, asked his American sponsors to help him plan for the islands' defense. Quezon wanted his old friend Douglas MacArthur, soon to retire as U.S. Army chief of staff, to be his military adviser, and Washington approved.

MacArthur's staff drafted plans for a "citizen army" of trained Filipino reserves ready to be mobilized in an emergency. By July 1941, the Philippine Army and the American garrison in the Philippines had been combined under one command, and MacArthur told Washington that 120,000 Filipino reservists had been trained and were ready to fight. "The Philippine Army . . . is progressing by leaps and bounds," he wired the War Department.[7]

In truth, the Commonwealth Army was more of a *levée en masse*, a force of reservists being quickly mobilized, than a standing army. The Filipinos were without adequate equipment or quarters. Their guinit helmets were fashioned from coconut husks and varnish; some had combat boots, but most wore rubber-soled canvas shoes that fell apart or rotted in the wet climate; in their initial training they used lengths of wood and stalks of bamboo instead of rifles and had only limited opportunities to handle or test-fire real weapons.

More than half of them were illiterate peasants drawn from the provinces. They came into the training camps speaking a hundred regional languages and dialects, and orders often had to be translated and retranslated three or four times before a man could understand them. During their first week of "training," they learned how to operate flush toilets and were lectured on the value of washing their hands before they sat down to eat. In the mornings they were taught how to march, stand in formation, tender a crisp salute. In the afternoons they worked in the camp gardens raising vegetables, and tended herds of livestock and flocks of fowl so they would have something to eat.

Their officers were often wholly ignorant of the most basic military subjects—map reading, troop movements, tactics, even simple self-defense. An American adviser once asked a Filipino officer to order his men to dig foxholes, and the Filipino, out of earshot, turned to a subordinate and whispered, "What is a foxhole?"[8]

Had they been well trained and well led, the Filipinos might have made superb soldiers. Generally a passive people, they followed the custom of *pakikisama*, Tagalog for "just go along with it" whatever the "it" was—the rule of government, the will of the family, the preferences of friends. And if going along put trouble in his path, well, then, the weary *magsasaka* (farmer) would just *bahala na*, "leave it to God, come what may." But wrong him, insult him, slander his family, question his honor, and the average Filipino would likely turn his bolo from cutting sugarcane to harvesting someone's head.

A handful of Americans in the islands, veterans of the Spanish-American War, had experienced this fury. After the United States invaded the islands in 1898, Emilio Aguinaldo, the leader of the Filipino revolt, and his peasant army fought pitched battles with the Americans, then became a guerrilla force that regularly harassed and ambushed the American troops who pursued them into the provinces. Impressed by the Filipinos' capacity to fight, the American Army created within its ranks a unit called the Philippine Scouts, ten thousand highly trained Filipino troops considered by some in 1941 to be the best light infantry in the Pacific.

Unlike the veteran Scouts, however, the much larger Commonwealth Army, only five years old, had no experience and little support. When the Japanese set sail from Formosa, the native force preparing to meet them was ill led and underequipped. Morale was high—the Filipinos shared their American overseers' contempt for the Japanese and were proud of their birthright and eager to defend it against the invaders. But without the proper equipment and preparation for the hard fight ahead, they were just "multitudes of men," as the ancient Roman, Vegetius, might have called them, waiting to be "dragged to slaughter."[9]

MacArthur knew of these deficits but never corrected them. Instead he concentrated on the politics of the moment, building morale and maligning his enemy. In May 1941 he told a reporter that the Japanese Imperial Army had suffered so many casualties in China, it was now a "third-class" force, a statement that said more about the general than the Japanese. Only a handful of American intelligence officers had the ability to analyze the strength and caliber of the Japanese troops, and these men had scant information in front of them. Japan was a police state in 1941, and everyone—natives, foreign residents, diplomats, and travelers—was under surveillance. So American operatives in Tokyo could only guess at the proficiency of the emperor's troops, and their best guess was sobering: the Japanese, they believed, were among the finest fighting men in the world, "aggressive, well-trained . . . superbly led," and "dogged in combat."[10]

AN ARCHIPELAGO of 7,100 islands lying on an axis some 1,150 miles long, the Philippines was too diffuse for a garrison to defend and too far away—almost 7,000 miles from American shores—for a battle fleet to reach them in time to thwart an invasion or relieve a garrison under siege. And for more than forty years, from December 1898 when America took possession of the Philippines, until December 1941 when the Japanese attacked, this conundrum, this classic problem of assembling "forces in space" and "forces in time," as Carl von Clausewitz called it, kept military planners spinning.

Across the years a succession of admirals and generals in Washington and Manila wrote and rewrote a war plan, code-named Orange, that tried to anticipate Japan's ambitions and America's answer. With almost every revision of Orange, and there were many, military planners reached the same conclusion: the islands would fall and the garrison would be captured or slaughtered. Brigadier General Stanley D. Embick, a respected strategist who had served in the Philippines, believed that if war came, America should abandon the islands, bide its time, build up its fleet, then return in strength to retake what it had lost. But to sacrifice territory without a fight, and to give up America's only major naval base in the western Pacific, was to risk the opprobrium of the other Western powers. All of which left American commanders in the Philippines in a tactical quandary: How was the army to defend the indefensible, and how could commanders convince their men to hold out for help when those commanders knew well that help would never come?[11]

In the decades before World War II, the top American officers in the Philippines talked about two strategies: an "active defense" of meeting the invaders at the water's edge, and a "defense in depth," which called for an orderly withdrawal down Luzon's central plain to the mountainous peninsula of Bataan whose east shore faced Manila Bay. There, in a last stand, the army would be able to deny the enemy the use of the bay and Manila harbor and would try to hold out for six months until the Pacific Fleet arrived to save them.[12]

Both stratagems were fictions, fictions because the generals who conceived them and the colonels in charge of translating them into action knew that the garrison would be outmanned and outgunned, constantly under siege and cut off from home. "Active defense" and "defense in depth" were euphemisms, military bunkum for what was really going to happen—the defeat, or annihilation, of the garrison.[13]

MACARTHUR had his own plan.

By 1940 Congress, now inured to the cries of the isolationists, voted for a military draft and for funds to rebuild the army and navy. It takes time, however, to retool factories and manufacture the matériel of war, time to stockpile armaments and mobilize men. That winter and spring the armed services were still understrength, and military planners wanted America to stay out of the war "as long as possible," long enough, at least, to get the country's factories going and enlist and train hundreds of thousands of men. At length Washington settled on a strategy to buy that time, a strategy that worried more about Europe than the Pacific. Germany seemed ready to reduce the British Isles and occupy all of Europe, so for the moment Washington decided to put "Europe First," as the plan was nicknamed. America would concentrate what resources it had on its Atlantic defenses; it would bolster the English and try to bluff the Japanese, long enough at least to let America build its stockpiles and prepare for a two-ocean war.[14]

Ignoring the shortages and the political realities back home, MacArthur in February 1941 sent the War Department a proposal to defend the entire archipelago, all seventy-one hundred islands. His plan called for his air force to bomb and shell invading ships as they approached the beaches, then, as soon as the invaders set foot on Philippine soil, his ground forces would attack and cast the invaders back into the sea. The stalwarts manning the beaches were to come from the ranks of the Philippine Commonwealth Army, an army that had never taken the field.

Although the War Department knew the truth—a former commander of the American Garrison in the islands had reported "the realities" of MacArthur's force "in precise and unflattering terms"—the rosy reports the general was sending to Washington were the only good news coming out of the Far East that winter and spring. And as the Japanese marched across East Asia and into the southern latitudes, any "good" news was welcome. Hope, not cold reason, ruled the halls of government during those anxious days of 1941.[15]

In July, President Roosevelt called the Philippine Army into active service, then he made the general commander of all American forces in the Far East. In August, MacArthur assured the War Department that his plan for the defense of the Philippines was nearing completion. And in October, he reported that he would soon have a force of 200,000 men, all of which led Washington to believe that their man in Manila was "ready for any eventuality."

When war came seven weeks later, MacArthur had under arms only half the number of men he'd promised. His army consisted of squadrons of unproven B-17 bombers and their green ground crews, a small garrison of guzzling Sundowners (as American troops in the tropics were sometimes called), 12,000 Filipino Scouts, and 80,000 Philippine Army reservists in tennis shoes and coconut-husk helmets. To these men, on the eve of war, Douglas MacArthur issued the following order:

"The enemy will be met at the beaches . . . [which] will be held at all costs . . . There will be no withdrawal."[16]

LUZON, Japan's primary target in the archipelago, was the largest of the Philippine islands, a roughly rectangular tract of land (like the shaft of a boot) 460 miles long and 140 miles wide at its extremes. The coastline ran for 2,242 miles, but only a handful of the hundreds of bights and inlets were big enough to accommodate an armada of troopships. The site most suited to an invasion, the largest anchorage with the longest landing beaches, strips of sand big enough to accept waves of soldiers and supplies coming ashore, was Lingayen Gulf on Luzon's west coast. The beach there was like a threshold; once the invaders had crossed the sand and debouched the defiles between the mountains, they would be standing at the gateway to a wide central plain that ran southeast between ranges of mountains 120 miles down the center of the island to Manila, the political heart of the country. The central plain was wide enough for ground troops to maneuver, and it had two paved highways, a number of side roads and trails, and miles and miles of railroad track. It was also a direct route to Manila Bay, one of the most perfectly formed harbors in the Far East. The central plain, in short, was an inviting pathway for an invading army, and its gateway was Lingayen Gulf.

By mid-December, Japanese aircraft had destroyed MacArthur's Far East Air Force, and after a devastating air raid on the U.S. navy yard at Cavite, home of the Asiatic Fleet, Admiral Thomas Hart sallied most of his ships south to the Malay Barrier, leaving behind only a handful of torpedo boats and submarines. Japanese planes, meanwhile, continued their attacks on American airfields and bases. And everyone on the island of Luzon was on tenterhooks waiting for the invading army to arrive.

The boozy belligerence and barroom burlesques of late November—"Let the Little Yellow Bastards come, we'll knock the living shit out of them!"—gave way to a frame of mind as dark as the banks of clouds that crept in low off the South China Sea and swallowed the tops of the mountains.

Alvin C. Poweleit, an army doctor from Newport, Kentucky, assigned to a tank battalion marshaling to move north toward the gulf at the first sign of an invasion, noticed that the daily bombings were beginning to "change the personalities" of some of the men. "For example," he wrote in his diary,

> Lieutenant Rue seemed absolutely listless, and Lieutenant E. Gibson lost all confidence in himself . . . Captain Sorenson had been a very fine man, capable and intelligent, until the war started, then he became despondent. Then when Company C was called into action, he fainted and went all to pieces . . . [Another officer] was drunk all the time. One day he asked me if the Army would release him if he shot himself in the leg. I told him it would be better if he shot himself in the head.[17]

On December 18 at his headquarters at One Calle Victoria, MacArthur received a report that eighty Japanese troop transports were headed toward the Philippines. Two days later the Japanese force was sighted forty miles north of Lingayen Gulf. The next day headquarters warned all commanders that an invasion was imminent.

Along the shoreline of the gulf, the men dug in. Their written orders were still the same—meet the enemy on the beaches. But here and there along the coast, officers from headquarters, inspecting the units dug in above the beach, began to whisper a word heretofore unheard by the men waiting at the water's edge: "withdrawal."

Withdrawal? "We must die in our tracks," Colonel Richard C. Mallonée reminded the officer from headquarters.

"Don't believe everything you hear," the officer said.[18]

The shoreline of Lingayen Gulf was shaped like a fishhook and ran for more than a hundred miles. To defend the entire country MacArthur had divided his command into three forces and his men were spread thin. At Lingayen Gulf he stationed troops at the most logical landing spots, above the widest beaches and at the gaps that led through the mountains to the central plain.

In the early morning dark of December 22, the Japanese launched their landing barges. Most of the invaders came ashore without having to fire a shot. They landed at unguarded strips of sand and immediately prepared to move inland. Only at the beach at Bauang did the two armies clash. Fire from Filipino machine guns riddled the waves of Japanese caught in the roiling surf, and soon the beach at Bauang was littered with bodies. But in preparing their position, the defenders there had buried their ammunition in the sand and it wasn't long before their guns started to jam and they were forced to withdraw.

By midmorning the Japanese had thousands of men on Philippine soil and were beginning their push toward the central plain. At HQ MacArthur ordered reinforcements forward to try to block the enemy's advance.

Colonel Mallonée, an adviser to the Philippine Army, was waiting with his artillery unit just south of the battle line when "an alarming number of stragglers" from the fighting along the gulf began to wander into his compound, each telling the colonel the same story:

> Always the story-teller was subjected to terrible mortar fire; always he continued bravely to fire his [weapon]; always his officers ran away—or if the teller was an officer, his superior officers ran first . . . always he was suddenly astonished to realize he was absolutely alone, all others having run away or been killed. Then and only then, with the tanks a few feet away, had he flung himself to one side where . . . Here the story has two variations. First he was captured but escaped that night; second, he hid until night, when he returned to our lines . . . The stragglers were very tired, they sought their companions, they were very hungry, and, sir, could they be transferred to the Motor Transport Corps and drive a truck?[19]

Some Filipino units stood and fought until they ran out of ammunition or until the Japanese brought up tanks, but many, especially those who had been used as cannon fodder, first at Lingayen Gulf and then at defensive positions on the central plain, were betrayed by their inexperience and fled. Of the 28,000 men under his command in northern Luzon, Lieutenant General Jonathan Wainwright, MacArthur's commander in the area, estimated that only 10 percent of his force—3,000 men at most—had been trained to fight.[20]

But it was not just a lack of training that betrayed the young Filipino reservists; it was their allegiance to their overseers, their faith in the great and powerful country they thought was protecting them. Filipino soldiers expected the American Air Corps to control the skies above the battlefield. Instead, the Japanese were "constantly overhead, destroying the morale" of the raw reservists who, according to an American colonel commanding them, "innocently and trustingly expected" the Army Air

Corps "to show up at any time." When the Americans failed to appear, Filipino "hope gave way to despair," and the frightened reservists fell back before the columns of attacking Japanese.[21]

As the Imperial Army began its push down the central plain, General Wainwright sent parts of two American units into the fight, the 26th Cavalry (Philippine Scouts, part of the U.S. Army) and a contingent of tanks, reservists from Minnesota, Illinois, and Kentucky who had been recently federalized and rushed to the islands.

The Scouts, astonishingly, were on horseback, one of the last mounted cavalry units in the U.S. Army. In an age of airplanes and armored vehicles, soldiers on horseback were either an absurd anachronism or the beau ideal of bravery.

Bill Gentry from Harrodsburg, Kentucky, was with the American tank crews assigned to support the cavalry, and he watched openmouthed as the horsemen moved their mounts into a position to attack the enemy tanks on the other side of a river. Gentry and his crew tried to convince the cavalry officer to hold his men and horses back. "Let us go over there, we can do something with our tanks," they said. "You can't do anything with those horses and sabres." But the cavalryman refused to listen. "Get your damn tanks out of the way," he said. "They are scaring my horses." Then, as Gentry watched, the Japanese started "tearing" the American and Filipino horsemen "apart" with their tank cannon and automatic weapons.[22]

When the slaughter was over, the Americans ordered their tanks forward to engage the Japanese, but someone somewhere had bungled the refueling. Only five of the dozens of tanks available to attack that day had enough gas to ride into battle and fight, five tanks against perhaps an entire column of enemy armor and an advance of thousands of foot soldiers.

Lieutenant Ben Morin of Maywood, Illinois, the commander of the five tanks, Second Platoon, B Company, 192nd Tank Battalion, positioned his command tank ahead of the others to set the example. He knew his men were afraid and nothing he could say would allay their doubts or lessen their dread, but at least he could take the lead, give them someone to follow.

Morin seemed young for such an assignment, only twenty-one years old, but he had spent four years in the National Guard and knew tanks and tank tactics. He also knew his men; tankers generally were a tight-knit crew, specialists working together in close quarters. Most of all Ben

Morin was a religious man, the son of Roman Catholics, and his faith steadied him.

Sometime after 1:00 p.m., the five tanks of the 2nd Platoon moved up Route 3, close to the town of Agoo, a short distance from the shores of Lingayen Gulf. The Americans rode to battle in M3 "light" tanks, thinly armored vehicles with a small single-shot cannon and an air-cooled machine gun, a cranky and sometimes unreliable weapon. The M3's turret was tall, giving the vehicle a high profile, an easy and inviting target, and its armor was thin and presented a flat instead of an angled surface to deflect incoming rounds.

Morin's platoon rolled forward unprotected. The Philippine infantry had fled south, and American units were regrouping or engaging other enemy spearheads. Morin looked on his mission as a kind of "last-ditch effort" to stem the Japanese advance onto the central plain—five tanks against a battalion, perhaps even a regiment of the enemy.

"We have to hold them, drive them out, drive them back or destroy them," the lieutenant told his men.

The column moved slowly down the road. Agoo was just ahead, a mile or so. The sun was shining and a breeze was blowing in from the gulf. Tanks and men moved forward in a miasma of road dust, exhaust fumes, and fear. Then all at once the enemy found them.

Shells slammed into the American column and "ripped through" the tanks "like a knife through butter." In the fusillade, Morin's lead tank lost its front hatch, exposing the men inside to rifle and machine-gun fire.[23]

Morin jumped down from his turret and tried to refit the hatch, but now the tank was ablaze, engulfed in searing flames and choking black smoke. Morin ordered his men to dismount and, hoping for rescue, looked anxiously over his shoulder for the rest of the column.

The other tanks had also been hit and had turned and were starting to withdraw. No way to reach them now. Morin and his crew were alone on the road. And in an instant the enemy was upon them.

Four Japanese tanks trained their cannon and machine guns on the Americans now standing on the road in front of their disabled and burning machine. The lieutenant looked at the enemy guns, looked at his men, put his hands up.

In that moment he felt disgrace rather than fear. He had surrendered—in all likelihood the first American taken prisoner in the Philippines in World War II—and he could not shake a captive's sense of shame.[24]

The Japanese rushed forward and forced the Americans to their knees, then they put pistols to the prisoners' heads. Kneeling there, Ben Morin looked for mercy in the eyes of the man pointing a gun at him. Finding none, he started to pray.[25]

> Hail Mary, full of grace
> The Lord is with thee . . .

BY THE END of December 22, the first day of the invasion, MacArthur's army was fighting a tactical withdrawal, a "retreat" by any other name. He had set a skeleton army of native reservists in front of 43,000 invaders, many of them seasoned by four years of war in China. Now he was falling back, back through the divides in the mountains, back down the dusty roads and dirt trails of the central plain, back to one defensive line after another, until there was no place left to fall back to, no place but the peninsula of Bataan.

The withdrawal had been planned well in advance, a complement to the old War Plan Orange, a plan MacArthur had originally rejected. He was back-pedaling before Lieutenant General Masaharu Homma's 14th Imperial Army. Now came a second enemy landing, this one at Lamon Bay in southeastern Luzon. The Lamon force was pushing north, the Lingayen force south. The general's grand scheme to defend the entire archipelago had left him between two pincers, and each claw had the same objective: close on the capital, catch MacArthur in the middle, and crush him. A textbook trap, as old as organized warfare.

The way out of the trap was textbook as well. On December 22, as the Japanese were wading ashore, MacArthur cabled the War Department: He was outnumbered, he said (another fiction), leaving him at "an enormous tactical discrepancy." He planned to invoke War Plan Orange and declare Manila an open city "in order to save the civilian population." Meanwhile he would relocate his headquarters to the tiny island fortress of Corregidor at the southern tip of Bataan, then, in a classic withdrawal designed to delay the enemy long enough to allow him to regroup, pull his forces out from between the pincers (sidestepping, in effect) to a "final defensive position" on the peninsula.[26]

Among the thousands of troops in central Luzon preparing to withdraw south to Bataan were a handful of men at Clark Field, salvage teams and a rear-guard of Air Corps ground crews, survivors of the bombings who had volunteered to stay and keep watch—eyes peeled, ears cocked, imaginations running riot.

December 25, 1941, Clark Field, Philippines
"We're expecting Jap parachute troops at any time," the Captain said. "We're gonna evacuate Clark Field completely."

"Parachute troops?" Q. P. Devore said to himself. "Can you imagine?"

Every night there had been a new rumor. Fifth columnists, saboteurs, now parachutists.

The captain wasn't joking. Everyone was pulling out, he said, and he ordered Devore to pick six "volunteers" to man a rear-guard listening post at the north end of the main runway, six men in foxholes facing toward Lingayen Gulf and the distant roll of battle.

Back at the barracks, the first man Devore asked was his best friend, Ben Steele.

"A parachute drop?" Ben said. "God, what the hell could six guys do out there against a parachute drop?"

"Well, yeah," Devore said, "it is kind of a suicide mission."

At dark they dug foxholes at the end of the runway. The captain made sure they were settled, then climbed into a white Plymouth convertible he had commandeered.

"If you aren't overrun, I'll be back tomorrow to get you," he said, then drove off.

Ben Steele thought, "God, we're all by our lonesome out here."

They adjusted their Lewis guns, checked their ammunition, and settled down to watch, six soldiers staring into the dark, whispering their worries. In the distance they could hear the sounds of battle, the vague report of the big guns from the gulf.

Here they were in foxholes at the edge of an empty air base, their enemy perhaps preparing to drop in on them. What man wouldn't be anxious waiting for that?

Then the big guns fell silent, and the men stopped talking and started listening. They scanned the sky and cupped their ears to the dark. It was quiet, lonely quiet.

"If they come," Q.P. said to himself, "will I fight or will I give up?"

Sitting next to him Ben Steele was thinking the same thing. "I don't know what I'll do. I guess I'll do what I have to."

They watched, they waited. The black night seemed to get blacker, then, at long last, gray. Soon morning was upon them, indigo, then light blue. The sun hung like a silken disk above Mount Arayat.

Just before noon, a white Plymouth convertible came roaring across the dirt runways, trailing a rooster tail of brown dust. The car skidded to a stop in front of the foxholes. The driver's-side door swung open.

"Get in!" the captain shouted. "We're goin'."

The sound of the big guns was back now, louder than the day before. The men tossed their weapons into the car, then tumbled in after them, and the convertible was out of sight before the dust had settled down again.

MORE LIKE A HIRED HAND

ONTANA'S BULL MOUNTAINS are more badlands than alpine
peaks, a cluster of hills and rises running east and west along
the lower Musselshell River. From a distance the rises look
like mounds of earth abandoned on the edge of the state's eastern plains.

In the summer the terraces and benches in the Bulls are covered
with sweetgrass, but in the winter when the Alberta clippers bear down
from the north, the plains and the Bulls turn into a bleak, snow-swept
wasteland.

The meadowlarks and mourning doves are gone now, and the sharp-
tailed grouse have left their sage-and-bunchgrass nests to winter among
the cottonwoods and pines. Hungry coyotes howl through the arctic
night, and in the early morning the frost- and snow-covered ground
around the ranch house at Hawk Creek is covered with their tracks.

THE WIND WAS PUSHING against the windows of the big room in the
main house, and Ben Steele lay there on his cot in the cold and dark,
waiting. Any minute now the Old Man would yell from the bedroom
for him to get up and light the potbelly stove.

He pulled the comforter over his head, grabbed it against his chest.

"Bud?"

He lay very still.

"You hear me, Bud?"

He poked his face out now but kept his eyes shut tight against the cold.

"Damn it, Bud!"

Off came the covers, noisily, so his father could hear.

At least he'd remembered to cut kindling the night before. Nothing worse than standing out in the vale of Hawk Creek in the frozen dark cleaving off strips of wood while an unseen audience watched from the hills.

He pulled on his moccasins and shuffled, shivering, to the woodbox.

HE GOT SO HE LIKED THE COLD, or so he would say. What he really liked was learning to stand it. Showing the Old Man.

"It's really cold today, Dad," he used to say at breakfast, as the Old Man handed out the day's work assignments.

"Cold?" the Old Man would come back. "God, I used to sleep in the snow with nothin' but a slab of bacon."

Maybe. But Bud hated it, the snow and bite of the wind. The Old Man would take him out to round up strays and he'd come back damn near froze to death. Next day, out they'd go again.

He'd say, "My feet are cold, Dad," and the Old Man would tell him, "Get off your horse and walk, that'll warm you up," but the cold went right through his overshoes, and he felt like he was tramping on frozen stumps.

"Stamp 'em," the Old Man said, but that only made the stumps hurt more.

Then one day, maybe he was ten or eleven, he stopped feeling the cold, or he just stopped complaining about it.

HE WORKED. He worked all the time. Started when he was eight, early even for a boy ranch-raised.

Whenever Bess would say, "That's no job for a kid," the Old Man would come back with, "He has to learn, he has to learn how."

The Old Man might give him some pointers, if the chore involved the kind of work the Old Man liked—roping, shooting a rifle, working a wild horse. Range work, cowhand work. Most everything else, often as not the Old Man would issue instructions and leave him to figure the rest for himself.

Before he could reach their withers, the boy learned to hitch work-horses without help. He'd lead the large animals into a bronc stall, climb the rails, and drop the heavy collar on them upside down so he could reach the buckle later to fasten it. Lot of bother for a kid.

He started driving a team and hay rake before his legs were long enough to brace him as he sat in the seat. He had to stand on the cross-bar, straddling the center pole and lean back against the pull of the horses. A hay rake was hard enough for a man to handle, much less a boy of nine.

Be careful, the Old Man would warn. "A team could run away with you, and you can get tangled up in those teeth."

He was okay. He had good balance, never lost his footing. Then one fine September day when the sun was shining and the wind was whistling in the bull pines, he was making a turn at the far end of a field and something, some rut or root, made the rake pitch.

Going down he grabbed for the center bar, his feet dangling, then he started to lose his grip, dragging on the ground a foot ahead of the sharp tines.

"Whoa! Whoa!" he yelled, as loud as he could.

By the time the team stopped, his toes were only inches from the teeth. He looked around to see if anyone was watching, if anyone had seen how close he'd come.

EVERYONE SAID the Old Man treated his oldest son more like a hired hand than a family apprentice. Bud didn't care. When he was young, he took a certain pride in his father's expectations. "The Old Man thinks I can do anything," he told himself. Even later, when he came to see that he was doing a whole lot more around a ranch than anyone else his age, he never complained.

His father was away a lot now. One business scheme after another, one card game and tumbler of whiskey, too. And his mother and Gert and his younger brother, Warren, took to saying, "Bud's the one who's running this place."

He liked that, liked the thought that his mother believed she could count on him. He was more her son than the Old Man's, though he'd never say so.

THREE

O<small>N THE SECOND DAY</small> of landings at Lingayen Gulf, a launch carrying Lieutenant General Masaharu Homma, commander of the 14th Imperial Army, landed at a makeshift dock at Bauang. The general slowly climbed the wooden gangway, his *tachi*, his warrior's sword, in his right hand and a smile on his face.

That look of kindness in his eyes always surprised the men in the ranks, accustomed as they were to the icy truculence of their iron-pants *ikans* and *sakans*, their officers, and the dark, unforgiving ethos of the Imperial Army code. But this *taishō*, this general, the men said, was different. He always seemed to have a gentle cast, even standing among the most ruthless-looking company.

Homma was tall for a Japanese, nearly six feet, and his size and soft physiognomy gave him a somewhat Western cast. He had been posted to London for several years and spoke and read English well. On assignment in India he had a British girlfriend. And all of this, his sometimes Western way of thinking, his public statements about the danger of going to war with the West, his apparent empathy for his men—all of it left him suspect among certain of his peers on the Imperial General Staff, especially the war minister, Hideki Tojo, and the army chief of staff, the humorless General Gen Sugiyama.

In the late fall of 1941, Sugiyama had summoned Homma and two other two-star generals, Tomoyuki Yamashita and Hitoshi Imamura, to his office. The Imperial General Staff had made the decision to attack Western bases in the Pacific, and it was time for Sugiyama to give Japan's top generals their assignments: Yamashita would lead the attack on the British at Singapore and Malaya, Imamura would move against the

Dutch in the East Indies, and Homma would direct the operations of the 14th Army and take the Philippines from the Americans. Then, turning to Homma, he added a caveat. Since most of the army was bogged down in China, the General Staff had committed only 200,000 troops to the campaigns in the southwest Pacific. The plan was to take territory quickly, leave a small garrison force to hold it, then move the battle units to the next fight. The General Staff, he said, had decided that Homma had just fifty days to take the Philippines; after that most of his troops would be transferred to Imamura for operations in the East Indies.

Imamura and Yamashita accepted the "honor" of their new commands with a nod, but Homma, who had risen to the upper echelon on his keen intellect instead of blind allegiance to his betters, was disquieted, and he assaulted Sugiyama with questions.

"This figure of fifty days, how has it been arrived at?" he began. What was the enemy's strength—did anyone know? Who decided that two divisions would be enough to take Manila? And what genius on the General Staff thought Manila could be taken in just seven weeks?

Sugiyama was simmering, and Yamashita and Imamura sat there stunned. Homma had violated the conventions of Imperial command— the unconditional acceptance of authority and orders. Worse, he seemed to question the competence of the Imperial General Staff, insinuating that the invasion had been poorly planned. And to speak so boldly, to be so pointed and direct, violated the strict etiquette that governed Japanese relations. Homma's questions and implications had embarrassed the chief of staff, and the *haji*, the shame, of this made Yamashita and Imamura most uncomfortable.

To allow everyone to save face, the two men convinced Homma that Sugiyama's target date was more a request than a directive. Homma would push his men to take Manila and destroy the enemy in fifty days; he would fight hard and he would fight well, and no one, they said, could ask more of him than that.[1]

In private, however, Homma was still troubled. He believed that Japan could not win a war with America and Britain, but he knew that to hold such misgivings, to begin a dangerous enterprise in such deep doubt, would be to put the men under him in great jeopardy. He had to quiet his concerns, he told his wife, Fujiko, in a letter he wrote from his headquarters on Formosa a week before the war. "This war is not one that is fought against any old enemy, and I don't think it will be easily won."[2]

Homma's command ship, the *Teikai Maru*, arrived on the early morning of December 22. "The ship sails along the northwestern coast," Homma wrote in his diary. "The sky is clear and the stars appear as if they are falling down." The first wave launched at 2:00 a.m. In his command post aboard ship, Homma waited and waited for word from the beach.[3]

The landing craft had been forced to negotiate a rough surf; many had been swamped and beached in the deep, wet sand, and the salt water had short-circuited their radios. Meanwhile, on deck the next wave of assault troops waited for the boats to return and carry them to the beach.

The delay worried everyone, especially the commanding general. "If we [are] counterattacked, we [are] almost helpless," Homma thought.

Then the weather calmed a bit, the task force shifted its anchorage, and the next wave of infantry on deck checked their weapons and tightened their straps and made ready to head for shore.[4]

THE JAPANESE WORD for infantry is *hohei*, literally "step-soldiers" or "soldiers who walk." And no modern army walked as far as the Japanese.

"A drop of gas is as precious as a drop of blood," the men were told. So they marched everywhere, often thirty-five miles at a stretch and under seventy pounds of equipment, ammunition, gear, and gun parts. They marched in the rain and under the boiling sun, marched for hours without a break on empty stomachs or short rations ("a half-pound of rice and some blackish potatoes" or tuna flakes). They had marched their way across the cold sweeps of Manchuria and barren flats of China, and from the end of December 1941 to the beginning of January 1942, every infantry or garrison unit that landed at Lingayen Gulf marched down the hot, dusty hardpan of Luzon's central plain. They didn't need trucks, they prided themselves. They could reach their objectives walking, "seventy-five centimeters" (one step) at a time.[5]

They felt all that walking, though. Their shoes were rough hobnailed half boots tight in the toes, hard on the heels, abrasive across the instep. And the socks were worse. Thin and heelless, they never lasted more than two days. Tasuku Yamanari, a farm boy from Hiroshima, had so many blisters—blisters on top of blisters—he wore several pairs of socks at once and at night dripped candle wax on them to "make it smoother in the shoes." Kozo Watanabe, son of a civil servant from Matsuyama, was more fortunate. In a storehouse along the way he stumbled upon some American socks, padded and three times as thick as the ones he'd been issued. Six-day socks, he calculated, strong enough to carry him all the way down the central plain.

When the men in Yoshiaki Nagai's unit set off on the march south, they were so happy to be ashore that many looked forward to walking. At least the roads weren't pitching and rolling under their feet.

Nagai had grown up on a mountain farm near Toyo City on Shikoku, tending his father's horses, and when he was drafted the army made him an equerry and hostler. His job was to lead a packhorse loaded with machine-gun parts and ammunition. The sun was baking the central plain, and Nagai, weak from seasickness, soon began to stumble.

"Not to drop out—that's the important thing," he reminded himself. "I must not drop. I don't care whether I die or stay alive. I must not drop out."

The veterans in the unit, the senior privates and leathery corporals and sergeants, thought the young conscript a milksop and scolded him.

"*Baka*," idiot, they yelled. Could he do nothing right?

He walked next to his animal, at the nose, and with every step he felt the weight of his overstuffed pack pulling backward and down. After two or three days walking, days of sweating horseflesh and choking brown dust, he began to swoon. He tried to play out more of the reins, and he dropped back several steps from the horse's head to its front flanks, where he could grab on to the gun trolley strapped to the horse's back. After a while this handhold was all that kept him from falling, but he could never quite keep in step with the horse, and the animal jerked him along in a kind of jig, mile after mile.

"Look at Nagai," one of the veterans guffawed. "He's dancing!"[6]

MACARTHUR'S MEN had been back-pedaling for days, retreating from the pincers pursuing them—a whole army on the run. Now with the invaders at their backs, the withdrawing Filipino and American columns, one coming up from the south, the other down from the central plain, converged on San Fernando, a junction of motorways and compass points northwest of Manila and the approach to the Bataan peninsula. There the columns merged into a single line of retreat that snaked its way south down the Old National Road toward Bataan, where the defenders planned to stop their running, dig in, and make a last stand.

The line of retreat stretched out of sight, from San Fernando southwest to Guagua, then southwest again to Lubao and onward to Layac Junction, the first major road crossing in Bataan on the Old National Road. Day and night for days on end the ceaseless regress clogged the road. To those watching from the barrios along the way, it must have seemed a procession without beginning or end, a cavalcade of vehicles large and small mingling with mobs of ragtag troops and refugees bent under bundles bulging with all they could carry.[7]

It was a dusty column. This was the start of the dry season, and the relentless tramping of feet and churning of tires and metal track on the dirt-and-gravel road sent up scuds of dust that hung in the air and formed an ocher cloud the length of the peninsula.

It was a noisy column, too. Civilian vehicles of every sort and size (taxis from Manila; sagging buses from the provinces; sedans, coupes, and convertibles by the score; even horse-drawn calesas and carabao carts) joined the queue of lumbering army trucks and ten-ton wreckers, tanks, half-tracks, and scout and command cars that bounced and rattled their way along the washboard road and across the potholes, axles clanking, gears grinding, engines aroar.

In between each cluster of vehicles came columns of weary troops, the dull thud of a thousand footfalls. They were dragging, these Filipino and American soldiers who had fallen back before the Japanese, first at the beaches, then on the long central plain, dragging along with the sheepish look of beaten men. "Keep moving!" their officers urged them. "Close it up!" But their pace never quickened. A lieutenant with an American tank battalion came upon a division of Philippine infantry by the side of the road "sound asleep from absolute exhaustion." A "pitiful" lot, the lieutenant thought. "They were all dirty, they hadn't eaten for many meals, and every single soul in that whole column was dead to the world."[8]

Some of the Filipino divisions had marched more than a hundred miles, marched so far so fast across rough roads and razor grass that their army-issue rubber-soled shoes had started to shred. When General Wainwright noticed his soldiers unshod, he told the quartermaster to issue new footwear, but, as the general discovered, the average Filipino had a foot "as broad as a bear's paw," and the American issue was too narrow. So most of the Filipinos "threw away what was left of their sneakers, tied the army shoes together by the strings, slung them over their rifles or packs, and walked into Bataan barefooted."[9]

By the end of the first week in January, the Old National Road leading from San Fernando to Bataan was as derelict as a garbage dump. The fields and drainage ditches that flanked the road were littered with the detritus of an army on the run: shoes, clothing, packs, empty ration cans, dead animals, broken-down cars and wrecked trucks, even wayward cannon.

The Japanese had pushed the defenders back, then back again. Now making their way south, the men on the run could hear the sounds of battle close behind them. And as they passed over the bridges that spanned the rivers and streams in northern Bataan, they sometimes saw wooden boxes piled at the ends by each anchorage. Most of the boxes were camouflaged with branches, but it was easy to see through the leaves and read what was stenciled on top in large red letters: DYNA-MITE—DUPONT.[10]

THE FILIPINOS and Americans who came down the road from San Fernando and settled into foxholes on Bataan formed a force of 80,000 that was organized in a classic order of battle: two corps, one to defend the east half of the peninsula, the other the west, each divided into divisions, the divisions into regiments, regiments into battalions. But to call the defenders of Bataan and Corregidor an "army" is to give that levée en masse a shape and character it simply did not have.

The Filipinos, for example (68,000), served in three different forces: the Philippine Army, the Philippine Constabulary—a militia and police force in one—and the Philippine Scouts. The Americans (12,000) came from the old garrison and the newly arrived units of conscripts, enlistees, and National Guard troops.

A third of the force had been trained as rear echelon: cooks, clerks, mechanics, radiomen, drivers, engineers, carpenters, medics, storekeepers, and so on (as well as planeless pilots, shipless sailors, civilian volunteers)—in short, supernumeraries so unfamiliar with the profession of arms most had never shouldered a weapon.

The majority of the foot soldiers, the infantry, came from the Philippine Army, and most Americans on Bataan thought "the P.A." a paper army. As the battle lines were forming, Captain Thomas Dooley, General Wainwright's aide-de-camp, noted in his field diary, "These Filipinos start running when the first shot is fired . . . It is generally accepted that all P.A. units will not fight, but flee to the hills and change to civilian clothes when a fight begins." Thousands of Filipino fledglings had indeed been routed during the withdrawal from the central plain to Bataan (Wainwright guessed that some 12,000 had run away), but thousands of others in their tennis shoes and coconut-husk helmets had stayed in their fighting holes until they ran out of ammunition or, when grim came to grim, until the Japanese overran them.[11]

As for the Americans, save a handful of holdovers from World War I, none of the line troops (infantry, artillery, armor) had ever faced an enemy in battle. The only unit of American foot soldiers was the 31st Infantry, a scant sixteen hundred men, part of the Manila garrison. On parade and on guard, the 31st was a model regiment, something of a legend in the service—its tailored uniforms precisely pressed, its ranks and files always plumb line perfect. Off display, however, these military mannequins did their best to keep from sweating their khakis. In the days before the war, the regiment held its field exercises in the cool of the morning, literally lolling under the palms, then after lunch they repaired to the barracks for a siesta.[12]

Ill-trained troops are often ill-led troops as well, and on Bataan, American officers, not Filipinos, ruled the field. They set the order of battle, staffed headquarters, controlled communications and supply. They led the Philippine Scouts and served as advisers and sometimes more in the Philippine Army. Some Americans were able men, clearheaded practitioners of the profession of arms, but the officer corps on Bataan was also filled with men who either were not ready for battle or were simply afraid of it.

Many of the junior officers and sergeants seemed to know nothing of the basics of fighting—how to set up a defense line, prepare a position to receive an attack, clear fields of fire. And some senior majors and colonels weren't much better. Enervated by age or illness, or just plain frozen with fear, several were caught cowering in their command posts. Colonel George S. Clark, commander of the 57th Infantry, a regiment of the elite Philippine Scouts, had a long record of solid service and an unusual rapport with his men. Then the bombs started falling, and Clark had a frightening revelation: air power leaves infantry exposed. For him, no hole was deep enough now, no bunker safe. And as the weeks passed, the colonel's dread deepened. He became convinced that Japanese pilots had been given one mission: Kill Clark! Any sound overhead sent the colonel running for cover. After a week or so of shelling and bombing, his men found him sitting in his bunker with a blanket over his head, trembling at the sound of the guns.[13]

BEN STEELE was tired and hungry but happy to be heading south, ahead of the sound of the guns. For a while the white Plymouth convertible had moved along at a good clip. Then south of San Fernando so many trucks and cars and refugees were on the road the Plymouth often sat idling or just inched along.

Sitting in front next to the driver, the squadron commander, Captain Jack Kelly, sometimes slipped into sleep. In the back Ben sat silently next to Q.P., occasionally catching his pal's eye. Where were they going? he wondered. And what were they going to do when they got there?

Soon the convertible turned southeast, and through breaks in the trees Ben Steele could see water—Manila Bay, he guessed—then he smelled the scent of the sea.

They were headed due south now along the coast, passing through one town after another—Abucay, Pilar, Orion, Limay. Between the towns were long stretches of dirt road flanked by fishponds and rice paddies and groves of mango trees and banana plants. Always to the left, beyond the ponds and paddies, was the blue of the bay, and to the right, to the west, a line of foothills fronting a phalanx of dark green mountains.

In the late afternoon they turned off the road and into a makeshift compound crowded with trucks, equipment, supplies, and men scattered in the bushes beneath the trees—the bivouac for their unit, the 7th Matériel Squadron.

"Okay, boys," said Kelly, "this is it, Bataan."

From where they stood Ben could see the bay to his left and front, and he reckoned that this place, this place called Bataan, was "some sort of neck." And now the captain was explaining how headquarters planned to close off the top of the neck, miles back up the road where they had come from. The army was going to dig in there and form a "front line," he said.

Ben Steele imagined infantry in trenches, hunkered down waiting for the enemy. And taking into account the length of the ride from where he imagined that front line was set to where he was now standing, he calculated he was far enough south to be safe, at least for the moment, and he wondered when they would get something to eat.

The field mess was serving rice and salmon flakes from cans. Rice and fish on Christmas? Back home his mother would be serving up turkey and potatoes, greens and biscuits and—

"I need two men for guard," the captain was saying, two men to stand by the road and keep the locals from wandering into the area.

The new guys, naturally, pulled the duty. Standing their post, Ben Steele and Q. P. Devore watched the boat traffic shuttle between a small pier on the shore just below them and the island fortress of Corregidor two miles out in the bay. Japanese pilots had been preying on the boats, and Captain Kelly, knowing that a pilot's aim was often askew, had advised the two sentries to dig a slit trench, a deep one. And just as they finished, sure enough, enemy aircraft appeared overhead, a couple of Zeros.

The first came in low, strafing the dock—Ben and Q.P. could see the boards jump as the rounds slammed into them—then a small bomber appeared, banked into a dive, and let its load go.

The missile made a strange sound, Ben Steele thought, "like the air was frying on top of you." They flattened themselves in the bottom of their trench, then came an immense *whomp!* and a painful ripping in their ears.

The bomb had exploded ten feet in front of their trench, collapsing the end of it and showering them with dirt and rocks. They coughed and spat and blinked and shook their heads.

"You should see the look on your face," Q.P. said.

"Yeah? You should see the look on yours," Ben Steele came back.

In the days that followed they stood sentry often, lolling around in the rear under the trees when they were off duty. Then one night, toward the end of that first week, two trucks rolled into the compound, and everyone was ordered to queue up at the tailgates.

"All right, fellas," said a sergeant in charge, "grab a rifle and at least four bandoliers of ammunition. You're goin' to the front."

The front? What the hell was he talking about? They were Air Corps, rear echelon, bunch of mechanics, fuelers, dispatchers, and clerks, not foot soldiers.

"Hey!" someone shouted, "I don't know nothin' 'bout infantry fightin'!"

"Well, son," the sergeant said, "you're going to learn."

THE JAPANESE took Manila, the capital, in twelve days. All that was left was to mop up the hinterlands.

Japan's generals were modern men, products of a military system that took its shape from the West, particularly the Prussians, and high on every officer candidate's reading list was the West's bible of belligerency, *On War* by Carl von Clausewitz.

The Prussian soldier-scholar refused to reduce a complex subject to simple maxims, but on two points, Clausewitz was clear: "the acts," as he called them, that were vital to victory were the seizure of the enemy's capital and the destruction of the enemy's army.

Like the strategists in Washington, the Japanese high command had been writing war plans for decades, and since 1919 those plans had called for the capture of Manila. The Japanese had also assumed that their enemy would try to fall back to Bataan, a natural redoubt obvious to any soldier who could read a map, but that assumption did not change their aim. With every new battle plan, Japanese strategists said essentially the same thing: they would take Manila first, then move quickly to destroy the American Army before it could withdraw to defensive positions on the peninsula. The problem was, the strategy called for one army to accomplish two missions at the same time.[14]

FOR MONTHS Lieutenant General Masami Maeda, Homma's chief of staff, had been trying to persuade his colleagues to change their plan of campaign, but no one, not the *bakuto*, the ambitious young planners on the Imperial General Staff in Tokyo, or his colleagues at 14th Army headquarters, would listen to him. And now Maeda was shuttling between the various field headquarters on Luzon, trying to convince divisional commanders headed for Manila to change their battle plans and intercept the retreating enemy troops headed for Bataan.

Maeda knew the islands well. In 1925 as a young subaltern, he had been sent to the Philippines as a spy and returned to Tokyo convinced that if war came to the islands, the defenders "would avoid a decisive battle . . . abandon Manila and withdraw to Bataan" for a "holding-out action." Fifteen years later, summoned to General Headquarters in Tokyo for a planning session on the eve of the invasion, he tried to convince those gathered around a large map of the islands that the enemy would surely hole up on the peninsula and engage the Imperial Army in a long and costly siege.

What was their main objective? he asked. To capture Manila? Or *teki ni katsu*, destroy the enemy? Bataan, he continued, gave the Americans what Clausewitz called the "benefit of terrain"; the peninsula was filled with precipitous gulches and gullies, difficult foothills and mountain ridges, and these natural "obstacles" would slow an attacking army and expose it to counterattack. Moreover, the enemy had likely dug thousands of trenches, bunkers, and foxholes, he said, turning the peninsula into a lethal labyrinth. If they did not catch the enemy on the central plain and destroy him before he slipped away to the thick jungles of Bataan, then "the power of the 14th army will not be enough."[15]

The men at Imperial Headquarters were political men, and in the army political men are careful not to challenge the prevailing opinion. Someone high up had decided that the "early" capture of Manila was going to be the 14th Army's "primary objective," so the majors and colonels standing around the map that day in November 1941 insisted, all evidence to the contrary, that Manila was the "central core" of American military strength. Take it, they argued, and the islands would fall. Let the *Americajin* withdraw to a narrow peninsula; they would be "easily bottled up and destroyed." Bataan? *Kudaranái hanashí ni jikán o tsubusú*—Why waste time talking about something so insignificant?[16]

ON JANUARY 2, 1942, less than two weeks after they had come ashore at Lingayen Gulf and Lamon Bay, the lead elements of the 14th Imperial Japanese Army strolled into the city of Manila.

A week earlier, to save "the Pearl of the Orient" from destruction, Douglas MacArthur had declared Manila an open city and quickly withdrawn his forces. Sixty miles north of the city at his headquarters in Cabanatuan, Lieutenant General Masaharu Homma, the 14th Army commander, was elated. That night, in the quiet of his quarters, he sat down to write in his diary.

"My wife, my children," he began, addressing the entry, as he often did, to his family, "we captured the enemy's capital twelve days after landing. Be happy for us. Celebrate for us!"[17]

The fall of Manila was indeed a great victory, a political victory. The day after the Japanese flag was raised in Manila, *The New York Times* opined, "This country now drinks the unaccustomed and bitter draught of defeat, [and] no reassuring explanations can ease the blow." But, as Masami Maeda had feared, the 14th Army had let the real prize slip away.[18]

By December 31, a Wednesday, most of the Filipino-American force had made its way onto the Bataan peninsula, and Homma and his staff knew for sure that their strategy (Tokyo's strategy, really) had been a mistake.

"We had the opportunity to pound them," Lieutenant General Yuichi Tsuchihashi, the outspoken commander of the 48th Division, told Homma. "And instead [we] allowed them to flee. So this is what it means to miss a big prize."[19]

"ALL RIGHT, FELLAS," the sergeant said, motioning for the men to climb into a large truck waiting to take them up the road. "You're goin' to the front."

Ben Steele eyed the rifle and the belt of ammunition he'd just been handed. He had grown up with a rifle in his hand, and the weapon made him feel better, a bit more secure. Now at least he could shoot back.

The truck joined a small convoy that headed north from Cabcaben, back up the same road Ben and Q.P. had come down a week or so earlier. In the back in the dark no one slept. Most of the men stared at the new rifles nuzzled between their knees. These guys, Ben Steele thought, "look about half scared of the damn things."

After the American air force was destroyed at Clark Field, some 1,400 Air Corps crewmen and technicians were gathered into a "ground" regiment, the Provisional Air Corps Infantry. They were to be used as a reserve force, ready to back up the guys manning the battle line. None of these clerks and mechanics, however, knew a thing about real soldiering; they were "infantry" in name only. A corporal from a pursuit squadron, for example, thought it was "funny to be carrying a rifle." And it was even funnier watching him learn how to shoot it. An Air Corps major guessed that most of his men "would have found [their] weapon more useful as a club." Some, in fact, were so flummoxed the major was sure that an enemy "could have approached at his leisure, rolled a cigarette, read the morning paper, and probably finished his shaving before bothering to dispatch the perplexed American warrior before him." Half "the Flying Infantry," as the Air Corps boys enjoyed calling themselves, got no training whatsoever. Along with the men of the 7th Matériel Squadron, they were simply put on trucks in the rear and told they were being driven north to a trench line.[20]

The convoy carrying Ben Steele and the rest of the 7th bounced north for more than two hours, one dusty mile after another.

"Where the hell are they gonna let us out?" he wondered.

Halfway up the peninsula the trucks finally stopped.

"This is where we're going to start the line," the sergeant said. "You guys go here," he said, pointing to one side of the road, then gesturing to an open area on the other side, "and you guys spread out through there."

They set up at the edge of a stand of mango trees with rice paddies in front of them. Their sector, they were told, was some two thousand yards long, part of a secondary defense line that stretched from Manila Bay, at a point south of the town of Orion, some fourteen miles west across the peninsula, to the town of Bagac on Bataan's west coast.

During the day Ben Steele and his comrades set aside their new rifles and took up the ax, the pick, and the shovel, cutting down trees, building bunkers, digging trenches—the hard labor of preparing a position for a fight. At night they climbed into their fighting holes and trenches and stared into the dark beyond the rice paddies, watching and listening for hours. The first few nights their imagination kept them awake, then the fatigue that comes from fear took hold of them, and one night on guard duty Ben Steele fell asleep.

Suddenly he felt something cold and hard poking him in the ear, then he heard the click of a trigger.

"You know what we can do to you for doing this?" said a voice above him, the voice of a lieutenant who had been checking the lines.

Ben Steele jumped up and grabbed his weapon back from the officer. The man didn't have to pull a cheap trick like that, taking his rifle and poking the muzzle in his ear. He could have just kicked him awake.

"You went to sleep on guard," the officer said. "I can court-martial you for this."

A battle was about to begin. They had their backs to the sea. And some of the men on watch with Ben Steele that night were so scared they were soiling themselves.

"Go ahead," Ben Steele snapped. "Court-martial me!"

HAWK CREEK

THE OLD MAN told him, "You don't point this at anything unless you're going to shoot it." Bud knew he meant kill it, of course.

Then he handed Ben Steele his first weapon, a short-barreled twenty-two rifle. The boy was seven years old. He was taught: grip the stock firmly but not too tight, sight with both eyes open, squeeze the trigger, don't jerk it.

He learned to hunt, how to stalk a prey and finish it. He would set out traplines too (the boy could dress out anything that walked or flew, a handy skill in hard times), but out trapping or hunting, often as not he'd sit there for a while and stare at the trophy before he took aim.

Sneaking up on a pond of mallards, he'd admire their colors, the jade-green head, the chestnut breast, the snow-white wingtips. Stalking sharp-tailed grouse, he'd crouch in the rushes for long stretches listening to the birds' comic cackle. When the time came, he'd always pull the trigger, get those cottontails his mother was waiting to make into rabbit pie, but it was almost as if he wanted to let his supper show him something of the world before he bagged it.

HE HATED SCHOOL, played dumb, and his mother knew it. The Old Man cursed and grumbled about his bad marks, and Gert, his sister, a couple of grades ahead, thought him so stupid she was embarrassed to call him her brother.

Bess would listen to all this and say, "Just leave him alone. He'll wake up someday and find out he doesn't know anything."

He didn't care. He sat there in a stone building in town or in some drafty wooden school shack in the hills and stared out the window at the shape of a certain coulee or the way the snow drifted against a fence, sat there taking note of things, though he could never say why or what for.

The best day of school was the last day of school. Final hour, closing minutes. "Have a good summer," the teacher would say.

He thought, "I'm free."

When his chores were done, when the work was finished, when the Old Man would finally leave him be, he could hunt, he could ride, he could roam Hawk Creek.

THEY HAD THE SAME STORY, the start of the family and the start of the ranch. Maybe that's why Bud loved the place so much. Hawk Creek was where he began, where he always felt he belonged.

At a cattle roundup in 1912 the Old Man, Benjamin Cardwell Steele (tall and strong in the saddle), met Elizabeth Gertrude McCleary (a pale Irish beauty in white lace). When they got engaged, the Old Man gave up running cattle on the open range and looked for a place to settle down. He'd always liked the Bull Mountains. Those hills weren't fit for farming, but a smart rancher who applied himself could make a profit there. Plenty of sweetgrass on the benches, plenty of water in the cool clear creeks.

He settled a section on the dry fork at Hawk Creek. "Prettiest place in the Bulls," he told Bess. And when she saw it, she knew he was right. Their vale was long and winding with a stream down the center. Sheltering the ranch front and back and running the length of the vale were ridgelines rising gentle and green.

With his brother James and a couple of hands, the Old Man set out to build a homestead. They cut trees in the hills, stripped off the bark, squared up the logs, raised the walls and the roof. A neat one-story, three-room bungalow, eighteen feet wide, forty feet long. Then came a barn and privy, storehouse, bunkhouse, icehouse, corrals, and a tack-and-equipment shed. Pretty soon there were chickens scratching in the yard and the cries of children coming from the house.

IN THE WINTER the vale turned gray and white. Bud was older now, just getting up, pulling on his boots. His father wanted him out before dawn to fetch some strays, and his mother got up early too to make him breakfast for the cold work ahead.

He finished his cocoa, stamped across the frozen yard, breath steam-

ing ahead of him, to the barn, where he saddled and mounted his horse. He had far to go but paused in the darklight to look back at the house. Did the same thing each time he rode off early. Something about the way the smoke came out of the kitchen chimney and drifted slowly down the darkened vale.

FOUR

A S BATTLEGROUNDS GO, Bataan was more brutal than most.
A thick thumb of land thirty miles long and fifteen miles wide, the peninsula of Bataan lay between Manila Bay and the South China Sea. Down its center ran a line of mountains, broken only by a wide defile from one coast to the other along the peninsula's belt line. Hugging the east coast of the peninsula, the flatland by the bay, was Bataan's main thoroughfare, the Old National Road.

The road was only two lanes, but it was a good road, dirt and gravel, half of it, then blacktop the rest of the way. The road began at Mariveles, the tip of the peninsula, and ran north hard by the bay forty-one miles to Hermosa. From Hermosa the road angled west for a bit, then turned northeast through Pampanga Province to the town of San Fernando, a junction with road and rail connections leading north up Luzon's long central plain.

Most of Bataan's major towns straddled the Old National Road. Between them were scores of barrios, and between the barrios were uninhabited tracts of jungle and lowland, a checkerboard of rice paddies, fishponds, bamboo thickets, cane breaks, and wastes of cogon grass. Sometimes the fields along the road were framed by clumps of banana plants or groves of palms and mango trees. And sometimes the flatland simply stopped at a wall of green, a dense tropical forest the men called "the jungle."

In places the thick jungle foliage screened the wind and blocked the sun, leaving the air damp and the light dim. Here beneath the canopy among giant ground ferns and tangles of liana hanging like thick cables from huge hardwoods lived wild pigs and monkeys, bent-toed geckos and fruit bats, buzzards and babblers, fantails and fishers, the wolf snake, the pit viper, the common cobra.

The humidity never dropped below 75 percent, even in the dry season, and with the temperature often over a hundred degrees, the jungle and wooded hills leading to the mountains felt like the inside of a hothouse. The air was still and suffocating. And always there was the smell of rot, the incessant decay of the tropics.

The mold and rot drew flies, ferocious flies that swarmed and bit like bees. And the leeches, spiders, mites, and mosquitoes were even more ravenous, spreading malaria (endemic on Bataan), dengue (breakbone) fever, filariasis, typhus, and scabies.

Although the dense vegetation favored the defenders, hiding their positions and hindering the enemy's movement, neither side could call that ground friendly. Nature was neutral in the battle for Bataan; its war plan called for misery on both sides.[1]

BEHIND THE SCENES, the staff of Lieutenant General Masaharu Homma, commander of the 14th Army Philippine invasion force, had been arguing for days, divided over "the problem of Bataan."

One group of officers warned their commander that he would be facing an enemy army of at least 50,000 men well entrenched in tricky terrain and determined to resist. Reliable intelligence, however, indicated they were low on rations, so instead of sending troops against them, why not just blockade the peninsula and starve the enemy into surrender?

Another group of officers wanted to attack. Relying on initial reports from the field, they were convinced that the enemy troops now holed up in front of them were little more than a mob, a rabble, "the remnants of a defeated army," 30,000 men at the most. The campaign for the Philippines was almost over, they insisted. A bit of mopping up, "nothing more than simply sweeping out the remaining enemy from the area." Attack, they urged the general, "annihilate" them.[2]

As the two groups wrangled, a telegram arrived from Tokyo: "Send a report on how you expect to proceed with the Bataan operations. The information is needed to make a report to the Throne."[3]

The meaning was clear: the Imperial General Staff expected Homma to attack the Americans and Filipinos, not lay back and starve them into submission, and they wanted a quick victory so the emperor would have the honor of announcing the end of the Philippine campaign along with Japan's other lightning victories in the southwest Pacific. The emperor occupied a powerful place in the heart and imagination of every Nipponjin. By law he was the supreme military commander, leader of the Imperial Army and Navy, and although he issued no orders and left the business of war to the Imperial General Staff, every man in uniform thought of the emperor as his military chief, his warrior champion. The soldiers pledged their lives to him, fought to honor his name, and there was no honor in waiting for a hungry enemy to give up.

The 14th Army, Homma assured Tokyo, was about to teach the Americans a lesson in "sheer brute force."[4]

EARLIER, Homma had gotten some bad news. His immediate superiors at Southern Army Headquarters had told him that the war in the southwest Pacific was going so well, they planned to attack Java ahead of schedule, and as part of the new plan they were taking one of Homma's best units, the 48th Division, and moving it south. In effect the general was going to lose almost half his command, his most experienced soldiers at that, along with much of his air force. The move would leave him shorthanded and heavily outnumbered, but there was nothing he could do or say in protest. "It is a bit too early to divert these troops, but it cannot be helped," he wrote in his diary. "It is absolutely forbidden to complain and whine about the situation."[5]

The new orders forced Homma to reshuffle his order of battle and take the 65th Brigade, a rear-echelon unit that had just arrived for mop-up and garrison duty, and press them into service as an attacking force. Code-named the Summer Brigade, the 65th was composed of older soldiers and fresh conscripts trained for police and peacekeeping chores. It was so lightly armed that half the men did not have rifles. By any measure, even that of its commander, Lieutenant General Akira Nara, "The organization was absolutely unfit for combat."[6]

Nara and his 65th Brigade had set sail from Formosa a week after the invasion force, and by the time their convoy arrived at Lingayen Gulf, Manila had fallen. Now, waiting anxiously for Nara on the beach as his men came ashore, was a high-ranking officer from Homma's headquarters.[7]

The officer explained the situation: the 48th Division was being transferred to the Dutch East Indies, and Homma needed Nara's brigade to replace the 48th in the order of battle. Homma "knew he was asking a lot" of a unit neither trained nor equipped for combat, the aide said, but the commanding general wanted the brigade to march south to the border of Bataan immediately and "mop up" what was left of the enemy.[8]

Akira Nara knew better. The coming battle would be no mop-up. Nara had studied American infantry doctrine at Fort Benning, Georgia, and had taught tactics at the Imperial Army War College in Tokyo, the tactics of attacking fortified positions—positions exactly like those he was likely to encounter on Bataan.

For the Summer Brigade, he thought, the mission was "impossible," but he agreed to attack. He would send his untrained, ill-equipped men into a lethal enfilade, knowing the consequences, because he was a Japanese general, and general-grade officers in the Imperial Army almost never argued their orders, even if they knew that following them might decimate or destroy their command.[9]

On his way south to the battle line, Nara stopped at Homma's headquarters to pay a courtesy call on his chief. He kept his doubts and disquietude to himself and put on such a great show of enthusiasm for his brother officers that one of them, Lieutenant General Tsuchihashi, commander the departing 48th Division, wondered whether anyone on the staff had warned the newly arrived Nara what he'd be facing.

"As a gesture of friendship from one classmate at the Army College to another," Tsuchihashi said, "I must tell you that you will be making a huge miscalculation if you think that those old soldiers [of yours] and the few supplies you have will be able to easily defeat" the Americans and Filipinos.

Never mind, Nara said, thanking him for his comments. Soon they would be celebrating their victory.[10]

So the Summer Brigade started walking. And since they had few horses and fewer trucks, they walked under the weight of all their gear 137 miles from the white sands of Lingayen Gulf to the torrid flats and steaming marshes of Pampanga Province (the gateway to the Bataan peninsula), more than seven thousand men and their officers, the hardest walk any of them could remember.

Colonel Takeo Imai, commander of the 141st Infantry, led the walk. "It was the dry season in the Philippines with hot winds whirling under the roasting sun" on an "endless road of burning pavement with no trees." It was so hot, Imai wrote later, the flowers and plants along the road looked like they were on fire, "reflecting" the rays of the "glaring sun."[11]

They walked at night too, but "compared with the daytime march under the hot sun the march in the evening had a touch of charm." Imai was bewitched by the "thousands of fireflies" that hung in the trees at the water's edge, some branches "so full of them, they looked like Christmas trees shining with small light balls."

Mostly they walked fast, as fast as Imai could push them. "Hurry up," he urged his men. "If you do not, the [enemy] will raise their white flags, leaving you no chance to distinguish yourselves in battle." Headquarters, he reckoned, was doing the clerks, cops, and sentries of the 65th "a samurai favor" by sending them against the defeated rabble on Bataan. Imperial Army planners, Imai supposed, must think "we are the perfect match for these Americans and Filipinos."[12]

FOR MORE THAN A DECADE the militarists and ultranationalists who controlled Japan had subjected the society to a program of agitprop that, by 1941, had left the Nipponjin among the most parochial people on earth, as hidebound as the "arrogant" white enemy they had been taught to hate. In newspapers, magazines, and movies, on the radio and the lecture circuit, and in every classroom in every school in every corner of the land, government pitchmen and pedants preached the glory of the East and the decline of the West. "Now, how about the Americans?" one such pamphlet began.

> The men make money to live luxuriously and over-educate their wives and daughters who are allowed to talk too much. Their lack of real culture is betrayed by their love of jazz music . . . Sex relations have deteriorated with the development of motor cars . . . The number of divorce cases in America is the greatest in the world [and] consequently, the beautiful family system is destroyed . . . They have lost their moral courage by relying on their material and technical wealth . . . They are governed by [nothing but] frivolous ideas [and] hence the poverty of their thought . . . America is, as everyone knows, a Kingdom of Gangsters [and] a country of bribes.[13]

And from this land of libertines came the most unfit and immoral soldiers imaginable. In the profession of arms, said a general named Kojiro Sato, "The Americans were the worst of all nationalities," sybarites in uniform who did nothing but gamble and drink. On assignment in

America in the 1930s, another Japanese officer was stunned that the American Army did not train on Sundays, and Japanese newspapers reported that American draftees, leaving home for training, "were seen embracing their girlfriends in public in train stations and weeping." No wonder, as the *Japan Times and Advertiser* wrote, that "many United States troops suffer from bomb-phobia." They had no pluck, no grit, no *shin no yūki*, true courage. Such soldiers would never stand and fight.[14]

ON THE EVENING OF JANUARY 7, the lead elements of the 65th Brigade began to marshal in southern Pampanga Province, the gateway to Bataan. Nara's formal orders were simple: "Capture the Bataan Peninsula" swiftly. And to make sure the brigade commander understood the urgency of those orders, Homma sent an aide, Colonel Motoo Nakayama, to pay Nara a visit at his battle headquarters in Angeles.[15]

In the seclusion of his command post, out of sight of his fellow officers, General Nara was no longer the eager hotspur bent on attack, and he pleaded with Nakayama for more time.

"But you can attack now!" Nakayama insisted. "The enemy is scattered."

Attack where? Nara wanted to know.

Nara had no idea where the enemy was dug in. He had no battle charts, no intelligence or reconnaissance reports, only an old road map supplied by headquarters.

"We should take aerial photos and make surveys before we move forward," Nara said.

"No!" Nakayama said. "You should attack immediately. It will be easy."

All the general had to do was form up in columns and march his troops down the Old National Road or into the jungle until he made contact with the enemy.

Just "chase them," Nakayama said, until they "collapse."

Nara knew the man well; he'd taught him tactics at the War College and remembered him as a mediocre student at best.

"Is this the order of Homma?" the general asked.

Yes, the aide replied. That was the 14th Army commander's order. "Please carry out the pursuit. The enemy force is only twenty thousand strong or so. As soon as you get there, start fighting immediately."

Osou! Attack! "Dilly-dallying serves only to give the enemy time for preparation."[16]

SERGEANT HIDEO SEKIHARA had come to believe that the war with America was a war "between the rich and the poor." And what he had seen on the long hot walk from Lingayen Gulf to the Bataan peninsula had convinced him he was right—abandoned American tanks, half-tracks, and trucks, all repairable but tossed away like so much junk. At one spot along the road he discovered a "mountain of bullets" under a tarpaulin. He'd never seen such excess.

"We cannot win this battle by the amount of matériel we have," he thought. "In order to win we have to have *Yamato-damashi*, Japanese spirit. Americans do not have our mental strength, the Yamato spirit. I am certain we will never lose. We never have, not in our history, but I must be ready to fight."[17]

Hideo Sekihara had been a star athlete in high school, a good student who wanted to be a teacher and coach. To please his father, however, he went into the family business making wooden barrels, *oke*. Then, on December 10, 1939, at the age of twenty, the *oke* maker was drafted into the Imperial Army.

Sixteen boys from Aoya had been called to service that month, and the morning they left for training camp, thousands of their fellow townsmen gathered at the train station to bid the boys a fond *wakare*. Shopkeepers closed their shops, farmers stepped away from their fields, children were marched out of their classrooms.

The ritual send-off, common throughout Japan, called for one of the young inductees to address the crowd, and his comrades pushed Hideo Sekihara forward.

He told the crowd that he and his fellow draftees were off to serve their country and their emperor, but they were not giving up the comforts of home just for the sake of his Imperial Majesty—May he live ten thousand years—they were out to prove themselves as well, he said, and they were grateful for the gift of this opportunity to do so.

The day was brisk and clear, and the wind off the water whipped the flags and pennants behind him. Then the mayor stepped forward to address the crowd. What a fine speech, the mayor said. Now it was time to salute all of Aoya's brave young men.

"Banzai!" he shouted.

"Banzai! Banzai! Banzai!" the crowd answered back.[18]

He was going to win a medal, Hideo Sekihara thought, the best medal the emperor could give.

BARRACKS LIFE WAS BLEAK. The training company was housed in a shedlike building two stories high with an unfinished wooden façade protected only with a coat of creosote oil. In the damp winter the wood-stove in the center never produced enough heat, and in the stagnant summer the room turned foul and stale with sweat and "belly wind."[19]

In the barracks the first-year privates, the conscripts, were like wretched vassals at the bottom of a feudal hierarchy, obliged to obey everyone above them, both their betters (superior privates, corporals, sergeants, lieutenants, and captains) and those senior to them in the same rank (second- and third-year privates). And this authority, enforced by law (the maximum penalty for insubordination was death), stood behind the "lessons" of Imperial Army discipline—the slaps, punches, floggings, and bloody beatings that daily, hourly took place behind the barracks walls.[20]

Maurice de Saxe, marshal general of France, believed that "the sever-est discipline" produced "the greatest deeds," and across the ages, East and West, men pressed into service often learned the lesson of discipline under duress. The Germans favored the whip, the French the fist. In the Imperial Japanese Army, this "encouragement" (bentatsu, it was called) turned the training camps of Hokkaido, Honshu, Shikoku, and Kyushu into alembics, a closed world of violence where men were subjected to the most brutal system of army discipline in the world. Here the civilian in a man, all he had been or wanted to be, was beaten out of him. What was left were hollow men, automatons living in a space, as one recruit put it, where "all the breathable air seemed to be exhausted," a "zone of emptiness."[21]

Most draftees hated the Imperial Army, and their discontent and bitterness filled the pages of their diaries and letters home. Army life was *ri ni kanawanai*, "unreasonable." That was the word they used over and over again, for the injustice was so great, the injury so painful, and the insult so severe, life in camp was beyond all reason.

It was unreasonable, for instance, to be slapped at almost every turn, slapped for spilling a few grains of rice or wearing a tunic with a button missing. "The ultimate purpose of [slapping]," a former army officer explained, "is to make them feel miserable, and thus to hammer it into them that absolute obedience is imperative in the army and that neither criticism nor protest is allowed . . . If the conscripts begin to give reasons for their deeds, they are hit for having tried to answer. If they keep silent, they are also hit. Either way there is no escape."[22]

When extra "discipline" was required, a recruit would be told to brace himself for a fist in the face.

"Soko ni shikkari tate! Megane o tore!" Stand firm there! Take your glasses off!

Men were beaten till their teeth fell out or their eyes swelled shut or they lost their hearing, "beaten like a dog!" one recruit wrote home, "beaten like a bag of flour!"[23]

When the first-year privates finally finished their pitiless apprenticeship, they were promoted to senior privates, stewards to a new cohort of conscripts. Now the bullied became bullies themselves. One group of primitives had created from itself another group of primitives, and all the groups from all the camps across all the home islands formed one great primal horde, 2,287,000 men who had been savaged to produce an army of savage intent.[24]

THE RIGHT-WING NATIONALISTS, rabid reactionaries, and ideologues who controlled the Imperial Army were determined to model it, indeed model all of Japanese wartime society, on the values suggested by another national myth, the legend of the samurai.

Almost from their beginnings, the samurai have stirred the popular imagination of the Japanese. Medieval poets and writers celebrated them in stories called "War Tales," heroic chronicles of fact and fancy that turned on the lives of the greatest fighters and most famous battles. Like the American cowboy, the samurai came to stand as an exemplar of the national character: indomitable even in defeat, virtuous even in his most vicious moments, most of all faithful—faithful to family, ancestors, feudal lord. And it was this legendary allegiance, this sense of supreme loyalty and a willingness to sacrifice everything to prove that loyalty, that made the image of the samurai the perfect paragon for a country at war.

The truth, of course, was a lot less appealing. The samurai of old were rough, practical men, more like mercenaries than gallants. Nothing mattered more to an ancient warrior than his military reputation, his

personal record of victories and defeats. That record determined a man's rank and rewards, and he would do almost anything to enhance it and gain advantage—betray a friend, deceive a comrade, switch sides in the middle of a battle, murder a loyal retainer to prove his allegiance to a new employer. And there was no opprobrium attached to any of this. The samurai thought of himself as a professional, and the mores of the day and customs of his profession gave him the license to act as he pleased.[25]

By the end of the seventeenth century, Japan's civil wars were over and the last of the fighting samurai were gone. Their descendants, some two million men who held the hereditary title "samurai" and received a samurai's stipend as well, no longer practiced the profession of arms. Samurai families still trained their sons in the martial arts, a part of their passage and heritage, but the samurai had become "domesticated." Half of them worked as civil servants doing paperwork, inspecting damaged buildings, directing public works. Some became politicians, others scholars and writers. And it was from the pens of the now sedentary sons of warrior families that the great myth came.[26]

In essays and broadsides, samurai intellectuals revised the history of their mercenary caste and gave it a set of ideals it never had. Loyalty was everything, the samurai writers said, and for the soldier, the warrior, there was only one true measure of loyalty: his willingness to self-sacrifice. The most famous of the books preaching this new morality, one whose words would echo across the battlefields of World War II, was the *Hagakure*, a miscellany of advice, anecdote, and instruction, each item intoning the same powerful theme:

> Bushido or the way of the [warrior], means death. Whenever you confront a choice between two options, simply choose the one that takes you more directly to death. It is not complicated; just advance to meet it with confidence . . . Every morning, with a calm mind, form a picture in your head of the last moment of your life . . . Every morning, be sure to take time to think of yourself as dead.[27]

The point was simple: purity of purpose through peace of mind. To daily embrace death was to be free of fear and hesitation, natural impediments to the ideal of self-sacrifice, which, in turn, was the ultimate expression of loyalty.

The political reformers of the nineteenth century borrowed this ideal, the spirit of Bushido or the "way of the warrior," applied it to Japanese society at large, and made it the way of the good citizen, a zeitgeist of allegiance, obedience, and sacrifice. By the turn of the century the sentiment of duty and loyalty was as strong in the Japanese people as the sentiment of freedom and self-reliance was in Americans.[28]

Who that is born in this land can be wanting in the spirit of grateful service to it? . . . Fulfil [sic] your essential duty of loyalty, and bear in mind that duty is weightier than a mountain, while death is lighter than a feather.[29]

NEARLY NINETY THOUSAND JAPANESE DIED for Dai Nippon in 1904 when Imperial Japan went to war with Imperial Russia. It was flesh-and-blood hurling itself against hot lead as wave after wave of loyal *hohei* charged up the muddy wastes of Port Arthur apparently oblivious to everything in their path. Against advanced Russian armaments, the Japanese carried single-shot bolt-action rifles, museum pieces that had little effect at long range. No matter, the *hohei* made themselves *nikudan*, "human bullets" or "flesh bullets," and walked point-blank into the Russian guns.

Most Western observers concluded that the Japanese were a people who celebrated self-sacrifice, or in the idiom of the day, they held life cheap. The cognoscenti, of course, knew otherwise.

"There never has been a race of men who really enjoyed sacrificing their lives for their country, or for anything else," Ellis Ashmead-Bartlett of the *Times* of London wrote.[30]

And the Japanese soldier was no different. *Atara wakai inochi o otosu*, "to lose one's young precious life," was as great a tragedy in Matsuyama as it was in the streets of Manchester, but the *hohei* had a feeling for his land and people that was rare among the soldiers of the West. To be Japanese was to be *futatsu to nai*, "second to none," an idea instilled in every child. And this feeling of being thoroughbred, along with the sentiment of loyalty and duty, produced a patriotism so powerful it became a weapon.[31]

Generals in every army take their lessons from history, and the Japanese generals who came to power during World War II preached the "fighting spirit," the *seishin*, of Port Arthur. The realists in the army, a handful of moderns unaffected by the slavish jingoism of their brother officers, understood that the West was rapidly developing new weapons that made old tactics—and old attitudes and sentiments—obsolete, if not appallingly prodigal. But the output of Japan's industries was limited and its natural resources few. The West would always have more assets, more tanks and aircraft, more trucks and guns. In comparison, Japan appeared poor, poor in everything except people.[32]

Millions of young Nipponjin of military age were available for service. Conscripts were called *issen gorin*, loosely translated as "penny men," the cost of the postcard calling them into uniform. And to an army poor in the pocket, penny men were the perfect weapon. All the army had to do was fill a young soldier with *seishin* and send him forward to skewer the enemy with his bayonet. "Plunge into the field of death willingly," an army pamphlet, echoing the *Hagakure*, advised young soldiers marching off to war. "Silently give your all."[33]

THE TACTICAL PROBLEM was simple enough.

Bataan was a peninsula and there were only two ways to attack such geography: storm it from the sea or mass at its neck, pushing the defenders from one trench line to the next until they came to the last trench, the last stand.

The backbone of mountains down the center of the peninsula left two approaches. Along the east coast was a relatively wide corridor of land, on the west coast a sliver of shoreline dwarfed by steep cliffs. Homma decided to divide his force in two and launch simultaneous attacks. The main push would come on the east coast by Manila Bay, where the mountains gave way to foothills, then tropical lowlands about a mile wide. On a large-scale map (at that point the only kind of maps the Japanese had), the east coast appeared flat and inviting. "The Plains," the Japanese labeled this terrain, and they planned to send two regiments down this expanse, chasing the enemy ahead of them. The "plains," however, were an illusion. The strip of land along the coast soon gave way to an undulating chaparral, jungle midland, then steep foothills. The hills were thick with plants, vines, trees, and tangled undergrowth.

Japanese intelligence had also been wrong about the enemy's strength. Some 68,000 Filipinos and 12,000 Americans were ready to defend the peninsula (roughly 47,500 of these men were classified as combat troops; almost all frontline troops were Filipinos). Homma had reinforced the Summer Brigade to 13,000 men, but the Americans had twice that number in front of them on the eastern plain, well dug in and waiting. Counting American and Filipino reserves, the Japanese were outnumbered three to one.

[*Japanese 65th Brigade, After Action Report, January 9, 1942*] The front line units, which had been waiting tensely for the zero hour, commenced the approach march at 1500 hrs . . . The roar of the artillery of both sides shook the northern portion of the BATAAN Peninsula. The enemy shells fell particularly furiously in the vicinity of [our staging area]. One shell made a direct hit on Artillery HQ, and in an instant the greater part of the Staff was wiped out.[34]

American artillery fire was withering. The men of Colonel Takeo Imai's 141st Infantry told their commander that the shells sounded "as if oil drums" were flying though the air, "letting out loud screams" overhead. Those shells, they said, made their blood freeze.

American cannoneers seemed to have every inch of open space—roads, trails, and fields—plotted on their maps. Even the watering holes, the streams and rivers where the Japanese filled their canteens, were in the Americans' crosshairs. "Especially astonishing" to General Nara and his staff was the enemy's inexhaustible supply of ammunition, enough ordnance to fire "countless shells day and night without ceasing."[35]

Nara went to the front to take a look, but "a vast jungle prevented a clear view of the battle area" and "the Brigade Commander . . . could see nothing but the furious enemy barrage in the direction of the coastal road," the road down which his Summer Brigade was advancing.[36]

To try to outflank the American line, Nara sent a battalion from the 141st Infantry west into the knotty chaparral and foothills of Mount Natib, but the men quickly became lost. In this group was a thirty-year-old sergeant named Nakamura, a machine gunner. Like many Japanese soldiers with a high school or college education, the sergeant kept a diary, pages composed under fire.

[*Nakamura, Diary, January 10, 1942*] Our trail becomes stiffer and stiffer as we advance into the mountains. An officer reconnoitering unit was sent out for the third time before night [to try to find the rest of the brigade]. Platoon commander died in action. I recalled my brotherly association with him since the organization of our unit. It is terrible to have to lose a man [on the first day]. I am downhearted . . . Everyone became silent after the death of our leader.[37]

The next night the two sides faced off in full-scale battle, the Summer Brigade hurling itself against units of the Philippine Army and the highly trained Philippine Scouts. The clash took place an hour before midnight in a sugarcane field south of the Calaguiman River and under a bright moon. The Japanese charged—their favorite tactic—and the Scouts and Philippine Army troops waiting in their fighting holes created a horizontal rain of rifle and point-blank cannon fire.

The first wave of *nikudan* were cut down, then came another wave of human bullets, then another.

In the morning, the cane field looked like an abattoir. Two hundred, three hundred *nikudan* lay dead in front of the Filipino positions. Japanese field officers reported that "the enemy positions were impregnable."[38]

Just before dawn, Sergeant Nakamura and his machine gun squad ran into the American line.

[*Nakamura, Diary*] Received artillery shelling and rifle shot rained about. It took the guts out of me.[39]

Ammunition was short, food stocks dwindled, and "the demand for water was enormous." The Imperial Army had very few trucks, and the trucks were easy targets. Nara's men switched to packhorses to traverse the heavy jungle and hills, but the animals could not negotiate the snarled traces or precipitous trails. The terrain was "so thick," Colonel Imai often felt he was "walking against walls." He kept running into "banyan trees, mahogany trees, mango trees, and the like, mixed with bamboo and thorns" and "vines of rattan and ivy." At night "the screams of weird birds shrieking in the dark or cries of the lizard" followed the boys from Fukuyama as they moved into position to continue the attack.[40]

[*Nakamura, Diary, January 12–13*] Two men from 4th Squad and one man from 3rd Squad were wounded. PFC Kobata was killed by artillery . . . Our food supply is now low—there are very few dry crackers left. I am [existing on] water only. No supplies can be brought from the rear because of the difficult route. We are getting weaker.[41]

By day the sun hung high and hot, baking the men in the open and turning the airless jungle into a suffocating shroud. A writer in the Imperial Army's Propaganda Corps, traveling with attacking units on Bataan, tried to capture the hardship in verse.

> Our troops plod wearily
> Through a furnace wind.
> There is no food,
> Our bellies must be filled
> With water.
> Drops of sweat roll out
> From under our helmets.[42]

By sundown the *hohei* would be soaked in sweat, then, as the temperature dropped and day gave way to night, their wet uniforms would cling to their skin and make them shiver. And all at once, from somewhere in the dark, would come the order to attack.

Each night they went forward, then attacked again.

"Whaah!" they yelled, charging into the darkness. "Whaah!"

And each morning the fields and jungle floor of Bataan were covered in corpses.

They attacked on January 11 and they attacked on the 12th, but, as they were wont to say, "without a good result."

"I am thoroughly disappointed," General Homma wrote in his diary. "Takeuchi [a regimental commander who led a flanking column west into the hills] took the wrong road and [got lost] . . . missing out on a good opportunity. What an incompetent fellow."[43]

But it was not incompetence that was killing the Summer Brigade; it was the exigencies of the moment. Without detailed maps, accurate intelligence, and reliable communication with brigade headquarters (their wires were continually cut by enemy shelling), the officers in the field leading the brigade's columns were left wandering in the dark.

Many led by instinct, which is to say the mindless reflex to storm ahead, and they positioned themselves at the most dangerous spot on the battlefield, the head of the column. Nara was losing so many lieutenants, captains, majors, and colonels that he had to order them to stop their bravado. "A person who cannot lead his men if not in a standing position is not a hero but a fool," he wrote in a battlefield directive. "There have been actual examples where three persons, the company commander and the platoon leaders [gathered at the head of the column], were killed at the same time."[44]

As the casualties mounted, the men in the ranks started to lose their *seishin*, their fighting spirit. Leading an attack, an officer might stop and turn to urge his men forward only to find himself alone in front of the enemy. "If a charge is to be carried out," Nara wrote in yet another directive, "it should be the creed of every officer and man in the force to charge en masse into the enemy's position, even if enemy shells are falling all around."[45]

On January 16, Sergeant Nakamura's unit managed to rout the enemy from a position in the foothills, but enemy artillery had the spot zeroed in and the new occupants soon found themselves under a "continuous rain of artillery shells."

> [*Nakamura, Diary*] I thought my end was near, so I took out my mother's photo. Yesterday and today are festival days at home. I wonder what the people are doing. I am praying for the health and happiness of grandma and the others from a fox-hole at the front.[46]

At last the Japanese changed tactics. Instead of ordering one infantry charge after another, Nara's officers first sent out infiltrators to probe the enemy strength, intrepid men like Sergeant Hideo Sekihara.

KIRIKOMI-TAI, they called themselves, men who slipped silently through the black and "cut deep" into the enemy's trenches. In a dangerous profession, *kirikomi* was the most dangerous of jobs, and Hideo Sekihara, the *oke* maker from Aoya, was well suited to such work.[47]

He was a *gunsō* now, a senior sergeant in charge of his own five-man squad. An hour or so before dusk, he and his men would gather at the edge of the battlefield, about five hundred yards in front of the enemy's position, and there, in the fading light, they would look through their binoculars and study the enemy trenches, noting the placement of machine guns and the other strong points on the line.

"Put every feature of the field in your mind so that you can walk it with your eyes closed," the *gunsō* told them.

Then they waited. *Kirikomi* required "sheer darkness," the blackest black. To muffle their steps they swaddled their boots in socks or rags. Halfway to the enemy's lines they would get down on their bellies and, as the *gunsō* had instructed them, crawl "like house lizards," right side, left side . . . right side, left side. Within a hundred yards of their objective they turned into "inchworms," undulating forward (again as they'd been taught), rising and falling, rising and falling slowly, silently until they reached the edge of the enemy trench line.

At this point, the *gunsō* always took the lead. He looked for a soft spot in the lines, a few yards left unmanned where he could slide into a trench unnoticed, then work his way left or right until he came upon an enemy on watch, almost always a hapless Filipino. If the man was facing away from him, Hideo Sekihara would reach out in the dark and tap him gently on the shoulder.

"Hi," he'd say, or sometimes "okay," or even "*magandang gabi*" (Tagalog for "good evening"), anything to get the man to turn toward him so he could drive his bayonet into the man's heart.

Sometimes he would stick the blade between the man's ribs and rip into a ventricle or slice through a major vein or artery, and sometimes he would stick the man in the diaphragm, or just below it, and thrust upward, as hard as he was able, into the body.

The first time he tapped a man on the shoulder, Hideo Sekihara started to tremble. He thought, "If I do not kill this man, I will be shot immediately." *Kore wa shinu-ka ikiru no mondai desu,* This was a question of life or death. After that he did his job without thinking.

Before the *kirikomi-tai* returned to their own lines, they scoured the enemy trenches for weapons, ammunition, food, clothing—anything to supplement the pitiful provisions of the Imperial Army.

More often than not, Sekihara and his men got away clean, but now and then one of the men would trip an alarm and then, all at once, the enemy trench line would erupt with rifle and machine-gun fire, and the house lizards and inchworms would have to crawl for their lives.

The gunfire always frightened the *gunsō*. It sounded like the roar of "a river in a flood," a rush of water at his back, chasing after him.

GENERAL NARA was fuming ("indignant in a towering rage" was how one of his operations officers described him in an after-action report).

"All units were attacking repeatedly . . . with no hope of victory in sight and with steadily mounting casualties," and Nara, who just a fortnight before had been so cocksure in front of his brother officers, was now worried about losing his brigade.[48]

His troops had begun the campaign without enough food or potable water, without enough ammunition and supporting arms. At the moment, they were reduced to eating dry biscuits and hardtack and foraging for roots and wild fruit. More than half the force was sick with tropical diseases, and almost every man on the front line had dysentery from drinking out of streams and rivers. By the third week in January, Japanese casualty lists were longer than the daily combat roll.

> [*Nakamura, Diary, January 22*] Last night a trench mortar shell about three feet long dropped near us. I thought it was my end. At dawn one enemy truck came directly towards us. The second squad attacked [it]. The truck swayed toward our heavy machine gun. Our machine gun opened fire. A man who looked like a driver was killed. Minami and Aoki of the 3rd Squad died in action.[49]

It was attack and counterattack, the Summer Brigade taking ground and pushing the enemy back, the Filipinos and Americans trying to hold the ground or regain what they'd lost. At last, late on January 22, American commanders began a staged withdrawal to a reserve battle line that stretched across the middle of the peninsula. To cover their withdrawal, American artillery pounded the Summer Brigade.

"I was completely paralyzed when I was suddenly attacked by the enemy at dawn," Sergeant Nakamura wrote in his diary. "Fortunately I spent the night in the fox-hole, safe."

The next day, January 24, somewhere in the southern foothills of Mount Natib, the sergeant's good fortune left him, and his diary abruptly ended.[50]

AFTER A FORTNIGHT of fierce combat around Mount Natib, the Summer Brigade needed to rest and refit, but Generals Homma and Nara were determined to pursue and destroy their enemy. Using maps captured after the fall of Manila, they ordered the regiments of the 65th Brigade to chase the withdrawing American-Filipino force south to what they thought was a thin line of outposts, but either the captured maps were wrong or the Japanese misread them, for they rushed head-long into the enemy's strength, a well-fortified second line of defense that stretched across the middle of the peninsula along the East-West Road. The line ran past the base of Mount Samat, a 553-foot spur with a commanding view of the lowlands.

Samat was the key, a strategic high point. Cannon emplaced there could shell the areas east and south. The heights looked down on the lowland coast, the East-West Road, and the narrow pass and hills be-tween Samat and Natib, an important piece of ground that made Samat worth fighting for.

On their maps, the Japanese named the area *Yoshi*, for the bulrushes and banks of reeds along its many streams and rivers. And into *Yoshi* they sent three units, among them the 142nd Infantry with Hideo Sekihara.

Twice his unit attacked the new enemy defense line, and twice the Filipinos and Americans repulsed them and counterattacked. By Janu-ary 29, Sekihara's Seventh Company, normally more than a hundred *ho-hei*, had just twelve men left uninjured, twelve men.[51]

Their captain was dead and the *gunsō* had been named company commander. Late that afternoon Sekihara got his orders: they were to hold their ground, the north bank of the Tiawir River, no matter what. And to a *hohei* such orders had only one meaning.

Hideo Sekihara gathered the walking wounded, about twenty men, and led them to a quiet spot near the river. Then he handed each man a grenade.

"If the time comes when you know we have lost the battle, you can blow yourself up," he said. "First pull the safety pin, then [arm it and] hold the grenade to your stomach, like so. See? Okay, then lie down on the grenade."

He spoke softly of these matters. He was sure he would never see these men again, and he tried to keep his feelings from overwhelming him. Earlier he had gone among the dead and scrounged the last of the food, mostly crackers and condiments, and now he offered these grim spoils to his men. They should share a last meal, he said, and talk of home.

There under the stars they told stories of their parents, their children, their favorite foods, dishes that made them think of home, of Japan. Most of all they longed for rice, *gohan*, a meal that always made a displaced Nipponjin wistful. They talked of *takuan* too, pickled radish, and *umeboshi*, pickled plums. They talked until their mouths began to water and their eyes filled with tears.

"This, comrades, is the graveyard of our youth," the *gunsō* said. "And this gathering is our farewell."

ON THE WEST COAST of Bataan, a separate Japanese force, some 5,000 men, had also been trying to push south. Here there was no beach, so the infantry had to take to the hills above the water. The hills were heavily forested, a hard and tangled hinterland with deep ravines, sudden drops, and breakneck gorges.

A single serpentine road, the West Road, had been cut into the face of the hills. The road began at Morong, and on January 14 that's where the main Japanese push south started.

Most of the fighting took place along the ridges, hogbacks, saddles, spurs, and ledges that looked down on the West Road, the only route to bring up supplies, weapons, and equipment. If the Japanese could fight their way down the West Road and through the heights above it to Bagac, roughly halfway down the peninsula, then pivot east and push across the East-West Road, they could turn the American flank and attack the enemy from the front and side simultaneously.

By January 17, the west coast force, the Kimura Detachment (named for the general who commanded it), had taken Morong and was starting to move south. Four days later at midmorning, part of the 3rd Battalion, 20th Infantry managed to slip undetected through the American line and set up a roadblock behind the enemy's front on the West Road. The Japanese officer in charge of the position, Lieutenant Minobu Kawaguchi, was just starting to reconnoiter his front when he heard the sound of vehicles approaching and quickly ordered his men to slip back into the woods and wait.[52]

Coming around the bend now were two armored vehicles, half-tracks mounted with machine guns. The lieutenant let the half-tracks pass, too much firepower, but somewhat behind them was a plain black sedan with two men inside, two American soldiers, a driver and, in the front seat next to him, a much older man.

The driver had his window down, and when the car came abreast of Minobu Kawaguchi and his men, they fired, point-blank. The driver slumped forward, the sedan ran off the road into a culvert, and the older man stumbled out of the passenger side and tried to take cover behind a fallen tree.

Earlier in the day headquarters had sent word it wanted prisoners, so the lieutenant tried to coax the older soldier out of hiding.

"*Anata-wa Nippon-gun ni houi sareteiru,*" "You are surrounded by the Japanese Army," he shouted in Japanese. Then, in English, he yelled, "Hold up hands. Come out!"

The American gave no answer at first, then he unholstered a pistol and fired a few rounds in Minobu Kawaguchi's direction.

The lieutenant was impressed. The older man's position was hopeless—surely he could see that—and yet he was fighting back.

Kawaguchi tried again. "Hold up hands. Come out!"

But the old one answered with another volley of pistol fire. Headquarters, it seemed, would have to find another prisoner. The lieutenant raised his rifle, took aim at the man's chest, and pulled the trigger.

Later that day when the rest of the battalion arrived, the lieutenant and a communications officer went through the American's pockets. His papers identified him as Colonel John Hoskins, commander of American artillery on the west coast.

Hoe-skins, Hoe-skins . . . Lieutenant Kawaguchi made an effort to memorize the name. After the war, he thought, he might try to find the man's family and tell them how bravely he'd fought, how well he had died.

Then he ordered his men to dig a grave, and there beneath a luan tree by the side of the West Road, the *hohei* of the 20th Infantry buried John Hoskins, Colonel, United States Army.

GENERAL KIMURA, commander of the west coast attack force, now decided to try an end run, an envelopment. On the black night of January 22 he sent the 2nd Battalion, 20th Infantry, some nine hundred *hohei* led by Lieutenant Colonel Nariyoshi Tsunehiro (by all accounts an extremely able officer who had won the admiration of his men), in eight landing barges from Morong south with orders to land on a beach behind the enemy's lines.

Tsunehiro's instructions were to sail down the coast twelve miles and come ashore at Caibobo Point, a good landing spot, then proceed inland a few miles to the West Road and cut the enemy's line of communication and supply to Mariveles, its main base at the tip of the peninsula.

Envelopment was an ancient stratagem, but unlike the ancient *bushi* and samurai, who relied on speed, surprise, and daring to encircle an enemy, modern infantry had to be careful outflanking a foe, for deep in enemy territory the enveloper could easily be trapped and become the enveloped.

Colonel Tsunehiro had been given fewer than five days to prepare the assault, and he embarked ill equipped and underprepared for such an assignment: His maps were large-scale and useless for reading terrain; his reconnaissance reports told him little about the enemy he'd be facing; Japanese artillery was too distant to support him; and his timetable was based on the assumption that the rest of the division would be able to push south in time to link up with him, so he and his men carried only enough ammunition, provisions, and water for a few days' fight.[53]

FROM THE SEA, Bataan's west shoreline was one set of cliffs and high bluffs after another: Ewan Point, Napo Point, Mabalan Point, Caragman Point, Cabayoc Point. With a good map and an experienced guide, the colonel might have been able pick out Caibobo Point from the others. At night with nothing but his instincts to guide him, he simply could not say where he was, and the navy coxswains driving the eight barges knew nothing of the swift tides of the South China Sea that were now carrying them way off course.

Soon one of the boats developed engine trouble, and as another took it in tow, an American patrol craft appeared on the scene and immediately attacked. It sank two of the troop barges, then broke off the fight and steamed away, apparently unaware of the rest of the flotilla.

Scattered by the attack, the flotilla split into two squadrons. One group of boats drifted south and came ashore in the darkness at Longoskawayan Point, not far from the tip of the peninsula, while the other group, barges carrying the majority of the landing force, some six hundred *hohei* with Colonel Tsunehiro, found itself drifting about halfway down the peninsula.

Dawn would soon break and the colonel did not want to attempt a landing in daylight, so he told his coxswain to head toward a small bay beneath a wide promontory, Quinauan Point.

FROM HIS SPOT in one of the lead boats, Private First Class Kiyoshi Kinoshita of the Sixth Company stared at the shoreline. Through the dark he could make out the contours of a ragged coast against a backdrop of black mountains.[54]

He was expecting a hard fight; they all were. Before the battalion embarked, the captain who commanded the Sixth Company called his men together.

"Most of the regiment is attacking the center, while we, the Second Battalion, will go on boats and attack from the side," he told them. "You will be landing in the middle of the enemy."

They had been in the boats for hours now, steaming along the coast, drifting, circling. Kiyoshi Kinoshita and his comrades were anxious to land—at sea a *hohei* feels helpless, a bull's-eye in an open boat, dead weight in the water.

At last the barges turned toward shore, fifty yards, thirty, ten, the hull scraping the bottom.

"Move quickly!" someone yelled, and the men in the bow vaulted the gunwales and landed in the surf along the rocky shore.

Facing them was an almost vertical cliff some sixty-five feet high, and in the darkness they quickly began their ascent. Grabbing tree roots, vines, fissures in rocks, and handfuls of earth, the raiders pushed and pulled one another up the face of the cliff, six hundred men struggling under the weight on their backs.

On top they quickly assembled into three companies, and Colonel Tsunehiro sent out patrols. One ran into some Americans on coast watch, and this skirmish, as well as the reports from the other patrols, must have convinced the colonel that a large enemy force was near, for he ordered his men to start digging.

Kiyoshi Kinoshita and his comrades began to hack out trenches and foxholes and firing positions among the tall trees, tangled vines, and underbrush on the shelf of land atop the cliff. With their entrenching tools and bayonets they chopped away at the stubborn roots in the jungle floor, and they clawed at the dark, moist jungle dirt until their hands ached and their fingers were numb.

THE JUNGLE canopy was high—in some places more than a hundred feet—and thick: towering almacigas and molaves with massive trunks and aboveground roots like giant dorsal fins, roots so big a man could shelter himself in the folds between them. In the middle story were balete trees with their bizarre tentacles or prop roots, and stands of benguet pine and green bamboo, bamboo so hard that bullets actually bounced off it. At ground level the understory was thick with thorny vines and creepers and chokers and stranglers, and everywhere—every square yard—there were winding lianas, wooden tendrils as thick as bridge cables, twisting and turning this way and that in tangles that hung from the trees and crowded the jungle floor.

Monkeys in the top story screamed protests at the interlopers below, and bent-toed geckos chirped at dawn like jungle roosters. The lizards and tree snakes, shy animals, stayed out of sight, but at night the rats came out, and so did the cockroaches and the itch mites and the red and black spiders. In the morning a man might wake in a swarm of mosquitoes and chase them off only to be assaulted by a cluster of flies.

The jungle canopy blocked the breezes and turned the point into a steam bath by day and a meat locker at night. The men had never known such asphyxiating heat, and they had never imagined that a jungle night could give them such a chill.

Most of all the jungle was a spooky place, a dim battlefield where the half-light created menacing shapes and shadows, a landscape that looked so riotous and malignant—the primeval trees, unruly vines, and woody lianas—it left a man feeling that nature was as dark and sinister as the enemy.

Quinauan Point was a fat finger of land, half a mile wide and three-quarters of a mile long, jutting out into the South China Sea. Years before, a logging company had cut a rough road from the tip of the point inland a few miles to the West Road, the only unfettered access. All else on the promontory, every square yard of ground, was tangled hinterland and jungle.

The terrain was so thick, so dense and ensnaring, it left each side blind to the other, but entrenched in the understory and perched high in the trees, Colonel Tsunehiro's men at first had the advantage. They sat behind the screen of jungle and waited for the enemy to walk into them. And they did.

For three days the Tsunehiro detachment beat back the enemy's assaults and probes. (The Americans had sent untrained troops to push the interlopers into the sea—first airmen and engineers turned provisional infantry, then the paramilitary Philippine Constabulary, gendarmes with rifles—but these rear-echelon troops were no match for Colonel Tsunehiro's men, who, unlike their comrades in the Summer Brigade fighting on the other side of the peninsula, had been trained well.) The colonel had deployed his men in an arc of trenches, each foxhole three feet deep, two feet wide, six- to eight feet long. Every day he tried to advance this line inland; the men would crawl forward from their holes, perhaps fifty or a hundred yards, then dig in again, advancing the arc. By the third day the line, which stretched some nine hundreds yards from one side of the point to the other, had moved about halfway to the neck. Even on the defensive, the Japanese always advanced.

When the fighting began, Kiyoshi Kinoshita was a runner for the Sixth Company, carrying messages and orders back and forth between his company commander and Colonel Tsunehiro, who had positioned himself just behind the center of the line. To call him a "runner," however, was a misnomer, for Kiyoshi Kinoshita spent more time on his belly than on his feet. The enemy appeared to have only one tactic— they just blasted away at the jungle in front of them, and they never seemed to run out of bullets. For every round a *hohei* fired, a hundred came back at him. It was astonishing, and it was effective. The defenders started digging deeper, and Kiyoshi Kinoshita went to ground so often he shredded the legs of his trousers and the sleeves of his shirt.

UNLIKE HIS TWO YOUNGER BROTHERS, who had enlisted as officers, he was *issen gorin*, a "penny man" or common conscript.

He had done well enough in school to win a position with the Ministry of Agriculture and Forestry, but the pay was a pittance, so after a year or so in Tokyo, he packed his kit and headed for Maizuru, a seaside town north of Ayabe, his home, to work as a welder in a shipyard. The radio and newspapers seemed to be clamoring for war, and in the noodle shops and public baths, young men of draft age were resigned to wearing a uniform. Sooner or later, they told one another, they would have to do their duty and swallow their discontent. Then, in January 1940, at the age of twenty-two, the penny postcard calling Kiyoshi Kinoshita to service arrived in the mail.

His father, an executive with a silk company, had taught him that a Japanese man had three obligations in life: to go to school, pay his taxes, take his turn in uniform. So with neither enthusiasm nor protest, Kiyoshi Kinoshita reported for training —four months of calisthenics, close-order drill, forced marches (day marches, night marches, heat marches, cold marches), rifle and bayonet practice, instruction in tactics, classes in military etiquette, and lectures on citizenship and the rewards of sacrifice.

Like the other recruits, he took his lumps, the daily cuff on the ear or crack in the mouth or open hand on the side of the face. "Private sanctions," the conscripts called this hazing, the bullying behind the barracks doors. None of them complained. No one ever did. Not openly. (Though some offered the public protest of suicide, slipping silently into the latrine at night to hang themselves.) Once in a while, a rare while, a strong-willed recruit, usually someone with an education and always someone with backbone, would offer some resistance. He wouldn't go against the grain, exactly. That would land a man in prison. Instead, he'd just stand up for himself.

One Sunday after their evening meal, the recruits (as was their duty) were cleaning up after the senior privates. Each recruit had a different job. Kiyoshi Kinoshita was collecting the mess kits and returning them to each man's cupboard, and in the rush, he apparently put one soldier's kit in the wrong place.

"My cupboard's on the second row," the senior private said. "You looked right at the shelf. Didn't you see it?"

Kiyoshi Kinoshita should have answered, "Yes, sir. I'm sorry, sir," because senior privates were always right, which is to say, recruits were always wrong. But Kiyoshi Kinoshita refused to offer the required obsequity.

He had just returned from a few hours' leave—he'd walked to the town, had a good meal, cleared the army out of his head.

"No," he told the senior private, somewhat dryly, "I didn't see it."

And just like that the man slapped him, slapped him harder than he had ever been slapped before, so hard his ears started to ring.

The unreasonable had turned into the intolerable, and Kiyoshi Kinoshita rushed his assailant, grabbed him by the legs, turned him upside down, and dangled him out a second-story window. He was going to drop the man on his head when he felt someone grabbing at him, pulling him, and as he turned to see who was interfering, he found himself facing a circle of senior privates.

In an instant he was on the ground. At first the kicks and punches stung, then it was just one dull thud after another. Pretty soon his eyes began to swell and his ears began to bleed.

When the "punishment" was over, the other first-year men picked him up and helped him to his cot. They soaked towels in cold water and applied them to the cuts, welts, and contusions on his face. The next day his platoon commander excused him from duty.

At first he was humiliated. He'd never felt so helpless, so powerless. Later, after he healed, a quiet rage took hold of him, and one morning toward the end of training when his company commander called him into the office and said, "You went far in school and you should take the test to become an officer," he answered courteously, "No, thank you, sir," because he had come to hate the army and everything about it.

To keep his sanity, his *tsuriai*, or sense of balance, he adopted a mindset common to most recruits. Instead of the iniquities of the army, Kiyoshi Kinoshita focused on his duty, his obligation to his country.

"To protect one's own country is something like protecting one's own family," he told himself. "It's something I have to do, just like obeying my father."

Several months later he still hated the army, but he was a senior private himself now, and with war approaching he had begun to feel a connection with his fellow *hohei*, that complicated transaction called comradeship.

They all ate their rice from the same pot. They all shouldered the same heavy load. Soon they would be watching one another's backs. After that they would be carrying home one another's ashes.

FOR FIVE DAYS at Quinauan Point, Colonel Tsunehiro's men fought the enemy to a standstill, even advanced a bit, a few more yards of ground. Then on January 28, the enemy apparently brought in fresh troops, regular infantry from the look of them (in fact, the crack Philippine Scouts), and the battle for Quinauan Point turned desperate.

The enemy attacked in the morning behind a whirlwind of gunfire. Colonel Tsunehiro's men hunkered down and dug deeper, dug furiously. The gunfire was so intense it shredded the screen of leaves and vines and kicked up clouds of dust and detritus from the jungle floor.

The colonel's men stayed low in their holes, waiting, then, with the enemy almost on top of them, they too let loose a volley of fire, then another and another. And so it went, back and forth, back and forth, almost till dark.

Late the next afternoon, following another day of frenzied fighting, Colonel Tsunehiro wrote a message to General Kimura at division headquarters.

Each company is fighting bravely, but there is no apparent promise of our completing our duty. [We are] surrounded by a superior enemy . . . The dead and wounded continue to mount, and our fighting strength is conspicuously declining. We are in a position of danger . . . We are already lacking in munitions and food. However, we are still fighting hard.[55]

Thereupon he added a poignant postscript.

"I pray for the success of Your Excellency's strenuous fight," he said, a doomed officer telling his commander he was grateful that the army was doing all it could to reach him. Then he signed off with, *Tenno Heika banzai!* (Long live the emperor!), a valediction that, under the circumstances, could be taken only as a dying declaration.

On the eighth day of battle, the enemy began its attack with a barrage of mortar and artillery rounds. The high-trajectory missiles came crashing down through the canopy and exploded on the *hohei* in their holes, then the barrage lifted, and behind a loud rattle of rifle fire the enemy advanced.

The Sixth Company was on the right side of the arc now, and Kiyoshi Kinoshita spent the day crawling back and forth with messages. He had to keep low, creep carefully under the heavy wooden lianas and across the green thorns and thistles that tore at his uniform and ripped into his skin. Sometimes, to catch his breath, he hunkered down for a moment in a depression in the ground or tucked himself into a nook between two finlike tree roots. The jungle soil was cool, the only relief from the smothering heat, but he had to keep moving.

He was thirsty—they all were. Some of the men had discovered a small spring in a ravine leading down to the beach, but it took a long time for a man to fill his canteen there, especially under fire. And the heat and dust and smoke and fear left their throats tight and their mouths as dry as rice paper and bitter as vinegar. They were hungry too, down to dry biscuits and bits of candy now. There was little forage on Quinauan Point, a few roots perhaps, some leaves and grasses they boiled to a sour tea. And they were so low on ammunition they often waited until an enemy was almost on top of them to fire. One officer, defending himself only with his sword, cut off his enemy's right hand before his enemy shot and killed him with the other.

After a week of such savagery, bodies, limbs, hunks of flesh, and viscera fouled the jungle floor. When they were able, the colonel's men dragged their dead comrades down a ravine to a natural cave in the face of the cliff, where, after picking the pockets of the dead for food and ammunition, they stacked the corpses in neat clusters, like cords of wood. Mostly, however, a man lay where he fell, or where a comrade could drag him. In such heat, of course, the remains began to rot, and the smell, the reek of decaying flesh, left the survivors retching.

So many men were wounded that the battalion surgeon had long since exhausted his kit. Those with severe wounds—men shot in the chest or stomach, men with burned or flayed flesh or splintered bones—tried to be stoic, to endure the consuming pain that settles in after the shock wears off, pain that left them bleary-eyed and breathless, but they could not keep up the pretense, the reserve that was always expected of a Japanese man. Sometimes, crawling past a hole on his way to a command post, Kiyoshi Kinoshita was arrested by the sound of suffering. "*O itai*" (oh-ee-tie-ee), a wounded comrade would yell to him, "How it hurts! How it hurts me!" Oh-ee-tie-ee.

He never stopped. The yelling of the wounded always drew more fire, and the Samaritans who answered the sorrowful cries and entreaties usually ended up casualties themselves or stacked in the cave at the bottom of the cliff. So he kept going, kept pulling himself through the creepers and ferns and across the moss beds and tangles of thorns.

On the ninth day the enemy began to push the battalion back, and the arc started to collapse on itself. Kiyoshi Kinoshita was with Colonel Tsunehiro in the center.

"Go to the Sixth Company and tell them they have to hold," the colonel said. "Tell the Sixth they have to fight until help comes."

The colonel knew by now that no relief would reach him; the division would never be able to break through the enemy's main line and drive down the peninsula in time to rescue what was left of the trapped battalion. And his men doubtless knew that, too. Their mission had failed. They were exhausted, outnumbered, and outgunned. Still, they would fight. The colonel knew they would fight. They were *hohei*.

LAFCADIO HEARN, the thoughtful Victorian who wandered Japan for fourteen years trying to get a sense of the place, thought loyalty a "religion" in Japan, a transcendent form of "affection." Loyalty, the government proclaimed in 1937, "is the basis of our national morality . . . In loyalty do we obtain life."[56]

To the soldier, "duty" was loyalty in practice, and to those who did their duty in time of war the government promised martyrdom. It built the Yasukuni Shrine on Kudan Hill in Tokyo, where the souls of all those killed in battle were installed as kami, soldier gods on perpetual duty protecting the fatherland. There was no greater glory, the government said, no better way for a man to bring honor to his family (and fulfill his filial piety) than to have his name inscribed on the rolls of the immortals on Kudan Hill.[57]

If self-sacrifice was the apotheosis of loyalty, then surrender was its apostasy. "Retreat and surrender are not permissible in our Army," General Sadao Araki told an American professor teaching in Japan before the war. "To become captive of the enemy by surrendering after doing their best is regarded by foreign soldiers as acceptable conduct. But according to our traditional Bushido, retreat and surrender constitute the greatest disgrace and are actions unbecoming to a Japanese soldier."[58]

Araki and his fellow ideologues were determined to create an army of human bullets and, like the Meiji politicians and strongmen before them, they too regularly hijacked history to do it. They took Bushido, that loose canon of moral instructions purporting to be the samurai code of behavior and belief, and created a code for the modern soldier, the *Senjinkun*, a pamphlet that served as a manual of battlefield morals. "Fight faithfully to the last," it reminded the soldier. "Even if it means dying on the battlefield, never give in to the enemy . . . Do what is expected of you, remembering that what you do will reflect on the honor of your home."[59]

Thus a man who surrendered, or was captured, betrayed not only his country but all those who had ever shared his name, living and dead. And the shame of that was more than most Japanese were willing to carry.[60]

"GO TO THE SIXTH COMPANY and tell them they have to hold," Colonel Tsunehiro told Kiyoshi Kinoshita. "Tell the Sixth they have to fight until help comes."[61]

He kept low, crept slowly. Any movement, a rustling of leaves, a swaying of vines, would set off a storm of fire. So he inched along, *zen-*

dosuru, "like a worm," first to the right and down the line, then forward toward the command post of the Sixth Company. Already the day was stifling. No breeze beneath the canopy to carry away the decay and rot.

From time to time the enemy fired bursts in his general direction. From time to time his comrades returned the fire. He stayed below it all, on the jungle floor, hugging the ground—"seeking cover," infantrymen called it—as if the reddish brown soil, the sweet earth, could enfold a man and keep him safe.

The command post was just ahead, but a tree felled by enemy artillery blocked his path, so he lifted himself up just a little to peek over the top, then, by degrees, he started to slide across the log and down the other side. And just then he felt a dull, heavy thud on his back, below his left shoulder, then an intense pressure, as if someone had poked him hard from behind and knocked him to the ground. *Itai!* He'd been hit.

The bullet mauled him. In an instant a sweet-smelling serum began to well up in the wound and spill down his back. The pain took his breath away, made his heart pound, soaked his body in sweat.

His left arm hung limp and heavy at his side. He fished a large white handkerchief from his pocket and tried to stuff it into the wound to stem the flow—

The message! He had to get to the Sixth Company and deliver the message.

The gunfire was more intense now as the enemy advanced. He started to crawl forward, dragging himself with just his right arm.

At the edge of the command post he encountered the company staff sergeant and made his report.

"The battalion commander says you should stand still until the help comes, until the relief comes," he said. "And—" He didn't get to finish because the sergeant was shot dead in front of him.

He crawled on, finally reached the captain, delivered his message, then turned around and began the long trip back along the line to the colonel's command post in the center.

He could sense he was seriously hurt. "This is a real miserable situation," he thought, but if he could make it back, crawl to the colonel's position, the doctor there could treat him. A bandage, some medicine, a drink of water, and a little rest, and he would be fine.

He dragged himself a few feet at a time. When he reached the command post, the doctor examined his shoulder.

"There is no way to treat such a big and serious wound," the doctor said. "The only thing you can do is wash it with seawater."

ON FEBRUARY 2, the eleventh day of the battle for Quinauan Point, the enemy brought in tanks. The Americans attacked twice that day, their tank cannon firing point-blank while their artillery and mortar rounds rained down on the *hohei* foxholes.

The battlefield was a wasteland—the denuded jungle, the brown dust and black smoke, the rotting corpses—and with the rumble of explosions, the unrelenting heat and thirst and cries of the wounded, Quinauan Point became *kono-yo no jigoku*, "a kind of hell."

Kiyoshi Kinoshita made his way to the edge of the point, stumbled down the ravine to the beach, and washed his wound with seawater, a remedy that brought him nothing but more pain. He was relieved of all duty now, save to survive.

One day passed, two. He grew weaker, more helpless. The blood vessels and nerves in his shoulder had been shattered, and the damaged muscles in his rotator cuff had left his shoulder, arm, and hand dead weight. His wound, still spilling fluid and blood, was suppurating, and he could smell the rot on his back. The foul emanation drew flies, swarms of them, a black blanket on the wound.

Dizzy and faint, he set himself down at the base of a large tree atop the point where many other seriously wounded men had gathered. The tree was near a steep ravine that led from edge of the cliff down to the beach. In the ravine was a natural spring where, during breaks in the battle, the men still able to fight went to fill their canteens. As they passed by his tree, Kiyoshi Kinoshita would beg them for water and ask for news of his comrades in the Sixth Company, still trying to hold the line.

The battalion's arc was slowly contracting, and the defenders were being squeezed into a pocket. From time to time Kiyoshi Kinoshita could hear the colonel yelling encouragement to the men in the foxholes.

Gambare! Gambare! he would shout. Keep going, men! Hold on! Hold on!

Every time he yelled, the enemy answered with more fire.

Now the dead lay where they fell, grotesques, tongues hanging, eyes bulging. The gas and sewage from the black and bloated bodies left the air rank and the men gagging.

Kiyoshi Kinoshita lost track of time. The sun rose, the sun set. It was light, it was dark. He started to think he was dying.

Gambare!

The colony of wounded around the palm tree had grown to more than a dozen now. Gut shot, many of them, others holding a mangled arm or leg. Now and then a man unwilling to face the shame of capture or so miserable in his suffering he no longer thought his life precious enough to preserve, would place the muzzle of his rifle under his chin and reach down and pull the trigger.

Kiyoshi Kinoshita thought, "This is the end now."

He passed out, came to, passed out again. When he awoke it seemed to him that the volume of fire had decreased. No one came by for water now, and he was so desperate for a drink he drank his own urine.

He thought he heard someone say that the colonel was dead. At all events he did not hear his beloved commander yelling anymore. He did not hear anything at all.

VARIOUS AMERICAN and Filipino units had attacked repeatedly during those last days. Their tanks blasted the Japanese out of their holes or kept rolling and crushed them where they stood. The evening of February 4 the Philippine Scouts leading the attack reported that they had forced the Japanese into a pocket roughly a hundred yards across and fifty yards deep. The Scouts could see the edge of the cliff and, beyond, the water. Alongside the Scouts were American airmen-turned-infantry, led by pilot William E. Dyess. "At fifty yards [from the edge] we could see [the Japanese] plainly," Dyess wrote later. Then, "suddenly, above the noise of the gunfire, we could hear shrieks and high-pitched yelling." Some of the Japanese were "tearing off their uniforms and leaping off the cliffs."[62]

Several score Japanese held out in the ravines and beach caves for another three days. They refused all offers of surrender, so on February 8 the Americans collapsed the caves with dynamite and called in gunboats to shell the last of the holdouts. A handful of Japanese, unconscious but still alive, were taken prisoner. Some six hundred *hohei* were killed at Quinauan Point and two hundred more at another landing. In effect, the 2nd Battalion, 20th Infantry was wiped out, the first Japanese unit in World War II to suffer a total defeat. Later in the fighting in the Pacific this kind of mass sacrifice became so regular the Japanese gave it a special name, *gyokusai*, "honorable death," and *gyokusai suru*, "to die but never surrender," became a rallying cry. But in those first days of the war, when such a large loss still shocked the Imperial General Staff, the Nipponjin used another word to describe the bloodletting at Quinauan Point. *Zenmetsu,* they called it. Colonel Tsunehiro and his men had been "annihilated."

GAMBARE!

Kiyoshi Kinoshita felt someone patting him on the cheek. Was he dead, dreaming?

He opened his eyes and saw . . . a *hakujin*! A white man!

He was in bed in a place of beds, beds in rows in the open and out among the trees. In a few of the beds he saw Japanese. In most he saw Filipinos. All around were *hakujin*, tending to things.

He thought, "This is an American soldiers' place. How did I happen to come here? How did I get to a place like this?"

His uniform was gone; he was in gray bedclothes.

"What am I wearing?" he wondered.

The *hakujin* who had patted him on the cheek was leaning over him now. Around the man's neck was a doctor's instrument.

All at once Kiyoshi Kinoshita realized, "I have become a *horyo*!" a prisoner of war.

The shame hit him hard, like another bullet in the back. His comrades were dead—he was sure of it—but Kiyoshi Kinoshita, orderly and messenger for the Sixth Company, was lying in an enemy bed.

He wanted to die, but he was weak, too weak to kill himself.

"This is miserable," he thought. "Why do I have to be a prisoner?"

He had betrayed his comrades, he had betrayed his colonel. They had died and he had lived, and the stink of that failure, that disgrace, would always be on him. *Haji*, they called it, a shame that ran deep.

His duty had been to die for his country ("Duty is weightier than a mountain, while death is lighter than a feather"), die with the *hohei* on Quinauan Point, but he had failed, and that failure turned his survival into an act of treachery.

Horyo! Prisoner of war. His mother, father, brothers, friends, neighbors—all Ayabe would know, or so he imagined. His shame would become his family's scandal. ("There goes the mother of Kiyoshi, the *horyo*!") The family would have to disown him. In a society where everyone was somehow connected, he would suddenly be estranged. How could he live? He was a *horyo*, and to everyone a *horyo* was dead.[63]

"I must get out of here," Kiyoshi Kinoshita told himself. "I must somehow change this situation of being a prisoner."

Each day he grew stronger. His left arm was still useless, but after a while he could make his way around unassisted, and he began to feel better.

The Americans were feeding him and caring for him, and for that he was grateful, but when he closed his eyes he could still hear the cries of his comrades—"*O itai*"—and the enemy's kindness only deepened his shame, so one day several weeks after his capture he leaned over to the man in the next bed, a *hohei* named Saito who had lost his right hand, and whispered, "Would you like to escape?"

That night as their Filipino guards slumbered, the two soldiers slipped out of their beds and into the jungle. Two cripples hanging on to each other with their good arms, running as fast as they were able.

They ran for days. One day they came to a hill and, still clinging to each other for support, clawed their way to the top, then down the other side into a valley with a river. They were very thirsty and helped each other down the steep bank and into the water. Dipping their faces to drink, they noticed a school of small fish swimming among the rocks. They were hungry, but one-armed men make poor fishermen, so they dined on earthworms that night and washed them down with river water.

They wandered and wandered, how long and how far they did not know. They lived on leaves and grasses, forage, belly-fill. After many days of wandering, perhaps twenty, they noticed something strange—it was quiet. What happened to the sound of the big guns? they wondered.

A while later in a field they saw some figures in the distance. Soldiers. But whose? They looked again and recognized the uniforms. *Hohei.* From the look of them, a Scout unit. They were finally home, in their own lines, among their own comrades.

Then Kiyoshi Kinoshita remembered, "I was captured. I was a *horyo.*"

The *horyo* were ordered to report to the military police. How did they come to be prisoners? the police asked. What happened in the battle? Where did the Americans take them? The police wanted to know everything.

Kiyoshi Kinoshita told them about being a messenger, about how he was sent to the Sixth Company to tell them to hold on, about being shot and losing consciousness. The police made him tell this story several times, and with each telling their reaction grew more grim.

At first they said, "How can you have survived until now?" Later they said, "Aren't you ashamed of yourself?" After his final recitation, an officer told Kiyoshi Kinoshita, "You are going to be put to death."

They returned him to the room where Saito-san, his fellow fugitive, was waiting.

"We are going to be punished," Kinoshita told him. "We are going to be put to death. You must get yourself ready."

For his part, he was prepared. "I have no private wish, nothing that I want, nothing at all," he told himself. "I am not afraid. I am ready to accept death."

The next day the two men were ordered into an automobile and off they went. The road cut through an area of undergrowth, then, ahead, Kiyoshi Kinoshita saw a break in the terrain, a flat, open place.

He thought, "This is the time I will be put to death."

The car, however, kept going. A while later they arrived at a hospital, and the two men were given uniforms. After they changed, they were driven up the road to Santa Cruz, and the car stopped in front of a big church.

"Oh," Kiyoshi Kinoshita thought, "here, here is where we will be shot. What a splendid thing it is to be shot like this at a church. My mind is pure, my heart is full."

The two men were given a meal, then they waited.

Two days later they were waiting still.

"Maybe we will not be shot," Kiyoshi Kinoshita began to think.

After that he was transferred from one hospital to another. His wound had healed and he was beginning to get some feeling back in his left arm.

At each place, he and a handful of other men who had been captured and repatriated during the campaign—amputees and cripples, most of them—were kept in separate quarters, apart from all other troops. The army apparently did not want these *horyo*, these men of shame, to befoul the ranks or stand as survivors, exceptions to the ethic of self-sacrifice.

When he was well, the army assigned Kiyoshi Kinoshita to a small garrison unit, then one day he was told they were sending him to Davao to work in a shipyard, his civilian job before he joined the army. So he went south and took up the welder's torch.

Here, as elsewhere, everyone knew he had been a *horyo*, but none of his superiors, or the men on the job, mistreated him, though from time to time someone might ease up next to him and, with the customary courtesy and respect, ask, "Why didn't you kill yourself?"

LEAVING

THAT DAY, as usual, Ben Steele, fifteen now, was working, mowing hay.

He'd cut only a quarter of the field, but already the meadow was filling with the scent of his work. At the far end he turned the team for another pass, back in the direction of the house, and as soon as he did he was surprised to see the Old Man coming up the road and cutting across the meadow. At breakfast his mother had told him his father had gone to town early on business and wasn't expected back till supper.

Bud pulled on the reins, stopped the team in the sun. It was hot in the meadow. The rimrocks often blocked the breeze.

"Unhook 'em and turn 'em loose," the Old Man said, as he approached. "We're leaving."

"What do you mean, leaving?" the boy said, looking down from his seat.

"We're just leaving the ranch, that's all!"

"But why? Why are we leaving?"

"We've lost the ranch . . . The bank . . . You know."

He didn't know. He didn't know anything.

"We have to move," the Old Man went on. "We have to get off the place."

"Get off when?"

"Now, like I just told you."

"What about the stock?" the boy said. "What about Buck?"

He still loved that horse, his old lineback buckskin. (Had him since he was seven, used to jump up and straddle his neck to get on. Got so he could ride that horse anywhere without a bridle, just touch his neck and he'd turn.)

The Old Man said that Buck and the rest of stock would be going to Uncle James's place a few miles down the creek. If they ever got out this way again, the boy could see him.

Then the Old Man turned on his heel and headed down the meadow to the dirt road leading back to the house.

Bud got down from the machine. The sun was hot. Birds were beginning to swoop down and feed among the clumps of cut hay and stubble.

Leaving Hawk Creek—he couldn't imagine it. There was a gnawing in his stomach, like a hunger pang, but more empty, and he was tired like he'd never been tired before.

From Gert later he got the story: the Old Man was mortgaged up to his gray Stetson, but he owned two hundred head of cattle free and clear, and the bankers, knowing he knew his business, urged him to stay on and try to turn a profit. Bess wanted to stay too. She loved the yellow clover by the roadside, the magpies making their nests in the trees, but the Old Man, he did not want to hear it. He owed on the land, owed on the machinery, owed on his taxes.

"We're leaving," he said.

FROM THE MUDROOM of the house they'd rented in Worden the boy could hear his mother light into his father.

"That's a job you should be doin'," his mother said. "Not that kid. Sending him out there, you'll get him killed this time of year."

"Aw," the Old Man came back, "that kid can do it as easy as I can."

Outside, beyond the mudroom door, the temperature was well below zero, and the thirty miles of broken ground between Worden and the Bull Mountains, where the boy would soon be headed, were frozen with ice and snow.

For a year now the family had been living in a thin-walled bungalow in a small town along the Yellowstone River, his father doing a little of this and a little of that and selling off what was left of the stock from Hawk Creek. The Old Man had made a deal to sell a nearby rancher a couple of workhorses, and he was sending the boy north on a borrowed saddle bronc to fetch them.

"You get with Fred Treible up there and he'll help you to tie those horses' heads together," his father told him. "Then you fasten onto them with a lariat and bring 'em into the valley."

He made it north okay, but early the next morning when he went to collect the animals he would be trailing, he discovered they were wild, fourteen hundred pounds each of unruly horseflesh.

A hired hand on the place helped him get halters on them, and around 7:00 a.m. Bud bundled up best he could against the cold and set out for the Yellowstone. He headed south first, across the hills toward the Dry Fork of Hawk Creek, then, keeping Steamboat Butte to his right, he planned to angle east toward Hubbard Creek, hoping to pick up the Bundy Road—if he could find it and it was passable—and use that old track to lead him to the river.

The horses fought him every step. He thought, "How the hell am I gonna break 'em and lead 'em at the same time?"

He yanked and tugged the beasts across the frozen prairie. After three hours, he'd gone barely a mile.

By noon he was hungry and half frozen but dared not stop. It was late afternoon by the time he reached the Bundy Road. At that point he was still some fifteen miles from the river, still wrestling with the knotheads on the other end of the rope.

Now darkness was falling and he was shaking with cold. He hoped he could keep to the road and not end up riding in circles till he fell frozen from his horse.

At last, in the blue light and a swirl of snow, he rode into Worden. It was well after midnight when he walked into the house so stiff with cold he had to stand for a while in front of the stove before he could bend to pull off his boots.

His mother tried to fuss over him. The Old Man stood nearby and said nothing, but the boy knew what he'd done. Knew the Old Man knew it, too.

FIVE

THE FIRST BATTLE for Bataan was going badly, and on February 8, 1942, at his new field headquarters, a large two-story house in the town of San Fernando some thirty miles north of the Bataan battle line, Lieutenant General Masaharu Homma, commander of the 14th Army and the man in charge of all Japanese troops in the Philippines, turned again to his officers for advice.[1]

Beleaguered in the field and beset by political enemies at home, Homma was in trouble.

Guam, Wake Island, and Hong Kong had been captured in the first three weeks of the war, and by early February, Imperial soldiers were marching hard on Singapore and coming ashore in the Dutch East Indies. Japan was taking the territory it wanted, taking it with just ten divisions, 200,000 troops, a relatively small number of men. The Imperial Army appeared invincible, and that chimera created a fervor back home and fear overseas. Quick strikes followed by fleet advances, swift victories, and stunning propaganda. The strategy seemed to be working—working everywhere except the Philippines. There a ragtag army of natives and the soft Western sots who sponsored them had dug in for a fight in a jungle wasteland, and suddenly there was a hitch in Japan's plan for early victory in the Pacific.

Homma had been given fifty days to take the islands. His deadline, January 26, had passed without a good result, and he knew that his countrymen, accustomed to waking to news of victories with their morning miso and steamed rice, would be disappointed. "It seems that the general public feels that since we captured Manila easily, the rest of the area is virtually won as well," he wrote in his diary. "This is immensely annoying to me. They should understand the difficulty we are experiencing here. Our opponent is the United States, an entirely different enemy from China. Of course there is no way for an easy resolution."[2]

More troubling, the general had learned through channels that the Throne—likely at the urging of its "advisers," which is to say his rivals on the Imperial General Staff—had refused to issue a general commendation to the men of the 14th Army, an accolade that by custom should have been theirs, and his, for taking an enemy capital. "I have no response when asked whether the Bataan battle will be over soon," he continued. "I only have fear."[3]

Most troubling of all, Japan's central strongman, General Hideki Tojo—war minister, prime minister, and one of Homma's old antagonists—was angry. Japan's other field commanders had brushed aside the British and bowled over the Dutch, but Tojo felt that against America, Japan appeared to be "blundering."

In truth, Homma's failure to secure the Philippines in fifty days had done nothing to delay Tokyo's timetable in the southwest Pacific. Indeed, the Imperial Army was ahead of schedule, but daily stories in the American press about the "valiant defenders of Bataan" had left Tojo "irritated." Frank Hewlett, for example, a United Press reporter, kept pounding out the same story line: "American and Filipino troops, after six weeks of battling here in the wilds of Bataan . . . have exploded the myth that the Japanese are 'supermen.'"[4]

THE MEETING at Homma's headquarters in San Fernando began in the middle of the afternoon. As was his custom, the general said little. As was their habit, his officers, divided into camps, were sharp-tongued and full of choler.

One side clamored to continue the attack. They argued that Nara and Kimura had repeatedly pushed the American line back. The 14th Army had the advantage, the initiative. If they would just concentrate their forces along Bataan's flat east coast, they could break through the enemy line and push the adversaries into the sea.

The other side wanted to break off the attack. To continue, they said, would be *jisatsu*, "suicide." Yes, Nara and Kimura had indeed made gains, but between them they had suffered so many casualties, an attacking force of nearly 20,000 men now could scarcely muster three battalions, fewer than 3,000 men, a handful against the enemy's horde. Take the peninsula under siege, they advised. MacArthur's men were already on half rations, and with Japan in control of the sea and sky, the situation was bound to get worse. The Filipinos and Americans had no hope of help. All the Japanese had to do was sit back and starve them into submission.

Homma sat in silence. To Major Moriya Wada, a young staff officer, the general looked troubled, "blue." The general's face, Wada thought, seemed filled with *anrui*, "hidden grief, tears in the darkness."

Since landing at Lingayen Gulf, the 14th Army had suffered 3,320 killed, 5,350 wounded, and 15,500 sick—men disabled by malaria, dengue fever, beriberi, dysentery, and other diseases. Homma had lost roughly half his army, more than 24,000 casualties. The 2nd Battalion of 20th Infantry, the unit that had landed at Quinauan Point, had, as the general later put it, "vanished without a trace," and its sister battalions, sent to its rescue, were decimated. An entire regiment wiped out.[5]

After hours of argument the general finally spoke. He was calling off the offensive, he said. With such losses the army was near collapse. If the enemy counterattacked, he told his staff, "we will have no choice but to hold up our hands and surrender."[6]

He ordered his officers to prepare a message for Tokyo, a plea for resupply and reinforcements. For a Japanese commander, no request could be more bitter, for it reeked of resignation and defeat.

> Under the present conditions, even if we continued our offensive, the chances of success are slim, and at the very least, huge losses will be incurred. In the worst case scenario, this will produce disastrous effects for the entire strategy of the Philippines . . . As the army sees the shedding of more blood and tears, we recommend the maintenance and reorganization of our present position. After increased troop strength arrives, we will think of an appropriate strategy for the changed conditions.[7]

And then, turning back to the long lists of casualties, the general's tears were hidden no more.

THE AMERICANS noticed the change almost immediately.

The enemy has "definitely recoiled," MacArthur told Washington in a series of cables in February. "Heavy enemy losses sustained in his ill advised and uncoordinated attack of the past two weeks have . . . dulled his initiative" and "he begins to show signs of exhaustion."[8]

Some of MacArthur's men were so buoyed by the news, they wanted to leave their foxholes and counterattack. "The situation looks rosy," one young army captain wrote in his diary. "If we can only get help here," he said, they could "clear" all Luzon of the enemy. "Hope this happens."[9]

Fueled by hope, the American rumor mill ground out one canard after another: Relief convoys were on the way from Australia; the war would be over by Easter; they'd soon be playing tennis and golf again.

The gossipmongers were everywhere, even in high headquarters. On March 7, MacArthur sent a radio message to General George C. Marshall, the army chief of staff in Washington:

"General Homma committed Harikari [*sic*], repeat, Harikari, because of his failure to destroy our forces in Bataan and Corregidor." The funeral, MacArthur went on, had been held in Manila on February 26 and Homma's "ashes were flown to Japan the following day." While he could not "completely substantiate this report," the general said, "it is believed to be correct." And in a postscript he added, there was even "a touch of irony" in all this—"his funeral rites, and, it is believed, his suicide, took place in my old apartment, which he occupied in the Manila Hotel."[10]

More melodrama from MacArthur, but any bit of good news, fact or fata morgana, suited the moment, and there had been few such moments in the first battle for Bataan.

The Americans had stalled and bloodied their enemy, but no one in the American camp was counting coup, for while the enemy's hardships were temporary (all Homma had to do was wait for Tokyo to reinforce him), the list of American troubles seemed intractable. And first on that list was hunger.

THE FILIPINOS and Americans had been living and fighting on crumbs. For six weeks their ration had been less than two thousand calories a day, a scant twenty-four ounces of food, half the minimum the average man needed for the hard labor of combat. And their stomachs were sore with hunger because MacArthur had made a fundamental mistake: in the rush to retreat, he'd left most of his rations behind.

Tons of provisions stockpiled in northern Luzon to support MacArthur's plan to fight at the beaches and along the central plain had simply been abandoned. At just one warehouse alone, the army quarter-master had left fifty million bushels of rice, enough grain to keep a garrison going for years.

The missteps—"mismanagement and indecision," one officer called it—were all MacArthur's. Somewhere along the line from West Point to Bataan, the general had forgotten the most fundamental lesson of warfare, the lesson on logistics.

Just as an army on the attack must keep its lanes of resupply open as it moves forward, an army that plans to fight a defense, holed up behind bulwarks, must stockpile its supplies in advance. (Many of his officers had implored MacArthur to give up his grand scheme and send the supplies to Bataan, but the general had refused to listen.)[11]

On January 2, after the Filipinos and Americans had completed their withdrawal to Bataan, the army quartermaster sat down to assess his stores. Roughly 80,000 combatants and 26,000 refugees had found their way to the peninsula, and the quartermaster figured that at full ration (four thousand calories, or roughly four and a half pounds of food per man per day), the garrison would exhaust the supplies on hand in less than a month.

Headquarters immediately put every unit on half rations, and the defenders of Bataan now had to fight on less than two pounds of rice, canned fish, or canned meat a day. After two weeks of such subsistence, the men were hungry, very hungry, and losing heart. When word of the grumbling got back to MacArthur, who was holed up underground in a command tunnel on Corregidor just off Bataan's southern tip, the general wrote a letter to his men, assuring them that "help is on the way from the United States . . . Thousands of troops and hundreds of planes are being dispatched. The exact time of arrival of reinforcements is unknown as they will have to fight their way through Japanese attempts against them," but help was coming. They could count on that.[12]

It was a lie, a Judas kiss. The American Pacific Fleet had been crippled in the attack on Pearl Harbor and was in no position to break the blockade of Japanese ships patrolling from the Bering Strait to the Coral Sea. The Philippines was cut off, isolated. Washington knew it and so did MacArthur.

EVERY DAY during the lull in the fighting, self-appointed sentinels from various units would climb a hill, shinny up a tree, or stroll down to the water's edge to squint at the horizon. Somewhere out there, beyond the line of black sea and blue sky, ships loaded with tanks and airplanes, men and food—great floating larders, as some imagined them—were steaming toward Luzon. They were sure of it. Washington had told MacArthur, and MacArthur had told them. Help was on the way.

Naturally there were naysayers, men convinced their country had forsaken them. And there were wise guys too, wags who liked to needle the optimists. (One joker hung up a picture of an old four-masted schooner and added the legend, "We told you so, help is on the way!")

When the Japanese got wind of this waiting game, the Imperial Army's honey-voiced propagandist, Tokyo Rose (the name used by several women broadcasters), took to playing a popular ditty on Japanese radio broadcast to the Philippines. "Here's one for the boys on Bataan," she would say:

> Red sails in the sunset,
> Way out on the sea,
> Oh! carry my loved one
> Home safely to me.

Everyone talked constantly of a convoy, one rumor following the next: The convoy was coming from Australia, from Hawaii, it was taking the northern route, it was crossing to the south, it was just off shore, just over the horizon, just days away. And each new report, each bruit or bit of scuttlebutt, was an occasion for a bet—a case of scotch or San Miguel beer, a couple of cartons of Luckies.

Tomorrow would bring rescue. America would never abandon them, they told one another. And they held as hard to blind hope as their enemy held to the idea of destiny. Tomorrow, they believed, tomorrow was going to be better than today.

THEY WOULD EAT almost anything.

When the canned meat ran out, they hunted and slaughtered carabao, a Philippine water buffalo. The quartermaster set up abattoirs, and the oxlike animals were slaughtered in the cool of the night, then cut into quarters, leaving the hairy hide intact to keep the flesh partially clean, which is to say at least half free of maggots. Once it reached the field kitchens, the meat was soaked in salt water overnight and pounded for hours to make it chewable. Even the best cooks, however, had trouble dressing the flesh of an animal that likes to spend its days wallowing in slime and swamp water. Reporter Frank Hewlett told his readers that he found the taste of carabao distinctive, "just short of rank."[13]

Soon almost every carabao on Bataan, some twenty-eight hundred animals, had been eaten, and the quartermaster began to slaughter the cavalry's mounts, packhorses, and mules. When these too were gone, the men turned to hunting wild pigs, jungle lizards, giant snakes. A veterinary officer who thought birds might make a good meal shot and cooked some crows. "He insisted that they were not bad at all," a comrade reported.[14]

Often whatever the men caught or collected went into a common kettle. When infantryman Dominick Pellegrino of Medford, Massachusetts, went to ladle himself a portion of his unit's "Bataan stew," he spotted the skeletal paw of a monkey reaching up from the depths of the pot. "I think I'll pass," he decided.[15]

Patrols "fished" the streams and rivers with grenades, and the quartermaster tried to organize a fleet of local fisherman to ply Manila Bay, but the Japanese bombed the boats. (During the attack a soldier in a nearby foxhole shouted, "If enough of those bombs hit the bay close to shore we will have fresh fish for dinner.")[16]

Mango trees were picked clean of their fruit, and by the end of February there did not seem to be a single banana left on Bataan. Some men tried eating grass and leaves, cooking them down like spinach to dress up their daily portion of bland rice.

Every morning at breakfast, Calvin Jackson, an army doctor from Kenton, Ohio, found worms and weevils in the porridge served at one of the field hospitals. "The bugs and larvae don't bother me," he wrote in his diary. "Most people try to skim them off as they float, but I just stir up the mess and [down] it goes."[17]

Like almost everyone else, intelligence officer Allison Ind of Ann Arbor, Michigan, could think of little save his stomach. He was hungry in the morning, hungry in the heat of the day, hungry at night, a monotony of unrelieved craving and want: "moldy rice . . . tasteless coffee [the grounds left white from many boilings] . . . flies . . . flies . . . moldy rice."[18]

By the middle of February, Ind and others were showing the first signs of malnutrition:

In the mornings before chow, one's legs feel watery and, at intervals, pump with pains that swell and go away again. If you move too rapidly, there is a hint of vertigo. The heart thumps like a tractor engine bogged in a swamp. These not-too-serious discomforts disappear immediately upon eating. For perhaps an hour one feels quite normal. Then lassitude. Between noontime and one o'clock is the worst for me. Seems as though I cannot sit straight, but must hump over.[19]

By the middle of March, well into the lull now, army doctors were reporting that "the physical fitness of [the] troops" is "seriously impaired," so serious that headquarters had to limit operations. The men simply lacked the energy to exert themselves; they had no stamina to mount long-range patrols, stage ambushes, launch frontal attacks. Some were so far gone they did not have the strength to crawl out of their foxholes or raise a rifle to their shoulder and take aim at the enemy.[20]

The average weight loss was staggering, between twenty and thirty pounds. "They need food," the chief surgeon, Wibb E. Cooper, told headquarters. "And lack of proper food is the basic cause of all the trouble."[21]

Living on a bare diet, the men quickly exhausted their reserves of body fat, then, bereft of the most basic nutrients (vitamins and minerals) they started to waste away.

Doctors noted that the command appeared ever "more emaciated." Men twenty years old had the feeble gait and haggard cast of octogenarians. They shuffled along head bowed, gasping for breath. Their skin, mottled and streaked like old marble, hung loose on their bones. Their faces were gaunt, the eyes seemed to protrude from their sockets.[22]

They felt awful, too. Most medical charts listed the same symptoms: dysesthesia (a burning and painful itch like pins and needles), edema (spontaneous swelling at the joints and in the arms and legs), gingivitis (bleeding gums), hypotension and hypothermia (rapid loss of blood pressure and body heat and the shivers and shakes that go with it), polyuria (frequent urination), and paresthesia (numbness in the hands and feet).

Many suffered from anemia so profound they could not walk. Others were chronically dyspeptic; the enzymes and acid in their empty guts left their gastrointestinal tracts painful and growling. A large number developed eye trouble; their optic nerves began to deteriorate, and men with twenty-twenty vision suddenly became quite nearsighted, saw the battlefield through a blur, suffered night blindness.

The most troubling ocular abnormality, however, was inorganic. Soldiers lost their foresight, their ability to see past the moment. Malnutrition, it seemed, had also laid waste to their morality.[23]

Hungry men, famished men, think of nothing so much as their next meal. They develop a kind of gustatory psychosis, "a pathological greed for food," and in their pursuit of something to eat they know no restraint, respect no right, suffer no attack of conscience. "Hunger," Woodrow Wilson said in 1918 at the end of his war, brings out "all the ugly distempers" in man—man the liar, man the cheat, man the thief.[24]

[*Field Memo to All Commands*] It has come to the attention of this Headquarters that organizations, individual officers and men are looting supply dumps . . . hijacking [food] trucks [including those headed for the front] . . . and hoarding supplies . . . Anyone caught doing this will either be shot or court martialed.[25]

FIRST THEIR STRENGTH. Then their moral balance. Finally their immunity to illness. On Bataan privation became a partner to disease. Run

down from malnutrition, thousands of soldiers were susceptible to the twin scourges that have haunted armies since ancient times: dysentery, which brought on a diarrhea so debilitating that doctors in the field hospitals feared their patients would collapse as they squatted over the straddle-trench toilets, and malaria, the blood disease that burned men's brains.

One bite from a delicate, dapple-winged female anopheles mosquito infected with the Plasmodium parasite, and six to sixteen days later a man would likely suffer an attack of "ague," the classic term for the cycle of surging fever, soaking sweats, and fits of chills and shaking that mark the onset of an attack of malaria.

The Philippines was one of the most malaria-infested countries in Asia—some two million Filipinos a year suffered from the disease—and, as prewar topographic surveys clearly showed, Bataan with its many streams and rivers was among the most fertile breeding grounds in the world for the mosquitoes that transport the malaria parasite. Millions of anopheles minimus flavirostris were waiting in the hills of Bataan as the Filipinos and Americans dug in, and sensing fresh prey, the avaricious insects immediately began to sally forth in search of a "blood meal."

Quinine, the drug used as both a preventative and a cure, was in short supply. By late February most of the command had been infected, and the disease was beginning to manifest itself in the ranks. By early March there were three hundred new cases of malaria a day; two weeks later, five hundred cases, then seven hundred. By the end of the month a thousand men a day were coming down with the disease.

To General Jonathan Wainwright, malaria "hung over" the army "like a black cloud, enveloping a land of men whose bones were lumping through their tightly stretched skin."

In a handwritten note from the field, another general advised headquarters that only half his command was capable of fighting. The rest of his men, he said, were so sick, hungry, and tired they could never hold a position or launch an attack.[26]

> He sailed at the dawning,
> All day I've been blue,
> Red sails in the sunset,
> I'm rushing to you.

The optimists still sat cockeyed by the shore, scanning the horizon, but by early March, well into the lull, most men knew, or strongly suspected, that a convoy was not coming.

"Had terrible breakfast—oatmeal and rice and [weak] coffee," Captain Thomas Dooley, aide-de-camp to General Wainwright, wrote in his diary. "Went to [headquarters] where General Wainwright discussed food situation w/General McBride . . . Very discouraging. Six out of eight of the last [local] supply boats that have tried to get thru to us have been sunk or captured. Rice supply will last 30 days. All other supplies a lot less—some items only 5 days . . . Frankly things look darker now for this force than ever before."[27]

The men blamed MacArthur, of course. The general of an army is the wellspring of its spirit, the source of its soul. Men draw on his strength, his courage, his love, and when they are troubled they ask him to carry their burdens, their doubts, their dread. He is the scapegoat who accepts their censure, the colossus who shoulders their worry.

> Dugout Doug MacArthur lies a shaking on the Rock,
> Safe from all the bombers and from any sudden shock.
> Dugout Doug is eating of the best food on Bataan
> And his troops go starving on.[28]

That broadside, a balladic takeoff on "The Battle Hymn of the Republic," must have stung MacArthur. No quality of character is more central to a soldier's psyche than valor, and Douglas MacArthur, cited often in his early years for courage under fire, was one of the most decorated officers in the United States Army. On Bataan, however, he had refused to lead from the field.

For the most part he stayed holed up underground on the island of Corregidor, a tiny cay shaped like a tadpole sitting just off the tip of Bataan, square in the mouth of Manila Bay. Fortified with long-range cannon and huge pit mortars, Corregidor prevented the enemy from entering the bay and using the port of Manila. The island had been formed from the detritus of an old volcano, hence its nickname, "the Rock."

Some of the rock formed a 390-foot hill, called Malinta Hill. A decade earlier army engineers had cut a tunnel through the hill—a shaft thirty feet wide and almost a mile long with dozens of smaller laterals running off it. In this honeycomb of reinforced concrete passageways, beneath tons of solid rock and earth, the supernumeraries of the various army and navy commands worked safely at their desks. At the last desk in Lateral Number Three sat the boss, the general.

> Dugout Doug, come out from hiding
> Dugout Doug, come out from hiding
> Send to Franklin the glad tidings
> That his troops go starving on!

MacArthur, his wife, Jean, and young son, Arthur, had arrived on the island Christmas Eve. At first they stayed in a cottage topside, then when the bombing became incessant they moved into the laterals. Malinta Tunnel was the army's communications and control center, its battle hub; only from there could MacArthur speak with all the elements of his command and with the War Department in Washington. For two weeks he stuck to his desk in Lateral Number Three; then, around January 7, he got a note from a trusted staff officer on Bataan. Morale on the peninsula was "sagging," the officer said. The general needed to come across the water, walk the battlefield, and buoy his men.[29]

MacArthur spent just one day on Bataan. At II Corps headquarters he stood with a gathering of staff officers and made a promise: their sorry lot, he said, would soon change. The battle for Bataan had captured the country's "imagination" and help was on the way, a convoy of men and planes "by way of Australia." When that help arrived, he told the officers, they would win back control of the air, retake lost ground, perhaps go so far as to launch a counterattack. And with that subterfuge still fresh on his lips, the general boarded a navy patrol boat at Mariveles harbor and returned to his underground office on the Rock.[30]

Twice the War Department had warned MacArthur that supplies being stockpiled in Australia likely would never reach him. "Previous losses in capital ships [at Pearl Harbor] have seriously reduced the capacity of the Navy to [provide Far East] convoys," General George Marshall, army chief of staff, cabled the Philippines. And to make sure MacArthur got his meaning, Marshall added a coda, the kind of thing a chief says to a commander he must leave to fight a lost cause. "Every day of time you gain is vital."[31]

Meanwhile on Bataan, hungry men were still scanning the skies and staring out to sea, convinced that their countrymen would never abandon them. Then, on Washington's Birthday, February 23, 1942, the president of the United States, sitting before a microphone at the White House, delivered one of his Fireside Chats on war, and after listening to him on shortwave radios in their tanks and foxholes, many of the men on Bataan—the loyal sons of New York and Nebraska, Maine and Montana, Alabama and Illinois—began to wonder whether patriotism was a virtue or merely the faith of a fool.

The president said Japanese forces had surrounded the Philippines, and that "complete encirclement" had prevented America from sending the garrison "substantial reinforcement." The United States, he went on, was in for a long fight, and to attain its "objective"—the destruction of both Germany and Japan—America would have to begin operations "in areas other than the Philippines." That had been the strategy from the beginning, the president said, "and nothing that has occurred in the last two months has caused us to change."[32]

So now they knew.

They were on their own. And they were expendable.

MOST OF THEM, that is. For weeks the president, the secretary of war, and the army chief of staff had been talking about getting MacArthur out, effecting an escape to prevent the propaganda coup that would come from the capture of a four-star general (the army's highest-ranking officer), especially this particular four-star general.

In less than two months of war, MacArthur had become so popular with the American people, they were naming babies, buildings, flowers (the MacArthur narcissus), dances (the MacArthur glide), parks, streets, and schools after him.

The newspapers painted him a hero: "the most articulate, great general in our history," "the greatest soldier since Grant," "hero of the battle for the Philippines whose courage and determination against overwhelming odds have already enshrined him in the hearts of all Americans." The popular columnist Bob Considine praised the general's "spirit-lifting, pulse-quickening, heartwarming communiqués."[33]

The communiqués were a labor of self-love, MacArthur's war work. He left siegecraft and the oversight of the army to his chief of staff, Major General Richard K. Sutherland, and busied himself writing his own actualities. Practiced in politics and publicity from his years in Washington, he sat at his desk in Lateral Number Three and either composed, edited, or approved every press communiqué issued from Corregidor. Anything "favorable to General MacArthur" got his initials; anything not was rewritten or redacted. And all to one standard—"their effect on the MacArthur legend."[34]

His gilded name was usually the only name that appeared in the communiqués, not the young Filipino privates or American corporals, not the 91st Philippine Division or the 4th Marine Regiment or any of the other proud bands of fighting men that served under him.

General MacArthur and his troops in the Bataan peninsula . . .

General MacArthur's small air force . . .

General MacArthur launched a heavy counterattack . . .

When those communiqués landed on the desks of newspaper editors and rewrite men, they framed their stories to feature the man most mentioned. Thus it was "MacArthur's planes" and "MacArthur's guns," "MacArthur's lines" and "MacArthur's men." Frequently the stories flanked a front-page portrait of the general looking tall and "tight-lipped." Bataan was an epic of survival—the story of a last stand, the Alamo of the Pacific—and it required an epic hero, Douglas MacArthur.[35]

He planned to die in battle, or so he said. In a cable to Marshall on January 23, he vowed "to fight it [out] to complete destruction." He reckoned he'd be destroyed "in a bombing raid or by artillery fire" but thought for a moment of seeking his finish "in a final charge." Whatever the end, he expected it to be "brutal and bloody." Radio Tokyo wanted his capture and imagined him hanging from a scaffold near the Imperial Palace. Perhaps MacArthur imagined the same thing. One day in January he summoned his aide Sidney Huff and asked him to find some bullets for a small Derringer, a keepsake from his father. When Huff returned, MacArthur loaded the tiny twin-barrel handgun and slipped it back into his pocket. "They will never take *me* alive, Sid," he said.[36]

For weeks Washington had been suggesting he leave, but he either ignored or rejected their entreaties. He was determined to "share the fate of the garrison," he told them. At last, on February 22, Roosevelt ordered him out. To his aides and staff MacArthur made a great show of protest: After huddling at length with his wife and Sutherland, he told his top officers he was going to resign his commission and "join . . . the Bataan defense force as a simple volunteer"—the general in a foxhole with the malnourished malaria-ridden men he had all but ignored in seventy-seven days of combat. His aides argued that he had been given a direct order, an official change of assignment, by his commander in chief. He had to obey, they said, or face a court-martial. He should go, go to Australia immediately and lead a rescue force back to the Philippines.

That seemed to convince him. "We'll go in the dark of the moon," he decided, and an hour after sunset on March 11, 1942 MacArthur, Jean, young Arthur and the boy's *Amah*, or Chinese nursemaid, and seventeen members of the headquarters staff boarded four patrol torpedo boats for a dash to the southern island of Mindanao where they would wait for a B-17 from Port Darwin to fly them south to safety.

Gathered at the dock on Corregidor to say good-bye were several officers of high rank, among them General Wainwright, MacArthur's choice as the new commander in the Philippines. MacArthur had conferred with Wainwright the day before and explained why he was leaving. Now he went through it all again—his plan to marshal the forces in Australia and rush back for a rescue, his reluctance to quit his command and desire to stay with his men, the president's unambiguous order to leave. Wainwright told him again that he understood. "He was going because he was a soldier, and a soldier obeys orders from his commander regardless of his own emotions, ambitions, hopes."[37]

And that was true, as far as it went. Orders, indeed, were orders, the incontestable "Word," and obedience was an officer's obligation, the base metal in the chain of command. To disobey a direct order was to violate the first rule of army life and undermine the orthodoxy of the profession. But there was another law (more an article of faith, really) that superseded the army's established codes and catechisms, a law as old as battle itself, the law of constancy: A soldier never leaves another soldier behind.

Combat is a countinghouse of killing and dying, and its cold math makes men feel worthless, worthless and alone. The loneliness never passes—it accrues with each corpse a man encounters along the way— but the first time a soldier stops under fire to tend another man's wound or haul him to safety, he begins to feel he is not so unimportant, so small, after all. Even in the cruel accounting of the battlefield, he has value. He is a comrade.

Comradeship is a kind of bargain men make with one another—a soldier never leaves another soldier behind—and that promise applies to every echelon. A private in the ranks keeps faith with his betters by trusting in their ability to command, and an officer repays that trust and shows his fidelity by sharing the fate of his men, standing with them on the deck of a sinking ship or digging in with a doomed garrison.

On the dock at Corregidor, the sun had set and the sky was becoming as black as the surface of the water. MacArthur made sure his wife and son were safely aboard the first boat. He stopped for a moment and looked up at Corregidor's heights and listened to the report of its big guns firing against the mainland, then he approached the small group of high-ranking officers waiting nearby.

"I shall return," Huff heard him tell Wainwright and the others. Then he boarded the boat, and the men on the dock turned back to face the enemy.[38]

BY THE END OF MARCH, Ben Steele and his comrades in the 7th Matériel Squadron were subsisting on rice—steamed rice, rice porridge, rice mush, rice soup. A few times a week the quartermaster would send up thirteen cans of salmon flakes and nine cans of condensed milk, but when the allotment was spread among 360 men, it provided just a teaspoon of fish and a splash of milk in each mess kit, scarcely enough to give their gruel some taste.

"This grub is pathetic," Ben Steele thought, "just pathetic."

For a while the boys searched for forage and game, rooting in local vegetable patches for turnips or camotes or roaming the countryside to shag papaya, guava, mangoes, cashews. Sometimes a man would bag a monkey or a big snake, or sometimes a patrol would spot some "big game," a stray carabao or swaybacked horse that somehow had escaped the quartermaster's roundup, and when that happened the patrol would carefully note the animal's location then rush back to their lines with the news, and the lieutenant would send for Ben Steele.

A man did not have to be a Montana marksman to bring down a big critter like a water buffalo or some old spindle-legged pony, but he had to be able to slaughter and dress the carcass quickly in the dark in the middle of no-man's-land with an enemy patrol possibly lurking, and Ben Steele was good at such work. One shot and the animal was down, then he was on it with his knife.

He slit the hind legs first, cutting the hide from the hooves up the hocks to the thighs, then along the flanks to the shoulders and chest, then up the neck to the throatlatch. When the skin was fully scored, he yanked it off the carcass, then slit the belly open, pulled out the guts, debrided the muscles around the joints, and hacked at the half-dressed carcass with a hand ax until he had cleaved it into quarters. Forty-five minutes start to finish. By sunup the patrol would be back on the line and the meat would be in the squadron's cooking pots.

In some of the other units, men were doing business on the black market, sneaking off to meet smugglers from Manila who crossed the bay in bancas loaded with sugar, eggs, and Filipino cigarettes, but this source of supply was unpredictable. Japanese launches mounted with machine guns plied Manila Bay, sometimes catching the bootleggers on the open water in sight of land. Days later when customers showed up to shop, they would find the food runners washed up on the sand, their bloated bodies mauled by Japanese bullets and the bites of voracious bay crabs.

When the rice ran short, Ben Steele and his squadron mates harvested palay from the paddies and threshed it themselves, but the yield was so small they were still hungry all the time. The hunger was worst at night when they were on watch, alone.

THE RESERVE defense line was now the main defense line—thirteen miles of foxholes, bunkers, and breastworks stretching across the middle of the peninsula. The Air Corps boys (provisional infantry) had been assigned to a one-mile sector not far from the bay. At their backs was a stand of trees, in front two abandoned rice paddies, roughly a thousand yards of open ground. On moonlit nights, Ben Steele and his comrades looked out on a gray no-man's-land of shadows and dark shapes, and on nights when there was no illumination at all, they sat and stared at a wall of black, imagining the enemy creeping along behind it.

Mostly Ben Steele fought off sleep and memories of home, especially memories that made his stomach growl. Roast pork and apple-sauce—that's all he could think of, roast pork and applesauce. His mother always added extra sugar to make the sauce sweet, just the way he liked it. After his watch he would spread a blanket on the ground next to his hole and fall asleep, and his daydream would become his night dream, only more vivid, the roast sizzling as it came out of the oven, the applesauce heaped in a big bowl in the middle of the table. Then he would wake up, grab his mess kit, and join the queue for a breakfast of "gummy" gruel that "tasted like wallpaper paste."[39]

Although the Japanese had pulled back during the lull, they were still firing on the American lines. Japanese dive-bombers came in the morning, Japanese artillery shells landed on them in the afternoon. One attack caught Ben Steele and another man in the open, and they flopped down in the dirt as the shells started to explode around them.

"Boy, that was close!" the other man said when the barrage lifted.

"You take that helmet off and you'll see just how close it was," Ben Steele said.

A piece of shrapnel had rent the top of the man's helmet and left a flap of metal sticking straight up. He was unhurt, but the more he looked as his helmet, the more unnerved he became, and soon the medics were hauling him off to a field hospital in the rear.

In fact, all the boys were on edge. Some went around angry, railing at their country for betraying them. And some sank into self-pity and sat down and wept. Naturally, with everyone miserable, no one wanted to listen to the bellyaching of or spend a night on watch in a hole with a man so scared he could not stop sobbing. ("You're making me nervous," Ben Steele told one of his sniveling watch mates. "Get the hell out of here. I don't want you around me.") So most men kept their frustration and fear to themselves and sat sullen faced, picking the bedbugs off their blankets or intoning a bitter bit of verse penned by an unknown hand.

> We're the battling bastards of Bataan
> No momma, no poppa, no Uncle Sam,
> No aunts, no uncles, no nephews, no nieces,
> No rifles, no guns or artillery pieces,
> And nobody gives a damn.[40]

At the end of March, the bombing and artillery attacks increased, a sure sign the enemy was preparing a second offensive.

Now the men were filled with foreboding.

"We're done," Ben Steele and his comrades told one another. "Only two things can happen to us now, we're going to be dead or we're going to be prisoners of war."

"And I heard the Japs don't take no prisoners," one man said.

A LATE SUMMER DAY in the small airless towns that sit in the valley of the Yellowstone. Down Main Street in Worden came a flatbed truck, a mound of firewood heaped high in back. Behind the wheel was Ben Steele, next to him his cousin Pat. As the truck came abreast of a block of stores it slowed down, then nosed to the curb.

They shouldn't have stopped. They knew they shouldn't have stopped. Ben Steele's father had told them to drive straight through to Billings. Straight through! he had said several times.

But they'd been hot loading the truck, hot driving down from the hills, and they thought they'd be only a few minutes, a few minutes cooling off with an ice cream cone.

In the heat of the day the sidewalks were empty, the street quiet. When Ben Steele came out of the store, he smelled the whiskey right away, then he saw it—a large dark pool gathering beneath their truck.

He was atop the mound of firewood now, tossing the logs to get at the kegs of whiskey beneath. There it was, the one that had toppled over when they stopped. The keg had popped its bung and the booze was pouring into the bed of the truck and leaking so fast onto the street there was a runnel of whiskey flowing along the curb.

"Oh God," Ben Steele thought, "the whole damn town smells of it."

"Get in the truck, Pat!" he said. "We gotta get out of here."

AROUND NOON one Friday morning in March 1934, a stranger knocked on the back door of the small house the family had rented on Broadwater Avenue in Billings. The three older children, Gert and Bud and

Warren, were in school. The two youngsters, Joe and Jean, were home with their parents.

The stranger was a customer come to buy a pint of whiskey. The Old Man had been bootlegging for almost two years now, making moonshine in the hills above Hawk Creek and, most recently, selling it from the back door of their rented house on Broadwater Avenue.

They were getting by, the family. The two-story cottage was crowded, but they were eating three meals a day and had a roof over their heads. In the hills, their mother reminded them, there were folks who were shivering in tents; in the city they were standing in breadlines.

The guy at the door looked legit, asked for the Old Man by name. Still, a bootlegger couldn't be too careful. Prohibition was nearly over, the state was going into the liquor business, and word had been going around that the governor didn't want backdoor bootleggers competing with the state's new stores. The sheriff's men were cracking down in every county, and one bootlegger after another was being hauled off to jail. Can't be too careful, they told one another. In hard times the police could always find a stooge to come knocking for a pint.

IN THE DISTRICT COURT OF THE UNITED STATES
DISTRICT OF MONTANA
BILLINGS DIVISION

. . . On or about the 9th day of March, 1934 . . . the defendant . . . at certain premises located on Broadwater Avenue . . . did then and there willfully, wrongfully, unlawfully, knowingly, fraudulently and feloniously remove and aid and abet in the removal of distilled spirits, to-wit, about 32 gallons, more or less, of whiskey, of which the United States Internal Revenue tax had not been paid.[1]

They led the Old Man off in handcuffs and hauled away his basement booze, but the revenue officers were so busy raiding other homes that day that they rushed off without checking the attic, and there, right above their heads in the dusty crawlspaces between the joists, were 150 gallons of the Old Man's best stuff.

Ben Steele always thought the sheriff knew about that upstairs stash, knew that he and his mother started selling the stuff not long after the authorities put the family's breadwinner in prison garb and shipped him off to a road gang in Washington State.

At three bucks a gallon out the back door, the family made $450 that summer. Bess stretched the cash as far as she could through the fall and into winter. When the money finally ran out, she started serving lard sandwiches for supper and wondered what she'd do for rent.

THE RAID made the *Billings Gazette.* "OFFICERS SEIZE KEGS OF WHISKEY," the headline read. After a while, Bud got tired of the taunting at school—"So your old man's a bootlegger, eh?"—and he started coming through the back door at Broadwater Avenue with bloody knuckles.

The Old Man came back at the end of the summer, sentence served, still scheming. With an old cowboy buddy he opened a beer hall in Worden, a legit place. Before a year was gone, he was broke and working for wages as a common laborer.

At least there was that, that and the $10 a week Ben Steele was bringing home from odd jobs. His mother always took the money with a smile, but he could see her worry, watched it grow week after week. When he could watch it no more, he quit school and took a full-time job as a camp tender for Jug Clark, a sheep man he'd ranched for summers. Thirty a month plus keep, and every month he sent every cent home.

Late that summer, another Dust Bowl summer that drove up the cost of hay, Jug Clark decided to put his sheep on a train and ship them west across the state to the Big Hole, an enormous mountain valley surrounded by towering peaks. Best hay in the state, and the biggest valley Bud had ever seen.

SIX OF THEM, the boss, four shepherds, and their eighteen-year-old camp tender, trailed eight thousand sheep from the railhead at Anaconda sixty miles into the long valley. Summer and fall were gorgeous, green and gold. Then in late November icy air started to slide down the mountain slopes and collect in the valley bottom. Come December the snow was up to the top of the fence posts and the temperature was the coldest in the state.

The shepherds and camp tender moved into a drafty farmhouse rented out as a kind of barracks. From dawn to dusk they bundled up in woolens and hauled and pitched tons of hay to the scattered bands. Nights they sat around listening to the wind howl and telling one another the same stale stories again and again. Ben Steele learned about boredom that winter, boredom and the company of men.

In the spring, when it was time to return to the home ranch, the camp tender, restless now, convinced the boss to let him ride ahead to Anaconda with their string of twenty horses.

He was on a pinto stallion named Patches, an ornery creature. At the end of the first day the boy was spent and looking for a place to stop and put up the string.

"Where you headed?" said a rancher's wife, serving him some fried chicken and potatoes.

"We wintered a bunch of sheep up in the Big Hole, ma'am, and now we're bringing them back to the Yellowstone."

"Wintered in the Big Hole?"

"Yes, ma'am."

"That's really something!" she said. "Let me see that coat of yours. Looks like you have some buttons missing."

He could have stopped anywhere, any ranch along the way for a bed of dry hay and a hot breakfast at sunup. That was the custom of the country. And he knew he could count on it, the kindness of strangers, count on it even in the hardest of times.

SIX

THE LAST WEEK OF MARCH 1942, and after more than a month's lull in the fighting, the revitalized 14th Army was ready to begin the second battle for Bataan.

Homma had 39,000 men now, well rested and well supplied. Determined not to repeat the mistakes of the first battle, his field officers had taken a month to teach their troops new tactics and fire discipline. No more blind charges across open ground, they told their men, no more attacks without bombing and shelling the enemy first.[1]

Nearly 150 big guns were positioned in front of the American line. Japanese bombers and fighters were armed with more than sixty tons of high explosives. And in jungle clearings, cane fields, and rice paddies just north of the American line, thousands of *hohei* were massed, bayonets fixed, waiting for orders to attack.

Among these nervous foot soldiers was Takesada Shigeta, a twenty-one-year-old private from the town of Yori in Yamaguchi Prefecture, a replacement to the 122nd Infantry, one of the regiments in the revitalized Summer Brigade.

HIS FATHER, one of the original "human bullets" (*nikudans*) in the war with Russia, thought Takesada Shigeta, the youngest of his five children, unfit for the army. The boy was stubborn and something of a *kojin shugisha*, an "individualist," and his father worried he wouldn't keep his promise, the promise all young conscripts made at their send-off ceremonies—to forget home and leave their lives on the battlefield.[2]

Father and son had never been close, so when Takesada reported to

Ogori station for the train ride to his port of embarkation, he was surprised to find his father waiting for him.

His father handed him a ten-yen note, a customary good luck gift to a soldier going away. The father tried to make small talk with his son, but Takesada, distracted by the moment and disaffected by this man who had always doubted him, just stood there and nodded.

At length the train arrived and Takesada Shigeta picked up his rifle, shouldered his pack, and turned to go.

Just a minute, his father said. He had something to say: "Go fight, and remember the promise you made at the shrine before you left for training—don't come back anything but dead."

Friday, March 27, 1942, south bank of the Abo-Abo River, Bataan Takesada Shigeta had never heard an officer speak so respectfully to a group of *hohei*.

"*Anata-gata wa . . . ,*" the general began, which was almost like saying "My dear fellows" or "My good men."

What courtesy! Takesada thought.

The general, Akira Nara, commander of the 65th Brigade, was standing on a small wooden platform that had been set on a rise above the river. In a clearing in front of him, hundreds of replacements stood in formation shoulder to shoulder listening.

"Thank you for your efforts and for coming here to fight," the general said. On April 3, a national holiday at home, they would begin their attack. While their families and friends were celebrating the anniversary of the death of the Emperor Jimmu, founder of the Imperial line, they would be crossing the Tiawir River, their departure point. Already, he said, the army's big guns were pounding the American lines. Listen! Could they hear the explosions? That's where they were going to attack. The fighting would be difficult, but they had been well trained, and the emperor would be with them. In fact, the general said, to bring them luck His Majesty had sent some presents, a royal gift of sake, and cigarettes for each man.

Standing in the middle of the formation, Takesada Shigeta tried to listen hard to what the general was saying, but he felt nervous, distracted. For days the old hands in the 122nd, the handful of men who had survived the first battle for Bataan, had been regaling the replacements with horror stories of the murderous fight and malevolent jungle that had consumed so many of their comrades.

"Fight hard," the general was saying, concluding his remarks. "We're depending on you."

When they had finished their sake and smoked their cigarettes, the replacements returned to their bivouacs, where their officers gathered them for one final ritual.

"This is the last chance you will have to prepare yourself for death," Takesada's captain said.

Then each man was issued a small paper bag. On the outside he was to inscribe his name and address, inside he was to put a lock of hair and some fingernail clippings, "remains" (in lieu of ashes) that would be interred in a stone reliquary at home, perhaps behind his parents' house or in some well-kept cemetery where his family would gather to chant prayers and whisper his name.

HE WENT INTO ACTION almost immediately. The big attack was scheduled for April 3, but parts of the 122nd Infantry and other elements of the 65th Brigade had been ordered to probe the enemy's outposts and look for weak spots in advance of the big push, and on March 28 Takesada Shigeta tightened his helmet strap and checked his weapon.

The men moved out slowly, deliberately, for the going was difficult. They climbed up hills and shimmied down escarpments; they forded rivers and picked their way through the tangles of thorns that tripped their feet and tore their uniforms. On open ground under a burning sun, their helmets became *nabe*, "frying pans," and Takesada Shigeta started to feel faint.

His company was positioned well back in the line of march, and as he and his comrades reached the heavily defended approaches to Mount Samat, they came upon what was left of the units that had preceded them, a grim parade of dead and wounded *hohei* lying by the side of the trail. Here was a man without a foot, there a boy with an arm shot away. Takesada Shigeta wanted to avert his eyes but could not stop himself from staring. These were landsmen, Yamaguchi boys!

Then his company too came under fire, and by the time the 122nd reached Mount Samat, half his platoon had been killed or wounded.

"The moment has come," he told himself. Time to give up all

thoughts of home, thoughts of Japan and Yori and his family. "There is no way for me to come back," he thought.

Still, like most young men, he loved life. And like most soldiers he could not stop himself from calculating his chances. All around him men were dying, and yet, curiously, he had remained untouched. And now he began to think, perhaps his moment had not come after all. Perhaps his *shukumei*, his "destiny," was to survive.

The thought came and went and came again, gnawing at his resolve, his determination to do his duty. The uncertainty was so irritating, he decided to test his fate, and one afternoon under fire he rolled on his back and stuck his arms in the air to see if he'd get hit. The enemy obliged with a volley of bullets. (He was sure he could feel the rush of air as the rounds whizzed past his arms and around his fingers.) Then he thought, "I should try this again to make sure." This time he raised his legs. Another volley, another escape. Now he was certain.

"I will never be shot," he thought. He was going to go home whole after all, instead of *hone to chitte*, a "bunch of bones in a box."

ON THE SAME DAY east on the same field, Second Lieutenant Hirohisa Murata, who had wanted nothing so much as to be a soldier, gathered a squad of sixteen *hohei* for a night patrol against the American outposts.[3]

He was young, this lieutenant, just twenty years old, but not without experience. His unit, the 61st Infantry, had been fighting in China when orders arrived transferring it to Bataan. The men of the 61st hated the wet and cold of China and imagined an easier time in the tropics, then they discovered they had only exchanged one tough piece of ground for another, frozen slop for sweltering jungle. The work was the same and it worried them.

The Chinese had run them ragged, sniping at their flanks, skirmishing in their rear, lurking in ambush around the next bend. Now, despite the assurances of their commanders that this new enemy would be easier, the men of the 61st expected another difficult campaign.

Their line officers were anxious as well. In other armies subalterns "directed" their men, reckoning risk and gain as they steered them toward the objective. In the Imperial Army, where "the object of all maneuver" was "to close quickly with the enemy" and apply the point of a bayonet, young lieutenants and captains led from the front. They were the bellwethers, vanguards of one whose job was to set an example of gallantry and daring so conspicuous that their men could not help but follow. In the West, leading from the front was considered above and beyond the call of duty. In the Imperial Army, however, such intrepidity was expected.[4]

In his first action in China, Hirohisa Murata was uncertain of himself, and he was sure his men could see it. He was nineteen, soft eyes, cherubic cheeks. He imagined his men asking, How is this "little boy" of an officer going to lead a platoon of His Majesty's *hohei*?

"I will take my helmet off and advance in front of everyone" in just a cloth cap, he thought. "It will make me look very brave."

His losses that day were heavy and so heartbreaking he worried he might not be able to summon the courage for the next day's fight. All around him the wounded were groaning, begging for help, or calling for their mothers and wives. From time to time one of the dying, sensing his end, would beg for *jisatsu*, and Hirohisa Murata would hand him his pistol or, out of pity, pull the trigger himself.

Now the lieutenant had been ordered to take a scout platoon south toward the Tiawir River and foothills of Mount Samat to probe the enemy's line of defenses along the East-West Road. To the Japanese, "probe" meant attack. Twenty-five *hohei* poking at a great beast hiding in the dark, trying to get it to snap back and reveal itself.

They set out after 8:00 p.m., Hirohisa Murata plus a communications officer named Kunoda and a platoon of scouts. The night was liquid black. All he had to guide him was a compass.

"We will use the inchworm tactic," he told his men.

The two officers advanced first. ("It is as if we are being sucked into the deep darkness," Murata thought.) As they made their way into no-man's-land, Kunoda pinned pieces of paper to the trees, then at a certain point he would double back, following the markers and bring the rest of the platoon forward to where Murata was waiting. And so they went, Murata and Kunoda, then the rest of the platoon; first the head, then the tail. Slow. Quiet. One length at a time.

The jungle was thick, the night black, and at first the two officers found themselves leading their men in circles. After a while Murata got his bearings, sent Kunoda back for the platoon, then sat on a tree stump in the dark, sword in his right hand, pistol in his left, to wait.

A few moments later, from somewhere in the black, somewhere

close, Hirohisa Murata heard voices, voices speaking English. They sounded urgent, these voices, excited. Then he heard gunfire, followed by the sound of exploding grenades. He was blind in the dark, but he could smell smoke from the explosions and hear the voices again, more urgent than before.

Maybe Kunoda and the men had run into the enemy on their way to him, or perhaps another patrol, also probing the American lines, had stumbled into a strong point.

Never mind. He had his orders, his standing orders, and the orders were to attack.

He turned toward the sound of the voices, raised his sword and, as he imagined it, "dove into the darkness."

March 28, 1942, American main line of resistance, near the East-West Road Every night the Air Corps ground crews could hear the enemy pushing against the outposts in their sector, probing the main line of defense.[5]

"Stay alert!" the officers yelled, but the men were spent and surly, and they snarled at such orders and cursed those who issued them.

"Officers," Ben Steele thought. "Worthless as tits on a boar."

Every day Japanese planes and artillery pounded them, then pounded them again. The bombing and shelling uprooted trees and left men with blood running from their ears and noses.

Ben Steele hunkered down like everyone else. He'd never heard such noise, seen such fury. And there seemed no way to stop it. When American artillery tried to answer, Japanese dive-bombers arrived to knock out the American guns. Then the enemy shelling would resume. Clearly they were coming, the Japanese. They would come out of the jungle by the thousands, and they would come soon.

More than 60,000 troops manned the American main line of resistance, which stretched fourteen miles across the middle of the peninsula just behind the East-West Road. Dividing the line roughly in half was the Pantingan River. The Americans guessed that the Japanese main thrust would come down the east side of the peninsula where more than 32,000 Filipinos and Americans were dug in defending that half of the line. Behind them were some 5,200 additional troops ready to counterattack and fill any gaps or breaches.

The Air Corps boys were assigned to a flat sector not far from Manila Bay, roughly 1,500 yards of ground along the south bank of the San Vicente River. Like the men on rest of the line, the Flying Infantry waited in foxholes, trenches, and bunkers that were topped with palm trunks, earth, and sandbags—all behind barbed wire and all protected with machine gun nests positioned to create curtains of impenetrable fire.

On a map, the main line looked solid, textbook bulwarks. On the ground, however, anyone with average eyesight and a modicum of military sense could see that most of the line was exposed. The trenches and bunkers had been set in the open instead of back in the jungle under the trees. Ben Steele and his Air Corps comrades and the rest of the 32,000 men guarding the east half of the peninsula were strung out under the sun like so much laundry, making it easy for Japanese air and artillery spotters to pinpoint their positions.[6]

On Friday, April 3, the Japanese let loose with their heaviest barrage yet, concentrating their shells and bombs on the two Filipino divisions holding the vital center of the entire line. From nine o'clock in the morning until three o'clock in the afternoon, almost two hundred cannon, some averaging as many as fourteen rounds a minute, fired continuously on the same spot. The explosions churned the earth, splintered the bunkers, collapsed the fighting holes, and plowed up the trenches. Japanese bombers joining the attack dropped so many incendiaries that even the green undergrowth and immature bamboo began to burn. Soon the middle of the line was a miasma of flames, smoke, and shrapnel, a place where a man could not see past his hand, hear beyond the ringing in his ears, or draw a breath without choking on the gray smoke and orange dust that formed a dome over the battlefield.[7]

Meanwhile, massed on the north bank of the Taiwir River and concentrated in front of the spot being pounded by Japanese planes and big guns was General Nara's refreshed 65th Brigade and the newly arrived 4th Division, both supported by tanks. The barrage lifted just after three o'clock, and, as Filipino medics were just beginning to pull the dead and wounded from their holes, thousands of *hohei* advanced on them. Came the whirlwind, came the Furies.

NOW IT WAS NED KING'S WAR.

In March on the dock at Corregidor MacArthur had handed command of the islands to Lieutenant General Jonathan "Skinny" Wainwright, a cavalryman and the senior officer in the Philippines, and

Wainwright, in turn, named Ned King, a quiet major general from Georgia, to replace him as commander of the Luzon Force, all the troops on Bataan, which made King the man with the final word on the battlefield.

At first glance, others might have seemed more suited to lead a last stand—Major General Albert M. Jones of Massachusetts, for one, a tough-talking tactician from a family of warriors, or Brigadier General Clifford "Blinky" (for the muscle spasms in his face) Bluemel, a fierce infantryman from New Jersey who demanded his officers fight till they dropped.[8]

King had been MacArthur's chief artilleryman, an adjuster of vectors, a plotter of parameters. He was good at what he did; Washington brass considered him one of the best cannoniers in the army. In January and February his big guns had shredded the Japanese, turning their attacks into shambles and forcing the battle into a lull.

King had grown up in Atlanta in the quarter century after Reconstruction, a son of the Old South with a lineage that led back to "the Lost Cause." (His grandfather, Captain Gadsden King, had commanded one of the batteries of mortars and cannon that fired on Fort Sumter, the start of the Civil War.) Like other young men of his era and class, he was groomed to be a gentleman. In high school he studied the classics. At the University of Georgia he took up the law. When he graduated in 1903 he went to work for his Uncle Alexander at King & Spalding in Atlanta, and in his spare time he indulged in some soldiering with a local militia and an artillery group in the National Guard. He did well in the service, rose quickly in rank and, preferring the regimen and rituals of army life to the law, left his uncle's employ and in 1908 accepted a commission in the Regular Army.[9]

He was a short, stout man with rust-brown hair and soft features, hardly a model of command. But he was smart and his training as a young lawyer had taught him to take care with details, a rare quality in the old army. By 1940 he was a brigadier general, regarded by his brother officers as even tempered and utterly reliable.[10]

On Friday, April 3, at his headquarters on Bataan, a tar-paper shack in a jungle hollow near Mariveles, King, commander of all Filipino and American troops on the peninsula, waited for word from his front lines.

Some thirteen miles north of his command post, the Japanese were attacking the center of his main line of resistance, but the reports from the field had been slow in reaching the general and he did not know whether the enemy had breached his line or whether his men were holding.

He'd done all he could to prepare, checked his lines, marshaled his reserves, tried to buoy his troops. Since he had nothing to offer them save himself, he visited them almost daily to buck up morale.

They had no chance of winning, of course, and Ned King knew it. The enemy was reinforced now, much too strong. His job, as one of his commanders described it, was "just a matter of holding on," holding on "as long" as Ned King could.[11]

His men had been on the line for thirteen weeks and the accumulated angst and deprivations were beginning to cripple them. Their bodies—nervous systems, endocrine systems, immune systems—were shutting down, depriving them of the basic hormones a man needs to think, fight, and survive. The hardships of living in the wild and the exertion of patrolling and being on constant watch left them enervated. A week of continual bombing and shelling, as well as the anxiety that comes from witnessing the casualties created by that bombardment—a procession of mangled limbs, crushed skulls, eviscerated torsos—sent men into a kind of shock, a state of mind in which they became disassociated from the present and felt nothing save a dull throbbing behind their eyes and the deadweight of their own bodies.

Thousands crowded the field hospitals and aid stations. The addled, the wounded, the sick, men so enfeebled by disease and malnutrition they had to be dragged from their holes to be put on a litter. With the entire command—80,000 troops and 26,000 Filipino civilians and refugees—squeezed into small pockets of open space in an area less than 200 miles square and with so many enemy salvos and sorties every hour, almost every shell or bomb hit something, or someone. Soon a large number of men began to show symptoms of "nerve fatigue."[12]

They forgot their training, lost their bearing and composure. Some still had the moxie for a fight, but most were apathetic, anesthetized. Filthy, soaked in sweat, wracked with fever, living on rice mush, and cowering in their holes under the ear-splitting cannonade, they had reached the point where they just didn't give a damn.

ON APRIL 3 AT 3:00 P.M., after five hours of constant bombardment concentrated on the middle of the American line, the Japanese attacked the gap they had opened with their bombs and shells and pushed a thousand yards into the Filipino and American breastworks.

The intense bombardment shredded and burned telephone wires. In the rickety barnlike building of two-by-two timbers and tar paper that was Luzon Force Headquarters, General King had to wait until evening when runners arrived with the details of the attack.

The center of the line had been hammered. Bunkers considered bombproof were blown down like straw huts, trench walls collapsed, men were set afire in their fighting holes. Three Filipino infantry regiments (part of the 41st, and all of the 42nd and 43rd) tossed their rifles and packs and ran for their lives, terror chasing after them.[13]

Their officers had tried to rally them, make them dig in and form a new line, but nothing could stop the stampede. They fled through the jungle and clogged the vital north-south trails needed to bring up reserves. No one at headquarters really blamed the Filipinos. Despite their perfunctory training, ancient rifles, coconut-husk helmets, and tennis shoes, many Philippine Army units had fought well throughout the campaign. And in the eyes of veteran American officers, even "the most seasoned troops would have been severely tried" by the fury of that opening bombardment.[14]

Late in the afternoon, Ned King learned that his center was in danger of collapsing. The Japanese were pouring into the gap left by the Filipinos, and the enemy was heading for the strategic Pantingan and Catmon valleys, natural corridors to the American rear.

The next morning, April 4, King ordered out of reserve and into the action the all-American 31st Infantry. The regiment had seen only limited combat and had been holed up since February 8 in a bivouac in the rear, but they could hardly be considered fresh troops.

Sickness and semistarvation had reduced the 31st to two-thirds of its original strength, some twelve hundred men. When the orders came to join the fight, many of the troopers struggled up from their sickbeds to join their comrades, but four hundred men told their officers they were too far gone to make the march. Along the way others collapsed and had to be left by the side of the trail propped up against a tree with a canteen of water and a rifle in their laps.[15]

On Sunday, April 5, General Wainwright came across the bay from Corregidor to take a look at Ned King's lines. He and his aide, Tom Dooley, arrived at King's compound as King and his staff were sitting down to breakfast. Dooley stared hard at the faces in the mess tent and thought, "Morale seemed very low. In my eyes 'DEFEAT' was written all over them."[16]

Around 10:30 a.m. the Japanese resumed their attack and finally captured the center, in effect driving a huge wedge into the American line. Now all the enemy had to do was pivot left, like opening a door into a room, to outflank Ned King, then sweep south and east though one sector of the line after another, driving the Filipinos and Americans ahead of them through the jungle and cane fields and across the rice paddies and swaths of cogon grass until they had their backs to Manila Bay.

That night Wainwright, King, and the other top American commanders decided to try to close the gap in the line with a counterattack.

In the early-morning dark on April 6, the counterattacking 31st Infantry started forward, but before the Americans could form fighting lines, they walked right into Japanese patrols. A battalion of the 31st, moving forward with fixed bayonets, ran into the Japanese at a trail junction and crumbled. The men tried to save themselves, tried to disengage and pull back, but the Japanese, as was their custom, pressed their pursuit and chased after the Americans. In the black of night with the enemy on their heels, the men of the 31st Infantry sprinted straight into a five-foot-high barbed-wire fence blocking the trail, and they panicked, a wild mob of American soldiers shrieking and wailing and dashing headlong into the dark jungle to save themselves.[17]

News of the failed counterattack reached Ned King sometime after first light and he and his staff began to wonder how much longer their troops, more a muddle than an army, could put up a fight. Most units had disintegrated, and along the east half of the defense line, what was left of the force was being pushed back, and back again. King considered forming a new line in his rear, but he had no idea how many men he could count on to keep up the battle.

At midmorning he called his field commanders to his headquarters. Many of his men had simply disappeared into the bush, and the general asked each officer to gauge the effectiveness of the outfits that were still intact.

What did the general mean by "effective"? one officer wanted to know.

An effective soldier, King said, was one who could walk a hundred yards without stopping to rest, raise his rifle to his shoulder, take aim, and shoot at the enemy.[18]

By that definition, the officers said, only fifteen men out of every hundred were fit to fight, and at the moment no one in the command shack could say exactly how many men were still under arms or in their fighting holes.

The Japanese were now threatening the extreme east section of the line, sectors manned by the Air Corps, the Flying Infantry. Another enemy attack force, the Nagano Detachment, was massing in front of them across the San Vicente River and was getting ready to push south through the paddies and fields and down the Old National Road.

At 7:00 a.m. on April 7, the Air Corps boys started to take incoming artillery, and in short order the Nagano Detachment, some four thousand well-rested *hohei* supported by tanks, attacked across the San Vicente, overran the Air Corps' forward outposts, and prepared to strike the Flying Infantry from the front.

"FIX BAYONETS!"

On the other side of the San Vicente River the 7th Matériel Squadron readied itself. Q. P. Devore checked his sidearm and made sure he had extra ammunition for his automatic rifle.

Stragglers from their sister Air Corps units were running through the 7th's sector yelling that the Japs were right behind them, which meant that the 7th had enemy closing in on it from the left flank and front. No way for them to hold now.

Ben Steele heard an officer shout at them to pull out. "It's every man for himself!" the officer said, but instead of joining the stampede, Ben Steele fell in with a group of men who had volunteered to hustle south and help man a new defense line.[19]

They marched in the jungle all day, through the night, and into the early-morning dark. At last, sometime before 5:00 a.m. on April 8, what was left of the Provisional Air Corps Infantry, 1st Battalion, 7th Matériel Squadron took up positions on the slope of a steep hill just south of the Alangan River. Some men scraped out shallow holes, but most, Ben Steele among them, just dropped where they stood.

NED KING had been shifting his line south, trying to position what was left of his east-coast units along a river, any river. He had tried to stop the enemy east of the Pantingan, then at the San Vicente. After the main line collapsed and the enemy took control of the Old National Road, he retreated again and formed a line behind the Mamala River. Now, midday April 7, he was dropping back one more time, this time to the Alangan.

He had committed all his reserves. What was once a fighting force of eighty thousand had been reduced to twenty-five hundred "effective" men. The Japanese had turned his right flank and forced him back so many times that he had lost seven miles of battlefield in five days, roughly half the area he had started to defend. In short, he had been ordered to conduct a defense in depth, and he was running out of both depth and defenders. So he asked himself a question that generals in extremis are sometimes forced to ask—generals, that is, whose notions of courage include conscience: What military purpose would be served by further resistance?

He could kill more Japs. Make them pay for every yard of ground, bleed them right up to the beaches at Mariveles. But to what purpose? What tactical advantage? Delay the enemy victory another forty-eight or seventy-two hours? And at what cost? The Japanese juggernaut had collapsed his line, turned his flanks, routed the 32,600 men on the east side of the peninsula, and now was rolling over every ad hoc group of troopers that King's officers could marshal to put in the enemy's path. In the end—and the end was clearly at hand—the enemy would annihilate him. His command would be destroyed, slayed en masse. Where, he wondered, was the military advantage in that?

Still, he hated the idea of surrender, the stain it would leave on his family name, the ignominy history would assign him—Mazaeus at Babylon, Cornwallis at Yorktown, King at Bataan.

Good commanders, however, are sometimes forced by circumstances, or the missteps of their superiors, to define duty differently. When that moment arrives, instead of the voice of authority, they heed a different call.

His army was just about gone, Ned King's aides told him. From reports and estimates, they reckoned some twenty-two thousand men lay sick or wounded in aid stations and field hospitals. Thousands of others had apparently chucked their arms and were wandering vacant eyed through the jungle or, like refugees, were streaming south from Cabcaben down the Old National Road.

Meanwhile, at the latest defense line, the one established along the Alangan, soldiers were poking one another to keep awake and pleading with their officers for food. When they didn't get it, many deserted, leaving parts of the line along the river unmanned.

The Japanese had been shelling the river most of the day. At two o'clock the barrage lifted and Japanese infantry appeared, then tanks. It looked like the enemy was about to break through, and if they did, their line of advance would run them right into the largest of the American field hospitals, a sprawling open-air infirmary with thousands of unarmed patients, doctors, and nurses.

Ned King had heard enough. He summoned his chief of staff, Brigadier General Arnold J. Funk, and ordered him to cross the bay to Corregidor to deliver a message to General Wainwright.

"General King has sent me here to tell you that he might have to surrender," Funk told MacArthur's replacement.

Wainwright had read the field reports and knew the situation was desperate. Like King, he too had been considering the unthinkable, giving up. (Days earlier in his diary he had written that "if necessary," he would surrender Corregidor.) But, at the moment, he could not countenance the capitulation of the main part of his army, the Bataan force. His standing orders—Washington's orders—were to fight to the last man.

"You go back and tell General King that he will not surrender," Wainwright told Funk. "Tell him he will attack. Those are my orders."

Funk tried one last time. "General, you know, of course, what the situation is over there. You know what the outcome will be."

"I do," Wainwright said.[20]

AT DAWN on April 8, in their new position on a small hill south of the Alangan River, the men of the 1st Battalion of the Flying Infantry woke up exhausted and hungry. When they looked around, they noticed the remnants of a field kitchen that had packed up and fled south, and in the debris was a barrel of boiled carabao meat. It smelled rank and had a white scum on top, but the men of the 7th Matériel Squadron gave in to their hunger and started to eat. A short time later most of them, including Ben Steele, were retching.

By late morning Japanese fighter-bombers and fighter planes had found them. The bombing set the hill afire and just then Japanese infantry appeared on a knoll behind them.

"Must be a thousand of them," Ben Steele thought.

"They're coming in waves," Q. P. Devore said.

The Americans took aim. The first volleys sent the Japanese to ground, but the enemy soon recovered and returned fire tenfold, and the Air Corps line started to break.

Platoon Sergeant Brown, a well-liked foreman, was shot in the stomach, and Ben Steele and another man rushed to his side. They stripped off their shirts and fashioned a litter and began to haul Brown up the hill. The underbrush was on fire, and the litter bearers had to soak their handkerchiefs and tie them across their faces to wade through the flames and smoke.

Near the crest of the hill they paused for a moment to catch a breath and check on the sergeant.

Brown was bleeding badly.

"Go on," he said. "I'm done for."

"We're going to help you as far as we can," Ben Steele said.

By the time they reached the top, the sergeant was unconscious, and the litter bearers set him down. Maybe he was breathing, maybe not—in the chaos they couldn't tell. Ben Steele found a canteen and nestled it in Brown's hand. Then, without ceremony, he turned away and hurried up the slope after the others.

In the smoke behind him he could hear the voices of other wounded, men they'd left behind.

"Help!"

"Help me . . . please!"

"Don't leave me!"

Ben Steele thought, "That might be me after a while."

Below in the draw between the two hills, he could see the enemy beginning to advance up the slope to where he'd left the sergeant and the other wounded.

"Whaah!" the Japanese yelled. "Whaah!"

Soon all he could hear was the sound of his own hurried footfalls.

At dusk in the company of a few dozen other stragglers, Ben Steele and Q. P. Devore emerged from the bush onto the Old National Road.

Now and then the big guns and pit mortars on Corregidor fired salvos at the Japanese positions, and the flashes from their muzzles lit up the bay and the sky and illuminated the press of soldiers and refugees crowding the road ahead of the advancing Japanese.

The soldiers in particular were a sorry sight, uniforms torn and filthy, listless and lost in the flow, a few carrying their rifles, but most without a weapon, save a bolo attached to a string and slung over a shoulder, all moving south, away from the sounds of a battle that seemed to be catching up to them.

At the turnoff to Lamao, Ben Steele and Q. P. Devore considered leaving the road to search for food and sanctuary, but as they started down a dirt track to the town, a Filipino emerged from the shadows.

"The Japs, they are already in there," he said, gesturing toward Lamao.

The only safe place seemed to be the bush and jungle so the two men slipped back into the undergrowth with Q.P. in the lead.

"Where you going?" Ben said.

"What do you mean?"

"You're going the wrong way."

"Yeah?" Q.P. said.

"Yeah. You go that way and you're going right back toward the Japs. You better follow me."

Soon they stumbled into a stream that was shallow and rocky and crowded with more stragglers, men busy dipping their canteens.

"We better fill up," Ben Steele said.

They worked quickly in the gloaming, then without warning there was the clank of tank treads and the report of small arms, and the men in the creek ran helter-skelter for the trees.

———

If a commander of military forces of the United States surrenders unnecessarily and shamefully or in violation of orders from higher authority, he is liable to trial and punishment.

—United States Army Field Manual[21]

By midday April 8, Ned King had made up his mind. The line along the Alangan had broken and the small groups of men still able to fight were putting up minimal resistance. His army was in flight, and the Japanese were now within a few miles of one of the large field hospitals.

King summoned his field commanders, his generals.

"There are six thousand sick and wounded in the hospital ahead of us," he began. "There are [twenty-six thousand] civilians [in the way too]. Only twenty-five percent of our men are on their feet. I should send a [white] flag across tomorrow morning at daylight. I'll so notify Corregidor" and General Wainwright.

Then he gave them orders to destroy all their equipment and weapons, but spare all buses, cars, trucks, and gasoline to ferry the sick and wounded to prison camp.

"Is there anything else any of you can think of?" he asked.

He looked each man square in the face, paused, then, as if he was thinking out loud, he said, "My career is over."

"Is there any possibility of any help?" one of the generals asked.

"None whatsoever," King said.[22]

Runners returning from the field reported that the Old National Road was jammed with bedraggled soldiers and terrified refugees, "a mass of sheep" straggling south. A half hour later King called his chief of staff and his operations officer into conference.[23]

Assemble the headquarters staff, he told them.

At midnight, surrounded by his department heads and aides, he made the inevitable official.

> I did not ask you here to get your opinion or advice. I do not want any one of you saddled with any part of the responsibility for the ignominious decision I feel forced to make. I have not communicated with General Wainwright [directly] because I do not want him to be compelled to assume any part of the responsibility. I am sending forward a flag of truce at daybreak to ask for terms of surrender. I feel that further resistance would only uselessly waste human life. Already [one of] our hospital[s], which is filled to capacity and directly in the line of hostile approach is within range of enemy light artillery. We have no further means of organized resistance.

They had known, of course, that the end was at hand, but hearing their commander say it, looking into those dark, empathetic eyes, the news, as one of them put it, "hit with an awful bang and a terrible wallop," for each of them "had hoped against hope for a better end." And several had tears coursing down their cheeks as they walked out into the night to perform their final duties.

Two junior officers had volunteered to find the Japanese lines and deliver the general's proffer of surrender and his request to meet with General Homma to discuss terms. The others, meanwhile, issued orders to all units to destroy anything of military value. Field officers now told their men that in the morning, they were going to lay down their arms.[24]

The senior ordnance officer, determined to keep Bataan's stores of dynamite and ammunition from the enemy, fired his fuses right away and the tip of the peninsula convulsed with explosions as the magazines, ammunition dumps, and ordnance warehouses began to blow up, one after the other. Soon shells were shooting skyward, filling the black cope of night with ribbons and medallions of color, fireworks at war. At first the men marveled at the pyrotechnics, the Fourth of July come early, then as the detonations crept closer, flak began to fall on the compound, and the final blasts stripped leaves from the trees and flattened the tar-paper-and-bamboo buildings in the command post.

THE SURRENDER PARTY set out around 9:00 a.m. on April 9 in two jeeps, each with half a bedsheet (white ensigns of surrender) flying from a bamboo pole attached to the side of the windshield. In the first jeep rode the operations officer, Colonel James V. Collier, and one of the junior officers who had found the Japanese lines and returned to guide the surrender party. Behind them in the second vehicle with two of his aides and wearing his last clean uniform was Ned King.

As the jeeps turned onto the Old National Road, a flight of five Japanese fighters swooped down and started strafing them. The Americans jumped for cover, the planes rolled out of sight, and the jeeps resumed their journey, but the respite was only temporary. The planes were soon back, and for more than an hour the Japanese pilots played cat and mouse with the men in the jeeps, a game that left the general and his aides constantly scrambling for cover.

Hunkered down under fire like that, a soldier's mind either shuts down or seeks distraction. Lying in the yellow dust by the side of the Old National Road that morning, Ned King turned to history. On the same day in 1865, April 9, General Robert E. Lee, one of Ned King's military heroes, surrendered the Army of Northern Virginia at Appomattox Courthouse. "There is nothing left for me to do," Lee told his staff, "but to go and see General Grant, and I would rather die a thousands deaths."

Now another son of the Old South, remembering that famous phrase, raised himself from the dirt of Bataan and went forward to give up his army.[25]

THE SURRENDER PARTY had been traveling for two hours now, and they guessed they were well beyond what was left of their front lines. As they rounded a bend in the Old National Road just south of the Lamao River bridge, a platoon of Japanese infantry, bayonets drawn, jumped out in front of them on both sides of the road.

One of the soldiers stepped forward and signaled them to stop. Close behind was an officer.

Lieutenant Ryotaro Nishimura, commander of the Fifth Company, 9th Infantry, 16th Division, had learned a number of lessons since landing at Lingayen Gulf, foremost: An officer should always double-check his target before he orders his men to shoot.

Three times in three months he had been ready to fire on some distant target, a cloud of dust or some figures in a tree line, only to discover that the quarry was really another unit of *hohei*.

Now moving fast across Bataan, the vanguards of the various attack wings kept bumping into one another, so Ryotaro Nishimura was trying to be especially careful. More than once in the last few days he had worried about killing his own men.

By April 9 his battalion had reached the Old National Road. Another division had secured the road up to Lamao River bridge. There they had established a command post in three small buildings fronted by a flagpole in a small parklike compound, an agricultural station just off the main road. Ryotaro Nishimura's company had been ordered to proceed beyond the command post, cross the Lamao River bridge, and scout the next section of highway south.

Almost as soon as they crossed the bridge into no-man's-land the point man spotted a cloud of dust beyond a bend, and Nishimura halted his company, formed two columns on either side of the road, and moved his machine guns up front, just in case.

The dust came closer—perhaps a tank, he thought—then closer still.

The lieutenant raised his monocular to his eye, ready to order his machine gunners to open fire, then the cloud stopped, the dust cleared, and the lieutenant spotted two small vehicles, American jeeps, one flying a large white flag.

The point man signaled the jeeps to stop and the occupants started to disembark.

One of them, Ryotaro Nishimura noticed, a man much older than the others, had on a clean uniform. This man must be a very high-ranking officer, Nishimura thought. He looked at his face—he'd never seen an

American before and could not read his expression—then he shouted the only two words of English he knew.

"Come here! Come here!"

The Americans were wearing sidearms, and Nishimura watched carefully to make sure they kept their hands still. He wanted to speak to the officer in charge and gave the group a thumbs-up with his right hand, a gesture the Japanese used to recognize someone in authority.

At length he made them understand they should follow him, and he turned around and led them back across the bridge to the command post where some staff officers and a translator took over.

Curious, the lieutenant lingered nearby, trying to eavesdrop on the proceedings, but he could catch only snatches of what was being said, and later, after the Americans were escorted away, he spoke to the translator.

"What was his rank, the one with the clean uniform. Who is he?"

"It is General King," the translator said.

"And did the Americans surrender or not?"

"*Hai*," the translator said, "they surrendered."[26]

COLONEL MOTOO NAKAYAMA, senior operations officer of the 14th Army, had no intention of talking terms with Ned King.

He would talk only to General Wainwright, he told King, and only about the surrender of all the forces in the islands, not just the Luzon Force, the 76,000 men left on Bataan.

Ned King tried to explain his position—he commanded only the troops on the peninsula, he said, not the forces left on Corregidor or in the southern Philippine Islands—and then pressed his terms: he wanted an armistice, wanted his staff to help arrange the stand-down, most of all wanted to be able to truck his tired and sick men to prison rather than have them march there.

Nakayama would not listen. If King did not have the authority to surrender all the troops in the islands, Nakayama said, the Japanese did not want to deal with the general. He could surrender his Bataan force to the division commander at Lamao, if that's what he wanted, but there would be no negotiations, no terms.

"Will you treat the prisoners well?" Ned King asked.

"We are not barbarians," Nakayama's interpreter said.

"Then I will agree to the unconditional surrender," Ned King said.

No American general had ever surrendered such a force, 76,000 men, an entire army.

He put his pistol on the table—they had asked for his sword but he'd long ago left it in Manila—then he sat back in his chair, crossed his legs, and folded his hands in front of him.

He had done his duty, the right thing for the right reason, as he saw it, but Ned King took no comfort in that stance. He had been a professional soldier for thirty-four years, and he could not shake the sense of shame that was beginning to settle on him.[27]

Q. P. DEVORE had lost his friend, Ben Steele. When they scattered at the stream, he had gone one way and Ben the other.

Now, at midmorning on April 9, he found himself atop a high hill among a large group of stragglers, strangers every one of them. Maybe Ben Steele had been captured, he thought, maybe Ben Steele was dead.

"I'm in this alone now," he thought.

A lieutenant in the group suggested they form a perimeter and build a fire to cook some rice, but just as they were starting to forage for wood, a dark apparition emerged from the tree line waving a white flag.

In broken English the Japanese officer called for the senior American. The lieutenant went forward to speak with him, then returned to the huddle of men.

"Jap officer says they've got us surrounded," he said. "They are going to give us a chance to surrender or fight on. I don't know what to do . . . Only thing I can think of is to take a vote."

Far below on the flats of the coastal plain, the cane fields and rice paddies were silent. Even the big guns on Corregidor had stopped firing.

"Maybe it's all over," one of the men said. And if that was true, what was the point of putting up a fight? If they gave themselves up, the enemy might feed them. This Jap officer seemed friendly enough.

"Okay," the lieutenant told the Japanese officer. "We voted, we'll surrender."

"Lay down your arms and pile your ammunition," the officer ordered, then he gave a whistle and, instantly, dozens of Imperial soldiers, more apparitions, came rushing out of the jungle.

"What the hell is gonna happen to me now?" Q. P. Devore asked himself.

The enemy soldiers stood the Americans in a line, made them raise their hands over their heads, and started to rifle their packs and pockets for valuables. A Japanese captain standing nearby noticed that one of the looters had tossed aside a string of rosary beads, and he picked them up and offered them to the next American in line—Q. P. Devore.

"I'm not Catholic," Q.P. said. "I don't use rosaries."

The officer offered again, this time at pistol point.

BEN STEELE had been running all night and when he could run no more he dropped to the ground and went to sleep.

When he awoke on the morning of April 9 he was among a small group of men on an old ammunition trail somewhere in the foothills of Mount Mariveles.

He looked around for Q.P.—he assumed his friend had been with him through the night—but saw only a handful of strangers, boys from different units, and, checking one more time, reckoned his buddy had disappeared or was dead.

He was too numb with fatigue to feel any sense of loss. He had been running for days, days of bombing and shelling and small arms fire, running to the rear, always to the rear, living on handfuls of rice and rotten carabao, living on empty. Now he had stopped running, stopped thinking, too. He looked neither forward nor back. He was breathing—that was his existence. He had his rifle, he had his helmet, he had his life.

All at once up the trail the group heard the sound of tanks, and the handful of men—there were no more than ten of them—dropped to their bellies in a small depression at the side of the trail.

The clanking got louder and louder. Then from the trees the tanks came into view, two of them, no—four, six, ten in a column, and with infantry.

The Americans took aim with their rifles and fired. Spitballs against steel.

The tanks returned the fire and the Americans flattened themselves in their hollow. The tanks clanked forward, stopped, advanced again. They were very close now, close enough to lower their cannon and fire directly into the hole where the Americans lay.

At that point—point-blank—some of the stragglers decided they'd had enough, and one of them draped a white undershirt over the muzzle of his rifle and held it up to the enemy. The others, meanwhile, began to remove the bolts from their rifles and toss them into the jungle, then, slowly, they rose to their feet and put their hands above their heads.

The hatch of the first tank popped open and a Japanese soldier emerged, carrying a machine gun. He climbed to the ground, settled himself behind the gun, and trained his sights on the Americans.

"This is it," Ben Steele thought. "It won't be long now."

He had always imagined he'd be afraid at this moment, but he felt nothing. That was the strange part of it. No terror, no sadness, no dread. He was tired, too tired to tremble. If he lived, fine, and if he didn't—

"It won't be long," he kept telling himself.

He hoped for a bullet in the heart or the head. Maybe it would hurt, maybe not. Either way, he thought, "I'm not going to suffer very long."

He wondered about heaven. His mother believed in an immortal soul. His mother—he could see her face in his mind's eye and was glad she could not see him, see this miserable son of hers standing with his hands raised above his head, waiting.

The Japanese lined them up and started to search them. They looked like hard men, these enemy soldiers. Beneath their large helmets their faces were dark, their eyes implacable.

The searching went on for a while. Maybe, Ben Steele thought, they weren't going to kill them after all.

A soldier rifled his pockets, took his wallet, camera. When the looting stopped, one by one the Japanese slipped off their packs.

"Kora! Kora!" Get over here! the Japanese soldiers yelled. Then they shoved their loads on their prisoners.

The packs were bulging. Strapped to the outside were pieces of heavy equipment—artillery rounds, cannon wheels, caisson axles, mortar tubes. Each pack must have weighed seventy pounds or more. Enormous, unwieldy loads.

The Americans had trouble shouldering the weight and started to stumble.

"Hayaku, hayaku!" Hurry up! the soldiers yelled, prodding the Americans with bayonets and rifle butts.

To men whose muscles had long since been wasted by malnutrition, the load was crushing.

"Oh, God!" Ben Steele said under his breath, "this is torture."

Like several of his comrades, he soon collapsed, and when he looked up, a Japanese soldier was standing over him, his leg drawn back.

Ben Steele covered his head with his hands. His body shook with each kick.

Some men pleaded for mercy—"No more! Please!"—but the Japanese took these cries for quarter as a sign of weakness and, worse, insubordination. The more a man yelled, the more blows he invited.

"They're enjoying this," Ben Steele thought.

He struggled to stand, gained his feet, and the great weight on his back started to propel him down the hill.

He concentrated on keeping his balance. Fall again, he knew, and he'd get another beating.

He stumbled down the trail and through the underbrush. Now and then a *hohei* would come astride of him and scream in his face, kick dirt on him, bang him with a rifle butt.

He was no better than a pack mule, he thought, a "dumb animal."

Bad enough they'd lost the battle, but this, good thing the home front couldn't see this—an American soldier as somebody's dogsbody, somebody's slave.

MAKING MAGIC

BEN STEELE heard Earl Snook calling for him.

"Take the truck, Bud, and run on up to Will James's place and bring him back, will ya?"

Fall 1937 and Ben Steele was going to school mornings and working for wages afternoons. He had found a job as an errand boy at the Snook Art Company, a painting and glass contractor and purveyor of art supplies. He liked working there on North 29th Street, downtown. Pay was okay, twenty-five cents an hour, and some of the workmen were real characters, some of the artists too. The owners, Earl and Eleanor Snook, had gotten real friendly with many of the quiet, serious-looking men who came in to buy sketch pads, canvases, pencils, and paint, in particular a well-known illustrator and author of children's books who called himself Will James.

Will James! The errand boy was excited.

"I'll get on up there, Mr. Snook."

Growing up, Ben Steele read everything Will James had written, all his stories of Montana and the West. He'd spent hours staring at the artist's illustrations, bucking horses that seemed so real that their riders looked ready to get pitched off the page.

He'd always been fascinated by the magic of art—that's how he thought of it, magic, the way someone could pick up a stick of charcoal or a pencil or a paintbrush and with just a few strokes on paper or canvas make a picture of the prairie or a cowboy running down a steer.

He used to watch the itinerant artists who set up their easels on street corners in Roundup, a town west of the Bulls. He'd stand there for hours as they turned out their three-dollar landscapes—the blue sky, the purple mountains, the big green pines, Montana—in twenty minutes.

At Hawk Creek he'd sometimes sit at the kitchen table with his mother while she painted flowers on her chinaware. He wondered, was there something of an artist in him, too?

Now and then he tried to sketch horses, Warren always hanging over his shoulder. "That's good, Bud," his brother would say, "real good." Same thing in grade school during art hour. "Great horse, Bud," the kids would tell him, gathering round for a look.

He didn't think so. Not compared to Will James. He'd pawed through the author's best seller *Smoky* so often, the pages were frayed and falling apart. No, he couldn't draw like that and likely never would. Art was like fishing; it was play, and he had to work. Still, he sure liked those books with their wonderful drawings.

"Come on in," Will James said.

The artist lived on a five-acre spread snuggled against the rimrocks on the city's north side. By then, his wife, worn down by his binges, had left, and most of his friends, save the Snooks, had given him their back.

James had been in an automobile accident that month and couldn't drive, and Earl Snook sent his errand boy out there to fetch the great man to town for supplies.

"You like art?"

"I do, Mr. James."

"Well, step over here."

The artist settled himself behind his drafting table and picked up a length of charcoal and started to draw. His hand swept back and forth, this way and that, up and down across the page, and it wasn't long before Ben Steele could make out the shape of a horse—the back, the neck, the withers, the legs. A dozen more strokes and, suddenly, there was a wild bronc bucking, snorting, and stomping in front of him.

"What do you think?" Will James said.

"Magic," thought Ben Steele.

SEVEN

B Y NOON on April 9, most Filipino and American field commanders had gotten the word to give up, and the jungle hills and hollows of Bataan were speckled with the white flags of surrender.

Like all men facing the dark, the defeated waited for the worst, convinced the worst wouldn't happen. They'd heard the stories, of course. Japan's reputation as a brutal occupier had been written across the world's front pages—the wholesale looting, the violation of women, the wanton murder of civilians, the execution of unarmed prisoners of war—but most soldiers thought such stories exaggerated, made up to sell newspapers, and they did not believe them, or did not want to believe them.

So what if the Japanese were barbarians? They had to abide by the law, didn't they? The international law of land warfare that prohibited the mistreatment of prisoners of war.[1]

"Everything is going to be all right," officers assured their men. "Just stick together, and don't worry."

AFTER THEY DESTROYED their gear and gobbled the food they had left, most men sat down where they were to await the enemy. They were beaten men now, trying to shake a growing sense of shame. Some told themselves that disease and hunger had defeated them, not the Imperial Japanese Army, but they could not shake the feeling that they had just flat-out given up, and as they smashed their weapons against the nearest tree, the first of many acts of obeisance that would be required of them, some men wept.

"The little bastards," said Corporal Brown Davidson of Denver, Colorado. "They've beaten us."[2]

A handful of Americans refused to surrender and either disobeyed General King's order or sought leave from their superiors and headed for the hills, hoping to slip through Japanese lines and make their way north to the Zambales Mountains, a staging ground for guerrillas.

Hundreds of Filipino soldiers tried to evade capture as well. They chucked their uniforms, borrowed civilian clothes from Bataanese villagers, and passed themselves off as locals or made their way to the peninsula's eastern shore and paid fishermen there to ferry them across the bay to Manila, Cavite, Bulacan.

Private Humphrey O'Leary couldn't decide what to do—dissemble and disappear, or talk some sense into his buddy Phil Murray.[3]

O'Leary was the son of an American expatriate who had fought in the Spanish-American War and had stayed in the islands to marry a Filipina. When the Japanese invaded, Humphrey O'Leary quit his job at his father's construction company in Manila and, since he held U.S. citizenship, joined the American 31st Infantry.

He was taller than the average Filipino, skin was lighter too, and growing up he often passed for white, a *puti*. Now, sitting in a circle of American soldiers down by the beach, waiting for the Japanese, he watched his white comrades, his friend Phil Murray among them, smear their faces with sand and dirt.

It was laughable, all this rubbing. *Loko-lokos*, idiots, what were they thinking, that they could pass as natives?

Humphrey leaned close to his compadre.

"Come on, Phil," he said. "Don't be foolish. You're too white. The Japs will see right through that."

Murray stopped rubbing.

"Tell you what," Humphrey said. "I'll stay, Phil. We'll sweat it out. We'll make this together."

CONFIDENT his April offensive would bring victory on Bataan, General Homma had ordered his staff to prepare a plan to clear the peninsula of prisoners. The campaign for the Philippines was not over yet; Homma still had to take Corregidor, the American fortress and command center blocking access to Manila Harbor. Bataan was to serve as a staging area for the invasion, and the Japanese had to move their prisoners off the peninsula before they could use it as a base to attack the tiny island out in the bay.

The evacuation plan stressed expediency: Guards were to marshal the prisoners in groups on the Old National Road, the peninsula's main artery, then start them marching north to a railhead in San Fernando, sixty-six miles from the tip of the peninsula. Along the way Japanese supply troops were to set up feeding and aid stations and provide trucks to ferry the sick and wounded. At San Fernando the prisoners would be put on trains to Tarlac Province, disembarking in Capas, the station closest to their ultimate destination, Camp O'Donnell, a Filipino training post the Japanese had converted to a prisoner-of-war camp.

Expecting the battle to last the month, the planners set April 20, more or less, as the day to complete their preparations. Since their intelligence estimates were at best a guess, they could not say how many prisoners they would have to manage, but they guessed no more than fifty thousand.

The plan seemed sound, as far as it went, which is to say like all military plans it reflected the miscalculations, misjudgments, misbeliefs, and misintentions of its makers. Of course, at war nothing runs true to plan.

WITHIN HOURS of the surrender, 14th Army Headquarters realized its estimates, and thus its plans, were worthless. Reports from the field indicated at least twice the number of prisoners and refugees headquarters had expected, 76,000 soldiers and 26,000 civilians.

Everywhere the Japanese looked, there were prisoners. On the roads, in the hills, on jungle trails—squads, platoons, and companies of them, twenty here, two hundred there, a thousand at the airstrip in Mariveles. None of the *hohei* had ever seen anything like it. What a spectacle.[4]

The scene reminded Private First Class Jinzaburo Chaki of a photograph in a Tokyo newspaper, a front-page picture from Malaya showing great masses of British prisoners at Singapore.

"We have done the same thing here on Bataan!" he told himself.

Like all victorious troops, the *hohei* at first were fascinated with their captives, eager to get a close look at the men who had been shooting at them.

Private First Class Tasuku Yamanari thought the Filipino soldiers looked "like children, hungry children" begging for the dry biscuits the Japanese carried in their kits. The *hakujin*, however, the white men, struck many *hohei* as *oni*, the devils they had been told about in training. Tall, hairy creatures with big noses and skin the color of a cadaver, ugly men, soft men, men without a fighting spirit, a will to win.

"How could they give up with this many soldiers?" Sergeant Tozo Takeuchi asked himself. And how could a *hohei* have anything but contempt for such men?

THEY KEPT PUSHING HIM down the trail, and his pack became heavier with each step, but Ben Steele wasn't going to let himself fall again and take another beating.

When the group of prisoners reached the Old National Road east of Mariveles, the Japanese soldiers took their packs back, and Ben Steele and the other men were made to join a much larger mob of prisoners squatting in the sun on the side of a hill facing Manila Bay.

He was glad to be rid of his load but worried about what was ahead. These soldiers looked angry.

Hate! Ben Steele thought. "Hate is sticking out all over them."

BY LATE AFTERNOON on April 9 most of the captured Filipinos and Americans had been gathered at assembly points along an eight-mile section of the Old National Road at the tip of the peninsula.

Corporal John Emerick of Norvelt, Pennsylvania, had been captured in the hills above Mariveles and was herded down to the airstrip there, then forced into line with hundreds of other men. An interpreter was telling them to empty their pockets and spill the contents of their bags and packs on the ground in front of them.

"You have guns, knives, anything," he said, "and we kill you. We kill you instantly. Right? Instantly."[5]

And then the searchers set to work picking through the men's pockets and rifling their clothing and gear, and it soon became clear that the search for concealed weapons was nothing more than a shakedown, a treasure hunt for cameras and flashlights and mechanical pencils and fountain pens (especially Parker Duofolds—"Pah-kah," the guards would demand, "Pah-kah pen"), sunglasses, mess kits, blankets and mosquito nets, safety razors and blades, terry cloth towels, extra clothing, rings and jewelry of all types, and, best of all, watches, American watches—that Hamilton or Bulova, that gold Lord Elgin with the jeweled works and pearl face.

The prisoners were too exhausted to protest and did not want to provoke the line of soldiers with pitiless faces holding those long bayonets, but as the Japanese stripped them of their possessions, many Americans started to seethe.

To them the signet rings, wristwatches, and fountain pens with gold nibs were more than graduation or birthday gifts or luxuries long wished for and purchased after months or years of putting money away. They were "personal property," and property was an expression of the pursuit of happiness, one of their unalienable rights. A section of land, an automobile, a quarter horse, a watch—emblems of the opportunity, part of the freedom they had sworn to protect.

THE HELL with the bastards. Some men dug holes in the dirt and buried their valuables where they sat. Others in silent rage tossed their keepsakes and curios from home into the bushes.

Here and there a man ripped the cuffs of his trousers or the seams of his shirt, then worked some small keepsake into the secret space.

Men with string or thread hung their watches and rings around their necks and down their backs.

One soldier secreted a ring in his mouth and secured it to a molar with a piece of dental floss.

Waiting to be searched, tank corps crewman Bernard FitzPatrick of Waverly, Minnesota, watched out of the corner of his eye as two guards worked their way down a line of prisoners and stopped in front of a soldier wearing a wedding ring.[6]

"Waifu?" asked one of the guards, smiling and pointing to the ring.

The American nodded and the guards moved on . . . and FitzPatrick got an idea. He turned his college class ring upside down so only the band was showing. The first guard passed by without noticing, but the second was suspicious and told him to turn his hands palm up. Bernard FitzPatrick hesitated. He'd worked hard for that ring, four years of studying and classes, and he did not want to give it up.

The second guard was shouting at him now, and the first was reaching to detach his bayonet from his rifle.

"For God's sake, Fitz," a friend said, "give 'im the ring. They just cut some guy's finger off because he wouldn't."

THE AMERICANS thought them "thieves," "thugs," "crooked bastards," but the average *hohei* was no more larcenous than his enemies. American pockets were full of "souvenirs," loot taken from Japanese prisoners or stripped from the bodies of Japanese dead.

Get rid of your Jap stuff, quick!

What Jap stuff?

Everything, money, souvenirs. Get rid of it![7]

The word went around quickly, and at the airstrip in Mariveles men began to toss away their spoils, most men, that is.

A Japanese private searching a young Air Corps captain found a few yen in the man's pocket. The guard hissed his disapproval and summoned an officer. The officer looked at the money, then forced the American to his knees. Some of the men standing nearby swore they saw a glint of sun on the officer's sword as he brought it down on the young captain's neck.[8]

Watching the officer wipe the blood off his blade, some prisoners started to think they'd gone back in time, awoken in another era. Who were these cold-eyed men who carried swords and cut off fingers and heads? Medieval marauders? A nightmare let loose upon the day?[9]

"ANYTHING CAN HAPPEN," Sergeant Richard Gordon of New York told himself. Anything.

Gordon and another soldier from the American 31st Infantry, Corporal Elmer Parks from Anadarko, Oklahoma, had been hiding in the bush high on Mount Bataan. When surrender came, they started down a trail to the Old National Road. Along the way they came upon an abandoned truck, cranked it up, and continued down the mountain. Parks was driving fast and almost ran over a Japanese soldier who jumped out from behind a banyan tree.

"What the hell do we do now?" he said, as the truck skidded to a stop.[10]

Gordon glanced around. The Jap seemed to be alone. They could shoot the bastard, run him over maybe and hightail it into the bush. All of a sudden Richard Gordon heard a rustle. More Japs, a lot more, surrounding them, hands reaching up and yanking them out of the truck.

They started on Parks first. One clown hit him on the head with a rifle butt and sent him sprawling, and the rest joined in with their fists and boots. Now it was Gordon's turn.

The first blow caught him in the face and filled him with fury. He had come of age in the streets of New York, a rangy kid from Manhattan's Hell's Kitchen, and when the punch landed square on his nose, he thought, "Son of a bitch! I've never put up with this kind of crap in my life and I'm not going to start now."

They hit him again, and again, and he thought, "Okay, so you take a beating, you take a beating and you live."

THEY SEEMED to go off without warning, stoics one moment, lunatics the next.

They beat the prisoners as viciously as their sergeants and lieutenants beat them—slapped them, punched them, kicked them, boxed their ears, bashed their skulls, broke their bones.

They beat them for looking this way or that, for moving or not moving fast enough, for talking or keeping still—beat them for everything and for nothing at all.

It was their duty to beat the prisoners, and for some their pleasure as well. The same sadists who had turned the training barracks back home into crucibles of cruelty roamed the lines of helpless *horyo*, inveighing them with orders they did not understand then slam-banging them for being *bakana*, stupid.

ARMY MEDIC Sidney Stewart, standing in the ranks at Mariveles waiting to be searched, watched a guard coming down the line punch a soldier in the face. The soldier was young, a fledgling, and afraid, and he cried out in pain—a form of protest, as the Japanese saw it, that always invited more punishment. The guard raised the butt end of his rifle and bashed the soldier in the head. The boy sagged to his knees, groaning, and the guard raised his rifle for another blow. This time, he split the boy's skull. The American twitched and shuddered in the dirt for a few moments, then he was quiet and did not move again.

Watching this, Sidney Stewart felt a "black hatred" begin to "boil" in his brain. He had thought himself a Christian man, small town (Watonga, Oklahoma), and full of faith. His religion had carried him through the bombing of Manila and the battle of Bataan, but this, standing there watching a guard bludgeon a comrade to death, this seemed to mock and reprove his piety, and the urge "to tear" his enemy "limb from limb," to "kill for the sheer pleasure of killing," overwhelmed him.[11]

APRIL 10, the day after surrender, the Japanese started their prisoners walking.

Groups of one hundred, two hundred, three hundred and more were herded into lines or loose formations (sometimes flanked by a brace of guards at either end, sometimes not) and told to get on the road. The ragged, disorganized groups of men set off at intervals. Half the 76,000 captives began the trek April 10 near Mariveles, at the tip of the peninsula, but every day for some ten days thereafter at various points along the thirty miles of road between Mariveles and Balanga, the provincial capital, roughly halfway up the peninsula, yet another rabble of Filipinos or Americans would come down from the hills or emerge from the jungle, and the Japanese would gather them into groups and head them north up the Old National Road.[12]

To label the movement a "march," as the men took to calling it, was something of a misnomer. During the first few days of walking there were so many men on the road, one bunch following closely behind another, they appeared a procession without end, prisoners as far as the eye could see, mile after mile after mile of tired, filthy, bedraggled men, heads bowed, feet dragging through the ankle-deep dust.

They walked the sixty-six miles in stages. For those who started at the tip of the peninsula, stage one was a stretch of road that ran east nine miles to Cabcaben. There the road turned north and proceeded along Bataan's east coast some twenty-seven miles, passing through the town squares of Lamao, Limay, Orion, Pilar, Balanga, Abucay, Samal, Orani, and Hermosa. At Hermosa the Old National Road turned west toward Layac Junction, then northeast for eleven miles across a torrid, sandy plain to Lubao, then continuing northeast to San Fernando—in all from Mariveles 66 road miles, 106 kilometers, 140,000 footfalls.

Some days the prisoners trekked ten miles, other days fifteen, twenty, or more. And hard miles they were. More than half the Old National Road on Bataan was a rural road—its base stone and crushed coral, its surface fine sand—built for the light traffic of the provinces. Four months of army convoys had churned up the hardpan, leaving potholes and sinkholes that tripped the men and shards of gravel that sliced up their shoes and boots.

They walked in the most torrid time of year, *tag-init*, the Filipinos called it, the days of dryness, the season of drought. From March to May the sun hung flame white and unshrouded in the Philippine sky, searing everything under it. By early afternoon the air was an oven, the hardpan as hot as kiln bricks.

LIEUTENANT SAMUEL GOLDBLITH of Lawrence, Massachusetts, started walking at Mariveles with a full pack—an extra uniform, underwear, socks, blanket, raincoat, shaving kit, stationery, mess kit, canteen, and a pink cotton towel, a keepsake from his wife's trousseau. It wasn't long before he had pitched everything save his canteen, mess kit, and Diana's pink towel, which he used as a mantilla to keep the sun from baking his head.[13]

Goldblith guessed he was bound for a prison camp somewhere in the islands, but where he could not say. One rumor had them being interned in Manila's Bilibid Prison, another had them bound for the railhead at San Fernando, but this information was of little use or comfort since few men were familiar with the local geography and had no real sense of the distances involved or the difficulty traversing them. They were walking, that's all they knew, walking in the heat and dust, eyes burning and throats parched, wondering where they were going and when they would get there.

Richard Gordon happened to be walking in a group that included Brigadier General Clifford Bluemel. Gordon had seen Bluemel in action and remembered him as "a spicy little bastard." Somewhere between Mariveles and Cabcaben, the Japanese had grabbed the general and started him walking, and along the way some of the guards decided to have a little fun.

They circled the general, then made him squat with his fingers locked behind his neck and started turning him in circles. When he lost his equilibrium and toppled over, they laughed—oh, how they laughed—and when he fought to keep his balance, his poise ("The man is a tough nut," Gordon thought), they kicked his feet out from under him and howled that much harder.[14]

The looting went on as well. Units of Imperial Infantry were encamped beside the Old National Road, awaiting new orders and watching the parade of prisoners. Though most prisoners had been stripped clean by the time they reached Cabcaben, now and then a *hohei* resting along the road would get curious.

Sergeant James Gautier, an Air Corps mechanic from Moss Point, Mississippi, felt a hand grab his shirt and pull him out of formation. Another shakedown, he reckoned. All he had left was his wallet, and the Japanese was flipping through the folds, looking for something of value when he came upon a snapshot of a woman.

"Waifu, Waifu?" the Japanese soldier said. Gautier nodded, then the soldier dropped the picture in the dirt, stepped on it, and ground it with the heel of his hobnail boot.[15]

So this is what it meant to be a prisoner of war, thought Robert Levering, a Manila lawyer from Ohio who had volunteered to serve on Bataan. This is what it felt like to "come to the end of civilization."[16]

PAST MARIVELES that first day, the highway ran flat for a few miles, then rose sharply in a series of steep switchbacks that had been cut into the side of an escarpment. The precipitous switchbacks were known as "the zigzag." Unfolded, this accordion section of road was less than a mile, but its angle of ascent—520 feet in less than two-tenths of a mile—was so acute that the back-and-forth climb was a tough one, especially at the height of the hot season. And for men left weak and exhausted by disease, hunger, thirst, and fear, the ascent was torture.

One hairpin turn after another blocked the marchers' view and made the climb seem endless: another incline, another turn, another incline, up, up again, up some more.

On the outside turns, the road dropped off sharply into deep ravines, stories deep, many of them, with boulders, stumps, trees, and tangled underbrush waiting at the bottom.

The labor of climbing the switchbacks under a tropical sun left the men gasping with each step, and it was not long before some of them began to collapse and crawl to the shoulder of the road.

The guards accompanying the first columns climbing the zigzag seemed to ignore the dropouts, but prisoners in later columns began to spot bodies at the bottom of the ravines, bodies wearing familiar uniforms.

FROM THE TOP of the zigzag the road ran flat and east, seven and a half miles to the seaside town of Cabcaben on Manila Bay. Along this stretch the marchers now began to encounter an increasing number of Japanese trucks, tanks, and horse-drawn artillery, all moving south to stage for the invasion of Corregidor.

Many of these trucks carried troops, and as these vehicles passed the columns of prisoners, Japanese soldiers would lean out with a bamboo staff or a length of wood or the butt end of a rifle and, like a polo player bearing down on a ball, swing their cudgels at the heads of the men marching along in the crowded ranks on the road.

They fractured a lot of skulls, smashed a number of jaws, dislocated scores of shoulders. Now and then a truck would swerve sharply toward a column, and the Japanese riding shotgun would throw his door open to catch a marcher flush in the face.

"Let's stay on the inside row in the column," Humphrey O'Leary told his friend Phil Murray. "If we march on the other side, the Japs will bash us in the head."[17]

Here came a truckful of soldiers holding lengths of rope as long as whips, lashing laggers on the road. One whip caught a prisoner around the neck, and the Japanese in the truck started to reel him in as the truck kept going. The poor man was twisting this way and that, dragging through the cinders. About a hundred feet later he was finally able to free himself, and he got to his feet, clothes shredded, skin lanced and bleeding, and looked back down the road.

"You bastards!" he yelled after the truck. "I'll live to piss on your graves."[18]

A MILE beyond the top of the zigzag, the columns of prisoners passed the entrance to one of the large American field hospitals, part of the headquarters and service area that had been tucked in the American rear. The Japanese had bombed and shelled the service area often during their second attack, fire that left the hospital in ashes. Now wandering among its charred ruins were scores of wounded Filipino soldiers who had been treated there. Many were still in their hospital pajamas or bathrobes, grimy now with dirt and soot. Their wounds and stumps were beginning to suppurate and their bloody bandages and dressings needed changing.

Major William "Ed" Dyess of Albany, Texas, an Air Corps pilot in the line of march, watched Japanese guards herd the sick and wounded Filipinos out of the hospital grounds and set them walking. To Dyess these "bomb-shocked cripples" had a look of "hopelessness in their eyes," and they stumbled along stoop shouldered for more than a mile before "their strength ebbed and they began falling back through the marching ranks" and to the side of the road.[19]

Zoeth Skinner of Portland, Oregon, came astride a Filipino amputee hobbling along on crutches. Japanese infantrymen camped along the way yelled and laughed at the cripple, poked him with sticks, tried to make him stumble. A while later farther up the road, Skinner noticed a tail of white gauze dragging in the dirt ahead of him. At the other end

of the tail, twenty feet forward, was a man with a bandaged leg, struggling against his wound, his dressing unraveling as he walked.[20]

AT FIRST the marchers tried to keep their sense of society, their culture of comradeship, and help one another. The lucky ones, men like Humphrey O'Leary and Phil Murray, were able to "buddy-up" and watch out for each other, but in the chaos of the surrender and the first commotion of captivity, friends became separated, and men like Ben Steele and Richard Gordon and Dominick Giantonio of Hartford, Connecticut, found themselves in the ranks of strangers, lending a hand when a hand was needed.

"Get up!"

"Let's go!"

"Don't fall, they'll get you."

Against despair, however, each man had to struggle alone. Ed Dyess got a "sort of sinking feeling" every time he saw a Ford or Chevrolet truck bearing Imperial Japanese Army insignia, prewar American exports (or a little piece of home, as Dyess saw it) packed now with enemy troops who jeered at him as they passed by.[21]

Colonel Richard Mallonée from Utah was a veteran of the old horse-drawn artillery, and when he felt low he distracted himself by studying the equipage of his Japanese counterparts. Each time a horse-drawn limber and caisson came along, Mallonée noted the condition of the animals—Were they in good flesh? Well-groomed and properly harnessed?—and the bearing of the men riding them.[22]

Lester Tenney of Chicago set goals for himself. Make it as far as "the next bend in the road," he thought, or up to that "herd of carabao in the distance." He also had a dream—"Without a dream," he figured, his "resolve would weaken"—a dream of home. He held hard to the image of his wife, Laura, his reason, he told himself, for living. And to keep his dream safe, he tucked a picture of her in his sock, telling himself it gave each step purpose.[23]

THE SUN was inescapable. It blistered their skin, baked their shoulders and backs, beat on their heads. Some men had managed to keep their helmets, some wore hats or caps or took rags and handkerchiefs and knotted the ends to fashion a sort of cap, but many men had no cover at all and walked bare-headed under the blazing sun.

The sweat soaked their clothes and streamed down their faces. It mixed with the thick dust and created a kind of gray sludge that ran into their eyes, stuck in their beards, caked on their clothing. They looked like ghosts of themselves mantled in gray, tramping along in a pall.

As each ragged group of men reached Cabcaben, the southernmost town on the peninsula's east shore and the place where the Old National Road turned north up the coast, they were halted and put in a holding area—a dry rice paddy, field, or section of runway at Cabcaben's jungle airstrip. From what the men could tell, there were a number of these marshaling yards in Cabcaben, places where the disorderly processions of prisoners from Mariveles were reorganized.

In the holding areas, the men were made to sit feet to back for hours at a time before moving on (the "sun treatment," they came to call it). At last, when they were ready, the guards rushed in among them, screaming, kicking, and flogging the men to their feet, then herded them onto the road where they were arranged into regular marching columns, three or four ranks across, a hundred to four hundred men in each column, with a handful of guards assigned to walk the flanks and bring up the rear.

By now the prisoners' hunger was starting to gnaw at them. They had been half starved before surrender and most had not had a scrap of food since. Even more pressing was their thirst. In the chaos at Cabcaben, only occasionally did the Japanese allow the prisoners to fill their canteens from a nearby stream. Most went without water and they rapidly dehydrated and began to suffer heat exhaustion: their temples pounded with pain, their heads felt afire, they became disoriented and wobbly with vertigo.

Back on the road, the guards yelled at them to pick up the pace.

"Speedo," they shouted, walking or riding bicycles beside the formations. "Speedo! Speedo!"

Some guards, laughing, started their columns running.

BEN STEELE was watching for socks.

Men were starting to blister. Big blisters, the size of a half-dollar, blisters in clusters, breaking and bleeding with every step. Some men used sharp rocks to make slits in their shoes and boots, makeshift sandals, but their feet were so swollen the skin just bulged painfully through the openings. Others removed their footwear and walked barefoot, wincing with every step.

He had to find dry socks or soon he too would be hobbled. Ben Steele pawed through packs and bags abandoned along the road. Finally, somewhere north of Cabcaben, he saw what he'd been looking for.

A corpse lay on the shoulder just ahead. The dead man was wearing garrison shoes, low quarters instead of work boots, and the laces were untied and loose.

Ben Steele removed one of the shoes, stripped off the sock, and was reaching for the other foot when, out of the corner of his eye, he spotted a guard headed his way and dashed back to his place in the column.

"What the hell were you doing back there with that dead guy?" said one of his fellow marchers.

"You gotta take care of your feet," Ben Steele said, "or you're not going to get very far."

MEN HAD BEEN FALLING by the wayside since the zigzag, but the guards had been so busy collecting all the captives and getting them on the road that they had paid the dropouts little attention. After the prisoners were put in columns at Cabcaben, however, the guards in charge of each formation started watching their prisoners more closely, and now when a man went down, a Japanese was soon standing over him.

"*Hayaku tate!*"

The order was unintelligible but the meaning of the kick that followed, the hard toe of a hobnail boot, was clear. Get up! Get up immediately or . . .

The fallen tried to raise themselves, tried to pull their knees under them, push up on all fours, but their heads, thick from fever, pulled them down, and their muscles, wasted by months of malnutrition, collapsed under them.

"*Hayaku! Hayaku!*"

THE JAPANESE type 30 bayonet was twenty inches long, overall, with a fifteen-inch blade. The weapon looked more like a Roman sword than a knife-bayonet, and when it was fixed to the end of a fifty-inch Arisaka rifle, it gave the *hohei* a kind of a pike, a five-and-a-half-foot spear.

The average Japanese foot soldier prized his bayonet. It was a symbol of his office, a twentieth-century warrior nodding to his samurai forebears. He would wear his bayonet home on leave in a scabbard. No other modern force spent so much time practicing with cold steel or developing in its men the stone heart to use it.

If a prisoner was straggling, lagging behind the formation or slowing it down, most guards would just jab him in the lower back or buttocks, a quick poke deep enough to hustle him along and make him rejoin the formation. (After a guard stabbed Sergeant Ed Thomas of Knox, Indiana, in the right buttock, he told himself he could run "all the way to Manila" if he had to.) If a man failed to raise himself, however, he usually got the blade to the hilt.[24]

A young American in Sergeant Tony Aquino's group had fallen face-first to the gravel roadbed, and a guard at the rear of the column ordered the marchers to halt. He kicked the young American in the ribs and shouted at him to stand up, but the soldier got only as far as his knees before he collapsed again. The guard kicked him harder. (Come on compadre, Aquino thought, get up, get up!) The young American raised his head (Aquino could see blood spilling from the man's mouth) and reached out, as if to ask the guard for help.

The guard put his bayonet to the man's neck, shouted, and drove the blade home. The American rocked back on his heels and rose up on his haunches, then the guard jerked the blade free, and the boy toppled over in the dirt.

So it was going to be a death march, Aquino told himself, "death on the road to nowhere." Falter and fall, he thought, and "there you will stay."[25]

When a sergeant in Joe Smith's column fell to the road, two of his comrades broke ranks to help. A guard from the rear of the column came running and shouting, and he beat the Samaritans back into line, then wheeled about and bayonetted the man on the ground. As Smith came abreast of the scene, the guard was struggling to free his weapon. He had driven the blade so deep that he had to put his foot in the small of the man's back and pull the rifle with both hands to wrest it free.[26]

THIRST is a warning, the brain reminding the body that its essence is being spent. On an average day, an average man requires two to three quarts of water. The body is liquid, 60 percent of the chemical equation of life, and the brain is always metering the balance. If the level drops just 2 percent, the hypothalamus sends out an alarm—the urgency for water, the craving to drink.

The men on the death march were drying up. As their bodies tried to conserve fluids, they stopped sweating and urinating. Their saliva turned adhesive and their tongues stuck to their palates and teeth. Their throats started to swell, and their sinus cavities, dry and raw from the dust and heat, pounded with a headache that blurred their vision. Some men got earaches and lost their hearing. A guard could shout "Hey!" (*Kora!*) all he liked, but a man down from dehydration, dazed and deaf with heat fever, would never hear the warning or sense the watchman's fatal approach.

THERE WAS WATER all along the route, plenty of it. On the way to nowhere the men on the death march passed one artesian well after another. In the towns the wells had spigots; on the outskirts they flowed freely from an open pipe, usually within a hundred feet of the road where parched men could see the water gushing in the air, see it bubbling, smell (or so some imagined) its fresh scent.

The guards were under orders to keep their columns moving. They might stop to make way for one of the convoys headed south, or they might pull up at a certain point to wait for their relief, but unless a superior had ordered them to stop, or they had covered the distance assigned them that day, they dared not allow their formations to line up for hours at a bubbling pipe. Japanese section chiefs patrolled the road, and any guard who failed to enforce marching discipline was yanked aside and beaten on the spot.

So the marchers had to sneak a drink on the run or during a rest break, and the only "water" within easy reach lay in the bottom of the drainage ditches, carabao wallows, and small stagnant pools beside the Old National Road.

During a rest a Japanese officer watching Ed Dyess's column allowed a few men to collect their comrades' canteens and fill them from a wallow. It was a foul drink, putrid and brackish. Gnats and flies swarmed above green scum on the surface, and the water gave off a "nauseating reek" that made the men retch, but Dyess and his comrades held their noses and "drank all [they] could get," aware that what they were gulping would likely lay them low.

From their first days in the islands, soldiers were warned not to drink from pools of standing water or slow-running streams, mediums for the pernicious microorganisms that cause dysentery. Some knew that tincture of iodine rendered the water safe, but only a few medics and a handful of others had a bottle of the disinfectant. The rest simply ignored the risk. And on the road north from Cabcaben to Balanga, it was not unusual to see soldiers crazed with thirst on their bellies around some stinking sump or muddy cistern. Just like cats, thought Richard Gordon, "lapping up milk from a saucer."[27]

SOME MEN were so dehydrated, the neurotransmitters in the brain started to shut down. In the pathology of dehydration, they became "functionally deranged." A few developed visions, hydrohallucinations— the cool mountain spring, the pristine waterfall. Most simply lost their minds, their sense of reason.

Only a madman would ask the enemy for water. Robert Levering thought one of his guards "seemed a little friendly" so he pointed to his mouth and mimed drinking from a canteen. *"Mizu nai!"* the guard shouted, no water, and gave Levering a good smack on the side of the head. Men who begged for a drink were clubbed with rifle butts, wooden cudgels, or golf clubs the Japanese had looted along their way. And it soon became clear to those men who had any sense left that the key to survival was not in finding a drink but in controlling the urge to seek one.[28]

BEN STEELE was drying up. His tongue was swollen and he felt himself gagging on it.

He looked at the sun. Not a prairie sun, he thought. This one was hotter, less forgiving. No trees, no buildings, no shade.

He stripped off his T-shirt and draped it over his head. Somewhere north of Cabcaben he got his first sun treatment in an assembly area. Must have been more than two thousand men sitting in that damn field.

Why the hell were the Japs doing that? Didn't make any sense. Mean bunch of bastards.

Back on the road he was choking again. Man next to him had some water.

"Hey, gimme a drink, will ya?" Ben Steele said.

The man kept walking.

"Come on buddy, I'm in bad shape. Whadaya say?"

"Here," the man said, relenting. "Don't take it all, you understand?"

Farther on, walking in the first rank at the head of a column, Ben Steele caught a glimpse of something at the side of the road. A half-gallon tin can . . . and it was half filled with water! An offering from one of the locals, he guessed.

Now he was the one with a drink, and other men began to pull at his sleeve and implore him.

"Water! Come on, water!"

When the can was empty, he would dip it in a rice paddy, a wallow, a drainage ditch.

He didn't share with everyone, just those he couldn't ignore.

"Gimme some water, dear God, please!"

"Here," he'd say, "don't take all of it."

THEY'D BEEN WARNED. Interpreters had addressed the columns: "You must maintain your organization. You must keep your position. No break, no break without Japanese permission."[29]

But at almost every artesian well along the way, some soldier insane with thirst would break formation and run for the pipe. Sometimes a guard would raise his rifle and drop the miscreant on the run, and sometimes he would wait and put a bullet in the prisoner just as the man reached the pipe and was bending down to the clear bubbling water.

When the men in Sidney Stewart's column came upon "a cool mountain stream," their guards shouted for the formation to stop. Stewart took a deep breath. The ground along the riverbank "smelled mossy and wonderful" and the water looked "so dear, so cool, so delicious."

"If only I could throw myself down into the water and lie there feeling it rush over my body," he thought.

The prisoners waited for the guards to tell them to drink, "waited and waited." After a time one man could wait no longer. He ran from the ranks, plunged his face into the stream, and in an instant a Japanese sergeant was standing over him, unsheathing his sword. What happened next happened so fast that Stewart caught it only in flashes—the sword clearing its sheath, the sound of a blade descending ("a quick ugly swish"), the head rolling down the bank into the stream, bloodying the water that hundreds of men were waiting to drink.[30]

North of Cabcaben, the Old National Road had been part of the battlefield, and the land on either side of the road, once lush with nipa palms and shady narras, had become a waste of black stumps and brown bomb craters. Littering this charred landscape were the incinerated hulls of tanks, smashed trucks, and twisted cannon, America's matériel "advantage" now a melancholy reminder of America's worst defeat.

Dead men and animals littered the field as well. More often than not, the corpses lay where they fell, marking their last stand. (During a rest John Olson happened to glance at an embankment and saw the body of a Philippine Scout, helmet still on, frozen in the act of climbing through a bush. Whatever had killed the soldier had caught him in midstep, and there he stood, "in suspended animation," Olson thought, one hand holding on to the bush the other reaching through it to clear the way.) A number of these remains were floating in the rivers and streams or lying half submerged on the banks, decomposing rapidly in the heat and defiling the water.[31]

Still, men stopped and drank, drank with the dead. Even water polluted by a corpse was better than no water at all. The bodies reeked and were so bloated their skin was beginning to split, but Zoeth Skinner drank his fill, and so did Robert Levering and James Gautier and Preston

John Hubbard. They held their noses and looked away from the grotesques floating nearby, swollen black from lying in the sun, and they drank that awful effluent by the canteen and bucket full. James Gautier forced himself to stick his head back into the water for a second drink. "Lord," he prayed, "keep me from getting sick."

BY THE THIRD DAY of the march, men were regularly dropping to the road or staggering out of formation—men with fever, men with dysentery, men too weak to go on. Now, however, instead of rushing up to dispatch the dropouts, the guards on the flanks started to ignore them.

"Why?" Sidney Stewart asked himself. "Why are they leaving them when they had killed them before?"

The answer was soon apparent. Stewart heard the report of a rifle behind him, at the very back of his column, then he heard another shot, and a third.

In other columns prisoners began to notice the same thing. Soon the men marching at the rear of those formations confirmed what their comrades were beginning to suspect—some of the guards had formed "cleanup" crews, or, as the marchers took to calling them, "buzzard squads."

"Oh, God, I've got to keep going," Stewart thought. "I can't die like that."[32]

By that point, the Old National Road was lined with fresh corpses. Hundreds of dead, sprawled on the shoulders, strewn in the drainage ditches.

First Lieutenant Ed Thomas of Grand Rapids, Michigan, caught sight of his captain and company commander lying in a ditch, dead from a bayonet wound. "His marching days are over," Thomas thought. And Bernard FitzPatrick kept passing corpses clad in faded blue hospital pajamas, Filipinos mostly, the cripples and amputees who had left their beds in the field hospital after the Japanese had assured them they were free to walk home.[33]

In the heat the bodies began to rot, and it wasn't long before great swarms of flies were feasting on them. During the day dogs and pigs joined the flies, and at night the smell of death lured large carnivorous lizards down from the hills, but it was the crows that commanded the carrion, crows standing wing to wing on the bloated bodies, tearing at the flesh, crows roosting patiently on the wire fences along the road or, as Private Wince "Tennessee" Solsbee noticed, always circling overhead, waiting for their next meal to drop.

"Y'all go away, big birds," he said. "I'm not fixin' to die yet."[34]

The bodies also attracted the attention of Japanese tank and truck drivers.

Murray Sneddon of Glendale, California, watched a convoy of trucks bear down on two bodies in the middle of the road. The first truck struck the first body with its right front wheel and left an imprint on the corpse. The trailing trucks followed the same line, and after they had passed, all that was left were two silhouettes in the dirt, outlines that hardly looked like men. It won't be long, Sneddon thought, before those bodies will be "nothing more than . . . oil spots."[35]

Richard Gordon stood horrified as a column of tanks crushed an American sergeant who had fallen asleep on the shoulder, and Brown Davidson came upon remains that had been run over so often, all that was left intact was a hand lying nearby. To Ray Hunt of St. Louis the remains on the road looked like "wet sacks." Major John Coleman of Wellington, Texas, thought them swatches of cloth, khaki cloth, until he stepped on one and slipped. "Good God," said Marine Private Irwin Scott of Dallas, "we're marching on our own men."[36]

BEN STEELE believed in God, but he did not think of himself as a man of faith, a religious man.

Back home he rarely spent Sundays in a pew and never wandered out to the prairie to listen to the tub-thumping evangelists call the Holy Spirit into their tents.

The Holy Spirit, he noticed, was nowhere in evidence on the Old National Road. How many of the men begging for a drink had gone to their deaths with the words "Please, God!" still on their lips?

He wasn't angry at the Lord. He was just being realistic. Faith wasn't going to feed him or slake his thirst. He had to focus on the next wallow or well or that guard, the one up ahead there raising his rifle and aiming at a Filipino who had broken ranks and was running to a stand of sugarcane. (The bullet caught the poor kid in the back and sent him sprawling, and the guard, over him now, was pulling the trigger again.)

Ben Steele thought, "Okay, this may happen to me, but all these other guys are alive and I'm not any worse off than they are, so I'm going to hang in there as long as I can. If there's going to be anybody left alive from this, I'm going to be one of them."

BY THE FOURTH DAY of the march, they were desperate for something to eat. Ray Hunt's hunger was textbook: The first day he felt empty, barren, vacant; the second day he had sharp pains in his esophagus; the third day he was obsessed with thoughts of food; the fourth day he felt nothing, a sure sign he was starting to starve.[37]

The men in James Gautier's column, resting in a field during a change of guard, started digging with their fingers for derelict vegetables—camotes, a native tuber, and radishes. They dug like dogs pawing at the dirt, dug here, dug there, dug so many holes the field "looked like it had been freshly plowed."[38]

Army doctor Paul Ashton of San Francisco was dubious when the men around him got the idea to eat a banana plant and started tearing away the stalk's leaves and outer layers to get at its core. The meat of the plant looked a lot like celery but tasted bitter like tree bark. Worthless, Ashton concluded. Might as well eat cardboard.

Captain Sam Grashio of Spokane, Washington, and his march mates made a meal of some horse feed, oats a Japanese hostler had chucked because they were crawling with weevils.[39]

As their formation passed stands of sugarcane, a few of the men around Sergeant Charlie James of New Mexico managed to snatch some stalks from a nearby field. Later James noticed that after he had chewed a hunk of cane and spit it out, the men marching behind him would scoop up the masticated mouthful from the dirt and "chew it again."[40]

The Japanese, meanwhile, were feasting on captured American food. A number of Imperial Infantry units were garrisoned along the road between Balanga and Cabcaben, and at intervals they had established what appeared to be food dumps—stacks of crates and boxes bearing American brands.

Ed Dyess's formation stopped across from one such cache, and an aging colonel boldly crossed the road, pointed to the piles of food, and in sign language he asked the guard for something to eat. The guard grinned for a moment, then picked up a can of salmon and smashed the colonel in the face, laying his cheek open to the bone.

Passing through Pilar, Paul Ashton spotted a food dump piled high with cases of Vienna sausage. Wasn't that thoughtful of the rear-echelon boys, he thought. The American Quartermaster Corps had been hoarding all that food during the battle, saving it, as it turned out, "for the Japanese."[41]

THEY LIVED in their keepers' world now, a world of conformity. *Deru kui wa utareru*, Japanese mothers warned their children, "The nail that sticks up gets hammered down."

Don McAllister was obviously doing something wrong. Each time a convoy passed his column, the Japanese in the trucks tried to hit him or kick him in the head. He seemed to be doing more dodging than most of the men around him and he wondered, "Why are they kicking at me?"

Then his friend Brown Davidson noticed something: circling the crown of McAllister's campaign hat was a bright red braided cord.

"Take that damn thing off your hat," Davidson said. "It gets their attention."[42]

Private Saturnino Velasco and his pal Corporal Freddy Burgos were also attracting more notice than they wanted. Mestizos, half white and half Filipino, they were conspicuously taller than their countrymen, and the guards had been hammering them.

Velasco was getting the worst of it. He had been a student at Ateneo de Manila University when the war broke out, and to distinguish himself from his classmates he had grown a beard, a thick red beard. Now at every change of the guard, some incensed *hohei* would confront him.

"Kora! Americajin?"

"No! No!" Velasco would say. "Filipino . . . Filipino."

"Filipino, no beard," the guard would come back, and Velasco would get another thumping.

Then he got an idea. The next time he saw an angry guard headed his way, he yelled, "Spaniard!"

The guard was suspicious. "You, Spaniard?"

"Yes, yes," Velasco said, nodding vigorously. "Spaniard, Spaniard." And he would snap to attention, shout "Viva Franco!" and give the Falangist stiff-armed salute. (He gave this performance several times a day until at length he found an old razor and hacked the rust-red whiskers from his face.)[43]

So they learned to dissemble. Men who since birth had been taught to stand out and distinguish themselves now were careful to conform, conceal, sublimate.

"Don't attract attention," they told one another.

"Keep your head down."

"Keep your mouth shut."

"Just keep moving."

BEN STEELE had a cowboy's constitution and a camp tender's legs (all those Montana mornings running miles after some horse he thought he'd hobbled the night before), and now, as he pushed himself forward, he reminded himself of all those years of hard work on rough ground and found it easier to keep on his feet.

As a rule he stayed at the front of the column, often in the first rank, a good vantage point to spot trouble or look for food and water.

Watching the guards on the flanks, he soon noticed they were leaving a lot of space between them. It occurred to him that at those distances, a guard would have to be a helluva shot to hit a man, so from time to time he broke from the line of march to run for water or stalks of sugarcane. (He thought of trying to escape too, but where would he go? Into the malarial hills? The jungle? Wander around lost until some Jap patrol bagged him?)

Early afternoons were the worst. The blistering heat left him heavy legged. Concentrate, he told himself. Left, right, left, right. When the guards stopped the column for a rest, he'd fall into an instant sleep, like many of the others, only to be stomped awake by the heel of a hobnail boot.

THE PRISONERS were *tekikokujin*, the enemy, and the Japanese hated them.

Gabbing in the shade of a tree or gathered around a pot of boiling rice beside the road, the *hohei* in bivouac, waiting to go back into battle, jeered as the prisoners passed by. *Kuda!* they yelled, worthless dogs, then they pelted the marchers with rocks and gravel and handfuls of mud.

Sometimes a group of Japanese soldiers would drop what they were doing, form a long gauntlet on the road, and force a column of prisoners to run single file down the middle, shoving them back and forth and

pummeling them so hard with ax handles and bamboo cudgels the prisoners could hear bones breaking.

One night on the road, Corporal Aaron Drake of Carlsbad, New Mexico, heard a commotion in the dark ahead of him, and a few minutes later the column came abreast of a burly *hohei* stripped to the waist, standing in the middle of the road slugging every man in line square in the face. (The blow that caught Drake, he thought, damn near fractured his cheekbone.)

The *hohei* were especially hard on the Philippine Scouts, the elite regiment of Filipinos that had mauled them in battle. The Scouts were known as dead shots, and someone in the Japanese chain of command reckoned that the best way to cull them from the ranks of their countrymen was to examine the trigger finger of every Filipino captive, and for a time Japanese guards made the *sundalos* extend their hands for inspection. When they found a man with a muscled forefinger—no doubt a carpenter, mechanic, pipe fitter, or anyone else who had made a living wielding a wrench, squeezing a pair of pliers, or gripping a hammer— they beat him bloody, beat him for being what he likely was not.[44]

IN THE AMERICAN COLUMNS were a number of officers forty and fifty years old. Those who had been in the field were accustomed to the hardships of combat and could keep up with the younger men, but those who had worked as rear-echelon adjutants or staff, plump majors and colonels, many of them, began to drop to the road or drift back toward the rear, the domain of the buzzard squads.

Zoeth Skinner couldn't help himself. Ahead of him in the line of march was an aging, overweight officer struggling to keep up, a major from the Quartermaster Corps. Like all frontline troops who had gone hungry during the battle, Skinner was sure the quartermaster had been hoarding rations, and he hated the niggardly "bastards" with "a purple passion."[45]

"Look at that old fart hobbling along," he thought. The idiot had on dress shoes, for Christ's sake.

Falling back and back again, the man was soon walking beside him. His eyes were bloodshot with anguish, and Skinner softened. What the hell, they were all suffering, he thought.

He offered to take one of the two musette bags the major had slung on his shoulders.

The bag was heavy. "You're going to have to do something here," Skinner told the officer.

When they stopped for a break, Skinner spilled out the contents.

"Okay, Major," he said, "let's see what the Christ you got in these goddamn musette bags you can't live without."

And there, among a pile of clothes and shoes and toiletries, was a marble desk set—two pens and a brass inkwell set in a piece of inch-thick stone a foot long, all mounted to a lead base.

"Sir, there's got to be two pounds of lead in this friggin' thing. This baby is going right now. I ain't packing that thing another inch."

The officer looked upset. "Jeez, that was given to me back in thirty-five and—"

"I don't give a shit when or why you got it," Skinner said. "You ain't going to be doing any writing where we're going."

Sergeant James Baldassarre of Boston was walking with a couple of colonels named McConnell and Mangunsen. As they neared a town, McConnell staggered out of formation and up to a house hard by the road.[46]

"Where you goin', Colonel?" Baldassarre asked.

The man looked gone. "I can't make the hike, Jimmy."

"Let's go, Colonel. You'll be shot."

"I've got to take a chance, Jimmy."

And just as he started to mount the steps, a guard raised his rifle, pulled the trigger, and put a bullet in the colonel's head.

A while later Baldassarre came upon the other colonel sitting in a drainage ditch, pulling off his shoes. His feet were sore, he told Baldassarre, so sore he could not manage another step.

A guard had spotted them and was running their way and Baldassarre, getting up to move, pleaded with Mangunsen to follow him, but the officer wouldn't budge.

The round hit him in the chest. His eyes were still open when Baldassarre knelt down next to him.

"Keep going, Jimmy," he said. "I'll be all right."

THEY WALKED on rumors and expressions of hope: "When we get to Balanga, we're gonna be put on ships to Manila, then traded for Jap prisoners, and we'll be home by Christmas." The promises were always empty: "Tonight you eat," a guard told the men in John Coleman's column as the formation approached the outskirts of Balanga, Bataan's capital city.[47]

How often had they heard that before, some Jap guard pointing up the road toward the next town, pledging *tabemono, tabemono,* "food, food there," only to find nothing waiting but more gray dust and the rank water of the wallows.

And yet, sure enough, when they reached Balanga, or Orani nine miles north, they saw feeding stations—cauldrons and wheelbarrows and oil drums filled with steaming rice, sometimes tea.

Corporal Bill Simmons of Commerce, Missouri, was asleep in a compound in Balanga, dreaming about food (a table of heaping platters and a large glass of ice water) when someone shouted, "Hey, I smell rice cooking."[48]

The men charged the pot "like wild starving animals," then someone yelled "for some kind of organization," and two men started ladling the porridge.

Men without mess kits lined up with anything they could find—old cans, palm and banana fronds, their helmets, their bare hands. (Richard

Gordon offered his cupped hands to a guard serving from an iron pot, and the guard laughed as he slopped the scalding mush into Gordon's naked palms.)[49]

Each man was given a cup of rice, a pinch of salt, and a half liter of tea. The rations were tasteless and too scanty to sate them, but to Simmons and his starving comrades even this bitter pittance "seemed like a Thanksgiving dinner."

Many of the marchers—maybe a third of the men who passed through Balanga and Orani, maybe more—got no food at all, for the Japanese, chronically undersupplied, habitually unprepared, and stoically indifferent to the distress of men who were their sworn enemies, simply could not, or would not, feed them.[50]

ON THE FOURTH or fifth day of the march, the Japanese appeared to abandon their original plan and were operating ad hoc. Many of the guards seemed confused now. Some marched their columns south, as if they had no sense of direction, then, realizing their mistake, turned them north again. Others kept re-forming their columns, as if shuffling men around would accomplish something. Orders were issued, countermanded, reissued.

There were simply too many *horyo*.

Balanga in particular was in chaos. Columns of prisoners converged on the city from two directions, the thousands who were marched up from the south, from Mariveles, and thousands more who were pushed across the East-West Road from the far side of the peninsula, from Bagac—in all 76,000 captives passing through a staging and rest depot set up to handle less than half that number.

In Balanga they at first left the prisoners standing around in the dusty streets, throngs of milling tatterdemalions staring with blank eyes at the rubble around them. Then guards began to confine the arriving columns in empty buildings or penned them up in barbed-wire enclosures and compounds on the outskirts of town. Soon it seemed as if every schoolyard, warehouse, granary, cockpit, tin pavilion, and factory shed in Balanga was bulging with Filipino and American POWs, and the fields and rice paddies outside of town began to resemble the stockyards of Kansas City or Chicago.

Guards packed the prisoners so tightly they had little room to sit or lie down. During the day they sat shoulder to shoulder with their knees to their chests, legs against the back of the man in front of them. At night they lay in the dirt elbow to elbow like canned fish.

For the first groups of men, the compounds were a respite from the road. But after several days, and many thousands of men, the overpopulated holding pens of Balanga and Orani had turned into cesspools, and a "noisome stench" greeted the weary, thirsty, and hungry prisoners who filed into them. Entering Balanga, Bernard FitzPatrick thought, "The whole town [smells] like a sewer."[51]

Thousands of men were suffering from dysentery, and the ground where the prisoners were forced to sit and sleep became coated with layers of excrement, mucus, urine, and blood. Japanese sanitation units had dug slit-trench latrines, but so many men were sick that the open pits (some eight feet long, two feet wide, and four- to five feet deep) filled after a day or so and started to spill over the edges. Hundreds of men, meanwhile, never made it to the latrines; they stumbled into the compounds too enervated, too far gone to take another step. Helpless against the exigencies of the disease—the wrenching cramps and resistless urge to evacuate—they soiled themselves where they stood right through their clothing, then lay down half conscious in a pool of their own filth.

Bud Locke of Hooksett, New Hampshire, looked in vain for a clean spot to bed down for the night. "Before long," he thought, "everyone [is going to be] a filthy, dust-covered, crap-smeared, stinking specimen of humanity."[52]

The compounds baked in the tropical sun and by midday the stench was so overpowering the men could taste it. Some heaved and retched, covering themselves in vomit. Others walked around hawking and spitting, as if they could expectorate the unspeakable taste that had settled on their tongues.

The stench brought the flies, of course, so many the air became dark with them. They swarmed the men who had fouled themselves and settled on the surface of the slit trenches. Colonel Ernest B. Miller entered a compound where the brimming trenches and surrounding scum wriggled with "a constantly moving sea of [gray] maggots."[53]

To many the degradation of those fetid pens was worse than any hunger or thirst. In one compound Murray Sneddon waded through "excreta of every type and kind." Already men "had fallen to the ground and fallen asleep wherever they could stand the stench." The next morning, rising with the sun, Sneddon noticed right away that "the foul-smelling mud had thoroughly penetrated" his uniform during the night. Getting to his feet he felt "some of the wetter ooze slowly flowing down inside [his] pants on [his] bare skin." And as the guards came through to marshal the prisoners back on the road, he imagined himself a medieval leper "required to notify all of [his] approach by crying, 'Unclean . . . unclean.'"[54]

Alvin Poweleit, a major from Kentucky who spoke Japanese, pointed to the compound his column was about to enter and told a guard, *ōkii benjo*, "big toilet."

The guard laughed. *Ōkii jōdan*, he came back. "Big joke."[55]

FEET BLISTERED, muscles worn from walking, most men sought sleep right away, but a few, dysphoric from hunger and thirst, wandered aimlessly about the compound calling for food and water and trampling the recumbent comrades at their feet.

"Bastard!" the trodden would yell. "Watch where you're walking, you son of a bitch."

Here and there others huddled in small circles talking in whispers about what they'd witnessed on that day's march: the sergeant crushed by a tank, the colonel bayonetted belly to back.

The nights were cool, and in their clammy, sweat-soaked rags the men shook and shivered. "Bone weary," Bernard FitzPatrick "fell into sleep as into a coma." The sick and injured, meanwhile, lay there babbling or hallucinating, flies grazing the length of them and feeding on their wounds. Most men moaned in their sleep, a night song of torment that continued till dawn when guards came rushing into the compound swinging their wooden spirit sticks and kicking the men awake with their hobnail boots to resume what Ray Hunt had come to see as the "man-killing march."[56]

"*Bangō! Bangō!*" the guards shouted. Get up! "Count off."

Getting to their feet, they ached. The damp ground left Ed Dyess so stiff his leg muscles had "set like concrete" and he could hardly straighten himself to stand.

Looking around and taking stock, the men who survived the night began to count those who had not—ten, fifteen, thirty. (Dying in their sleep, the survivors agreed, was the only kindness any of them were likely to get.) Dead from dysentery, exhaustion, dehydration, and malaria, the bodies lay in heaps. Flies, roundworms, and maggots picked at their eyes and crawled in and out of their mouths and noses.

"Oh God," said Lester Tenney, shuddering at the sight, "please have mercy on their poor souls."[57]

IN MANY COMPOUNDS the Japanese left the bodies where they were, and it wasn't long before they started to decompose. By the time the next group of prisoners arrived, the reek of these rotting grotesques had mingled with the stench from the swamped latrines, and the compounds became unbearable.

"For sure, I'm [going to] go mad," Richard Gordon thought.[58]

In other pens the prisoners were ordered to bury their dead, but as the gravediggers started to collect the inert figures from the muck, they discovered that many were still drawing breath, men too wasted to move or speak, the near dead, blank faced and empty eyed, unconscious and slipping away.

At a compound in Orani, a burial detail came upon three of these comatose souls and started to carry them to a nearby shed, a makeshift infirmary. A Japanese sergeant, standing next to a row of freshly dug graves, halted the litters, tipped the stretchers into the open holes, and ordered the prisoners digging the holes to bury these men along with the dead. Suddenly, one of unconscious men came to his senses, and when he realized what was happening to him, he reached up, grabbed the edge of hole with both hands, and pulled himself to his feet. One of the guards barked an order at one of the gravediggers, a Filipino, but the digger just stood there. Angry now, the guards put their bayonets to the Filipino's throat, then, as Ed Dyess watched, the Filipino "brought his shovel down upon the head" of the man in the hole. The man toppled "backward to the bottom of the grave," indifferent now to the dirt the diggers were throwing on top of him.[59]

Captain Burt Bank of Tuscaloosa, Alabama, was forced to bury a man alive, and so was Robert Levering. Bernard FitzPatrick watched two Americans inter an unconscious friend, and Murray Sneddon looked on as two of his comrades were forced to drag a delirious Filipino into a grave.

In Lester Tenney's group, when two diggers refused to bury a malarial comrade alive, a guard shot one of them, then ordered the other man to bury the malaria patient together along with the man who'd just been shot. When he felt the dirt hit him, the sick man started screaming. Lester Tenney watched all this as long as he could, then he hid his face in his hands and threw up on himself. "Is this what I'm staying alive for?" he thought.[60]

NORTH AGAIN. Always north. No sense of time, no sense of place, no sense of purpose. On the road all that mattered was to keep moving, one foot in front of the other, left, right, left, until the guard yelled *Yosu!* "Stop!"

Even the strongest and most fit among them felt enfeebled, and as they marched from Balanga north to Orani, they stumbled along, shifting their weight from one foot to the other, the columns yawing to and fro in unison, automatons in slow step.

By midmorning the sun was on them again, baking their brains and filling their eyes with an aura. It was like "looking through a fog," they said, or a veil of tears.

The heat left them dull witted, etherized. Men would find themselves passing through this town or that with no sense, no memory at all, of how they had gotten there. And these blackouts, these stupors, frightened them. Were they just sunstruck, hallucinating from the heat, or did the spells of catatonia suggest something much more serious?[61]

They dream-walked, many of them. Murray Sneddon shut his eyes and imagined himself on "a clean mattress with snow-white sheets." Many a man envisioned a waterfall spilling over rocks or a cool green valley filled with wildflowers and meadowlarks.[62]

Such drift was dangerous. A few cataleptics came to at the point of a Japanese bayonet. So some of the men played mind games to keep awake. Ernie Miller pictured a calendar and started checking off the days. January 1, 1942, January 2, always pausing to reflect on the holidays or days with special meaning. By the time he got to September 1, the sun was setting and that day's walking was done. Lester Tenney concentrated on the image of his wife, Laura (he still had that photo tucked in his sock). Robert Levering had grown up on a farm in Ohio, and as he walked the blistering road, he imagined himself a boy again, following behind a plow, his bare feet enfolded "in the fresh, cool furrows."[63]

BEN STEELE would not allow himself to drift.

This was no nightmare with bugbears chasing him up the road. The beatings, shootings, and stabbings were real, and he knew he wasn't going to wake from them.

Here was a blond-haired boy half collapsed on the shoulder, desperately trying to push himself to his knees, and here came a Jap to finish him. The boy groaned, that's all, just groaned as the bastard stuck him in the back.

Turn away, Ben Steele thought. Turn away from the horror and hurt of it. Just another corpse by the side of the road.

No room for loathing or hate. A Jap spits in your face, so what? To hell with the bastard. Just keep walking, he told himself. "Make the best of it."

Men were still clawing at him for water, but by the time he had reached Balanga, walked some thirty miles, he'd become selfish with his can.

Sure, he could sympathize with a guy and want to help him, but he'd been carrying that water all day, careful not to spill a drop of it, and the can held only enough to last a couple of hours.

"It's survival of the fittest," he thought. "You gotta look out for yourself."

WHEN WAR CAME to Bataan, the *tao*, the local people, at first fled and scattered. Some wanted to stay close to their herds and crops and hid in the fields and fishponds until the shooting stopped and they could return to what was left of their homes. Thousands of others abandoned their barrios and fled south down the Old National Road to an "evacuation center" that the Americanos had set up at Mariveles. The rest of the people, townsfolk, most of them, packed what they could carry and headed for the hills. A few had a rough idea where they were going, but by and large the rugged hill country was terra incognita, and they soon became lost.[64]

"The Japanese are there, walk this way."

"No, compadres, you will run into the *Hapón* if you go that way."

So they just kept hiking, kept climbing into the wooded hills, until they were sure they were safe. They built lean-tos or sought shelter in caves and under outcroppings. In the morning half-light they came out of hiding to cook a meal over a campfire, then slipped back into their warrens until dark when they could emerge again and sit together in a circle, staring at the stars and the explosions that were lighting up the night.

In the hills they had little to eat—banana stalks and papaya leaves cut into strips and boiled, and rice, dirty rice, they made into *lugao*, a kind of watery gruel. They got sick in the hills, dysentery at first, then malaria. The little ones suffered the most. At first they were colicky, then listless, then still, very still. Their parents cried over the bodies (quietly), said prayers, wrapped them in rags, and buried them there. No funeral Mass, no burning incense, no stone to mark the grave. *Bahalá na*, they told themselves, come what may they would leave it to God.

The thousands of refugees who had fled south to the evacuation center at Mariveles fared no better. Their crowded camp was in the open and they were bombed by the Japanese. So many were killed (how many no one could say), it took four days to gather the dead. After surrender the Japanese ordered the refugees out. Go home, they said. Walk north, north up the Old National Road.

The road was crowded. Long columns of prisoners, *sundalos*, on one side, a steady stream of refugees on the other. The parade of people was so long, Rosalina Cruz could not see either its beginning or end.

Ay! Susmariosep! Oh, Jesus, Mary, Joseph, she said, crossing herself. There were so many of them.

When war came to her home on Bataan, Rosalina Almario Cruz was sixteen years old and pregnant. She and her young husband lived with her family (her father, mother, brother, and five sisters) in Bagac, a seaside town on Bataan's west coast. Her father and husband were away when the shooting started and were cut off from home, so Rosalina's mother, following the lead of her neighbors, took her family into the hills, then a few weeks later led them south to the evacuation center. Now they were walking north toward Orani, thirty-three miles up the Old National Road, there to find a boat that might take them to Manila and the rest of their kin.

For the most part the Japanese ignored the refugees. They were allowed to stop at will, eat if they had food, drink from the artesian wells, nap in a field off the road.

Six months pregnant and weak from malaria, Rosalina Cruz found the walking hard, but her misery seemed small compared to the suffering of the *sundalos* marching beside her. She could not look at the stumbling line of prisoners across from her without being overcome by a feeling of tenderness. She had never seen men so low, so miserable, the tattered clothes, the sad eyes.

"I pity their suffering," she thought.

And they in turn pitied her, the pretty young girl holding her belly and gasping for breath as she walked.

"Can you make it?" they would say. "It must be so hard for you."

When she was able, which is to say when the guards were not watching, she would pour some water from an earthen jar into a coconut shell and slip it to one of the men begging for a drink.

She was very afraid doing this, for the guards had no feelings at all. They stabbed the soldiers who fell. Whenever she saw a guard running up to a man who'd gone down, she would look away and say to herself, "I should not remember this." She knew they might stab her too, but she could not stop herself from filling the coconut shell and passing it to one thirsty man after another.

"Please! Please, can you give us something to drink?"

"*Ay, Diyos!*" How could she refuse?

After a while, the Americans began to hand things back, or toss them at her—jewelry, money, anything of value they had managed to hide from their swag-seeking captors. At first Rosalina Cruz could not imagine what they were doing and was afraid to pick up the rings and gold chains and wads of pesos. Then she thought, "I guess they are throwing those things because they think they will not be needing those things anymore." And that only deepened her *áwa*, her pity for them. "They think they will be killed," she told herself. So when an American soldier, a pleasant but sad-looking man, tossed his bankbook at her feet, Rosalina Cruz bent down and picked it up and brushed it off.

She said nothing to the man but made sure he could see she had hold of the little ledger, the record of his life savings, and hoped he saw that she meant to keep it safe.

WITHIN A DAY of the surrender, word spread across Luzon that the Japanese were marching Filipino and American prisoners of war up the Old National Road out of Bataan and through Pampanga Province to the railhead at San Fernando. Now from provinces near and far, Filipino kith and kin began to make their way to Bataan and take up positions along the road, hoping for a glimpse or perhaps a word with their soldier.

In the neighborhood of Batac in the town of Abucay, Armando Pabustan, nine years old, stood next to his mother, Rosalina Maxali, behind a long iron fence that fronted the Batac Elementary School, a white one-story building next to the road. They'd gotten there early, an hour before dawn, to wait in the cool and dark. Now with the light came the columns of men.

The boy was hoping that his father, Damian Pabustan, a soldier in the Philippine Army, had survived the fighting and was among the long lines of soldiers passing in front of him.

His mother told him to watch carefully. There were so many men, all wearing the same thing, all dirty and tired. They would have to study each face, note each man's way of walking. They would have to hope, and they would have to pray.

They kept coming, the men, one group of *sundalos* after another. They were so *payát*, thin and haggard, hanging on to one another as they walked, the guards punching, kicking, and beating them.

Whenever Armando looked at his mother, she was crying, and the boy became convinced his father was dead, but he continued to search among the faces coming up the road. And then, *Ay! Ay!* There was his father in the middle of a column of soldiers.

He crossed the yard, rushed through the gate, and threw himself into his father's embrace. His *tatay* felt thin. He must be sick, the boy thought.

"Where is your mother, Armando?"

The boy pointed toward the fence.

"You must get away from here now," his father said. "Go back to your mother."

But he did not want to go. He was holding his father around the waist, hugging him, and he would not let go.

"Have you eaten anything, Father?"

"I haven't had any food or water for three days."

His father glanced at the fence again.

"Go over to your mother," he said.

But the boy wouldn't move.

A guard who'd been watching came over to break them apart, and Armando buried his face in his father's midriff. Suddenly he felt a pain in his back, the toe of the hobnail boot. And here came a second guard, grabbing at him, catching the scruff of his shirt, pulling him from his father and tossing him to the road.

Kora! Kora! the guards shouted, shoving his father back into line.

"Take good care of your mother," his father yelled back to him.

Then the column of men moved on, past the fence, past the school, down the road out of Abucay, out of sight.

THERE WERE THOUSANDS of them waiting, townsfolk from the dusty burgs and barrios along the Old National Road, waiting to do whatever they could for the men slogging their way north.[65]

They filled tins and earthen pots with water; they made rice balls stuffed with meat and vegetables and wrapped them in banana leaves; they boiled eggs and picked fruit and collected panocha, small cones of dark brown sugar.

They set the water beside the road and at first tried to hand the victuals to the soldiers as they passed by. Soon the guards had had enough of this, and they started to beat the people off with clubs and rifle butts, so the people started tossing their treats into the columns.

In Lubao, where there were a number of two-story buildings, people packed the upper windows and rooftops and showered the soldiers with hunks of bread and rice balls and cookies and chocolate bars. Enraged by the disruption, the guards stomped the food into the dirt and beat the prisoners who stooped to retrieve it, but there were too many *tao* and too few *hohei* to stop them.

From the side of the road children would dash into the columns, shove something into a soldier's hand—a banana leaf full of rice, a small melon, a sugar cookie—and dash off before the guards could kick or club them. After a while some of the guards relented; as long as the columns kept moving they let the men shag what they could.

North of Orani, Bernard FitzPatrick spotted a Chinese man in a dark *ch'i-fu* standing beside the road with his arms crossed, hands hidden in the robe's wide sleeves. Now and then, when the guards were not looking, the man would pull something from a sleeve, a sugar cake or banana, press it surreptitiously into a prisoner's hand, nod a greeting, then fold his arms again and wait for the next column to come along.

As FitzPatrick's formation passed into Pampanga Province, a small boy gave him a piece of sugarcane and an old Filipino handed him some panocha.

"*Vaya con Diyos, compadre*," the old one said.[66]

RICHARD GORDON loved the army—the good order and discipline, the clean white sheets, starched uniforms, and stacks of pancakes at morning chow. He felt more at home in a barracks than he ever had growing up in a tenement in New York's Hell's Kitchen, but now, dragging himself along in a ragged column of defeated men, he began to think that the "training" he had gotten coming of age in Manhattan's gritty Irish ghetto might keep him alive in the dog-eat-dog world of the prisoner of war.[67]

By the third day of the march Gordon noticed that his comrades had lost all respect for authority. At a well or water hole, if an American officer tried to organize things and ensure every man a drink, the officer was either ignored or knocked down in the rush. He wasn't part of an army anymore, Richard Gordon told himself, he was a member of a mob. Gone was the close society that had given him so much comfort. Now when he watched soldiers fighting over a filthy scrap in the road or clawing one another to get a drink, he was embarrassed for them.

Perhaps it was this feeling that moved him one morning to take a chance and leave the line of march to answer the appeal of an aging colonel calling out from a stretcher beside the road.

The colonel was desperate: his legs were broken, he said, and his litter bearers had abandoned him the night before. He'd survived the night, but he knew the buzzard squads would be out in the morning, so at first light he started pleading with the passing columns for help.

"Please!" he yelled from his litter. "Please, someone!"

Hundreds of soldiers had passed him by, he said, pretending not to hear or see him.

"Come on fellas," Richard Gordon was yelling now. "Come on, some of you Joes, gimme a hand."

But each time a man started to leave the column and head toward Gordon and the litter, the other marchers jeered him. Had they come to hate their officers that much? Gordon wondered.

He kept up his pleading and finally found a volunteer, then another and a third.

Their load was bearable at first, but the stretcher became heavier and heavier, and by noon the four sweating Samaritans were imploring others to spell them.

That night, after they had settled down in a compound, two of Gordon's helpers snuck off. The next day he found replacements, but that night, Gordon's second with the colonel, they too abandoned him.

Gordon was tired. That afternoon he'd almost passed out carrying the colonel, and now, in the early morning dark, he was worried about his own health, his own chances. Sometime before first light, his conscience surrendered to his instinct to survive, and Richard Gordon walked away from the stretcher before the colonel awoke, slipping into an anonymous mass of men moving slowly toward the road.

TO KEEP HIMSELF GOING, to make sure he didn't fall back to the buzzard squad, Zoeth Skinner tried to distract himself by counting the dead, the corpses that were accumulating in the drainage ditches and along the shoulders of the road.[68]

"Nine."

"Eighteen."

"Thirty-two."

At first he thought himself demented ("fifty-four . . . one hundred and seven"), but he kept counting anyway ("two hundred and twenty-six . . . four hundred and fifteen").

He counted Filipinos and he counted Americans. Sometimes he recognized a patch or an emblem on a uniform and made note of the unit. Here was an artilleryman sprawled in the gravel, there in a wallow was a Philippine Scout.

Once in a while he noted a man's injuries—how many bullet holes in the chest or stab wounds in the back.

Somewhere before or just after Balanga, his grim census reached a thousand.

"Holy shit!" he said to himself, "You better stop this crap or you're going to go wacko."

SO MANY were dropping to the road, Ben Steele thought, it was better to stay aloof, not to get close to anyone, but north of Layac Junction, about fifty miles into the march, he lost his resolve and befriended a march mate.

They had talked a bit while walking, talked about where they'd been, where they might be headed, what might happen when they got there. Talking made the walking easier, the heat a little less intense. That night sitting together in a compound they chatted some more, and Ben Steele felt better for the company.

Next afternoon on the road, he noticed his new friend beginning to wobble, and a mile or two later the man's legs gave out and down he went, grabbing for Ben Steele's leg as he hit the ground.

"Come on, Ben! Help me."

He and another man hauled the dropout to his feet and started to drag him along between them down the road. They hadn't gone far before a guard rushed up and screamed at them to let the invalid go. His helper obeyed, but for reasons beyond all understanding, Ben Steele hung on to the man, and the next thing he knew his buttocks were on fire.

The guard's blade had penetrated to the pelvis. Blood was beginning to course down Ben Steele's leg and flies were starting to swarm the wound.

He looked at the man he was holding, hoped he'd understand, then let him sink slowly to the road at the guard's feet.

"No!" the man said. "No. Please. Help me, please."

AS A TRANSIT CENTER, San Fernando, sixty-six miles from Mariveles, had always been a busy city, known for its gaudy Easter and Christmas festivals and as the location of the large Pampanga Sugar Company. Coming up the Old National Road from Guagua and Bacalor, the long columns of exhausted prisoners could see the sugar company's tall red-brick smokestacks rising in the distance, and, knowing that familiar landmark, some began to spread the word that at last they had reached their destination. Here, they'd been told, they would be put on trains and hauled off to prison camp.

The first columns arrived on April 13, the others across the two weeks that followed. Without enough trains and guards, the Japanese supply and transportation officers in charge of the movement of prisoners were overwhelmed by the logistics and the staggering number of men, and San Fernando, their final collection point, was soon a shambles.

As in Balanga, men were being held like livestock in barbed-wire pens all over town, even in the side streets. Some were fed and fed again; others got nothing, not even a mouthful. If there was a schedule, it wasn't apparent; one column of men might be put on train as soon they entered the city, while other groups languished for forty-eight hours or more in their foul enclosures. Most men had walked at least fifty miles.

On average they had covered the distance in five to seven days, days of depredation and duress. They were weak and sick and had reached their limit.

For the Japanese support troops and staff officers billeted in San Fernando, the parade of men shuffling through the city was quite a spectacle, and Imperial soldiers turned out in large numbers to gawk and ogle at their trophies.

"They're staring at us like animals in a zoo," Ben Steele thought.

Meanwhile large crowds of Filipino civilians gathered along the streets, searching the passing columns for their husbands, sons, fathers, brothers.

As the prisoners waited in the holding compounds to entrain, they began to exchange stories, lurid catalogs of what they had seen on their long, brutal march north.

Here, for example, was a Filipino soldier talking about a massacre he said he had witnessed while hiding in the jungle. Hundreds of men, he said, prisoners with their hands tied behind their backs, had been bayonetted to death in a secluded spot near the Pantingan River. Impossible, thought doctor Alvin Poweleit, and yet there was something "sincere" in the man's voice, something authentic.[69]

A week or so later, Captain Pedro L. Felix, bleeding from bayonet wounds and shaking with malaria, appeared at his family's house in Manila. Felix, a staff officer with the 91st Division, Philippine Army, said he'd been in hiding and on the run since April 12, the day the Japanese massacred hundreds of his comrades at the Pantingan River.

ON APRIL 11, what was left of the 91st Division and two other units surrendered near Bagac on Bataan's west coast, and the Japanese ordered them to begin moving east, on their own, along a dirt road, Trail 8, across the middle of the peninsula toward Balanga. On the morning of April 12, the prisoners, roughly fifteen hundred Filipino officers and men (their American advisers were left behind, Felix said), came to the Pantingan River and were taken into custody by Japanese infantry from the 65th Brigade encamped there. The Japanese used the prisoners as laborers to help repair a small wooden bridge, then they marched them across the river and up a series of switchbacks into the dark green foothills of Mount Samat, stopping, finally, about a mile and a half above the river at the intersection of Trail 8 and another jungle road. Here, spread out in the rough terrain, were more clusters of Japanese troops.[70]

Just then, about noon, a Japanese army command car came up Trail 8 and stopped about thirty yards from where the hundreds of prisoners were being held. An officer alighted, big brass, Felix thought, judging from the obeisance paid him, and one of the Japanese soldiers standing among the prisoners told Pedro Felix that the officer was in fact the commander of the 65th Brigade, General Akira Nara.

The general called a conference, and all the Japanese officers in the area—the four in charge of the prisoners and others from the infantry units encamped along the trail—gathered around him. When the meeting was over, the general left, and almost immediately the Japanese began dividing the prisoners into two groups, officers and NCOs in one group, privates in the other. The privates, roughly eleven hundred men, were told to start walking east on Trail 8 toward Balanga. The Filipino officers and noncoms, meanwhile, some four hundred men, were formed into three columns, then more Japanese soldiers appeared, carrying strands of telephone wire.

They bound each man's hands behind his back, then leashed one prisoner to the next, creating chains of men. The chains, fifteen to thirty men in each, were marched to the edge of a ravine. The first chain was told to face the ravine; the other rows of men were lined up to the rear. Standing behind the first chain of prisoners were Japanese soldiers with fixed bayonets, as well as officers and noncoms with their swords drawn, waiting.

A Japanese civilian who spoke Tagalog stepped forward to address the prisoners.

Mag kaibigan, pasensya kayo. Kung kayo ay nagsurrender agad, hindi namin kayo papatayin. Ngunit maraming napinsala sa amin. Kaya pasiensia kayo. Kung mayroon kayong gustong hingin, magsabi lang kayo.

Dear friends, pardon us. If you had surrendered early, we would not be killing you. But we suffered heavy casualties. So just pardon us. If you have any last wish before we kill you, just tell us.

Some men asked for a cigarette, some for food and water. Many begged for their lives.

Pedro Felix, the last man in the first row facing the ravine, asked to be executed by rifle shot or machine gun fire. At least, he said, "kill us facing front," facing their executioners.

The Japanese refused.

Then an officer gave a signal.

From his position on the extreme left, Pedro Felix glanced down the line and saw three heads go flying.

He took a deep breath and held it.

The first thrust caught him in the right shoulder. The second came out his front. He dropped to his knees and fell on his side. The third stab hit his backbone, a thud. The fourth was like the second, through and through.

He was tumbling now—the chain of men had been pushed over the side—and came to rest halfway down the slope. He tried to lie still, dead still. Japanese soldiers were prowling the slope, finishing off anyone who moved.

Felix bit his lip and tried to hold his breath. Lashed to him on the right was Luciano Jacinto, a young lieutenant. His compadre was writhing and kicking, and in his death throes he flipped the lower part of his body on top of Felix, shielding him from the buzzard squads prowling the slope.

That night Felix slid out from under the corpse, raised his head a little, and looked around. It was quiet. He was alone, he thought, alone among the dead.

His pain at that point was unbearable. Why keep suffering? he asked himself. And he started to push his face into the soft earth of the slope. He pushed until he was exhausted, then gasping, rolled over, took a deep breath, and rested.

He had more strength than he'd realized, perhaps enough to get away, and he began to think how he might free himself from the chain of dead men.

He wriggled this way and that, and after much effort was able to get the connecting strand of wire to fall across his mouth so he could gnaw it. Three hours later he had finally chewed himself free, but his hands were still bound behind his back.

During his chewing he thought he had heard someone groaning, and now he called out in the dark.

Ano, buhay ka pa? Nakakalag ka na ba? Anyone still alive? Have you freed yourself?

"I'm alive," a voice came back.

His name was de Venecia, a lieutenant. A big man, he'd been bayonetted eleven times. He was weak but able to free Felix, who then freed him.

Both men were thirsty, and Felix crawled among the corpses, checking canteens, but could not find a drink, so he and de Venecia decided to leave the killing ground to look for water.

Too weak to stand, they dragged themselves backward on their buttocks along the bottom of the ravine. Soon de Venecia stopped.

"I can't go any farther," he told Felix. "Leave me here. If you reach Manila, contact my family."

Felix built a fire—at least he could make the dying man warm—then set out again. Sometime before dawn he reached the banks of the Pantingan River and happened upon three more survivors. In the days that followed, the four men made their way north, then east across Mount Samat to Pilar, where a Filipino doctor dressed their wounds. From there Felix joined a group of Bataanese refugees on their way to the relative safety of Bulacan Province. And on April 24, dressed like a peasant and riding in a horse-drawn calesa, he arrived in the Malate section of Manila, his home. He had returned from the dead, he told his family. And then he began his astonishing story.

PRIVATE YOSHIAKI NAGAI, a hostler with the 122nd Infantry, had come down with malaria, and by the morning of April 10 was so sick he had to hold on to his horse's harness to keep himself standing. Teeth clenched, head pounding, his face dripping sweat, he finally stumbled into the regimental bivouac along the Pantingan River and collapsed. A friend put a cool cloth on his forehead and he soon fell into a deep sleep.[71]

The next morning his squad leader sent him to the regimental surgeon, who gave him a shot of quinine. He slept well that night, but in the morning when he tried to raise himself and join his comrades in their breakfast circle, he still could not keep his feet.

Small groups of Filipino and American soldiers had been giving themselves up since the afternoon of April 9, and now more and more of them were beginning to appear along the Pantingan River. No one had ever seen anything like it, not even the men who had fought in China.

"What a lot of prisoners coming out," they said.

To Nagai these *horyo* looked hungry and "worn out"—gaunt, bearded men, some groggy and reeling in the heat, most carrying back-packs or gunnysacks on their shoulders. Down the trails and out of the bush they came, dropping their loads and raising their hands, one after another, so many it seemed like they'd never stop.

These miserable *horyo*, Nagai thought, were a sure sign of victory.

"We have won," the *hohei* told one another. "We have won the battle."

The more they reflected on their good fortune, the more, naturally, they began to think of those comrades whose luck had run out. The Summer Brigade had taken heavy casualties, and hundreds of wooden boxes and cans of *nakigara*, "remains," were waiting to be sent home. Now, here, with their hands up, were the ones responsible for all that loss, all that mourning.

Here were the men who had "rained" bullets and shells on them day after day. America had fought with its factories, Nagai thought, Japan with its "flesh and blood."

Living so long with danger had changed him, he thought, changed his comrades, too. Looking at the *horyo* emerging from the hills he felt more than *kirai*, simple scorn. He found himself filled with *dai-kirai*, hatred.

For months he had hated the enemy in the abstract, the enemy as evil. Now, by the Pantingan River, he hated them in the particular.

Here were the very men who had made his life so hot, so hard, so damn miserable. *Hai,* yes, he knew the rules, he'd read the *Senjinkun*, the military code—"do not punish them if they yield"—but he thought, "How can we stick to the rules?" Comrades had been killed, good Matsuyama boys butchered.

"How can I forgive them so easily?" he asked himself.

Besides, these *horyo* had disgraced themselves. In the middle of a battle they had laid down their arms and raised their hands, a shameless act for any soldier. Should such men be received with respect? What did they think they were going to get, "a welcome, a bath, a rest?"

He wanted revenge, assumed his comrades felt the same way. They had been trained to "destroy" the enemy, to exterminate him. Well, here he was.

And just then, sometime after breakfast, the word came down, no one knew exactly from whom or where. It spread from platoon to platoon, company to company, upriver and down, then among the men camping in the hills.

Korosu no da, "We are going to kill them," kill them all.

Well, this was just "a continuation" of the two sides "killing each other," Nagai thought, not an epilogue to the battle but an extension of it. If there was a difference between fighting and butchery, he didn't see it. And neither did most of his comrades.

They cared nothing (knew nothing, most of them) of international treaties and conventions protecting prisoners' lives and rights.

Rights? *Horyo* didn't have rights. Their lives belonged to the Imperial Army now, and the Imperial Army wanted its due.

"We are going to stab them to death," the *hohei* were told. "And soldiers from each company should be in on it."

It wasn't an order, exactly. More like an opportunity. The prisoners were going to be killed, this was something that had to be done, and it would be agreeable, harmonious, if a few men from every unit in the regiment took part in the work.

Some men volunteered right away, but a number held back.

"I don't feel like stabbing those who put their hands up," they said.

"Just do it once," their comrades came back.

Kekkō da, "No thanks," the dissenters said.

"Then we will go."

And off they went. A short time later, several returned, looking bewildered and asking to be relieved.

"It's too much for me," some said. "Let me change with someone."

Yoshiaki Nagai wanted to take part in the killing. He had been at battle for ninety-nine days and "every day" had "started and ended with madness." It was always kill or be killed. He had reached a point, he thought, where he could kill "without feeling anything."

"I would really like to go and join my comrades and help kill the prisoners," he told himself, but he was still weak with chills and fever and could barely stand up. Never mind. At least he could watch, bear witness to their work.

He crawled to the trail above the ravines and "like a toad clinging to the roadside" found a place where he "could see everything."

The killing began right after breakfast. The prisoners were gathered at a secluded spot on the trail, divided into files of fifteen to thirty men, then they were marched a mile or so to the killing site, a section of trail along a precipice above a ravine. Between the staging spot and killing ground was a ridge, so the remaining prisoners could not see or hear what was happening to each file of men after it had been marched away.

At the ravine the first file was made to sit on the ground next to the precipice, facing the void. A soldier held each prisoner tightly by the scruff of the neck. Behind stood other soldiers, the executioners, with rifles and bayonets and swords. At a signal, the soldiers released their grip and the executioners drove their blades home, aiming at a point from behind where they guessed they might skewer the heart. When they were done, they kicked the dead and dying into the ravine, and another file of prisoners was marched into place.

When the second line of prisoners saw the blood on the trail and the bodies below, they grew restive, and as soon as the soldiers loosened their grip on them, they leaped into the ravine. Some tumbled and bounced down the steep slope, breaking their bones; others crashed directly on the bed of rocks below.

"They had to give it a try," Nagai thought, watching from a distance. "They knew they would be killed."

After that the lines of prisoners were made to face away from the ravine, and after they were stabbed or beheaded on the trail, the soldiers picked them up by their arms and legs and *ichi, ni, san,* "one, two, three," flung them into the gorge.

Now and then Yoshiaki Nagai noticed an American in the group; the white men were sunburned (the color of pomegranates, he thought) and easy to pick out. One of them, perhaps a young officer, Nagai guessed, had been bayonetted only once and was still alive, flailing about in agony, facedown on the trail. He looked "like a frog swimming in water," Nagai thought. A *hohei* standing nearby, apparently seething with vengeance, stepped forward and hoisted a large rock above his head.

"Look at this!" he said.

Then, yelling his dead commander's name, he smashed the wounded American in the head, cracking the man's skull.

By late afternoon Nagai was too sick with fever to keep watching,

Rare and believed to be unpublished photograph of a secret planning meeting of the Imperial Army General Staff, November 1941. This was likely the final gathering of Imperial Army commanders prior to the attacks on Pearl Harbor and Clark Field in the Philippines—the beginning of World War II in the Pacific. Masaharu Homma first row, fifth from right. Hideki Tojo (the prime minister and war minister) first row, ninth from right.

(Courtesy of Masahiko Homma)

ABOVE: General Edward P. (Ned) King (center with hands clasped) with three of his aides, discussing the logistics of surrendering his command with a staff officer and interpreter from the 14th Imperial Army at the Balanga Elementary School on Bataan, April 9, 1942, within a few hours of raising the white flag (Courtesy of MacArthur Memorial Library and Archives)

BELOW: The American generals Jonathan Wainwright (far left) and Ned King (third from left) with Japanese captors aboard what is believed to be the boat that carried them to prison camp in Formosa, May 1942 (Japanese Propaganda Corps photograph, courtesy of Ricardo T. Jose Collection)

TOP LEFT: Fallow rice paddy enclosed with barbed wire, April 1942, one of the many fields used by Japanese guards to hold and keep track of the prisoners along the route of the death march. This is what the POWs called "the sun treatment."

(Japanese Propaganda Corps photograph, courtesy of Ricardo T. Jose Collection)

TOP RIGHT: Filipino and American prisoners on the death march, April 1942

(Japanese Propaganda Corps photograph, courtesy of Ricardo T. Jose Collection)

BOTTOM: Bloated bodies of two American soldiers and one Filipino soldier in one of the drainage ditches that lined the route of the death march, Orion, Bataan, April 16, 1942

(Japanese Propaganda Corps photograph, courtesy of Ricardo T. Jose Collection)

Masaharu and Fujiko Homma,
wedding photograph, Tokyo,
November 1926
(Courtesy of Masahiko Homma)

General Masaharu Homma
visiting wounded Japanese
soldiers during the battle of
Bataan, January 1–April 9,
1942 (Japanese Propaganda Corps
photograph, courtesy of
Masahiko Homma)

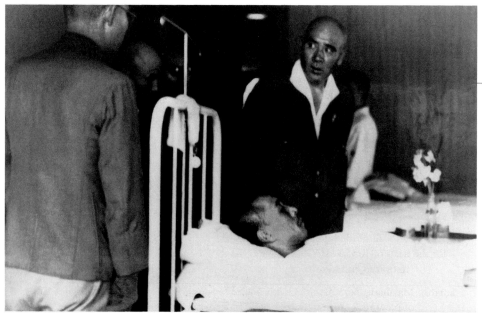

TOP: Great Hall of the high commissioner's residence, Manila, converted to courtroom for the trials of Tomoyuki Yamashita and Masaharu Homma. Photograph taken during testimony in Homma trial, January–February 1946. (Courtesy of Robert Pelz)

BOTTOM: Masaharu Homma, right, with one of his six defense attorneys, Lt. Robert L. Pelz of New York, during his trial, January–February 1946 (Courtesy of Robert Pelz)

ABOVE: Hawk Creek, Montana—the small valley where the Steele family established a homestead and ranch during the 1920s (Courtesy of Ben Steele)

BELOW LEFT: Bess Steele with her two eldest children, Gert (left) and Ben (right). Believed to be 1919. (Courtesy of Ben Steele)

BELOW CENTER: Young Ben Steele in the saddle at Hawk Creek, approximately four years old, with his father, "the Old Man." Believed to be 1921. (Courtesy of Ben Steele)

BELOW RIGHT: The Old Man, Ben Steele Sr., with his brother-in-law, John McCleary, circa World War I (Courtesy of Ben Steele)

Ben Steele, official prison
photograph at Omine-
machi coal mine prison
work camp, fall 1944
(Courtesy of Ben Steele)

Ben Steele, portrait taken after liberation
in Spokane, Washington, 1945
(Courtesy of Ben Steele)

Ben Steele, self-portrait at the
Cleveland Institute of Art, 1946,
age twenty-nine
(Courtesy of Ben Steele)

Ben Steele, self-portrait at
home, 2008, age ninety
(Courtesy of Ben Steele)

and he crawled back down to the company bivouac to rest. The executioners had been working in shifts—slaughter, it turned out, was hard work—and they would return to the bivouac to eat, drink, and trade stories.

"I killed seven," one said.

"Seven? That is nothing. I killed twelve."

The afternoon gave way to evening, the evening to night. Lying there, looking up at the moon, Nagai could hear the shouts of the executioners up on the trail ("Yaah!" they yelled with each thrust) and the screams of the captives echoing in the valley.

"It's still going on," said the men in bivouac, sitting around their fires.

The next morning most of the regiment moved out. As they climbed the trail from the river, their line of march took them past the execution site.

The ravine was filled with the dead.

"They are piled up to the edge of the road," Nagai noted. "If I sat on the edge and stretched out my arm, I could touch them. I think there must be a thousand."

His head was "splitting" and he was dizzy, and his platoon commander let him ride in the back of a truck. As they passed the headquarters area, he watched a formation of *hohei* performing a ceremony to break camp and mark the victory. They stood at attention, then presented arms while a bugler sounded the call to colors.

Yoshiaki Nagai thought the trumpet had an especially "bright sound" that morning. It echoed off the mountains and through the hills.

"We won," he told himself. "We won."[72]

PRIVATE ISAMU MURAKAMI thought his father—a farmer, fisherman, and logger—a most unusual man, at least for the times. Other parents seeing their sons off to war told them, "Don't come back alive" or "Go and die for your country." But his father hated the war and blamed the military for putting the country on a path to defeat and ruin, and the day Isamu, his oldest, reported to the Fifth Light Machine Gun Company, 122nd Infantry for embarkation overseas, his father had tears in eyes.[73]

"Don't volunteer for anything," his father said, sobbing. Isamu had never before seen his father cry. "Just come back."

Isamu Murakami thought of himself as a good soldier who hated the army and the war, and on April 9 when the guns fell silent, he was elated, but surveying the corpses scattered around him, *tekihei*, "enemy soldiers," as well as *hohei*, his moment of exultation flew away like a startled bird and all that was left was simple relief.

"How," he wondered, "did I manage to survive?"

Maybe it was his destiny, or just luck. He couldn't say. Then, looking around again, another thought occurred to him.

"Why" he asked himself, "did we have to have this war?"

He was thirsty and wandered down to the Pantingan River to get a drink. Upstream he saw some Filipino soldiers getting water. Obviously they had yet to surrender. He watched them for a moment, decided to leave them alone.

"I'm thirsty and they're thirsty too," he told himself. "I'm not going to report that I saw them."

The regiment bivouacked along the Pantingan and awaited new orders. One day passed, then another. They cleaned their gear and bathed in the river and cooked rice for their midday meal. On the third day, Isamu Murakami and four other men got word that the company commander wanted to see them.

The officer explained that each company had been ordered to send five men to a spot above the river for "special duty," men who had excelled in bayonet training.

A lieutenant came to fetch the group, led them up the hill and into the jungle to a section of trail above a ravine. Assembled there were many many *horyo*, hundreds, in fact, Filipinos mostly, but a handful of Americans, too. Some of the prisoners were blindfolded and tied with rope, some with wire.

Isamu Murakami sensed that something ominous was about to take place and did not like it. Several other men there were uneasy as well.

"What are we going to do?" one of them asked.

"*Shobun*," an officer said. They were going to "kill them."

Then the officer called Murakami's name, told him to step forward. Isamu hesitated.

"Just kill one and then you can go back to your unit," his company sergeant said.

Isamu just stood there.

The sergeant tried again.

"There are lots of officers here from other units," he said softly. "Their men are killing the prisoners and our company commander wants to show them that our men can do this, too. You should do this as quickly as possible, just one and you can go back." Then the company sergeant said, "Or you will be killed by the company commander."

The officer was growing impatient and barked at the sergeant.

"Why don't you tell your men to do it quickly? This is the order of the emperor!"

Isamu Murakami thought, "I have no choice."

In training he had stabbed large dolls stuffed with straw, but this—this was different.

He stepped forward with his rifle at the ready. The man in front of him was a Filipino, face pale, eyes filled with fear.

Isamu Murakami tightened his grip on the rifle, flexed his knees, and thrust the weapon forward ("Yaah!") at a point where he imagined the man's heart was.

He heard a kind of click or snap, like a stick breaking. He guessed he'd hit a rib, so he twisted the blade, hard, finished the stroke, and yanked the bayonet free.

The Filipino sank to his knees, blood pouring from the wound.

"*Owatta!*" Isamu shouted, almost defiantly. "I'm finished!"

"*Kere!*" The major yelled back. "Kick him down!"

Murakami put his heel on the figure twitching in the dirt and shoved it over the side and into the ravine.

"Follow him," the officer told the next man, and so it went, man after man down the line.

With each thrust there was a scream, then an echo in the hills. And when the ravine began to fill with bodies, it too issued a complaint, a chorus of moaning and crying.

"Why do I have to do things like this?" Isamu Murakami thought.

He toweled the blood from his clothes, wiped his weapon clean, and tossed the towel into the ravine.

"You can go," the officer said.

He ran. He ran as fast as he could, and when he looked back over his shoulder he saw many of the others running as well, as if someone or something was chasing them from the killing ground.

Back at the bivouac he chanted a prayer for the man he had killed, for all the murdered men moaning and crying in the valley, but the prayer didn't work. That night the dead came to him in a dream, one after another.

"Don't come only to me," he told them, "but if you want, please appear in front of the emperor and ask the emperor how he would feel if he had been ordered to stab you."

KILL THE PRISONERS? thought Private First Class Takesada Shigeta, a machine gunner with the 1st Battalion, 122nd Infantry. It didn't make sense.[74]

"Why do we have to kill those who come out of the jungle with their hands up?" he asked himself. "The battle is over. This is not a situation of kill or be killed."

On April 12 at the Pantingan River, the men of the 122nd Infantry Regiment were given an unusually large ration of sake, in fact all they could drink. Not long after the ration was issued, they were told that their unit was going to kill prisoners of war.

"Those who want to kill the prisoners," a noncom said, "just go ahead. Kill the ones you want. Kill as many as you want."

The men who volunteered for this duty tried to convince the others to join them.

"These prisoners aren't real prisoners," the volunteers argued. "They're not yet imprisoned so we can't call them prisoners. It would be hard for us to kill the prisoners in a camp, but these men are still the enemy and we're still in the middle of a war. We have to kill them."

The killing began in the late morning. All along the river and at bivouacs in the hills, working parties of executioners were assembled and marched to the spot. From all the coming and going along the river, Takesada Shigeta got the impression the executions were taking place at several spots, and several hundred *hohei* were taking part.

Though it was not put to them that way, the men assumed they were acting on orders.

"Someone must have given an order," Takesada Shigeta thought. "The regimental commander, someone. Someone must have said something. Without an order we would not be killing the prisoners."

They worked through the morning and into the afternoon, worked in shifts, drinking and killing, drinking and killing.

Takesada Shigeta stayed in camp by the river and watched the killing parties leave and return, men sweating and thirsty and covered in blood.

"I killed only one. No more than that," one man said,

"I killed six," another said.

By early afternoon the sake barrel was half empty.

"Drink and go!" they yelled,

"All right, I'll go!" a man said.

Takesada Shigeta wanted no part of it.

He thought, "It was good enough to have the enemy surrender."

And others apparently agreed.

"I don't want to kill them, either," he heard more than one man say.

As the afternoon wore on, however, some of the executioners began to resent this display of individuality, and one of them started to pester Shigeta. Soon he was nose to nose with the man, shouting and yelling. And now their sergeant was stepping between them.

He should either go to the killing site, the sergeant told Shigeta, or take his machine gun to the hill above the ravine and make sure none of the bodies at the bottom tried to escape or crawl away.

Takesada Shigeta asked his good friend, Kozo Hattori, who had also recused himself from the killing, to join him.

"Let's go up or else we have to kill them," he said.

When they finally reached their position on the hill, they looked down and were struck dumb.

The ravine was filling with bodies, and issuing from the pit was a sound neither of them would soon forget, cries of agony echoing in the valley and off the hills. Neither man had ever heard anything like it—a chorus of moaning, pain, and lament that never seemed to stop.

The day was hot and humid, and with a light wind blowing in their direction it wasn't long before the smell of blood, a thick and frightening fragrance, reached the two *hohei* sitting on the hill.

At first they just watched. The prisoners were led forward five and six at a time to a spot on the road just above the ravine. Some wore blindfolds, rags and towels knotted behind their heads. Others just stared straight ahead, facing their executioners.

Takesada Shigeta thought, "Imagine standing in front of the prisoner and watching his eyes at the very moment you pierce him with your bayonet."

After a while of looking down on all this, he went into a kind of trance.

Again and again he told himself the same thing, "The battle is over . . . The battle is over."

At length the two men realized that the sergeant who had sent them up the hill would wonder why they had not yet fired their machine guns, so just before dark they loosed some short bursts at the empty slope opposite them, but the firing only made the moaning in the valley sound louder, and this unsettled them even more and they stopped.

The killing went on till dark. By the time Takesada Shigeta and Kozo Hattori were called down from the hill, the battalion had packed up and was beginning to move out, north, to a bivouac by the Abo-Abo River.

Sitting around their campfires that night at the new position, none of the men spoke of the slaughter.

"They were all in high spirits a few hours ago," Takesada Shigeta thought. "They were saying, 'I killed this many or I killed that many.' Now none of them are willing to talk because it wasn't an honorable deed."

He still felt numb, felt nothing, really, neither pity nor fear. The next day the 122nd gathered the remains of its dead for cremation and shipment home. The day after that the unit prepared to move off the peninsula and take up its next assignment.

Takesada Shigeta was sure he had put the Pantingan River behind him, but that night, unable to sleep, he "meditated deeply" on the blood-soaked trail in the jungle and the valley full of bodies below. At length he closed his eyes but could not sleep. An eerie noise began to nag at him, a chorus of moaning and crying he knew would never stop.

ONE LAST LOOK

BEN STEELE hated this part of the job, sitting here in the pickup in front of Casey's Golden Pheasant, waiting for the shepherds to stumble out of the saloon, their loyal sheepdogs lying on the sidewalk in front.

Same thing every payday, Jug Clark's men couldn't wait to drink up their checks. So he'd sit there, just like Mr. Clark had ordered, sit behind the wheel watching the front door till they came rolling out into the afternoon, then he'd help them onto the mattresses in the bed of the truck, dogs jumping in after them, and haul the ossified load back to the ranch.

Next morning Jug Clark would tell him, take a bottle out to so-and-so's camp, just enough for one drink, some hair of the dog to straighten him out for work. Half the time the shepherds were shaking so bad when he rode up, they'd spill the cure down the front of them.

They weren't a bad bunch, though. Many were old cowboys who'd lost their rides and maybe a wife or live-in woman along the way. The work was lonely, that's all, out there with the sheep night and day, week in week out. Drove most to drink. And made a few of them mean.

BY THE FALL OF '39, he'd graduated from high school, left Snook Art, and signed back with Jug Clark as a camp tender. The ranch was doing well and so was he, making $40 a month and still sending most of it home.

He had grown up well, twenty-two years old now, five foot ten, a lean 150 pounds with a shock of dark hair, an open face, and an easygoing manner. He got on well with almost everyone, unless, of course, they didn't want to get along with him.

That summer he had a run-in with a shepherd named Blacky Halco, a new man from Wyoming country. The sheepherder started giving him a bad time as soon as Ben Steele rode into his camp.

"I'll bet I can outshoot you with this six-shooter and you using that rifle you got in the buckboard there," Halco said.

The camp tender had several stops to make that day and long rides between them.

"I didn't come out here to shoot a competition or anything," he said. "I'm here to tend your camp."

Halco was a big, hard-looking man.

"That so?" he said. "Well, the last outfit I worked for I killed the camp tender."

Ben Steele finished unloading the wagon and stacking the supplies, then got back in the buckboard and rode slowly away.

"Next time I go to that camp," he promised himself, "I'm going with the rifle loaded."

When Jug Clark got wind of what had happened, he kicked the shepherd off the place. Later word reached the ranch that Blacky Halco had walked into a bar in Hardin with a handgun, shot two men point-blank, then turned the pistol on himself.

THE REST OF THE SUMMER was a cowboy's dream. Clark owned ten thousand acres north of the Yellowstone and had grazing rights on another ten thousand south of the river in the massive foothills of the Pryor Mountains. The practice there was to leave the prairie unfenced, and when the wind was up, the grass looked like an ocean, one wave of green after another.

His job in the Pryors was to search for water and good grazing, and Ben Steele traded his wagon for a saddle horse. He always rode at a walk or a trot, never a run. Too much ground to cover for that, fifty square miles of range. No point getting pounded.

Sit back, ride the pockets, relax. Up this slope, across the ridge, down the back side to the next. Lay the reins left, right, nudge the horse along with a touch of the heel. He'll go where he's told. "A good horse will take you anywhere," the Old Man used to say. And he was right.

He loved riding the Pryors. Green swells in front and behind, mile after mile under a bowl of blue. No trees here, no buildings, wires, fences. Just land, so much of it a rider could go all afternoon without seeing anything but grass, mountains, sky. Open country, they called it, free range. It wasn't free anymore, but that didn't matter. That didn't matter at all. On and on. The country, the horse, the rider.

IN THE EARLY FALL OF 1940 his parents drove out to the Clark ranch for a visit. They came in a car they'd bought with his money, $400 of savings. ("The car's yours, Bud," they told him. "We're just holding it for you.")

His mother was eager to speak with him. She'd been thinking, she said. He was twenty-two years old, time he considered his future. Back east Congress had just passed the first peacetime military draft, and the first call-up was scheduled for later that month.

"You really ought to get in before they draft you," she said. "Maybe if you do, you could, you know, do what you want in the army."

He knew she wanted something better for him. After all, how long could he work as a hired hand? Later, after his parents left, he kicked the army idea around with Jug Clark.

The rancher was against it. His future was here, Jug Clark said, on the banks of the Yellowstone. "You know, Bud, I've always told you, someday I'm gonna give you your own band of sheep."

Someday. He began to think that maybe there was something in what his mother had said. He could travel, he could see the world, he could have an adventure. Hell, he'd never been out of Montana.

He'd miss the ranch, no getting around that, the creak of saddle leather, the murmur of the wind. But maybe it was time.

In mid-September he borrowed Jug Clark's car and drove to Billings, found the enlistment center in the Stapleton Building, and signed the papers to become a private in the United States Army Air Corps.

Three weeks later, October 9, in the company of his mother, his father, his little brother Joe, and little sister Jean, he stood on the platform of the Billings train station on Montana Avenue waiting for the westbound Northern Pacific, the train that would carry him to boot camp in California.

His mother kept stealing looks at him. They chatted some, nervous talk. Did he have the sandwiches she'd packed? Was he excited about seeing California? Would he remember to write?

The train rolled into the station. He hugged his mother, shook hands with the Old Man, said good-bye to the kids. Then he stepped up and into the coach and settled himself in a seat by the window.

Standing on the platform, his mother tried to smile. He knew what she was thinking. She'd been reading the newspapers, reading the rumors of war. Never mind, he wanted to tell her. He'd be all right. He'd be just fine. Like always.

The train started with a lurch. He turned in his seat and looked back, looked back as long as he could.

EIGHT

GUARD was shoving him in the back, pushing Ben Steele to get on the train. Since dawn the Japanese had been rousting prisoners from holding pens throughout San Fernando and herding them toward the railroad station.

As they walked through the streets toward the waiting trains, many men, convinced the worst was behind them, began to say things like, "I think we're gonna be okay" or "Things will be better now." A few told their comrades they looked forward to riding in comfortable coaches the rest of the way.

At the depot they found boxcars waiting, old French Mercis, "Forty and Eights," as they used to be called, narrow-gauge boxes just big enough (about twenty feet long and roughly seven or eight feet high) to carry either forty men or eight mules and horses. Now the Japanese were shoving a hundred men and more into these ancient wood-and-metal carriages, packing them in tight, shoulder to shoulder, belly to back, and slamming the doors shut, leaving the men in the stifling dark.

Almost immediately men began to struggle for breath. Some panicked—the Japanese, they were sure, meant to kill them, suffocate them—and they started pounding their fists on the boxcar walls.

"I have to get out!" they screamed. "Oh God, please God, open the doors!"

Sitting atop the cars the guards stamped their feet on the roof and screamed back.

"Ketsu-no-ana damare!" "Shut up, assholes!"

Loading each train took time; men might be left for an hour or more in a closed car before the train finally started with a sudden jolt. A hun-

dred men in two hundred square feet of space, stinking men all of them, sick men, too, standing in their own waste.

By then, of course, the sun was up and the boxcars were beginning to bake. In the hot, smothering dark some men lost control and began to claw, punch, and grab at one another, anything to get from the middle of the car to the sides where they might find a crack in the wooden slats and suck some fresh air.

A number of men in the middle fainted, and a number of others died. (The cars were packed so tight that the lifeless figures were often left standing for the three-hour trip.)

Ben Steele was lucky. One of the last men in the car, he found a spot on a side wall and could breathe between the slats. A man standing behind him tried to muscle him out of the way—"Move, you fucker, or I'll break your fucking neck"—but Ben Steele was willing to take punishment, and return it, to keep his spot. Behind him men were dying— he could hear their death throes, for Christ's sake!—but he held his ground and his pity and fought for his sliver of light, his few breaths of fresh air.

SOME GUARDS kept the doors closed all the way, but others opened them as soon as the trains picked up speed, and they allowed the men to take turns in the open doorways.

In the towns and villages down the line, people had gathered along the tracks with food and water. Many of the trains were driven by Filipino engineers, and they slowed their engines as they passed through the stations so the locals could toss their gifts into the open doors or run alongside the platform holding up cans of water. Most prisoners shared what they shagged, but in every car there was at least one man who turned his back and a deaf ear to the pleas of his comrades.

After twenty-two slow miles of this, the trains finally stopped at the station at Capas, Tarlac and the prisoners spilled out and onto the platform. The living were ordered to drag out the dead, and they set the bodies alongside the tracks, shoulder to shoulder, faceup in the sun. Then the prisoners formed up again and started walking on a road that ran west toward the Zambales Mountains in the distance.

Most men wondered whether they were about to make another march—"Where the hell are we going now?"—but officers who had worked in the province before the war guessed they were headed just down the road about three miles to the site of what was to have been a temporary cantonment for a division of the Philippine Army—a steaming 617-acre tract of abandoned rice paddies and rolling grassland with rows of partially completed barracks and buildings, Camp O'Donnell.

WHEN BEN STEELE SAW BARBED WIRE and watchtowers, he was relieved.

"At least," he thought, "this is where we're going."

They entered the camp through a main gate then walked up a rise in front of a two-story headquarters building. Beside the building was a watchtower topped by a large Japanese flag ("the flaming red asshole," the men called it). To the right of the tower, facing the headquarters building, was a makeshift parade ground. Here the arriving columns finally stopped.

Japanese guards in fresh white shirts and wielding wooden cudgels scooted among the prisoners shoving them into ranks.

"Narabe!" they shouted. "Line up!" "Kiotsuke!" "Attention!"

They searched them again (yet another shakedown) and after a long wait (another sun treatment), the door to Japanese headquarters opened, and a middle-aged officer appeared on the porch, followed by a much younger man. The two descended the steps, crossed to the front of the parade ground, and mounted a raised platform.[1]

"Watashi wa Tsuneyoshi Yoshio Taii de, kono shūyōjo no shocha da." "I'm Captain Yoshio Tsuneyoshi and I'm the commandant of this camp," he said through his interpreter.

Since April 11, when the first two hundred prisoners reached O'Donnell, Tsuneyoshi had made it his practice to address each group of arrivals. Colonel Michael Quinn of Kansas City, Kansas, among the first men in O'Donnell, thought the commandant a "funny-looking creature, dressed in a white shirt, like our sport shirts, a pair of very baggy shorts, [polished] riding boots with spurs," and a sword that hung loosely from his belt.[2]

"Kimitachi wa meiyoaru horyo ja nai," the commandant continued. "You are not honorable prisoners of war; you are captives! So don't expect to be treated well." It was a shame, he said, that he couldn't kill all of them, but the code of Bushido demanded that true warriors show mercy, and as a true warrior he was bound by the code. Still, he wouldn't hesitate to shoot a man if he disobeyed any of the camp rules or, of course, if he tried to escape. Let any man try to slip away, he said, and nine of his comrades would be executed. Obedience, that was the key; if they obeyed orders and instructions, he said, they might go home, and if they didn't, they would die. Then he delivered a harangue on race and politics that varied somewhat from one group of prisoners to the next but, essentially, went something like this: America was finished in East Asia; Japan had seen to that. And Nippon would keep fighting till it had won the war, even if the war lasted a hundred years. "You will always be our enemies," he said.[3]

Some men were dispirited by the performance, but most, like Air Corps mechanic Cletis Overton of Rolla, Arkansas, stood there watching the commandant "just a-screamin' and a-carryin' on" and thought to himself, "this guy's crazy."

Afterward, the new arrivals were turned over to their officers. Tsuneyoshi had appointed General Ned King "prisoner commander," which made him responsible for the maintenance of the camp and the behavior of his men. King was ordered to instruct all prisoners on the camp rules, and while he later delegated this job to subalterns, when the first groups of men came shuffling and staggering through O'Donnell's front gate, King was there to greet them.

> You men remember this—you didn't give up, I did. I did the surrendering. I surrendered you; you didn't surrender. I'm the one that has the responsibility for that. You let me carry it. All I ask is that you obey the orders of the Japanese so we do not provoke the enemy any more than he already is.[4]

He believed what he told them, and no amount of sophistry from his staff could convince him otherwise. His army was the largest army under American command ever to have been captured, and the dark dishonor of that act belonged to him. Everything that followed from his surrender—the bodies that still littered the Old National Road, the bodies they pulled from the boxcars, the bodies beginning to pile up in this hellhole of a camp—all of it was his responsibility. He was sure, he told them, his career was over. He'd be cashiered, court-martialed, maybe even jailed when he got home. It was up to him to carry the blame, he said, suffer the censure and disgrace.

And his men loved him for that. They loved him because he was sharing their fate, their misery, their stinging loss. Whenever he addressed them in O'Donnell, they would afterward talk of his eyes, so heavy with sadness.[5]

BEN STEELE didn't like all the bowing ("Like this, from the waist," the interpreter instructed). It made him feel like a slave. And to the Japanese, that's what he was. Tsuneyoshi had chosen his words carefully. To be a *horyo*, a prisoner of war, was indeed a disgrace, but a *horyo* at least was still considered a soldier, a failure of a soldier to be sure, but a man-at-arms nonetheless. But a *toraware no mi*, the commandant's phrase, was a captive, and a captive was nothing more than chattel, part of the spoils of war, like a horse or a cow, something to be used, then discarded. And the same idea was behind all the bowing. In Japan one bowed *atama o sageru*, as a sign of respect. Here, however, the guards in the clean white shirts weren't looking for respect; they wanted *kuppuku suru*, a bow of complete submission, something a Montana boy found hard to give.

He was hot and tired, one of 1,188 Americans that came out of the boxcars that day, April 18, 1942. After the speeches and instructions, the men were turned loose to find their barracks, and as Ben Steele wandered away from the formation toward a group of prisoners who had arrived earlier, he noticed a familiar face.

Q. P. Devore was astounded. His pal Ben Steele had lost so much weight the guy looked like a walking cadaver.

"Goddamn, Ben," Q.P. said. "I can hardly recognize you."

They settled down to talk. Q.P. had been lucky. He'd been taken prisoner midway up the peninsula and had been part of a small group of men that had been picked up by a truck on the way to San Fernando. The ride had spared him many of the deprivations of the march, and compared to many others, he seemed in good shape, better shape at least than his emaciated buddy.

Don't worry, he told Ben Steele. "The word around camp is we're gonna be out of here pretty soon. They say thirty days. The Americans are gonna clean the Jap plows in thirty days. They'll be back."

THE JAPANESE had divided O'Donnell into two prison camps. The Filipino camp sat on one side of the road from Capas, the American compound on the other. The facilities, if they could be called that, were the same: open-air barracks buildings constructed of bamboo poles and rattan lashings with half walls of woven sawali and roofs of nipa leaves or corrugated tin. The men slept on shelves that ran the length of the buildings. The barracks were organized by units, the Air Corps here, the artillery there and so on.

As a cantonment for a division of 20,000 native troops, the camp might have been adequate, but the Japanese jammed more than 56,000 (9,270 Americans and almost 47,000 Filipinos) into that small square mile of steaming grassland and jungle scrub.[6]

[*Diary of Captain Alvin Poweleit, prison camp doctor, April 17, 1942, Camp O'Donnell*] The medical situation [is] disastrous . . . I wonder how long a person can stand this situation. I know I'm losing weight, but I'm still in better condition than most of the other men. I finally got to sleep and woke up about daybreak as the Japanese guards tramped through the area.

[*Poweleit Diary, April 18*] As more prisoners poured into camp, more sick were placed in the hospital. Already the [hospital] area was filled with [sick] prisoners milling around defecating anywhere, until there was nowhere to stand that was not defiled by human waste. Men were lying, sleeping and dying in their own waste . . .

[*Poweleit Diary, April 19*] A large group of prisoners [1,188] came in [yesterday]. They were more pitiful than the previous group. Practically none of them had blankets. Only a few had towels. Some wore shorts, and many were bare-footed. These prisoners had swollen legs which were covered with sores, some with maggots crawling over them . . .

Shortly after midnight a storm broke . . . The rain came down in sheets. The men who were able, ran into the various barracks, while the rest just laid on the ground. Each time the wind died down, you could hear the men coughing and moaning. In the morning all over this one area (between our barracks and the main hospital) were the dying and the dead.[7]

The 617-acre site had only one artesian well with a working pump in its reservoir. The pump pushed the water through a narrow pipe, five-eighths of an inch in diameter. The pipe delivered water to both camps, but with only a few spigots for each side, the men had to queue up for a drink. On the American side, one of the faucets was reserved for the exclusive use of the hospital huts, and that left just two faucets for general use, two water faucets to slake the thirst of nearly nine thousand men.

To make matters worse, the Japanese, always short on petrol, issued restrictions on the number of hours the well pump could run. So the water lines were often more than half a mile long—two thousand men standing in line for twenty hours or more, standing there from well before dawn till well after dark to get just one canteen, one quart, of water.

Before long, some of the men in the barracks organized themselves into water brigades, eight to ten prisoners taking turns fetching water for the others, especially those too weak to walk. The designated Gunga Din attached the canteens to a bamboo pole and took his place in the long queue that wound its way through the camp.

[*From the notebooks of Colonel James V. Collier*] As [the water line inched forward, thousands of empty aluminum canteens] striking [against one] other tinkled like bells . . . The tinkle of the canteens could be heard almost any hour of the day or night. I believe I shall hear that doleful tinkling—a mournful sounding of the doom of the damned—as long as I live. On many more occasions than I like to remember, a man who was told to move along as the line had started to move [again] was found to have quietly passed-on.[8]

Army medic Sidney Stewart looked at the men in the water line and thought of the catatonics he'd seen in hospitals back home. "They [stood there looking] at the ground, shuffling their feet. None of them talked . . . Out of their blank eyes came a stare of detachment, of receding within themselves, trying desperately not to be a part of all that was around them."[9]

When the pumps were broken or the Japanese shut them down, the line would stop, and Marine Irwin Scott would sit on the ground where he was, take a nap, and dream, the same dream each time: He was stretched out "in an old enamel bathtub with claw feet . . . under a waterfall," his "head back, mouth open, catching the clearest blue water" anyone had ever seen.[10]

BEN STEELE started praying.

He'd never asked God for anything, but he'd been having one malaria attack after another, terrible chills followed by long sweats that left him dry, dry as an alkali flat. He'd been thirsty on the march, thirsty on the train, thirsty waiting on the water line.

He tried to distract himself, think of something else, anything else, but his mind was fixed on water—the cool, crystalline spring at Hawk Creek, the April rains along the Yellowstone.

In the barracks he tried to lose himself in sleep, but the sleeping shelves were made of split bamboo and the planks dug into his hips and back, keeping him awake. His throat felt raw, his tongue swollen.

"God," he prayed, "please help me find a drink."

He begged his bunkmates to share their canteens. "Come on, just a sip. What the hell's the matter with you guys?" Finally, one man relented.

"Here," he said, watching closely. "Remember, fella, just a couple of swallows."

On the third day of his thirst, Ben Steele returned to the water line. Two hours, five hours, eight hours. In the afternoon, the Japanese shut down the line and he walked away thirstier than before.

His malarial attacks were becoming more frequent. Sometimes he shook so violently he thought he could feel his brain rattling against his skull. One day, he fainted.

When he came to, he was facedown in the dirt, and men were stepping over him, walking around him.

He eased himself up on his elbows, looked around. Nearby was an officers' barracks. He crawled there on his hands and knees and propped himself up under a window.

He could hear men inside, talking. He could also hear a canteen cap clanking against the side of the flask. The officers had water! (He remembered some of the men saying they'd seen officers hoarding five-gallon cans.)

"Please, sirs!" he yelled, as loud as he could. "Please, can I have a drink?"

No one answered. Maybe they didn't hear him.

"Please, sirs! I need water!"

He passed out again, came to, passed out a third time. It was late afternoon now. He waited for the sun to set, and with great effort dragged himself back to his barracks.

"Damn, Ben, you look awful," Q.P. said.

"I'm sick," Ben Steele said.

From somewhere his friend fetched him a few gulps, then, glancing furtively around the barracks, Q.P. reached into his pocket and took out a small brown bottle.

"Quinine," he whispered. "Here, take one. Found 'em in a medic's bag along the road on the march."

At the edge of the camp was a small stream polluted by runoff from nearby barrios. American officers tried to keep their men from washing and bathing in, and drinking from, this viscous brook—only the camp kitchens were authorized to draw water there, water they boiled to cook rice—but many prisoners, Ben Steele among them, were so crazed with thirst they would volunteer to haul water for the camp mess just so they could sneak a drink from the pestilent creek.

[*Poweleit Diary, April 20*] The sick were crammed shoulder to shoulder [in the hospital] buildings. Most of them had no clothes on, nor blankets . . . Coughing, groaning and moaning were continuous.

[*Poweleit Diary, April 23*] Most of our cases were malaria, dysentery (bacillary and amoebic) and beriberi . . . We had all kinds of undiagnosed cases. Some are possibly dengue fever, yaws and tropical ulcers . . . Practically all the men had some type of scurvy (Vitamin C deficiency). Their gums were bleeding and their teeth were loose. Some of the dysentery patients developed corneal ulcers which perforated and collapsed the eye globe. There was nothing that could be done for these poor souls.[11]

THEY ATE RICE. Rice with stones, dirt, and weevils. They steamed it, stewed it, made it into soup. Sometimes they supplemented the rice with vegetables—camotes, a poor-man's sweet potato, kangkong, a spinach-like vine commonly known in America as swamp cabbage, as well as other assorted, and often unidentifiable, leaves and weeds. Once in a while they got meat (beef or carabao), but the ration was so small—one pound twice a month for every fifty men, or a third of an ounce per prisoner—it appeared as nothing more than flecks floating in the dirty rice.

Starving men will eat anything, and much of the camp was picked clean of weeds and cogon grass. Army Corporal Johnny Aldrich told himself, "If cows and horses can eat grass, I can eat grass, too." He tried it raw first but couldn't get the bitter stuff down, then he took his forage to a friend in the camp kitchen, who boiled the long blades into a brown and green stew.[12]

They ate in the open, sitting or squatting in the dirt, spooning or fingering their food with one hand and swatting away the flies with the other. On the average they were given eighteen ounces of food a day (fifteen hundred calories and thirty grams of protein), half of what a healthy adult man (under ideal conditions and doing moderate work) needed to live. For sick men—and almost all of the Americans and Filipinos at O'Donnell suffered from something—this prison-camp "diet" was a disaster.

The lack of nutrients aggravated and accelerated their malaria, dengue fever, blackwater fever, diphtheria, and pneumonia, and left them suffering from a host of painful, and lethal, conditions: wet beriberi (with its gross edema), scurvy (which made their noses bleed and their

teeth fall out), pellagra (a feeling of pins in their skin accompanied by severe diarrhea), nyctalopia (night blindness), amblyopia (day blindness or loss of vision), tinnitus (ringing in the ears), vertigo (severe disorientation), burning feet, conjunctivitis (severe itching and burning in the eyes), and gross peripheral neuropathy (their limbs went completely numb).

Far and away, however, the worst of their maladies was dysentery. So many men had come into camp with it (a third? half?) the slit trenches they dug—and they dug them regularly—filled within days. And like the foul holding pens of Balanga and Orion along the route of the march, Camp O'Donnell started to look and smell like a sewer. Men who were too weak to walk fouled themselves wherever they happened to be when the urge seized them.

Without enough sulfa drugs to stop it, dysentery was soon epidemic. The barracks became so noxious, men started sleeping outside on the ground, if they could find an unsoiled patch of dirt for a bed. Coming up the road from Capas some weeks after the camp opened, Medical Corps Captain John H. Browe of Burlington, Vermont, caught wind of O'Donnell miles before he ever set eyes on it.

"This," he thought, "must be the smell of a charnel house."[13]

Within a week of the prisoners' arrival, O'Donnell was aswarm with bluebottle or blowflies, a great buzzing mass of them, and their eerie vibrato filled the camp day and night.

[*Poweleit Diary, April 26*] Sunday morning was clear and nice. The chaplains held services but many who attended last Sunday were not there to attend this one.

[*Poweleit Diary, April 27*] A number of our doctors were sick with malaria and dysentery. Actually we have only about twelve medical officers who were able to work. The rest were sick. Each time a [new group of men arrived] with a doctor, the doctor was as sick as his men so the workload was not eased . . . I was called over to see a couple of men who were having difficulty breathing. I looked in their mouth and saw what appeared to be a large black membrane. I am sure that this was diphtheria . . . A tracheotomy was attempted using a piece of rubber tube and a safety pin, but these cases were so far gone that it was impossible to do much for them.

[*Poweleit Diary, April 28*] Tuesday morning we tried to get some diphtheria anti-toxin but it was a useless attempt—a waste of time. The Japanese did not care. They were busy trying to win the war.

[*Poweleit Diary, April 29*] Nothing much to do but try to comfort the sick without medicine, giving them guava tea which did not do much good. We attempted to enforce some sanitation rules but made little progress.[14]

Every man was forced to look inward. Those who saw nothing—and there were many of them—abandoned all hope of ever seeing home again. It was almost as if death itself had become contagious, and men who should have survived, men in halfway decent shape, lost their will to live.

Men of faith found themselves praying for their lives. Every night Second Lieutenant Philip Brain of Libby, Minnesota, slept outside on the ground with his canteen for a pillow (so no one would steal it), staring at the stars and thinking of "a different world" and the loving God he believed was looking down on him.[15]

In that miserable place, however, many a man mislaid his religion. Mormon Gene Jacobsen, an Air Corps supply sergeant from Montpelier, Indiana, lost his capacity for forgiveness. "I'm going to do everything I can to survive," he promised himself, "and then I'm going to get even with these sons of bitches."[16]

Zoeth Skinner, who had grown up relying more on his wits than on his parents, believed in himself. Lying in a camp hospital hut with malaria, he noticed that most of his ward mates were too sick to feed themselves.

"Hey, buddy," he'd ask, "you going to eat that chow?"

"I can't eat nothin'," they'd always say, too weak even to raise themselves off the floor. "I just can't."

So Skinner ate the food, ate it right there in front of them.

"I'm going to do what I need to do to live," he told himself.[17]

SOME MEN WERE SELFLESS, buddies from the same unit looking out for one another, keeping an eye on the sick and weak, giving a bit of comfort to the dying. Empathy, however, and the altruism that sometimes accompanied it, was the exception that proved the cruelest of rules: In prison camp, more often than not, men revealed what Darwin called "the indelible stamp of [their] lowly origin."[18]

When his malaria got worse, infantryman Richard Gordon dragged himself to one of the huts in the hospital compound and encountered a short man wearing a white armband with a small red cross, sitting at a wooden crate, a makeshift ward desk.

"I'm sick," Gordon told the American medic. "I need something."

The man could see Gordon's tremors, hear his teeth chattering.

"We don't have any quinine for you," he said. "Sorry."

But there in front of him on the crate Gordon could see a brown bottle of white tablets, medicine Gordon recognized from his visits to the field hospitals on Bataan.

"That's quinine, isn't it?" Gordon said.

"Yeah, that's quinine," the medic said, "but that's my personal stock."

"Your personal stock? What the hell—"

"Yeah, mine, pal. And you can buy it, two dollars apiece."

Gordon thought, "You little son of a bitch!"

"I'll see you in hell first," he told the man and dragged himself away.

He could feel himself failing and he staggered around the compound, not knowing where to go or what to do. At length he wandered into the kitchen shack, where he'd been assigned to work, and curled up in a corner. He was conscious, he could hear and see what was going on around him, but he was shaking so violently all he could do was lie there.

"What's the story with that guy?" he heard someone say.

"Don't worry about him," someone else answered. "He's had it."

He thought, "I'm right here next to them and they're talking about me dying." Was he really that bad, that close to the end? Then he felt someone cover him with something, empty rice sacks. Were they trying to keep him warm or drape him with a winding sheet, a shroud?

"Dick? Dick?"

He knew that voice. It was Fred Pavia, a comrade from the 31st Infantry. Pavia was from New Jersey, just across the river from Manhattan where Gordon had grown up, and fighting together the two had become close.

"I looked for you in the barracks, Dick. Figured I might find you here. You don't look good. I'll be right back."

A while later Pavia returned and held out his hand. In his palm were two capsules. Quinine, Gordon guessed.

Next morning his fever broke, and he was back on his feet. Some weeks later, looking at a list of the dead, Richard Gordon spotted Fred Pavia's name. Cause of death: complications of malaria.[19]

BEN STEELE tried not to think ahead. No daydreams, no ideas but in things. Food, water, medicine. Survive, exist. Another hour and day.[20]

He'd walk by a barracks hut and see a man sitting in the dirt sobbing, and he'd think to himself, "The hell with you. What a waste of goddamn energy. Where the hell is crying going to get you?"

Then, maybe that afternoon or the next, he'd be wandering the compound and hear shouting coming from a hut and see another man miserable and in despair, and he'd feel something, an impulse.

So he'd go into the hut and up to the men who were shouting at the man in despair and say, "What's going on here?" And they'd tell him, "This guy's shitting all over the place and we're going to throw him out." And then they'd grab hold of the man, drag him from his sleeping shelf and across the rough bamboo floor, and Ben Steele would say to them, Stop! Please stop! "That's a helluva way to treat a sick man." And now the pack would turn on him. "Keep your goddamn mouth shut," they'd say. "And get the hell out of here."

[*Poweleit Diary, May 7*] We learned this Wednesday that Corregidor had surrendered along with all the Philippine islands . . . Corregidor's surrender had a depressing effect on everyone in camp in spite of the Japanese rumors that there would be peace. No details of the surrender could be learned.[21]

The Japanese had been bombing and shelling Corregidor since late December. Many of the big guns on the tiny island fortress had been knocked out, but not all of them. And from deep in Malinta Tunnel, General Jonathan Wainwright, MacArthur's successor, still led what was left of his command—scattered combat units in northern Luzon and in the southern Philippine islands. So General Masaharu Homma, eager to end the campaign, issued orders to reduce the fortress to rubble and "exterminate" its garrison.[22]

On May 5, Homma sent two thousand *hohei* ashore. At that point the island's beach force of four thousand marines, sailors, and Filipino soldiers had been bombed and starved to the breaking point. They fought the invaders fiercely, fought them for nearly a day. After that, the Japanese landed tanks, and without the weapons to stop those armored cannon, American commanders knew the fight was finished.

More than a thousand wounded lay in the hospital lateral of Malinta Tunnel, and Wainwright, worried about flame-throwing infantry and tank cannon wreaking slaughter in the tunnel, radioed President Roosevelt that further resistance was pointless.

> With broken heart and head bowed in sadness but not in shame I report to Your Excellency that today I must arrange terms for the surrender of the fortified islands of Manila Bay . . . With profound regret and with continued pride in my gallant troops I go to meet the Japanese commander.[23]

When word of Wainwright's decision reached MacArthur, the "hero" of Bataan—on April 1 in Australia he had been awarded the Congressional Medal of Honor for "conspicuous leadership"—refused to meet with reporters. The next day, May 7, MacArthur's press aide issued a brief written statement from the general:

> Corregidor needs no comment from me . . . I shall always seem to see the vision of its grim, gaunt, and ghostly men still unafraid.[24]

In Washington, the commander in chief seemed to understand something MacArthur did not: the Philippines command had always been expendable. Roosevelt radioed Wainwright that those who had stayed behind in "complete isolation" had turned "a desperate situation" into "a heroic stand."

On May 6, 1942, the nine thousand Americans and two thousand Filipinos on the island also became prisoners of war, guests of the emperor.

TOWARD THE END of April, O'Donnell's hospital was more a death house than an infirmary, a place for only the sickest of men, the terminal, the half dead. Its crude, unfinished huts, set up on stilts, formed a quadrangle in the northeast corner of the camp—five wards, long open buildings of wood and bamboo. No beds, furniture, blankets, pillows, or sheets. Patients lay shoulder to shoulder in rows on the rough, hard plank floor.

The surgeons, physicians, and medics who tended the hospital's eight hundred patients had few supplies and almost no medicine, only a trickle of pills and patent cures from the Japanese (a bit of quinine, sulfa, iodine, and slaked lime for sanitation) plus what they had carried into camp from the field hospitals on Bataan—adhesive tape, gauze, plain old aspirin.

Roughly a third of the patients suffered from malaria. Doctors, pooling the quinine on hand, calculated they had only a quarter of a tablet per patient. Not even a palliative. So rather than "waste the drug," as one of them put it, they decided to practice pharmaceutical triage. Only patients with a chance of survival or remission were given a dose. And when the potential survivors outnumbered the supply, doctors staged a quinine lottery to see who might get lucky and live.[25]

Most of the hospital's other patients had dysentery, O'Donnell's black plague. And the worst of these were gathered together in one building, "Zero Ward."

Zero Ward patients had long since stripped off their clothing and now lay naked on the hardwood floor in pools of filth. Without soap or water to bathe the patients or scrub the ward, medics could do little to improve the place. They tried to trowel the filth out the door, then spread lime to mitigate the stench, but the lime splashed on men with open sores, and their screams soon made the medics stop.

In the end, the patients of Zero Ward just lay there, waiting to die, two long rows of living skeletons side by side along each wall from one end of the ward to the other, half conscious, most of them. The flies found them, of course, and it wasn't long before maggots were spotted in their mouths, ears, and noses. Then the ants arrived.

Army Captain Merle Musselman, a doctor from Nebraska City, attended Zero Ward during the late April rains when a leaky hospital roof left the patients wet and shivering. At night, seeking warmth, they would "worm together across the floor in an unconscious effort to share body heat." And in the mornings when Musselman and his colleagues entered the ward, the doctors would come upon "a large mass of intertwined bodies," the living snuggled up to the dead.[26]

HIS MALARIA WAS SO BAD he could barely get to his feet, so Humphrey O'Leary found himself on his way to Zero Ward.

The ward was full when they carried him in, and since he looked half gone, they took him back out again and laid him on the ground in the crawl space beneath the building, among four other hopeless cases. In the morning when he awoke, he was cold, very cold. One of the men lying beside him was holding his hand, and the man was dead.

Since he'd survived the night, the medics gave him a spot on the ward floor. At least he was off the wet ground. That morning, a man he knew well, Bill Young from Manila, was also brought into the ward. Bill was in bad shape too, worse than Humphrey. His back was covered with suppurating sores and the ulcers were infested with maggots.

"You guys have got to clean this man up!" O'Leary shouted.

"We're too busy for that," one of the medics said. "Besides he's—"

"Just give me the stuff," O'Leary said. "I'll do it."

With a basin and some filthy rags, O'Leary did the best he could. His friend seemed to revive a bit, then around noon, Young became delirious. O'Leary yelled for the medics again. The medics called for a priest.

"What's the matter here?" Army chaplain William Cummings said when he arrived.

"Father, this man is really delirious," O'Leary said. "You better give him extreme unction."

The priest anointed the dying man and turned to O'Leary.

"I'd better give you last rites, too," he said.

"Shit, Father! I look that bad?"

"Yeah, soldier, you do."

That afternoon Humphrey O'Leary happened to catch the glance of the man lying against the opposite wall. The man was staring at him, giving him the eye. Probably trying to put a name with a face, O'Leary guessed.

"I know you?" O'Leary asked.

"No," the man answered. "I'm looking at your boots," cavalry boots O'Leary found on the side of the road during the march.

"What about my boots?"

"When you die," the man said, "I'm gonna pick them up."

"Fuck you, you son of a bitch," O'Leary said.

He grabbed his boots and wedged them between his head and the wall behind him. He hardly slept that night, watching his property, a waste of time, as it turned out. The next morning the vulture was dead.

"Goddamn," O'Leary thought. "Now I feel sorry for the son of a bitch."[27]

IN SHORT ORDER the ground beneath Zero Ward became the camp's de facto morgue, the place where they stacked the bodies for burial.

At first the numbers were modest, four Americans dead one day, three the next, nine a few days later. Then on April 28, twenty-two Americans died; on May 11, thirty-two; on May 19, forty-three. The Japanese wanted to cremate the bodies but agreed to the Western custom of burial. Now, with a death rate between twenty-five and fifty a day, the camp required standing burial details, one group to dig the graves, another to bear the bodies to the cemetery. Barracks chiefs picked men at random for this work, but most of the men on the burial details were volunteers.[28]

They were burying friends, many of them, and they reckoned that if it came to it, they too would want to be put in the ground by those who'd known them, those they could count on to carry their memory, whisper their good name.

Many signed up for the grim duty day after day. Like the Samaritans who shared their food and water, the gravediggers and pallbearers were also trying to hold on to their humanity. For them the will to live sprang from impulse rather than instinct, the impulse to be human and do human things—tend the ill, inter the dead.[29]

The burial parties formed up after dawn. The gravediggers collected their tools (old spades and makeshift shovels fashioned from truck parts and discarded metal) and headed up a rise to the American cemetery, a flat piece of ground outside the main camp, some eight hundred yards from Zero Ward. The pallbearers, meanwhile, gathered with a graves registration officer in front of the morgue and began to bring out the bodies.

Grizzly work, collecting those corpses. Many had lain around the compound for days before they were hauled to the morgue, and in the tropical heat these derelicts had started to decompose. To Army medic Sidney Stewart, they were "no longer recognizable as the bodies of men," just "yellow balloon-like forms," stacked in the dirt, some with their limbs frozen at grotesque angles. The "horrible smell" of these "shrunken skeletons . . . hung in the air" and "clung to the ground" like a "thick, pungent gas." It stung the nostrils and made the eyes water. Grabbing a limb to pull on a body, a pallbearer might come away with a sleeve of skin and a month's nightmares.[30]

Irwin Scott noticed that a few of the dead lay facedown, one arm outstretched, one knee drawn up as if they had crept to the morgue to die.

"I swear to God," he thought, "they crawled under that building to save us the trouble of having to carry and drag them there."[31]

The bodies were put on litters fashioned from wooden doors and shutters or blankets strung between bamboo poles. Many had no dog tags, and the graves registration officer, Captain A. L. Fullerton, did his best to identify and make a record of each body and the plot of ground where it was to be interred. Then four men would pick up the litter and join the line of other bearers, and the silent procession, in the company of a guard, would pass through the camp fence behind the hospital, down a slight incline, and work its way slowly along a streambed toward the cemetery.

The graves were six feet wide, ten to twenty-five feet long, and three to four feet deep, communal graves for five, ten, fifteen men and more. After several days of rain, the water table would rise and the holes would be half full of liquid mud. By the end of May, the burial parties had to weigh the bodies down with stones to keep them from floating up before the diggers could cover them.

The first burial parties treated their dead comrades with tenderness and respect. They lowered them carefully into the holes, laid them respectfully side by side. Later, as the death rate rose—in May, the diggers seemed to be burying men from dawn to dusk—the burial parties tossed the bodies into the holes as if they were piling up firewood, one recumbent form pitched on top of another. At first Richard Gordon, a regular on the detail, was horrified by the "crack" of skull hitting skull, but by his third time out he too was tossing corpses and turning quickly away.

JOHNNY ALDRICH volunteered for the burial detail almost every day. He wanted to keep busy. Men who didn't, he'd observed, seemed to just "lay down and die."[32]

Aldrich grew up a Catholic in New Brunswick, New Jersey, the fifth of thirteen children born to two bookkeepers. He left school after the eighth grade and joined the Civilian Conservation Corps. He liked the job, the life—the barracks, the discipline, the company of men—and in 1940 enlisted in the army and was assigned to the Quartermaster Corps as a carpenter and electrician, then sent to the Philippines and stationed at Nichols Field.

Every Sunday he went to Mass in Manila with a group of other Catholics. After church they enjoyed a meal together, bought candy for the local children. Before long Johnny Aldrich had a pal, Tom Wolfington of Norristown, Pennsylvania. The two went hiking and bowling, drank beer together. On base they often found themselves paired on the same job. So when Wolfington fell desperately ill in O'Donnell and was hauled off to Zero Ward, Johnny Aldrich went to see him right away.

He found his friend in "real bad shape," pale and gray and "skinny like a rail." Worse, the sick man was hacking and coughing constantly, "like he had tuberculosis or something."

The next day, when Aldrich returned to the ward, the medics told him that Tom Wolfington had died during the night and his body was waiting in the morgue to be buried.

Johnny Aldrich got himself on the burial detail that morning. He helped pull his friend from under the hut, helped put him on a wooden-door litter, helped carry him the eight hundred yards to the graveyard. With three other men he lowered him, ever so gently, into the wet hole.

He wanted to say a prayer over him, some short requiem for his repose, but the Japanese had forbidden such rituals, so Johnny Aldrich stepped down into the grave and slipped his hand under Tom Wolfington's neck, lifted the head a little, and gave his dead friend a kiss.

When he climbed out, the guard rushed up furious and slapped Aldrich, slapped him hard, then hit him again.

Johnny Aldrich looked down at the hole, took out a scrap of paper and a stub of pencil, and noted its location: row X, column Y, "fourth or fifth man down in the hole."

Then he said to himself, "Forget about it. Worry about tomorrow."

THE FILIPINOS were dying at the same rate, and since their overall numbers were higher, so was the number of their dead, six Filipinos for every American. One hundred a day, two hundred and fifty, three hundred.

At first Filipinos volunteered by the score to bury their dead comrades. A Catholic people, they were determined to keep the sacraments. (Sometimes a Filipino chaplain would sneak into a burial party and in lieu of last rites surreptitiously recite the Twenty-third Psalm.) Whenever a burial procession left camp, Filipino soldiers standing by the entrance would snap to attention and salute the litters as they passed the gate.

Later when the death rate climbed into the hundreds and the corpses became commonplace, the men stopped taking notice, stopped saluting. Officers had to comb the camp to come up with even a handful of men willing to dig graves and carry the bodies down the road. They were refusing the duty, they told their officers, because they were afraid of being contaminated and made sick by the touch of the dead.

BEN STEELE hated going near Zero Ward. The moans and cries of the dying, the stink of the sick, the morgue with its stacks of the dead. But he'd been assigned to the burial detail by his barracks chief and, thinking the work worthwhile, he went willingly. The next day he volunteered for the duty again, same thing the day after that.

Some days his detail would get to the graveyard only to discover that ravenous dogs had gotten to the bodies, and the diggers would have to scrape a new hole and reinter the corpses. At that point, the third week in May, burial parties might put thirty bodies in one hole, put them down in layers, walk on each layer to compress it, then toss dirt on top and stomp the dirt down.

Ben Steele, gravedigger, buried two friends, Bob Schope from Billings and Walter Mace, a married man from Spokane. Mace was an Air Corps buddy, and when he came down with dysentery and was taken to Zero Ward, Ben Steele went to see him and was shocked.

Doctors had been giving their patients charcoal (an absorbent) from the kitchens to try to control their diarrhea, and poor Mace had soiled himself so often his legs and lower torso had turned black.

"Listen, Ben," he said, "I'm not going to make it out of here, so when you get home, if you get home, go see Peggy. Talk to her. Tell her. You promise?"

"I will, Walter."

Then Ben Steele helped bury him.

He'd been on the detail two weeks, and he thought he should volunteer for some other work, work that might get him out of camp and perhaps something to eat.

Work parties were leaving camp all the time now, a hundred, two hundred men in each group, working in nearby fields cultivating crops, doing one kind of labor or another. And often when they returned, the men smuggled back vegetables or extra rice or even a bit of meat.

On the afternoon of May 21, word spread that a large work detail, three hundred men, would be leaving the next morning. To where and for what, no one could say. Ben Steele didn't care.

"There's got to be a better place than this," he thought. "If I can get on that detail, I'm going to go. I've got to get some food, some water. I've got to get away from all this shit."

In the barracks that night he convinced Q. P. Devore to join him.

"We'll get something to eat," he said.

Early the next day, the two men signed up, and when the trucks rolled in they climbed aboard together. From the truck bed, Ben Steele could see the men already queuing up for the water line. And he told himself, anything would be better than that. But Q.P. had this queer look on his face. He seemed nervous, unsure. And now he was getting off the truck. He couldn't say why exactly. Just a feeling. He didn't like the look of it.

"That's okay," Ben Steele said. "Don't worry. I'll bring you some food. We'll probably be back tonight."

"A FINAL DETERMINATION"

BILLINGS, MONTANA, early summer 1942. Waiting for word has been hard on them both. Bess goes long periods without saying much. And the Old Man, he seems tired all the time. They read the papers. They listen to the radio. They hope for news.

Since December and the attacks on Clark Field, they've had only two pieces of mail from him. The first was a Christmas card, sent, they guessed, before the Japanese attacked. On the front was a photo of a farmer walking behind a plow hitched to one of those Philippine oxen. It read, "A Merry Christmas and A Happy New Year from the Philippines," and it was signed "Love Bud" in big script.

A few weeks later, a telegram arrived, a "Holiday Greeting by Western Union." At the top was a drawing of a Santa next to a Christmas tree with a small boy peeking out from behind a fireplace. Message: EVERYTHING OKAY NEVER FELT BETTER IN MY LIFE MERRY CHRISTMAS LOVE BENJAMIN STEEL [*sic*].

ACROSS THE LATE WINTER and through the spring, they followed the story of the fighting. April was the cruelest month. Its headlines left them anxious and alarmed. "Bataan Forces Lose Ground" . . . "Desperately-Pressed Bataan Forces Battle Jap Hordes and All Types of Warplanes" . . . "36,853 Americans, Filipinos Slain or Face Captivity."[1]

In June the Old Man's heart broke down. The family knew he was sick, but the "old fool," as Bess called him, had refused to see a doctor. When it finally happened he was out working on a government road crew. He started to sweat and sat down on the road. Just some pulled muscles, he told the crew chief. The chief called a doctor; the doctor told Bess it was a coronary.

He's got to stop working, the doctor said, stop reading the papers, stop all the worrying about Bud.

They worried all the time, Bess told the doctor. There hadn't been any word from the boy since December. How could they stop worrying?

Then, two weeks before Labor Day, a letter arrived from the War Department.

August 14, 1942.

Dear Mrs. Steele:

According to War Department records, you have been designated as the emergency addressee of Private Benjamin C. Steele, 19,018,989, who, according to the latest information available, was serving in the Philippine Islands at the time of the final surrender.

I deeply regret that it is impossible for me to give you more information than is contained in this letter. In the last days before the surrender of Bataan there were casualties which were not reported to the War Department. Conceivably the same is true of the surrender of Corregidor and possibly of other islands of the Philippines. The Japanese Government has indicated its intention of conforming to the terms of the Geneva Convention with respect to the interchange of information regarding prisoners of war. At some future date this Government will receive through Geneva a list of persons who have been taken prisoners of war. Until that time the War Department cannot give you positive information.

The War Department will consider the persons serving in the Philippine Islands as "missing in action" . . . until definite information to the contrary is received. It is to be hoped that the Japanese Government will communicate a list of prisoners of war at an early date . . . In the case of persons known to have been present in the Philippines and who are not reported to be prisoners of war by the Japanese Government, the War Department will continue to carry them as "missing in action." . . . At the expiration of twelve months and in the absence of other information the War Department is authorized to make a final determination.

Very Truly Yours,
J. A. Ulio
Major General,
The Adjutant General

The letter left Bess undone. Her sister, Sue, sent a note to Gert in Bremerton, Washington. Come quick, it said. Gert drove straight through. The doctor was there waiting at the house on Broadwater Avenue when she finally arrived.

It was all too much, the doctor said. The war news, the Old Man's heart attack, the letter from the government—"in the absence of other information the War Department is authorized to make a final determination."

Bess had stopped eating, cooking, taking care of the other kids. She had told the doctor she was sure her son Bud was dead, and she blamed herself for losing him. She was the one who'd urged him into the army, who'd told him to get a new life.

The doctor had put her on tranquilizers and sleeping pills but, he told Gert, there had been no improvement. All she did was sit in the parlor and stare at the walls. Maybe Gert could get through to her, the doctor said.

"Look, Mother," Gert began, "it isn't your fault. You understand? You didn't realize what was going to happen. How could you? Even they didn't know. He was just like all those other boys who joined the army.

"Do you hear me, Mother? Are you listening? It's not your fault, Mother. They all went to war. Nobody made them. They just went."

NINE

TEN TRUCKS loaded with prisoners rolled slowly out the front gate of Camp O'Donnell and down the asphalt road toward Capas. Glancing back, the men could see a wall of dark gray thunderheads gathering above the Zambales Mountains and the camp.

"I'm damn glad to leave that death trap," Ben Steele thought. "Anything is going to be better than that."

Where the work detail was going, none of them knew. A couple of men guessed they'd be put to work salvaging armaments and equipment from the battlefield, but others thought the detail had been assembled for more arduous labor. Guards had come through the barracks the day before looking for men who were "fit." "Maybe get eat," the guards said, knowing they would fill the quota with anyone who could walk.

Rolling south, most of the prisoners in the trucks thought themselves lucky to be leaving O'Donnell. No more water line or burial details. Gone were the flies, gone was the filth. And for the moment that was enough.

Down the main highway on the central plain, past Clark Field (a grim sight for the Air Corps boys), through San Fernando and east around Manila Bay into the city itself, stopping for the night at a one-story, white-stucco school building on Park Avenue in the suburb of Pasay.

The Japanese were using the school as a way station for prisoners being transported between prison camps and work sites throughout the big island. A handful of captured Navy doctors were in temporary residence at the school. And a small group of Air Corps mechanics captured in the southern islands and brought to Luzon were also being quartered there that night.

The mechanics were in good shape—they had been treated well

since their capture—and now, as they stood on the porch of the Pasay schoolhouse watching the grimy and ragged men from O'Donnell slowly get off the trucks and stumble into formation in the courtyard, they were shocked at the sight of them.

"They're more dead than alive," thought Sergeant Louis Kolger of Richmond, Indiana. "Their eyes—they're vacant. And look at their ribs, you can see their ribs!"

Kolger and his comrades from the south could not understand what the hell had happened to the men in the trucks. They seemed to walk listlessly around the schoolyard or just stand there staring into space. Hard to get anything out of them except a yes or a no or a passing glance, an empty look.

"It's like, they've resigned," Kolger thought, "like they're a bunch of sleepwalkers."[1]

The Navy doctors in temporary residence were also shocked by the men from Bataan and asked the guards to let them examine the prisoners. It didn't take long to see they were quite sick—not one seemed fit enough to work—and the doctors tried to convince the Japanese to take the most serious cases off the detail.

The guards refused. Their orders, they said, called for a work party of three hundred men, and in the morning three hundred men were going to get back on those trucks. At least, the doctors pleaded, hold back the five with highest fevers and replace them with men who'd come up from the south. To this their keepers agreed, and the next morning, 3 officers and 297 enlisted men, Louis Kolger newly among them, were rolling south under a tropical sun.

They drove for hours along the western shore of Laguna de Bay, then stopped for the night at a lime kiln outside San Pablo. The next afternoon they boarded railroad flatcars, heading south and east, across the neck of land that connects the main part of Luzon island to the wild uplands and jungle wastes of the rugged Bicol peninsula.

The train rolled slowly through the lush countryside, across the day and into a bright moonlit night, a good night, Louis Kolger thought, to escape.

"That guard is going to be nodding off and I'm going to jump this train," he told himself. He watched and waited, one hour, two, three. Then he felt his eyes get heavy. Suddenly it was morning and the guard he'd been watching was yelling for the prisoners to get off the train.

They had been traveling for almost three days. Half the men appeared weaker than when they started. And now, the Japanese were ordering them to start walking.

Five men were so sick their comrades had to carry them on litters fashioned from old doors. Other men, meanwhile, were made to shoulder sacks of rice and crates of canned goods. And the guards ordered a score of prisoners to carry their bulky packs and heavy equipment.

The prisoners had no idea where they were, no idea where they were going. Just before they got off the train, one of the men had seen a road sign for the town of Calauag. Calauag? That was in southeastern Luzon off the main part of the big island, more than 155 miles from Manila on the way to nowhere.

BEN STEELE had a temperature of 103° (the navy doctors at the school would have held him back had it been two degrees higher). Walking north on a winding one-lane dirt-and-gravel road through the thickly wooded jungle of southern Luzon, he could feel his temperature spiking, his temples throbbing, his face burning with fever.

They walked through the afternoon and into the night. The moon came up and turned the jungle silver, a place of dark shapes and shadows. They were in hill country, that much they could tell. Up one slope, down the next, then up another. Waves of hills.

Ben Steele was tired and so were the others. They kept switching off on the litters, stopping to adjust their Japanese packs. No one said much. Most of them were too weary to talk, too sick. The guards, for the most part, let them be, content with the pace, tolerant of the frequent stops.

Five miles, ten, fifteen. The sky was turning from silver to steel blue then gray as banks of monsoon clouds rolled in from the south.

They had forded a number of rivers and creeks and now they came to another, spanned by a small wooden bridge. Crossing the bridge the guards turned the column left, parallel to the river, then down through the underbrush to the riverbank and downstream another two hundred yards to a large, flat point bar of rocks at a bend in the river below the bridge.

The rock bar was wide and long. It ballooned out from the shore some 30 feet into the river and stretched roughly 125 feet along the shore. Behind the rock bar was a dirt and grass embankment, the beginning of the dark green jungle. All along the river, a wall of trees leaned out ominously over the water.

The weary and bedraggled group put their loads down on the rocks and looked around. There was nothing there. No bamboo buildings, no nipa shacks, no canvas tents. Nothing but the rocks under their feet, the shallow, slow-moving river at their front, the deep green jungle at their backs.

"Is this the end of the trail?" someone said.

"Where are we going?" another man shouted. "What the hell is going on?"

Ben Steele thought, "This must be just a place to stay overnight, a campsite. We're going to move on to another place."

Then the gray sky turned black and it started to pour.

"There's nowhere to get out of the rain," Ben Steele thought. "This isn't good."

THE RUGGED RAIN-SWEPT BICOL PENINSULA is really a jumble of sub-peninsulas, isthmuses, and islands—volcanic derelicts that spread out eastward from Luzon's southern end. In every season tropical storms soak Bicol's sharp peaks and rocky hills, and in the years leading up to the war, the tropical rain forest was tall and thick, a place Joseph Conrad would have called "a colossal jungle, so dark-green as to be almost black," baked by a "fierce" sun that made its wild groves "glisten and drip with steam."[2]

To be sure, there were towns and villages in Bicol, occupied mostly by migrants from Luzon's crowded cities, but there weren't many of them, and since much of the terrain was inhospitable and uninhabitable, the majority of locals lived on less than 10 percent of the land, farmers and foresters, most of them, leaving the rest of the peninsula a silent and teeming wilderness.

The Japanese had arrived on the peninsula during their second landing, coming ashore at points between Atimonan and the southern city of Legaspi, the terminus of the Manila railroad. The peninsula was important to them; there were iron mines in the area and some of the interior plains were suitable for airfields. The problem was the roads. Most were seasonal. Route 1G, for example, from Calauag north along Bicol's westernmost shoreline, seemed to stop in the middle of the jungle a mile or so north of the Basiad River.

Most of the Japanese heavy equipment, bulldozers and earth movers, were tied up elsewhere on Luzon repairing and extending airfields, so any clearing of jungle, any taking off hills and filling depressions—the work of road building—would have to be done with pick and shovel. Work for captives, work for prisoners of war. And so on May 21, a clerk in the Japanese military bureaucracy in Manila sent a requisition to the Japanese headquarters building at Camp O'Donnell asking for three hundred prisoner-laborers to build a section of road that would link Route 1G out of Calauag—the Old Tayabas Road—to the highway coming up from Legaspi. Three hundred men to hack at jungle roots and fill wheelbarrows with jungle mud and make a road through the wilderness.

THE MEN slept on rocks that night, and the next day guards issued picks and shovels and wheelbarrows, then marched them into the jungle to work.

It was clear they were preparing a roadbed, and some of the men thought maybe this was a temporary job, something they would finish by the end of the day and then move on to someplace else, someplace more permanent and with shelter. But that night the guards led them right back to the rocks, and they knew that this long stretch of riverbank, this point bar of rocks and stones and gravel two hundred yards below the wooden bridge, was where they were going to stay.

There, the river formed an S, with the bridge in the middle. On the lower bend of the S was the rock bar bivouac of the prisoners. On the inside of the upper bend, upstream from the bridge, was the Japanese encampment. The Japanese lived in tents with wood walls and floors, while their bedraggled captives were made to sleep in the open on the rocks. Of all the shocks and jolts they'd suffered since December 8—the bombings, the invasion, the defeat, the march off Bataan, the dunghill that was O'Donnell—this stone shelf in the open at the edge of the jungle was the worst misery of all, the lowest of the legacies that had come from their losing.

Their second night on the rock bar, some of the men started to pry up stones and make a bed in the mud. At least, they reckoned, it was softer than the rocks. Ben Steele, perhaps remembering how he'd slept on the open range encircled by a lariat to keep out the snakes, gathered up loose rocks and built a low stone wall around himself. Soon others were building walls too, but these first urgent attempts to improvise a bit of shelter gave them no comfort. Their mud mattresses leached groundwater and collected rain, and the men would wake up in a puddle of muck and their own piss, stiff and sore from the early morning chill and from sleeping cramped in a circle of stone.

The mosquitoes found them right away. In the dark the insects swarmed the rocky encampment. To fight them off the men built fires of wet wood and tried to sit in the thick smoke. Then they'd get into their sleeping pits and try to hide their faces in their shirts, shove their hands in their pockets, anything to keep from exposing their skin. (The few who had mosquito nets shared them, a dozen men sleeping with their heads together in a circle, the net stretched across their faces.) In the morning, many a man awoke with a kind of second skin, a black mat of mosquitoes in his scalp, on his face, down his neck.

IT RAINED almost every day, not all day but every day, monsoon rain. Low rolling clouds like billows of smoke, lots of mist, a thick mist that clung to everything, and rain, sheets of pounding rain slapping the leaves and roiling the river. The rain turned the jungle dark, and in the perpetual gloom some men began to believe that they had been forgotten.

Their government had forgotten them, of this they were sure, and it seemed that God had forgotten them, too. He had sent them into a wilderness, into the heart of darkness, and set them down by a river on a bed of stones.

Now the jungle was their enemy too and it showed them even less pity than the Japanese. Their captors were merely indifferent to their fate. They could live or not; the guards didn't care. Nature, however, seemed bent on destroying them—the heat, the wet, the rot and disease. And they were alone, alone and utterly exposed in a world that hissed and snapped and stirred in the dark, shadows of men sleeping on rocks by a bend in a river on a ragged peninsula at the end of the world.

All they had was one another, and as comrades often do, they buddied up, many of them, picked a partner, another man to share camp chores, nurse them through the chills and fever, break the long spells of loneliness. They hoped a partnership might preserve them, but because hope had so often lost its currency among them, and because it was clear to everyone that their chances of surviving in this wilderness were few (men were dying now, and the scent of death had started to mingle with the musty smell of the damp earth), they buddied up for another reason as well. Here at the end of the world they wanted someone to save them from oblivion, a buddy to carry their memory, if it came to it, and comfort their kin.

BEN STEELE buddied up with Dalton Russell, first sergeant to the 7th Matériel Squadron. They had met in training camp in Albuquerque, and although first sergeants and privates were never close, the young cowboy from Montana had taken a liking to his supervisor. Most of the squadron had.

Russell was young for a first sergeant, just twenty-six years old, which made him something of a prodigy in a prewar army of hoary bootlickers. He had graduated with honors from Troy High School, Montgomery County, North Carolina, in 1934, the class valedictorian, lean, dark-haired, and handsome. In those days of Depression and want, even a top student had trouble finding a job, so he joined the Army Air Corps and married Donnie Harrison, a blond, blue-eyed nurse he'd met back home in Denton. He was a good manager of men and rose quickly in rank. Near the age of those under him, he wasn't afraid to get close to his soldiers, or let them know him.

Ben Steele, addled with malaria, didn't know Russell was part of the detail until they got off the train in Calauag and started walking in the moonlight. The first sergeant remembered the young cowboy right away. "You were the only soldier on base who had a horse," Russell said.

After a couple of days and nights on the rock bar, the two started to stick together and, like some of the others, decided to move back off the rocks and build a bamboo and palm-leaf lean-to against the embankment at the edge of the jungle. Some nights the lean-to would give them comfort; other nights the wind and rain would tear their shack down, forcing them to seek shelter between the buttresses of a towering yakal tree or return to the rocks, living, as Ben Steele liked to say, "like reptiles."

THEY ATE what they'd carried in from Calauag—mostly rice and cans of corned beef hash (a dish the Japanese disliked). The beef, however, was too rough on intestinal tracts ravaged by dysentery, and it passed right through them. So they lived on the rice, low-grade rice (unlike the polished white grains the Japanese kept for themselves) that often still had the chaff on it.

Instead of a rice pot, the Japanese gave them a rusty old wheelbarrow coated with dried concrete. They scraped off the coating as best they could, built a fire in a trench in the middle of the rock bar, and rolled the wheelbarrow over it. At first they used too much water and ended up with a watery rice slop. Even after they adjusted the recipe, the rice always tasted of rust, river water, and old concrete.

Their day began before dawn when guards came onto the rock bar and poked them awake. One man looked worse than the next, eyes rheumy, hair unshorn, face hirsute and filthy. (They could peel off the mud in strips.) Stiff and wet in the predawn chill, they sat up slowly, scraping off the mats of mosquitoes, coughing and hacking up phlegm from the damp, shaking from night sweats or swooning with fever. Every morning, one man at least was carried up the bank and into a section of jungle set aside as a graveyard. After the morning count, the men lined up at the rice wheelbarrow for their morning gruel, then they drew their picks, shovels, and wheelbarrows and marched off to work.

Even with heavy equipment, the job of reshaping the Bicol jungle would have been difficult work. Now they were using hand tools to hack the shoulders off hills, dig out massive roots, haul loads of wet fill—weak men working all day, struggling to swing eight-pound picks or push heavy wheelbarrows through a gumbo of mud that swallowed everything that touched it.

Sometimes the muck was so thick that five men were needed to move one wheelbarrow, two pushing from behind and three, trussed up in harnesses of vines and ropes, pulling like horses from the front. They worked barefoot and in loincloths, most of them, saving the rags they called clothes (which they wrapped in palm fronds and left back at the rock bar) for their nights and the mosquitoes.

Most of all they were sick. Every man jack of them was sick with something, and every day that passed, fewer and fewer were able to march off to work in the jungle. On their first day at Tayabas Road only two-thirds of the men in the detail were able to report for the morning labor call. Two weeks later, fewer than half were well enough to work.

BEN STEELE had awoken in a fever sweat, and the malaria attack had left him flushed and fuzzy all day. Breakfast had been awful too, the rice half cooked and hard raw. And now under a blazing morning sun in a clearing in the jungle, he was chopping at tree roots and lianas with a spade. Thick and hard those roots, like hacking at metal cables. His hands were bruised and tender and his shoulders ached. Worse, the sun was making him light-headed, faint. He stopped, tried to gather himself. The air was still, the clearing stifling and incendiary. "This is goddamn grueling," he thought, then—

When he came to his senses, he was lying under a tree. Nearby, a guard was beating a slacker. When the guard noticed Ben Steele stirring, he motioned him back to work. The afternoon rain had been heavy, and he slogged through the muck until dark.

Back at the river, the lean-to was down again. He cleared away some stones on the rock bar to make a sleeping pit. Too weak to stand in line for rice, he asked Sergeant Russell to bring him his gruel. Afterward, he made his way to the river to wash himself. His hair was long, his whiskers too, full of clumps of mud, leaves, and grass.

He sat for moment on the rocks, letting the wind dry him. Then it started to rain again, a driving night rain. His body began to shake and his teeth chattered (keep that up, he told himself, and he'd grind them right down to the gums). "Damn, I'm freezing," he thought. "I'm like to shake to death in this downpour."

EVERY MORNING there were more bodies on the rocks. After a month at the site, the dead had filled up one jungle graveyard and the living had started another. The infirm, the men too sick to work, dug the graves. Once in a while, someone would stand at the edge of the hole and offer a sentiment. Preston Hubbard, an Air Corps signalman from Clarksville, Tennessee, occasionally acted as an unofficial chaplain. His eulogies were short and his service always included the Twenty-third Psalm, by Hubbard's lights an apt text. In the green gloom of the Basiad River, he could easily envision "the valley of the shadow of death."[3]

They buried them as they were born, naked, their filthy rags stripped for the living to wear. If they died balled up or contorted, they were put in the ground that way, sitting hunched over. Less digging, the men reckoned, too many roots to go down deep. The diggers made crosses from sticks and pounded the rough rood into the damp earth at the top of the hole, then paused for a prayer. "The Lord is my shepherd . . ."

"Poor guys," thought Ken Calvit, an Air Corps mechanic from Alexandria, Louisiana. "Here they are, seven thousand miles from home, lying on the ground naked, covered with flies, covered in shit, sicker than hell, nobody to even hold their hand, nobody to comfort them, nothing. What a way to go."[4]

Men dying of cerebral malaria groaned and wailed for days, their song of suffering filling the hospital grove and spilling out onto the rock bar. At the end, their wails would fall to whispers, faint cries to friends and family, then, finally, an inarticulate rattle and rasp. At that point, the worms had already started their work, and everyone was eager to get the bodies underground.

BEN STEELE and Dalton Russell were agreed.

"If they don't get us out of here," Ben Steele said, "neither one of us is going to make it. We gotta get out of here some way. We're burying more dead every day and soon we're going to be one of them."

They were huddled in their rebuilt lean-to, staring out at the heavy rain and gray gloom. "We ought to try," Russell said. "You're right, we're gonna die if we don't get out of here."

Many of the others, watching the boneyard fill, were also thinking of escape, and sometime in June, six men took flight. It was easy to elude the guards; there weren't that many of them. Besides, it was the jungle, not the Japanese, that was really imprisoning them.

As soon as the missing men were discovered, the Japanese asked for "volunteers" to help search, but after several days of beating the bush, they gave up. Some in the detail were sure the escapees were holed up with friendly villagers or had found a guerrilla camp in the hills. Most men, however, suspected that the runaways had been consumed by the jungle or had waded downriver and gotten caught in the current and washed out to sea.

After that, Ben Steele and Dalton Russell talked about eventualities rather than escape.

"If one of us gets back," the sergeant said, "we should agree to see the other one's family."

"Fine," said Ben Steele. He'd heard so much about the sergeant's blond wife, Donnie, he could almost see her pretty face. And he reminded Russell that if the sergeant was the one who ended up making the condolence call, he should make sure to get some of Bess Steele's roast pork and applesauce.

FOR THE FIRST FEW WEEKS, the Japanese pushed the men to work harder, part of a bet the guards had going. The keepers had divided the kept into teams, five prisoners to each guard, the guards haggling to get the biggest and strongest men. After the teams were picked, they set the wager, so much for the one that moved the most wheelbarrows of earth. With yen to win or lose, the guards drove their charges hard, rewarding good work with a banana or coconut, a short rest or water break. Slackers were scolded with stinging strokes from a punishment stick. The sergeant of the guard was particularly pitiless. He'd been wounded and hobbled at Lingayen Gulf, he told the captives, and he seemed determined to get even. He beat three men so hard with a bolo scabbard, they damn near died. After that, the men started calling him "the Killer."

Sometime during the second or third week in June, after roughly a month working on the road, the prisoners began to notice a change in the guards. The beatings became less frequent. And every now and then, either at the jungle work site or back at the rock bar, a guard might wander over to where a prisoner was sitting and nonchalantly toss an *okurimono*, a little "present," on the ground.

Irwin Scott was so sick with malaria when the detail arrived at Calauag, his comrade Bill White of Albuquerque had to carry him most of the way to the Basiad River. Scott couldn't work, of course, and in the mornings was left back at camp with the infirm. Every afternoon when White returned from digging on the road, he would try to help his friend. First he would fetch him a cup of gruel and insist he eat it. Scott always refused (he was ready to give up), but White kept pushing the rice on him until the canteen cup was empty. Then White would pull his friend to his feet (Scott screaming execrations) and drag him across the rocks to the river to cool his fever and wash off the crud. After a while Scott started to show some improvement and White made his friend crawl to the water on his own, kicking him in the backside when he balked.

"Leave me alone!" Scotty would yell. "Lemme die."[5]

"Aw, go on and crawl down there," White would say. "You're dirty. You need to wash yourself."

"Why can't you just leave me the fuck alone? We're all gonna die here. Nobody gives a damn what happens."

"Oh, yes they do," White said one day. "Watch."

A few minutes later, a guard appeared at the edge of the rock bar. He looked around till he spotted White, then started walking slowly and casually in their direction.

"Here he comes," White whispered.

As the guard passed the two men on the rocks, he dropped a small bundle wrapped in a green banana leaf and wandered off as if nothing had happened. White unwrapped the package. Inside was a rice ball and a tiny white hand-folded envelope that held two pills.

"Go ahead," White said, handing the rice and pills to Scott. "Eat them."

"What is it?" Scott said.

"The pills are quinine."

"Bullshit."

"Taste it."

Bill White was right.

"The day after I brought you into camp passed out," White explained, "that guard came walking by like he was checking something, and when he saw you he tossed me a folded banana leaf. 'For him,' he said, and he pointed at you. That's the only words he said." Every two or three days the guard returned with another *okurimono*, and White slipped the pills into the gruel he had been forcing Scott to eat, the spiked slop that had been saving his life.

One guard gave Louis Kolger a whole bottle of quinine, and another tossed Ben Steele a couple of pills. Air Corps radio operator Paul Reuter of Shamokin, Pennsylvania, noticed that even the Killer was handing out *okurimono*. He was still beating his workers with his scabbard, but at night he'd sidle up to the men he'd thumped and slip them some quinine and Japanese fruit juice.

The cynics in camp said the Japanese were just looking out for their own interests, tending to their human livestock, their draft animals. But their extra attentions had no effect on the work. Every day fewer and fewer Americans were able to answer the morning call. No, the Killer and his comrades weren't helping their captives because they wanted to get more production out of them. To some of the men it was almost as if the enemy, moved by the abject misery of the place, was starting to feel sorry for them.

TWICE IN JUNE the Japanese culled the sickest prisoners from the detail and put them on a truck and drove them 173 miles north to Manila and a hospital for prisoners of war that U.S. Navy doctors had set up in the city's Bilibid Prison. One of those trucks rolled into the prison compound on June 19, the day Army doctor Captain Paul Ashton happened to arrive at Bilibid with some five hundred patients from one of Bataan's captured field hospitals. Ashton had just settled his patients in their beds (straw mats on concrete floors) and was strolling around the prison compound getting the lay of the place when the truck from Tayabas Road stopped just inside the front gate.

Thirty invalids were in the back, men so emaciated, filthy, and malodorous no one moved to help them. "They were not in uniforms," Ashton noted, "just nondescript shirts and pants, rags really, and caked with muck. They looked wizened and dehydrated . . . quite the sickest" and most "broken men" Ashton had ever seen.[6]

Who were these wretched derelicts? Ashton wondered. And what kind of "frightful" hell had tossed them up? When the prison medical staff learned that there were more such cases at the road-building site, they asked the prison commandant if they could send someone down, and Captain Ashton—intrepid surgeon and irritating swashbuckler— was the first to volunteer.

In 1940, living in San Francisco, Paul Ashton had almost everything he'd ever wanted—a pretty wife (Yvonne Toolen was as beautiful as a "fairy queen," he thought) and a good job as a surgeon at Letterman Army Hospital. All that was missing was a little "adventure." He'd spent "a lifetime sitting in chairs studying," and now he yearned for some "excitement," some "color," so he put in for a transfer to the Philippines, arriving in Manila in June 1941 and assigned to the 12th Medical Regiment, Philippine Scouts.

On Bataan Ashton had become a triage specialist, operating in the open or under a tent next to the front lines. His first job, of course, was saving lives, but he thought himself a fighting man as well as a doctor and was just as willing to take lives as save them. He kept a .45 automatic strapped to his hip and told anyone within earshot that he was ready to use it against the nearest Jap. (Riding in an ambulance once, he came under fire from a Japanese Zero, grabbed a Browning automatic rifle, and started shooting at the plane.) He could be abrupt and abrasive, but he was a steady surgeon, ready to carry his doctor's kit into any foxhole or jungle waste.

Ashton convinced Major Charles Brown, a doctor from San Antonio, Texas, and a few army medics who'd chased around on Bataan as his assistants to accompany him to Tayabas. The medicos likely arrived at the site on Monday, June 22, almost a month to the day since the detail left O'Donnell to start working there. It was dark when the truck carrying the six men from Bilibid came up the road from Calauag, crossed the bridge, and stopped at the riverbank. Ashton, an avid memoirist, never forgot his first impression of the place.

> The headlights of the truck revealed the rock-covered river bank . . . It was a warm tropical night, and as our eyes became used to the dark, we could see many people sleeping amid the rocks on the bank. Few of them had anything to lie upon.
>
> The next morning we awakened early, and at dawn the red sun was filtering down into our clearing. Smoke from a few small fires curled straight up and many people were stirring around . . . The jungle was the first I ever saw that was truly impenetrable . . . The sun only shone on the camp when directly overhead, since we were surrounded by tall jungle trees. The place rarely had a chance to dry out, and the mosquitoes were [astonishing].

Ashton started asking questions, talking to the ambulatory, making an inventory of the sick: "everyone had diarrhea or dysentery"; most

had malaria too; a handful suffered from dengue fever and couldn't eat. Half the detail seemed to have some kind of respiratory problem, and several of these were developing pneumonia. Others were either yellow with jaundice or covered with jungle ulcers, which were suppurating and attracting flies. A number of the infirm were infested with worms, nematodes, deposited as larvae by flies and mosquitoes. (A local guerrilla, Bernabe de Leon, who sold snacks by the bridge and spied on the Japanese, one day came upon an American on a path in the jungle near the river. The man was only half conscious, sitting on the ground with his back against a tree. His head was leaning back and inch-long worms were crawling out of his closed eyes.)

The doctors did what they could to treat this catalog of disease. Ashton brought what medicine was available, morphine mostly. He ran out of paregoric, the treatment for dysentery, his second or third day on-site and tried homemade remedies: riverbank clay mixed with water and decanted into a silt the men could swallow, and spoonfuls of powdered charcoal ground from burned boxwood, a treatment that left most of the detail black faced from their noses to their chins.

The weak were too weak, "even [to] feed themselves," and with "the flies, bugs and leeches . . . legion," Ashton, Brown, and the corpsmen spent their days circulating among the men on the rocks and under the tarp "fanning away the bugs" that would "congregate on the skin," inflicting "multiple bites that would cause ulcerations, especially on the cheeks and foreheads." Their "uncontrolled diarrhea" compounded the problem, and the doctors and corpsmen were "constantly" dragging men to the river and "cleaning and bathing them."

Watching all this, the Japanese conferred a kind of unofficial authority on the doctor. The detail's American commander, Captain Henry Pierce, did not have Ashton's moxie, and his second in command, Lieutenant Thomas Rhodes, had been caught stealing food from their stockpile and the men despised and shunned him. Into the void stepped Ashton. "Few of the guards on the road job seemed hateful or vicious" to him. Instead he saw them as simply ignorant and inept. At first he tried arguing with them. Couldn't they see that if they treated the men better, they'd get more out of them? When that didn't work he took to haranguing them, standing on the rock bar and shouting tirades upstream toward their camp.

He also treated a few of their soldiers for diarrhea and became friendly with one of them, a *hohei* who apparently had been distributing *okurimono*. One day Ashton noticed the man missing from the site and asked after him. The soldier was *byōki byōin* (sick in hospital) in Calauag, and the guards asked Ashton if he would go there and look at the man.

> It was a ramshackle barn where fifteen Japanese soldiers lay on the ground on rice straw, some shivering with malaria, some with diarrhea . . . A couple even had my charcoal on their chins . . . [No doctors or orderlies were around.] They prepared their own food or friends brought it to them. Otherwise they got nothing. I had occasion to ruminate on the sort of help or consideration [we could expect] from people who cared for their own in that manner.

After that, the Japanese took to calling Ashton *shōsa*, "Major," instead of the captain he was, and made him a kind of honorary noncommissioned officer in their unit. Every morning at dawn, however, Ashton reverted to being their antagonist, "the fly in their rice," as he liked to think of himself, holding back as many sick men as possible from the job site.

In the weeks that followed, the death rate increased—three, four, five men a day.

> The stronger men became weaker and several startling cases of sudden death occurred even in the strongest when attacked by dysentery which we could not prevent . . . Our graveyard was growing by leaps and bounds at the edge of the clearing. Most of the men died in black face, and their hats and rags, taken to be washed as best we could without soap, were given to survivors. We had no shrouds for the emaciated corpses covered with bug bites and leech ulcers . . . I said or thought a few words for each man as his last rites.

SOME MEN WENT INSANE. The detail's executive officer, Captain Jerry Gonzales of Magdalena, New Mexico, spent a whole day trying to put both his shoes on the same foot. (He died June 19, and his men, out of respect, buried him in uniform, the only man so interred.) Another soldier—(Hatten, some of the men called him)—developed an obsession with his mess kit. Every morning he'd become angry at his breakfast and beat his tin canteen cup into a lump, then he would spend the rest of the day banging it back into shape again.

Steve Kramerich was crazy and knew it. Sick with cerebral malaria, he'd been assigned a spot under the hospital tarp. One afternoon he dreamed he had amnesia. "This is horrible," he said to himself in his dream, and he awoke with his heart pounding. When he looked around, he saw some dirty men in ragged clothes sitting nearby cooking something. Who were these men, he wondered, and why were they sitting in the open around a campfire? And all at once he realized that his dream was no dream at all.

Steve Kramerich, an army signal corpsman from Lebanon, Pennsylvania, could not remember who he was. He wandered over to the circle of men, asked what they were doing. (Maybe they knew him, he thought.)[7]

"We're fixing a little chow," one of them said.

He stood there for a while, hoping to hear something that would jog his memory, make him remember his name.

The next morning, still amnesic, he found himself walking through the camp and came upon a man in uniform, holding a long rifle. What a strange-looking fellow, Steve Kramerich thought, and he ambled up to the man and introduced himself.

"And who are you?" Kramerich asked.

The man holding the rifle looked annoyed, barked something unintelligible, and motioned for Steve Kramerich to go away.

"But I don't know you," Steve Kramerich said.

The man was getting irritated now, shaking his rifle at him.

Steve Kramerich said to himself, "This man has a gun. I better not do anything foolish." And he tootled away, more befuddled than before.

BY THE MIDDLE OF JULY Ben Steele was spending all day in his lean-to at the edge of the rock bank. His malaria was so advanced he was having daily attacks. "Each one is tearing me down a little bit more," he thought. "I'm getting weaker every day."

The week before, digging on a hillside barefoot and in a G-string, he had stepped on a sharp stick. The point punctured the ball of his foot, and within twenty-four hours the foot became infected. The infection spread up his leg, which started to swell. Blood poisoning, Ashton told him.

On top of all this he was suffering from beriberi and the painful edema that comes with it. His ankles were swollen and grotesque, "as big as melons," he thought. He could no longer stand and had to depend on Sergeant Russell for almost everything.

Through it all, he had struggled to keep his spirits up. A few days after they'd arrived at the rock bar and learned they'd be living without shelter, he told himself, "The type of life I've lived, dealing with the elements, I think that's going to help me take care of myself here." He thought about the year he'd worked in the Big Hole, how the crew had slept on a hillside in the rain for days that spring with nothing but their bedrolls for cover, shivering at night and working "sopping wet" during the day, making the best of it. But a rainstorm in a Montana mountain valley was like a sprinkle set against the massive monsoons that rolled in from the South China Sea and enveloped the thick jungle of the Bicol peninsula. At home on the prairie, he might best the elements, but here at the end of the world, sleeping on rocks, he was no match for nature and knew it.

At first he called on God for help. Every day he prayed for deliverance: Please, God, he would say, let this work detail be over before they all died. And he begged the Almighty to show him how to continue, how to survive. Then the beriberi crippled him and he gave up praying and looking to heaven for help.

He thought, "After going through the battle, the march, O'Donnell, now this? We're just a bunch of guys that nobody gives a shit about. We've been let down by everybody—God, our country. All those promises, nothing happened. We've been sacrificed."

He didn't believe in anything anymore. He'd lost all hope of ever leaving the river and the rock bar. He thought, "I'm about as low as you can get without being six feet under."

Every day he could feel himself failing some more. He was so sick and wretched, he thought, "I don't care whether I live or die. I just don't give a damn."

He wasn't afraid and he wasn't angry. He was dying. And he wondered, "How soon? How soon?"

THEY'D REACHED THE END. After eight weeks at the site, on or around July 25, Paul Ashton told the Japanese that no one was able to work.

None of the men who remained were "fit for duty" and the total census of the working party had shrunk to twenty, including the two corpsmen and myself. Of the remaining seventeen, at least seven were moribund. [Everyone] was entirely depleted by the multiple diseases that consumed them. Dysentery had dehydrated them, removing essential chemicals and fluids; malaria with chills and fever had thinned their blood, turning the urine to black water. Their bellies were bloated, yet their extremities thin. Their wizened faces gave them an appearance of advanced age. The far-off lack of focus in their sunken eyes (as a myriad of flies walked drunkenly searching between the parted lips and eyelids, and upon the mosquito-ulcerated cheek bones) revealed their merciful preoccupation with the beat of some other drummer.

The Japanese told Ashton to get his men ready for transport to Manila the next day.

BEN STEELE was half gone. Maybe he heard the news, maybe he didn't. He was delirious. All he could think about was getting a drink. Where was Russell, where was the sergeant? Never mind. He pulled himself slowly across the rock bar to the river and lowered his face into the water.

MEANWHILE the Japanese were telling Ashton that they refused to transport seven men who were lying unconscious under the hospital tarp. Space was tight, the guards said. No point carrying men who wouldn't make it. Ashton knew better than to argue. He knelt down among the comatose men and lingered for a long time.

The Japanese were screaming at him to "Speedo! Speedo!" but Ashton ignored them. He was going to give his patients one last treatment, and he was not going to be rushed.

As a medical student in San Francisco, he'd studied with a professor who had given large injections of morphine to patients with terminal tuberculosis. "G.O.M.," the professor called the treatment, "God's Own Medicine."

Ashton reached into his medical bag and took out a syringe. He filled it with God's Own Medicine, then went from man to man, giving each a shot. ("They were yet alive," he noted, "but quite oblivious to what was being done to them.") He was not going "to leave them . . . without water or help," he told himself, and he was not going to leave them "for the ants to eat" either.[8]

SIXTY-THREE MEN had been buried at the site and six had disappeared during an escape. A hundred and twenty-four men had been returned to the Bilibid Prison hospital on two earlier trips; thirty of these had died en route or in the hospital. Out of the original detail of three hundred, nearly one-third, ninety-nine men, were dead.

At 5:45 p.m. on Tuesday, July 28, trucks carrying 107 American prisoners of war and one corpse—Oliphant, James L., Sergeant, U.S. Army, 38912574—rolled into the courtyard at Manila's Bilibid Prison.

Waiting for them were Navy doctors and corpsmen. Commander Thomas H. Hayes, Bilibid's chief surgeon, noted their arrival in his diary:

Eight big truck loads arrived. It was the last of the [work detail] and the medical officer came with them. Two lasted long enough for us to lay them out on stretchers under a mango tree where they immediately expired. Another dozen in extremis we laid out on the ground until the Japs would release them to us for bedding down. The rest—horrible walking creatures—like Haitian Zombies, the living dead—dirty, bewhiskered, hollow cheeked, sunken eyes, some too weak to stand. Others still up on their pins, fighting to the last ditch to carry their few remaining articles . . . Pitiful broken human hulks."[9]

Pharmacist's mate Clarence Shearer, standing nearby, started to catalog their condition: "All very pitiful . . . suffering from Malaria, dysentery, beri-beri, pellagra, and general starvation . . . With [our] food issue [here at the hospital] scarcely more than sufficient to prevent starvations; with the supply of anti-dysentery and anti-malarial preparations meager and uncertain, it is going to prove extremely difficult to save the majority of these individuals."[10]

TEN

BILIBID PRISON was a sprawling seventeen-acre quadrangle (a penitentiary the size of five city blocks) in the center of Manila on the north bank of the Pasig River. Behind its high stone walls, topped with barbed wire, were long one-story cell blocks and barred dormitories radiating out from a central rotunda and watchtower like spokes from the hub of a wheel. It was an ancient prison, built by the Spanish in 1865, and neither the Americans nor the government of the Philippine Commonwealth had maintained it. Most convicts were being transferred to a new jail in a suburb south of the city, and many of the crumbling cell blocks and ramshackle barracks were being used as temporary office and storage spaces for several departments of the Philippine government.

The Japanese quickly returned the place to a lockup. They used one part of the old adobe and concrete prison as an overnight staging center for prisoners in transit between the many forced labor sites in the islands. Another part of the prison housed disciplinary prisoners (so-called hard cases). A third part was given over to administrative offices and barracks for the Japanese guards. The rest of the old jail, roughly half the compound, was a central hospital for all prisoners of war in the islands, a place, putatively at least, where the sickest men could be sent to get well, which is to say, to keep from dying.

Patients and their doctors lived in nine of the cell blocks. They also occupied several L-shaped dormitories set in each corner of the compound. Once upon a time all the buildings had been whitewashed; now the façades were gray and ocher and streaked with soot and grime. The roofs leaked, most of the pipes and electrical fixtures had been purloined by the locals, and almost everything else inside the crumbling prison was rusted and rotting or in disrepair.

Not long after surrender, the Japanese moved a group of American Army doctors into the derelict compound but, overwhelmed by the number of patients, the doctors mostly warehoused the sick instead of trying to treat them. Then in early July 1942, the Japanese brought in a group of Navy doctors and corpsmen led by Commander Lea B. "Pappy" Sartin and his chief of surgery, Lieutenant Commander Thomas H. Hayes. Sartin, now the senior man, took a look around at the "filthy and degrading hell hole" and immediately ordered his 26 doctors, 11 dentists, and 165 corpsmen, pharmacist's mates, and orderlies to scrub it down and effect repairs. The Navy men took inventory of the medicine and equipment they had been able to salvage from the places where they'd been captured, infirmaries in and around Manila and the hospital on Corregidor, then they established wards, treatment rooms, and a space for surgery.[1]

Pappy Sartin set down the rules, but Hayes was the hospital's real ramrod. A day or two after he arrived, he visited each ward to see what was waiting for him.

[*Hayes, "Notebook," July 4, 1942*] A walk thru the length of the wards, each holding about eighty cadaverous animals that once were men, is one of the most desperate, heartrending sights conceivable . . . At best many must die. In this prison the war is not over.[2]

Hayes was impatient and impolitic ("outspoken" and "aggressive" in official reports), but he was such a good doctor and medical administrator that he thrived at every post ashore or at sea. He grew up by the ocean, the Tidewater region of Virginia, and after graduating from George Washington University Medical School, he joined the Navy and was commissioned in 1924. By May 1941, he was a lieutenant commander, the chief surgeon at the U.S. Naval Hospital, Cañacao, Philippine islands, Cavite Naval Base, eight miles from the capital. On December 10, 1941, the first day of air raids that would soon destroy the base, Tom Hayes proved to be the right man at a critical moment. He kept three operating teams working continuously, treating more than 1,330 casualties, then, under fire, he helped organize the evacuation of the hospital and move the wounded to dispensaries in Manila. On December 22, as the Japanese were coming ashore at Lingayen Gulf, Hayes was named chief surgeon to the 4th Marine Regiment, the unit defending the beaches of Corregidor. When the island fortress surrendered in May, Hayes ordered his doctors and corpsmen to stuff their pockets with gauze, bandages, tape, bottles of medicine, surgical instruments, medical records, anything of medical utility they could take with them into prison camp. What was left they secreted under the blankets of the stretcher cases—supplies that made the hospital in Bilibid more than just another prison camp charnel house.[3]

On July 28 Hayes happened to be in the prison yard as a long line of trucks pulled into the compound, a convoy carrying Dalton Russell, Louis Kolger, Irwin Scott, Preston Hubbard, Ken Calvit, Ben Steele, and a hundred and one other "heavy sick," as they were labeled, human wrecks from the miserable jungle work detail at Tayabas Road.

> I stood in that yard and just looked. All the bitterness and the hate that has kindled and built up in me in these past two months of captivity seemed to well up within me at that moment. At no one other moment in my life have I ever hated with the intensity of that moment. And then again I swore and vowed that I would never be satisfied nor content on earth until every vestige of Nippon was destroyed—until I have personally known the feel of ramming a bayonet into their guts, starving them, looting them of all they hold dear . . . Until I die, every one of them is my avowed eternal enemy. Goddamn 'em.[4]

THE TRIP from Tayabas Road had been long and rough, a day's travel across bad roads. When a truck hit a rut or pothole, the men in back would bounce and moan, and Ben Steele, delirious, would come to for a moment and think, "I'm all but dead."

Now, in the prison yard, someone was slipping arms under him, lifting him up, setting him down on a stretcher.

How did he feel? one of his bearers asked. He would be okay now, they said. They'd take care of him.

They carried him across an open area and into a building. The first thing he thought was, "I have a roof over my head."

They set the stretcher by a wall, spread a cotton pad on the concrete floor, rolled him onto it.

"How about some soup?" one of the corpsmen asked.

The soup tasted good.

"Thank you," Ben Steele said. "Thank you."

Then he began to weep.

HIS FALCIPARUM MALARIA (the worst form of the disease) had turned the blood in his brain to sludge, and he was unconscious for long periods of time. His beriberi was advancing rapidly—his ankles were swollen to the size of melons and the edema had climbed up his legs and into his scrotum. The wound in his right foot that had given him blood poisoning was suppurating, and doctors thought they detected the first signs of gangrene. (During a moment of lucidity, he was sure he heard one of the them say, "You could lose that leg, you know? You hear, soldier?") His lungs were gurgling and his temperature was spiking, sure signs of bronchial pneumonia. He still had dysentery, and he was jaundiced, a liver infection, doctors said.

Some days he knew he was alive, some days not. On one such day a priest appeared, Father William T. Cummings, a short, plucky Maryknoll brother who had served his order in the Philippines before the war and, after the Japanese attacked, had volunteered for service in the army.

Father Cummings opened his Mass kit, took out a prayer book, a rosary, a tin of holy oil. He dipped his thumb in the oil, made the sign of the cross on Ben Steele's eyes, ears, nose, and mouth.

"Through this holy anointing, may the Lord forgive you whatever sins you have committed . . . Amen."

Ben Steele lay very still. His eyes were closed, his senses swimming, but he could hear the voice and he could recognize the prayer, the last rites. (Along the death march and later in Zero Ward at O'Donnell, he'd watched priests kneel at other men's sides and absolve them of their sins before death released them from their misery.) Now he felt neither joy nor fear, just sick, heavy sick, and tired.

"I'm ready," he thought.

He survived the week. His edema got worse, though. He was hideously swollen now. Then he went into a coma again, and Cummings returned with his rosary and tin of holy oil.

"Okay, Ben," the priest said, "why don't we try this again."

The other men in the ward, watching all this, took Ben Steele's moaning and babbling as death throes. And after the priest left, a few of them crawled over to where Ben Steele lay and began to divvy up his kit—his web belt, mess gear, canteen, and the crackers an orderly had set at his side.

The next morning Ben Steele was still breathing. The day after that he was able to sit propped up. Now he could look around a bit, get a sense of place, check his pitiful few belongings.

"You goddamn bastards!"

Where the hell was his gear?

"Give me my stuff back. Damn you guys. You wait till a man gets buried before you do that."

TO THE MEN who had been on the death march, then in O'Donnell, then on a grueling work detail, the gray stone walls of Bilibid Prison seemed warm and enfolding.

The doctors and orderlies, however, hated the place. The circumstances of their capture and early custody had not been nearly as harsh as that of the patients. Accustomed to the white, antiseptic chambers of a hospital, the navy men were appalled by the sooty squalor of Bilibid.

Every morning when he opened his eyes and was "confronted by four walls and faced with another dismal day as a prisoner of war," Stanley Smith, a dentist from Sandwich, Illinois, felt the shock of confinement. To Smith and Tom Hayes and the other medicos, Bilibid was a Bastille, a melancholy tomb.[5]

> [*Hayes, "Notebook," July 30*] All day rain. Raw damp & cold. Held a [leadership] council meeting tonight [with five senior doctors]. Things look a little desperate. Information from the outside plainly indicates [extra] food becoming almost unobtainable . . . There isn't a chance in a million of any Red Cross Relief ship or any thing of that kind . . . There is every reason to believe that as far as we are concerned, our country has scratched us off the list and charged us up to loss.[6]

Every day at 6:00 a.m. the Japanese rang an old bell in one of the guard towers, summoning the men for *tenko*, roll call, and those who could walk stood formation outside their wards, while the invalids were counted where they lay. When the count was correct—and it always took the mistrustful guards many *bangō* (count-offs) to get the tally right—the bell would ring again, and everyone would return to quarters and wait there for breakfast. Around seven o'clock, one man from each ward

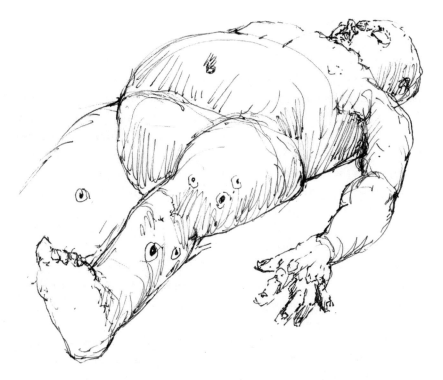

would go to the central galley and return with a five-gallon can of *lugao*,
rice gruel, to distribute equally among patients, doctors, and staff. Then,
around eight, the doctors would begin rounds, two or three doctors to a
ward, wards crowded with eighty to a hundred men, some on pads on
the concrete floor, others on old iron-and-spring cots or beds cobbled
together from scraps of wood.

Here, for example, on a thin cotton pad on the concrete floor in
Ward 11, a dim prison dormitory, is Army Air Corps Private Benjamin C. Steele, serial number 190-18-989. The patient presents symptoms of multiple infectious diseases, indications of starvation, and an
infected puncture wound of the right instep. His pulse is 110, irregular
and thready; his blood pressure is 95/50 but difficult to hear because of
extensive edema; he has a fever of 103°. He is often not oriented to time
or place and must be forced to eat. His treatment protocol involves quinine for the malaria, carbasone and emetine and liquids for the dysentery, sulfa powder for the foot infection and incipient gangrene, and
complete bed rest for his jaundice and pneumonia. A treatment plan
with one notable omission: it did not address the most serious and easily

treated of Ben Steele's maladies, the one turning him into a fleshy elephantine grotesque, beriberi.

Diseases born of starvation respond to a simple cure; give a swollen or emaciated starveling the food he needs and his improvement will be marked and dramatic. That knowledge, that ancient and obvious medical certainty, left the prisoner-doctors of Bilibid frustrated and depressed. For want of a few vitamins and minerals, simple sustenance, men were dying. Every week a burial detail quarried fresh graves in the boneyard by the back wall. And in their early months in prison there was little that Pappy Sartin, Tom Hayes, or the other forty clinicians at Bilibid could do to stop the digging.

[*Hayes, "Notebook," August 24*] Our dysenteries and beriberis still die. We have improved the general mass of the sick but even at best, with our supplementary [food bought from merchants at the gate] we are not able to produce a planned ration. None of us will ever be really well.[7]

Beriberi is a disease of the nervous system and heart caused by a thiamine (vitamin B_1) deficiency. There are two forms of the disease. Dry beriberi affects the nerves and the extremities, particularly feet and legs, and some of the men in Bilibid were in so much pain they could not walk or even stand. Wet beriberi weakens the heart, affecting circulation and blood pressure. Without thiamine, the body's cells begin to break down and the walls of the arteries and veins grow so weak and porous they allow pints of fluid to leach into the surrounding tissue and body cavity, turning a man into a bloated hulk. The fluid in turn puts pressure on the body's organs, and when they start to fail, death is sure to follow.

Ben Steele looked awful. The fluid in his body had pooled everywhere. The swelling that had started in his feet and spread to his ankles, legs, scrotum, and abdomen finally reached his chest and head. His body was so bloated (the term is "anasarca"), that his skin looked like the surface of an overinflated balloon—smooth, shiny, stretched hideously tight. Sometimes the liquid in his head would pool on one side of his face and he'd wake looking deformed, his eye sockets so swollen he'd have to hold an eye open with one hand so he could see to eat with the other hand.

Looking himself over, he thought he weighed three hundred pounds. He was so misshapen it was impossible for him to do anything but lie flat or sit propped up against the stone wall. There were many nights when he could hear the fluid sloshing around in his chest and he was afraid his heart would drown. Many days he was so sick he couldn't eat, couldn't do anything for himself, really, and since the corpsmen and orderlies were always too busy to tend an invalid properly, his doctor on Ward 11, Lieutenant Gordon K. Lambert, assigned an ambulatory patient in the ward—a man with his own troubles—to help him.

STEVE KRAMERICH was as crazy as ever. He came into Bilibid from Tayabas Road with severe cerebral malaria. The daily doses of quinine he was taking had done little so far to stop the amnesic spells and the bizarre behavior that had started on the rocks by the river. His doctors recognized his pathology right away. His comrades, meanwhile, thought him just plain loony.[8]

One day on Ward 11, for example, he spiked a fever of 105°, and the corpsmen dragged him into a cold shower to lower his temperature. He was addled and woozy, and as he stood in the shower stall watching the water circle the drain at his feet, he got the idea he was being sucked down into city's sewer system. And he started to scream.

In the weeks that followed, he suffered one malarial delusion after another. One day he might be Jesus Christ standing in an open window, arms outstretched, shouting to heaven, "Father, forgive them for they know not what they do." The next day he might see himself as a fallen angel exploring the precincts of hell. He was sure Bilibid was hades, he told his bunkmates, because the clock on the central guard tower, long since broken, of course, never changed time. "Forever and ever," Steve Kramerich kept mumbling as he stared at the clock. "Forever and ever."

For a while Dr. Lambert thought that intravenous quinine might stop Steve Kramerich's delusions, but the man was still "nuttier than a fruitcake," as his comrades liked to say, so Dr. Lambert took Steve into the compound for a stroll and a talking cure. Steve talked and Lambert took notes.

He was still seeing visions, he said, still hearing voices—the wards as circles of hell, the rain on the roof as a chorus of the damned. Then he accused the doctor of being Satan in disguise, said he was keeping him alive just to torture him.

The doctor had heard enough. "Soldier, you need a job," he told Steve Kramerich, something to occupy the mind, and he ordered him to work as a corpsman's assistant on Ward 11, work with one particular patient, empty the invalid's bedpan, fetch the man's food, chat with the poor fellow, a patient named Ben Steele.

[*Hayes, "Notebook," August 25*] To gather round a lugao bucket and dip out your ration with a wooden stick, to drink from a hollowed-out coconut shell a watery slop made from a river weed and some tough gourds, to squat about a fire with some dozen practically naked comrades and beat mongo beans or boil a tenth run of coffee in a blackened tin can—you can't do these things day in and day out, with nothing to look forward to tomorrow except this mud and heat and flies and stink, half-starved and yet not wanting the stuff that comes to fill the emptiness of your guts, you can't do this and then snap back into a world that couldn't ever believe that this could happen to us.[9]

Lunch was at noon, dinner at six, rice and rice, just like breakfast. The Japanese insisted they were supplying the prison with enough raw grain to yield two cups of cooked rice for each man every day, but the daily ration was usually less, closer to ten or twelve ounces. Other than carbohydrates, rice has few nutrients. Filler food, for the most part.

The prisoners got the worst grade of rice, the dregs of each shipment. The grains were often spoiled or moldy, each sack laced with worms, weevils, small rocks, dirt, rat droppings. Everything, of course, went in the pot. There were men who couldn't stomach the worms. They'd sit hunched over their ration, meticulously culling them out, white worms about as long as a finger joint, with two tiny black spots near the head. Paul Reuter ate it all, the whole squiggling mush, but he always took a moment to flick off the worms on the surface. Just couldn't look 'em in those two black eyes before they went down.

The rice tasted "moldy and musty," "dirty and soggy," "like raw dough," "like wallpaper paste," "like dishwater." Some men found it so vile they had to "choke it down." To others it tasted like nothing, a meal that left the American palate sour and unsatisfied. Still, they ate every ounce. Especially the men from O'Donnell and work details. They licked their cups clean, then checked in the dirt at their feet for any grains that might have dropped there.

Twice a day the cooks served soup, which is to say hot water with a bit of meat ("a sliver," "a ribbon," "a thread") or a tiny piece of fish (always rotten) and a "vegetable," usually worthless thistle, muddy water lilies from the nearby Pasig River, or other weeds of unknown origin. Almost every day the men found scraps of garbage in the soup, the tops of carrots or camotes or radishes, refuse from a restaurant or Japanese army mess.

Pappy Sartin and his doctors tried to supplement this subsistence ration with extra food from local merchants. (The doctors pooled the little money they'd smuggled into prison with the $10 to $12 a month the enemy paid them for "working" in the hospital.) Some of this fund went to set up a special diet kitchen for the heavy sick that procured foods high in protein or other nutrients—peanuts, duck eggs, most of all, mongo beans. Mongo beans, about the size of small lentils, were cheap, ubiquitous, high in thiamine. Some men ate them raw or stewed or let them soak in a wet towel to sprout, then boiled them and served them over rice. Every ward had a mongo bean garden, tins and jars and buckets growing the beans.

> [*Hayes, "Notebook"*] This mongo bean is a life saver to us and as long as we can get them we can stomach the rice and eat a sustaining quantity as well as acquire a vitamin intake of which we are so much in need. We buy these beans at 45 centavos a cup (canteen), about one centavo's worth [in prewar prices]. But they go a long ways and so long as I live I will always attribute my survival to this lowly bean.[10]

Everyone was hungry all the time. Men picked through the garbage outside the galley for scraps—scraps of scraps, really. They chased after the dogs, cats, snakes, and rats that wandered into the compound. The Catholic chaplains had contacts outside the walls who from time to time would smuggle in peanuts and chunks of crude horse sugar, and for a while an unusual number of Bilibid's patients expressed an interest in converting to the Church of Rome. "Son," Father John E. Duffy told a would-be catechumen, "you don't want to be a Catholic. You're just hungry."[11]

They dreamed about food, dwelt on it night and day. Men formed "food clubs" to trade recipes—Brandy Pottage, Virginia Brunswick Stew, French Apple Pie—or talked about their favorite restaurants.[12]

"Prison life goes on," Tom Hayes often wrote. "Mongo [beans] night & morning, lugao, dry rice, & watery soup . . . days of scratching for existence, groups gathered about open fires with improvised utensils fashioned from tin cans, gasoline tins, pieces of wire, parts of galvanized roofing, cooking up odd concoctions of all possible edible combinations of anything edible and available . . . At night one lies courting sleep and looks at the reflection on the stony floors of the cold black bars that stand between us and the moon."[13]

BY NOVEMBER 1942, Ben Steele was doing better. He was still sick with malaria, beriberi, dysentery, and jaundice, but after three months in Bilibid he seemed on the mend. The spike of protein in a duck egg Dr. Lambert had given him had activated his kidneys, and the terrible swelling that had distorted his body had slowed. He was still an invalid, but against all odds and his doctors' expectations, he had survived. As they say in Montana, he'd been near enough to hell to smell the smoke and was happier than a kid pulling on a dog's ears, just to be breathing.

Meanwhile, he'd made a new friend, a landsman, or as close to one as Ben Steele would find in Bilibid, a man named Merrill Lee. Raised on a ranch in Lincoln County, Nevada, Lee too had been a working cowboy. A double hernia had landed him in Bilibid's hospital, and since the Air Corps had trained him as a cook, the doctors put him to work in Bilibid's galley. It was a good job—the cooks always looked suspiciously healthier than the rest of the prison's company—and Merrill Lee was hoping to finish the war in Bilibid, whenever the war was going to finish.

The two men met by chance. Lee had gone to Ward 11 in search of a doctor, and glancing around the room, his eye happened to fall on one of the patients. The man was swollen with wet beriberi, and he was lying next to a filthy old mattress, scratching lines on the floor with a chunk of charcoal.

Lee, curious, wandered over to take a look, and there, taking shape on the floor, was the drawing of a cowboy—the broad-brimmed hat, the boots, the bowed legs, a corral, a snubbing post, two horses.

"Damn!" Lee said to himself. "That's my life."

"Hey there, I'm Merrill Lee."

The man on the floor looked up. "Oh yeah, I'm Ben Steele."

"Where you from, Ben Steele?"

"Montana, out the Bull Mountains way, north of Billings."

"Well, I'm from Panaca, Nevada, Lincoln County. And what you're drawing there, that was my life. That's what I'm living for, to get back to that kind of life."

It was like two men meeting on the open range, two solitary horse-men coming upon each other in the middle of nowhere after days or weeks riding the benches and badlands and waves of buffalo grass alone.

"What kind of outfit you got?" Merrill Lee asked.

"Well," Ben Steele said, "the Old Man used to run about three hundred head on six sections."

"Funny thing," Lee said. "I was up in Montana working in Yellowstone Park just before the war."

"By God, that's just down the road," Ben Steele said.

Nearly every day thereafter, Merrill Lee visited Ward 11. And every day he brought Ben Steele a canteen cup brimming with stewed mongo beans and a nice crust of burned rice as a side dish.

Lee would sit down on the mattress while Ben finished the snack, then he'd watch Ben draw, watch him for hours and hours, day after day. Sometimes, in the torpor of a tropical afternoon, Merrill Lee would get drowsy, and he would lie back on Ben Steele's mattress and shut his eyes and lose himself among the sorrels and bays, corrals and snubbing posts.

BEN STEELE'S LIFE as an artist began in the dark interstices of his disease, the periods of waking rest when he was left to lie on an old and moldy mattress on the concrete floor of Ward 11. He'd never felt so helpless, useless, and low. Propped up slightly against a gray adobe wall, he spent most of the day staring at his bloated limbs and balloon of a body.

The more he took stock of himself, the mound of flesh he'd become, the more he thought about his life, the life he'd lived at Hawk Creek and in Billings. He kept drifting back to that day in the studio when the great Will James invited him in and started drawing. He knew that James was largely self-taught, and as he lay on the thin mattress on the floor day after day, Ben Steele wondered whether he too had the talent to make magic. After a while, he could imagine himself drawing, and he started drawing horses in his head. Then, sometime in early November, when he began to lose some of his aqueous bulk, he dragged himself across the floor to the ward's stove and grabbed a burned stick from the woodpile and started to scratch on the concrete floor.

His scratches didn't look like much at first, just rough black lines on the gray concrete. This drawing business was difficult, more to it than he'd thought. "I have to make something that looks like something," he told himself. Finally, after weeks of scratching, a memory started to take shape—a horse straining against a halter in a corral.

Every day after that, after *bangō* and breakfast, he would settle down to draw. His new friend Merrill Lee started bringing him paper, old government record sheets the cooks were using as kindling for their fires. Some of his bunkmates brought him pencil stubs and twigs of charcoal. He drew in the morning, he drew in the afternoon, he drew under the yellow lights. Horses, cows, sheep, ranch buildings, his beloved hills at Hawk Creek. He sketched the contours of the land, the prairie architecture, the animals and objects of his youth, but since he knew nothing of the geometry of composition, his renderings were all surface, pictures on one plane with animals and men that looked more like cutouts, paper dolls, than the animated figures he'd watched Will James create.

One day, one of the prisoners who occasionally wandered over to watch (the "artist" from Montana had become something of an attraction) started going on about "angles" and "edges" and "lines of convergence." Ben Steele asked the man what he was talking about. "Perspective," the man said. He was an engineer, and like all engineers he'd been trained as a draftsman. Every sketch, he said, needed depth and distance, and the way to create the feeling of depth was to find a drawing's "vanishing point."

Okay, vanishing point. What was that?

By mid-December Ben Steele was able to stand and take a few steps. Pretty soon he could make his way across the compound to the ward where the engineers slept. Every few days he took another lesson in "picture planes" and "eye level." His teachers were patient. They explained that all the lines in a sketch should run to a point of convergence, the point where the lines vanish from sight. Vanishing point, they told him, was the secret to creating perspective, and perspective was the magic he was looking for.

He practiced every day. One day, sitting cross-legged on his new bunk, a sleeping platform fashioned from scraps of wood, he decided to draw the interior of Ward 11. The ward was an L-shaped building with plenty of angles and vanishing points. He drew them all, every pillar, crossbeam, joist, rafter, and brace. And afterward, sitting back and looking at what he'd wrought, he thought, "Hell, everything worked! Worked beautifully." It was like, well, "a revelation."

He kept at it, one sketch after another, convinced that it was art (along with a timely duck egg, many cups of mongo beans, and doses of quinine, carbasone, emetine, and sulfa powder) that had saved him. Here, he thought, was "a way to put all this other misery aside." All he had to do was take up a pencil and start to draw, draw his way around his disease, past the guards, over the wall, and across an ocean home.

[*Hayes, "Notebook," December 6*] Some lousy rumors got abroad today— of no value whatsoever. Usual hooey . . . They are the same rumors [we] have heard a dozen times before, and each time proven childish banter. But each time hope springs in the human breast that "this time, it may be right."[14]

"The hope of ultimate release" is "part of the will to live," wrote Terrence Des Pres, a chronicler of survival. And every day in Bilibid, every single day, this particular hope got a boost from rumor.[15]

Every prison, barbed-wire pen, and work site in the islands had a rumor mill. The grist for these grinders came from any number of radios hidden in Filipino homes and tuned either to KGEI in San Francisco or other distant English-language stations. Civilians with news would throw messages wrapped around rocks over Bilibid's outer wall. Merchants allowed to trade with the prisoners, Filipino clergy visiting Bilibid, and other interlopers also passed along the latest bruit and buzz. Occasionally this "news" had some truth to it, but the mongers in Bilibid who purveyed scuttlebutt could not resist the temptation to embellish it. Many men, desperate for the least bit of light, hung on every word of this nonsense. Tom Hayes, Bilibid's resident cynic, listened and laughed.

The dope is "Big things to happen in Luzon in a matter of hours," implying arrival of an American Force. Of course that is plain unadulterated hooey . . . To bed before I begin to think.

Scuttlebutt began to flow about hearing bombings about midnight last night . . . If the [rumors] keep on as they have in the past few days they will have MacArthur calling up from the Manila Hotel and inviting us to lunch in about a week.

The last wild rumor of the day comes in that Wall Street bets 2 to 1 the war will end in November, Lloyd['s of London] bets 29 to 1 it will end in December.

Gobs of rumors . . . Formosa has fallen and Hirohito is asking Roosevelt to permit Tokyo to be an open city. My! My! [Or] Hirohito has requested that Roosevelt keep Tokyo an open city and Roosevelt is supposed to have replied "Get out of Manila."[16]

Just beyond their ken, of course, the actualities of war were playing out across two oceans. For the first six months of 1942, the Tripartite Pact countries, Germany, Italy, and Japan, the so-called Axis powers, had pushed the Allies, the Americans, British, French, and Dutch, off their colonial possessions and out of their overseas bases. Allied losses were heavy: 894 ships sunk and more than 192,600 American, British, and Dutch soldiers, sailors, marines, and airmen captured (along with at least another 100,000 native troops under their command).

Then, in May, as General Wainwright was surrendering to the Japanese on Corregidor, the American Navy, steaming in the waters between Australia and New Guinea, won a strategic victory at the battle of the Coral Sea, the first serious challenge to Japanese advances in the Pacific. In Europe, meanwhile, the British increased their air raids over Germany, and a thousand Royal Air Force bombers raided Cologne.

In June, Germany and the Axis rolled over the British in North Africa, but in the Pacific at the sea battle of Midway, a tiny atoll held by the Americans, the American Pacific Fleet sank four Japanese aircraft carriers in a dramatic victory.

The next month the Japanese consolidated their position on New Guinea, but again the Americans were able to mount an offensive and bomb Japanese possessions in the Solomon Islands, including Guadalcanal.

In August, the Allies suffered a setback as six thousand British and Canadian troops tried to conduct a surprise raid on Dieppe in occupied France; half were slaughtered and the survivors were lucky to escape. Meanwhile, U.S. Marines in the Pacific landed on Guadalcanal, built an airfield, and held it.

The year ended with the Japanese being beaten and pushed back in the South Pacific. On New Guinea and Guadalcanal, *hohei* fell in great numbers.

[*Hayes, "Notebook," January 2, 1943*]. Thirty eight Jap bombers went over today. Couldn't tell from our site, of course, whether they were coming in or going out. Probably for the south. Cold in the early mornings now.

We stand bango long before day break . . . I am reminded that this is 1943, and as I recall, the year Mr. Churchill had decided upon as when Britain would make her offensive.

The greens, the water lilies and pechay [Chinese cabbage] are still shoveled out of a truck on delivery to our galley. And they still stink and are cluttered and mixed with egg shells and other debris that plainly tell its source as being some slop chute or hotel garbage barrel. It makes no difference if we refer to it as "greens in the garbage" or "garbage in the greens" it is still garbage, but they are still greens—and we eat it.[17]

They had been prisoners of war, most of them, for more than half a year now, and like all convicts across time, they had come to accept what Dostoevsky called the "drab, sour and sullen aspect" of life behind bars and barbed wire. They lived on hope because hope was all they had. And they sat around all day speculating about the date of their deliverance and composing anapestic epigrams to cheer themselves.[18]

We'll be free in '43
Mother's door in '44

Men lost hope, of course. In the squalor of prison life and throes of disease, a number of the sick just gave up. Irwin Scott could see it in their eyes, "dull eyes," he and other patients used to call it, eyes that went "blank."[19]

"It's like you can look right through them," Scotty thought, "and you know they are going to die."

So Scott and some of his comrades tried to cheer the cheerless, sit and talk with them, tell them anything—MacArthur has landed on Mindanao and will be in Manila in a week!—"all kinds of lies" just to get their comrades to continue. All the talk "seldom did a damn bit of good," however. Once a man had lost his will to live, he usually surrendered his life. "Three days," Scott discovered. "Every damn one of them dies in three days."

Friends never let friends die alone. Steve Kramerich's Air Corps buddy Kenny O'Donald was debilitated by dysentery and could not shake the disease. And when O'Donald died in the Isolation Ward, Kramerich was sitting at his side.

"He looks like a hide stretched over a skeleton," Steve Kramerich thought. "If his mother and father could see him, they would never stop crying."[20]

SOMETIMES camaraderie is based on compassion, one man seeing his suffering, or abject loneliness, in another.

Zoeth Skinner struck up a friendship with Bobby Robinson, an aging civilian who had been in the Philippines most of his adult life and was a patient with Skinner on Ward 1. Robinson had served during the Spanish-American War and had stayed in the islands, working as the manager at one of Manila's most famous gin mills, the Legaspi Landing. By 1941 he'd survived two Filipina wives, married a third, and had a handful of children of various ages. Despite nearing his dotage (some of the men guessed he was going on seventy), he reenlisted at the beginning of the war, reassumed his old rank as a first sergeant in the 31st Infantry, fought in the battle for Bataan, and made the march off the peninsula, the sixty-six-mile trek that killed men a third his age.[21]

Skinner liked and admired Robinson; with his gray grizzle and rimless eyeglasses, he looked somehow wise, authentic. Both men were classified as convalescents and had been assigned to light work sorting POW mail at Japanese headquarters. The headquarters was two blocks from the prison, and every morning, as the two walked the route with a guard, they saw Robinson's third wife standing at the curb outside the front gate, holding his youngest child high for him to see. Robinson always stopped to look before moving on, and every morning, Zoeth Skinner noticed steam on the old man's glasses and tears rolling down the old man's cheeks.

FOR MONTHS "the laity," as Tom Hayes liked to call the men on the wards, had been awaiting the arrival of mail from home and food packages from the International Red Cross. Patients working the docks (convalescents strong enough to do manual labor were drafted as stevedores) reported unloading pallets of cartons marked with the Red Cross logo and labeled "Prisoners Parcel" or "For American Prisoners of War." So where, the men wondered, had those packages got to?

Every occupying army has profited while doing its "duty," and some of the Americans in Bilibid knew that a certain amount of these "relief supplies" were going to end up in the pockets of Japanese soldiers or as goods on the local black market. And sure enough, in the early winter of 1942 some of the guards were seen smoking American cigarettes.

"It will be very interesting to see how much of [the shipment] we get," Hayes wrote in his secret notebooks. "Entire cases are taken by the guards at the pier and of course, every agency handling them gets their cut."[22]

Finally, a week after Christmas 1942, the eleven-pound boxes, along with some mail and medical supplies and vitamins, were distributed to the various work sites and prisoner of war pens throughout the islands, and since Bilibid was so close to the docks, the prisoners in the hospital were among the first to get the boxes.

Ben Steele was excited, the whole ward was, guys ripping open their packages, laughing and joking and spreading the contents on their bunks:

Biscuits, lunch, type C	8 oz. pkg.
Cheese	8 oz. pkg.
Chocolate, ration D	two 4 oz. bars.
Cigarettes, pkg. 20's	4 packs
Coffee concentrate	4 oz. tin
Corned Beef	12 oz. tin
Fruit, dried	15 oz. pkg.
Liver paste	6 oz. tin
Milk, whole, powdered	1 lb. tin
Oleomargarine	1 lb. tin
Orange concentrate	4 oz. tin
Pork luncheon meat	12 oz. tin
Salmon	8 oz. tin
Soap	two 2 oz. bars
Sugar	8 oz. pkg.[23]

Ben Steele grabbed a chocolate bar. He peeled the wrapper from the end, bit off a corner, and let the candy slowly roll around in his mouth. (Save the rest of the bar, he told himself. No telling when, or if, they'd get another package.)

Then he eyed the margarine. How long had it been since he'd tasted butter? He stuck his finger in the can, smeared a gob on a cracker. God, was that good!

Around him guys were swapping for their favorites.

"Anyone want to trade butter for some coffee?" Ben Steele asked.

And right away he had a taker.

"How about cigarettes?" he asked, "I'm giving cigarettes for spam."

Everyone knew that these few supplies would not last long. With some prudent self-rationing, they might stretch the contents several weeks and augment their regular daily ration, but after a month or so they would be right back to their cups of verminous rice, spoiled fish, vegetable peelings, and a handful of peanuts in the cup of sewer water they called soup.

Still, Ben Steele was happy. There were plenty of prisoners, Tom Hayes among them, who thought Bilibid a hell on earth, a place of "doubt, depression, disappointment, diversified disease, hunger, hate, heat, pestilence, poor prospects [and] pauperized prisoners."[24]

Not Ben Steele. He didn't mind the dank adobe and dim barracks, the foul emanations of his bedfellows, the clock whose hands never moved. He was doing all right. Most of his swelling was gone. The rest was just a matter of time. He was still weak, still sick, and he was hungry all the time—who the hell wasn't?—but, on balance, he thought, "Bilibid is the best damn prison I've been in so far." Roof over his head, wooden bunk, guards more annoying than anything else. And the doctors, the doctors had brought him back to life. Dr. Lambert still stopped by to check on him, chat with him. Kind of like a father. ("I think I will

always worship that man," he told himself.) All he had to do was get better, then live day to day until the day the war was over. Wait, that was the thing, just wait.[25]

ONE AFTERNOON in February 1943, Ben Steele was crossing the inner compound on his way to the galley to see Merrill Lee. For more than a month he'd been feeling well enough to get around and had slowly been exploring the half of the prison that served as the hospital. He'd visited a couple of the Air Corps men in other wards, taken a look at the prison store (such as it was with its handful of items—horse sugar, bananas, and a few peanuts—that no one could afford), looked in the library, and taken general stock of his surroundings. Around the corner from his ward, he noticed a rusty metal door in one of the prison's interior dividing walls. The portal was painted orange, and it appeared to lead to another section of Bilibid. On this particular day, passing by that door, he heard screams coming from the other side, the kind of screams made by men who are being beaten.

"What the hell's going on over there?" he asked Merrill Lee, when he got to the galley.

"That," Merrill Lee said, "is where they keep the special prisoners."

ON THE ISLAND OF PALAWAN, a long, narrow strip of land between the Sulu and South China seas, on the night of Tuesday, February 2, 1943, Don Schloat, a tall, lean twenty-one-year-old Army medic from Los Angeles, waited until his fellow prisoners had fallen asleep, then slipped out of his barracks, scaled two high barbed-wire fences, and scampered down an embankment between some palms and through the undergrowth toward the beach below to begin an escape.[26]

His partner, a man he knew only as Hanson, was right behind him in the drizzle and mist. It was roughly one in the morning, they guessed, which would give them about five hours of darkness to get as far as possible from the airstrip work camp.

They walked north along the shore, keeping an eye on the sea and sky, and when the first glow of light revealed the horizon, they headed inland to find a spot to hole up the rest of the day.

Their hiding place was a tangle of roots, hanging vines, and dangling branches in a mangrove swamp. After a while, from somewhere outside the tangle, they heard a commotion, a kind of clatter! Monkeys, they thought. A short time later, they heard another noise. Sounded like the door of an automobile slamming shut. Then they heard barking. They thought about abandoning their hiding spot, changed their minds, watched and waited.

Schloat was sure that by now the guards back at camp would have held *bangō* and discovered them missing and sent out search parties.

Suddenly, from somewhere very close, they heard a voice, a flat, matter-of-fact voice.

"What will you do?" it said.

Through the tangle they could see a man in uniform, and he was pointing a small silver-plated pistol at them. The man was Kempei Tai, the Japanese secret military police.

"What will you do?"

Schloat and Hanson had agreed they would never be taken alive. They'd both seen fellow prisoners beaten almost to death for making escape plans, and they knew the enemy's standing order: Anyone caught trying to escape would be executed.

Hanson jumped to his feet.

"Don't shoot," he yelled, raising his hands high above his head. "Don't shoot. We surrender."

The Kempei Tai man motioned them forward, and as they stepped over the vines and roots and out of the tangled grove, they saw that the policeman had company, Negritos, Philippine bushmen the Japanese used as trackers, standing nearby with long spears.

Maybe it was his experience as a medic, someone who'd watched how other men handled pain, or maybe it was his sense of self-possession, the staunch Presbyterianism of his youth. Whatever the case, Don Schloat guessed what was coming and started to gird himself.

He thought, "You're going to be punished terribly. Whatever happens now, eventually you're going to be killed, executed, decapitated. So don't allow yourself any hope. Don't allow yourself fear. Be numb, completely numb."

The Kempei Tai man had brought an interpreter. The interpreter was holding a *bokutō*, a wooden practice sword the Japanese used as a punishment stick, and he rushed the two prisoners and started to beat them on the shins.

The prisoners were put in a truck and hauled to Puerto Princesa and headquarters, a two-story cement building with cells in the basement. "Looks like a fortress," Schloat thought.

Guards separated and questioned them. "Where were you going? Who else was involved? Why did you want to escape?"

Between questions, the prisoners were beaten.

"Ride with the blows," Schloat told himself. "Feel nothing."

They beat him across the day and through the night and into the next day. Then they told him, "Tomorrow morning you will be beheaded in front of your people."

Instead, they denied him food and water, deprived him of sleep, gave him another beating.

"Don't faint," he thought. "Don't let yourself get hungry. Don't let yourself feel pain. Don't let yourself hope."

But it was hard not to hope, for his reason kept getting in his way. He reasoned that every day he survived, he made his death less valuable as an object lesson for his fellow prisoners. If the Japanese were going to kill him, he thought, they'd have killed him straightaway, walked him into the compound, made him kneel in front of his comrades, and left his head rolling in the dirt.

They asked him to sign a confession, a document written in kanji. He signed. Who cared? If they were going to kill him, they were going to kill him anyway.

A month passed, another month. Off and on, a Filipino or two would be thrown into jail with him. One had a mirror, and Schloat was shocked to see himself: his hair was falling out and his scalp and face were so white his blue eyes seemed to glow against his cretaceous skin. He had a full beard too, and it was bright red. He looked bizarre, he thought, a haggard albino in a crimson frame.

Finally, in late April 1943, nearly ninety days after he went over the wire, he was told that he and Hanson were being taken to Manila to be court-martialed.

The hearing was quick, the verdict reached in minutes. Hanson was given four years in jail, Schloat five. Sentences to begin immediately in Bilibid Prison, the section for special prisoners.

THEIR "CELL" was a wooden box, one of ten such boxes, or enclosed rooms, that had been built inside a regular adobe cell block, a kind of box within a box. This particular chamber was roughly ten feet wide, thirty feet long, and twelve feet high, a long narrow I of a room. At one end was a short barred door, four and a half feet high and two feet wide. On either side of the door was a small observation window for the guards. The floors, walls, and ceiling were polished mahogany, Schloat guessed, beautifully joined and fitted. At the rear of the room were two traps cut into the floor; beneath one was a drain, beneath the other a shallow tin box the prisoners used as latrine. Overhead a single naked lightbulb burned day and night. The room was otherwise bare, save for the prisoners, ten in this case, all escapees.

Their hair and beards were clipped short, and they were issued baggy gray shorts and a plain blue cotton jacket and trousers with coconut-shell buttons. They were to wear the blue uniform only for morning and evening *bangō*, which took place at the far end of the room, standing at attention. (*Gohyaku yonjū ichi*, Schloat would shout, "five hundred and forty-one," his prisoner number.) At all other times they were to wear only their shorts.

From seven in the morning to nine at night, all day every day, they were made to sit and face the wall. Just sit.

A Japanese-Filipino guard, a slob of a turnkey the prisoners called "Mister-Big-Number-Three," read them the rules:

> You are not to talk to each other.
> You cannot lean against the wall.
> You must sit on opposite ends of the room with your backs to each other while facing the wall.
> You must not look up at this door or window.
> While sitting, you must not put your hands on the floor to rest.
> You can sit [with] your knees [up] or cross-legged. In any other position you are breaking camp rules.
> Whatever you do, you must always face the wall.
> And you must never talk!

Breaking any of these rules invited a slap in the face, a cuff on the ear, a punch, but these beatings were nothing compared to the real torture, the real punishment that was taking place in the special prisoners section of Bilibid Prison, brute boredom.

"You must always face the wall . . . You must never talk!"

Five prisoners facing one wall, five the other, their arms folded and resting on their knees. Ten men, sitting all day, staring at a blank wall.

DON SCHLOAT wondered, naturally, why he was still alive.

At every prison and work camp in the Philippines, the Japanese had warned their captives that if they were caught trying to escape they'd be shot or beheaded. Don Schloat had lived in the shadow of that falling sword since the morning he and Hanson had been caught in the mangrove swamp. Why had the Japanese spared them? Why had the enemy spared any of the other special prisoners? And what were they sparing them for? For this? Sitting all day in front of a blank wall?

"How long can I sit here?" Schloat wondered. "Just sit and wait. How long is this going to go on?"

The more he asked the question, the more time became his torturer, present time, the moment that never passes. It is "the now that is agonizingly slow," he discovered. "How many heartbeats are there in an hour? Must I count them all?"

At first he thought he might escape "the interminable present" by slipping into the past, taking himself back to the locations that had defined his life: 2650 West Pico Boulevard, Los Angeles, his home; the Wilshire Crest Presbyterian Church where he sang in the choir; Los Angeles City College where he had studied entomology and the Los Angeles County Art and Natural History Museum where he'd worked as a summer volunteer mounting insects.

But how could he think about where he had been without remembering where he was? There was simply no escaping the stillness of the moment. Besides, thinking about home made him sad, and being sad made him weak.

So he tried some other tricks. He studied the section of wall in front of him. "Sometimes I feel I am almost a part of it. I am flesh, and it is wood, but we are both made of atoms. Can the atoms of my body pass through the atoms of wood and the steel bars beyond to freedom? If no guard is watching, I will press my hands against the wall, atom to atom, testing the reality of the walls, hoping to see my hand go through— The wall remains impenetrable. I wonder what Hanson's thinking, Hanson behind me facing the opposite wall."

AS THE MONTHS PASSED, the ten men in the wooden box found that when the guards were out of earshot they could whisper to one another. And when one of the ten died, and another became so sick a Japanese doctor thought he was dying, the survivors started to scheme.

For reasons none of them could explain, the Japanese did not want their special prisoners to die in the box. When a man became mortally sick, the guards always removed him, picked him up and carried him out through the orange steel door in the wall that led to the regular prison hospital.

Schloat and a couple of cell mates thought, why not make themselves so sick, so malnourished, they too would appear to be dying? And, one by one, they secretly started to starve themselves, passing their pitiful ration of rice to the other men in the box.

It was a risky gambit, and Schloat knew it. "How," he asked himself, "could the pretense of dying be done without dying? It cannot, of course." All the same, he was desperate.

Don Schloat got thinner, weaker, more worn and wan. Finally, after several weeks starving himself, he looked so bad the guards called a Japanese doctor, and on October 22, 1943, after almost five months in a wooden box, Don Schloat was put on a stretcher and carried though the orange door in the wall to the regular prison hospital, a "grinning skeleton" with only one thought: "What bliss!"

BEN STEELE was getting his strength back. He'd even gone on a day-long work detail at the docks. He came back weak and exhausted, but at least he'd kept his feet.

That fall the Swedish Red Cross ship *Gripsholm*, chartered by the American government to effect an exchange of a limited number of Japanese and European civilian internees, made port in Manila with more Red Cross boxes and with mail and parcel post packages for the prisoners of war. Ben Steele got a small parcel and twenty-five letters from home.

In the parcel his mother had packed some personal items, including socks, red socks, and in one of the socks she'd stuffed candy, hard candy that had melted into the fabric. Ben Steele filled his canteen cup with water, added the socks, and gulped the sweetened liquid down, red dye and all. Then he tore into the letters.

In one was a black-and-white photograph of the entire family that had been taken during an outdoor birthday party for Gert's daughter, Sandy, at the folks' house in Billings. They were all there—his parents, brothers, and sisters—smiling, but it was not the faces that caught Ben Steele's eye, it was what was on the table behind them—the platter of fried chicken, the chocolate cake, the large wedges of watermelon.

"Holy God!" he thought. "They don't have a clue. They really don't know what we're going through here."

He had tried not to think about them. Easier that way. During the battle, on the march, and at Tayabas Road, each time a memory of home worked its way up from his subconscious, he'd force himself to think of something else. Then the bundle of letters and the package arrived. Now he missed them, missed them a lot, especially his mother, and he read her letters over and over until the paper started to tear at the folds. She was "concerned," she said—that was the word she used in almost every letter—she was concerned about him.

BY THE BEGINNING of 1943, the Axis powers had started to lose ground in both the Pacific and European theaters of war. In January the British Royal Air Force bombed Berlin, and the Allies in conference at Casablanca agreed that their goal was nothing less than the unconditional surrender of Germany, Japan, and Italy.

In February, in the Solomon Islands in the Pacific, the Americans, after six months of combat, had defeated the Japanese at Guadalcanal. Meanwhile, troops under the command of American Admiral William Halsey were advancing rapidly through New Guinea to Bougainville.

That June, submarines from the U.S. Pacific Fleet started a campaign against Japanese shipping, and by September they had sent more than 160,000 tons to the bottom.

Through the fall of 1943, U.S. Marines moved deeper into the central Pacific and defeated fierce Japanese garrisons on Makin and Tarawa in the Gilbert Islands.

In his Fireside Chat on December 24, President Roosevelt told his fellow Americans that at last he could "do more than express a hope."

Increasingly powerful forces are now hammering at the Japanese at many points over an enormous arc . . . [The Allies] are all forming a band of steel which is slowly but surely closing in on Japan.

These setbacks put pressure on Japanese lines of communication and supply, and in all Japanese-held territories, especially in the southwest Pacific, there were shortages of men, matériel, manufactured goods, and food.

For the prisoners of war at Bilibid hospital, the shortages were proof that America was at last winning, but after a year and more of captivity, they no longer expected the cavalry to come riding over the hill at any moment, and "We'll be free in '43" and "Mother's door in '44" gave way to "Keep alive till '45" and "Golden Gate in '48." In his notebooks, Hayes wrote, "General change in attitude can be noted. The war is no longer expected to be over next month or next week."[27]

A few thinking men, Hayes among them, also began to worry about how the enemy, so seemingly indifferent to the fate of their captives, might behave in losing.

"I have never been able to convince myself that the Japs would [just] move out of here in the face of attack and leave us to be relieved by our own forces," Hayes wrote. "I can't be convinced they would . . . allow us to continue [on] our way unmolested."[28]

In a war driven by ideas about race, which is to say, hate, the threat of extermination was ever present. And the Japanese hated white men such as Hayes as much as Hayes and his comrades hated the Japanese.

"Shades of the days of the Tripolitan Pirates," he wrote, "days of the Moslems and Turks when our seamen died & rotted in Oriental prisons! The white man is sure as hell serving in bondage to the Yellow boys to-day . . . The American people back home can't realize yet what it means to [be] . . . reduced to [an] animal existence with less care and attention than animals in our zoo."[29]

Japanese military leaders made no attempt to hide their animus, either. To hate the *ketōjin*, the hairy white foreigners who had denied Nippon its due, was part of the propaganda at every army training camp in the Japanese home islands. But as a practical matter—and the Japanese, a most practical people, were always looking for something that was *jitsuyō*, "capable of being turned to use"—prisoners of war were an obvious source of labor, especially in a country where every man, woman, and able-bodied child was either pressed into military service or put to work in the fields, rice paddies, and overburdened factories.

Not long after the fall of Bataan in April 1942, the bureau chiefs at the War Ministry in Tokyo met to decide what to do with the 192,600

Dutch, British, and American POWs they'd captured in their conquest of the southwest Pacific. The generals reminded one another that Japan had not ratified the Geneva Convention and thus was not bound by the proscription against using prisoners as slaves. So, "all prisoners of war [will] engage in forced labor," they decided. First they would set up work camps in Japan proper, then in Formosa, Korea, China, Manchuria, and throughout the occupied territories of the southwest Pacific, 160 camps in the home islands, 367 camps overall.[30]

The commanders of these labor camps were ordered to keep their chattel busy. Do "not let them remain idle for even a single day," Hideki Tojo, the war minister, said.[31]

And work them they did. By the fall of 1942, in a brief on labor conditions in the home islands, the Japanese Prisoner of War Information Bureau was able to report, "The use of [POW] labor alleviated in some measure the labor shortage" in the country at large. The *ketō*, of course, were not as efficient as Japanese workers, only "60–70 percent [as good] in special labor such as coal unloading," the brief said, but "it is generally admitted by all the business proprietors alike that the use of P.W. labor has made the systematic operation of transportation possible for the first time, and has not only produced a great influence in the business circles, but will also contribute greatly to the expansion of production, including munitions of war."[32]

In the Philippines, the first draft of American prisoners to leave for Japan, five hundred men, set sail from Manila aboard the *Nagaru Maru* on September 5, 1942, some five months after surrender. These innocents, still filled with hope and perhaps a little hooey handed out by the Japanese, boarded their ship convinced that the Red Cross had negotiated a prisoner exchange. Later drafts either knew better or the Japanese dropped all pretense. Whatever the case, no one wanted to go. They knew that the Allies, their liberators, were fighting their way north from the Solomons to the Bismark Sea, from the Marshalls to the Marianas, and simple geography told them that the Philippines would likely be liberated long before America would be able to push north of the islands and mount an invasion of Japan.

THE JAPANESE captured some 20,000 Americans in the Philippines, and from that first day of captivity forward the victors used their prisoners of war as slaves. Several of these work details and labor gangs, especially the ones building airfields, were quartered in self-contained camps, places with bamboo barracks, barbed-wire enclosures, and permanently assigned guards, but most work details—cleanup parties, road gangs, field crews, and the like—drew their labor from the central American prisoner of war camp, a large, flat, open piece of land on a treeless plain outside the city of Cabanatuan in the central Luzon province of Nueva Ecija.

Camp Cabanatuan had replaced Camp O'Donnell. At first it had all the same ills—appalling living conditions, feeble and corrupt army leadership, feculent Zero Wards of dying men. Then the Japanese put Marine Corps Lieutenant Colonel Curtis T. Beecher of Chicago in charge. Beecher, a decorated hero of World War I and by every account one of the most competent field officers in captivity, set about turning a cesspool into a place of survival. He ordered the sprawling camp cleaned up, organized the men, lobbied his Japanese overseers for more medicine, supplies, and food, and the monthly death rate dropped from several hundred to a handful. In 1943 the camp census averaged between three thousand and four thousand men. And everyone, including the officers, worked. Prisoners drove trucks, repaired machinery, performed various chores and menial labor. Every day two thousand men tilled and tended the fields of a two-hundred-acre plot adjacent to the camp, a farm that grew vegetables exclusively for Japanese mess tables on Luzon.

It was from Cabanatuan, for the most part, that the Japanese drew their cargoes of prisoner chattel to ship north to the slave labor camps in the Japanese home islands. Five hundred this month, eight hundred the next, a thousand after that. And as the calls for more men increased, the doctors in Bilibid came under pressure from the Japanese to move as many patients as possible off the sick lists and into Cabanatuan, patients the doctors knew would likely end up on drafts designated for Japan.

BEN STEELE wasn't well yet, but at least he was on the mend. The beriberi was under control and his malaria was in slow remission. Christmas was coming, Christmas 1943, his second in Bilibid Prison. Services were scheduled in the chapel in the compound and the ambulatory planned to serenade the invalids with carols. Maybe Santa would deliver a Red Cross treat or two.

For weeks the doctors had been discharging men from the hospital, sending them to Cabanatuan. Some of the men in Bilibid were so desperate to stay in the hospital they were buying stool samples from comrades with dysentery and passing them off as their own. Ben Steele just sat and waited and sketched.

Sitting cross-legged on his bunk with a makeshift drawing board in his lap, he usually attracted an audience. One day a short, gruff Japanese sergeant, a man the prisoners called Captain Bligh, sat down next to him. For a moment, Ben Steele worried he'd made trouble for himself. The sergeant was pointing to the drawing—a generic sketch of a Japanese guard—and going on and on, yammering about something. Finally someone summoned an interpreter. Seemed the artist had misdrawn the guard's leggings, and the sergeant was trying to get him to do it right.

His drawings were getting better, the subject matter more varied—portraits, prison scenes, landscapes. Meanwhile, some of the officers approached him with a secret project. The cruelty they'd all suffered was criminal, they said, and no one was "taking any photographs of this stuff," so maybe he should start drawing it, create a record of atrocities for the reckoning that was sure to follow the war.

He'd never thought of art as documentary, as an accounting. To him a drawing should aim to capture the raw energy of the world, the mysterious force of life. Like someone looking at a well-drawn picture of a horse and feeling the animal under him, feeling its muscles, its natural aversion to having anything on its back. That was the kind of art he wanted to create.

Still, he understood. In their secret diaries and reports, a number of American officers had already started a chronicle of the enemy's misdeeds. Now, here was a young artist who could help record that malfeasance, a man who could make his comrades' misery come alive.

So with an eye out for the guards, he started drawing scenes of suffering, scenes he remembered. He drew men on the long march off Bataan falling to their knees and begging for water; he drew the Japanese guards who answered those entreaties with a bullet or bayonet. He drew the daily death parade and burial details at O'Donnell. He drew the rocky hell of Tayabas Road.

This was dangerous business, and everyone knew it. As soon as each drawing was finished, Ben Steele would give it to Father Duffy, who would hide the young artist's growing body of work in the false bottom of his Mass kit.

Ben Steele produced more than fifty such scenes and, from time to time, kept sketching his West as well. He drew every day, drew his pencils down to the nub. Rather than sharpen them and waste precious lead, he carefully picked the wood away from the core until, at the end, he was left holding nothing but a short rod of lead between his fingertips.

At some point during all this drawing, he got the idea that "this is what I want to do when I get home, go to art school." Art, after all, had saved him, sustained him. It distracted him from his constant hunger and gave shape to his days. To almost everyone else in prison, the sameness of the days produced a numbing apathy. They woke to the bell, stood *bangō*, ate *lugao*, went to bed. Then they got up and did the same thing all over again, day after leaden day. Ben Steele got up and started to draw.

HE GOT THE WORD from the doctors right after the New Year in 1944: they had reclassified him from convalescent to well, and he was listed to go to Cabanatuan. He knew that Cabanatuan was the staging point for drafts to Japan. Everyone said it was going to be cold in Japan, very cold. And he didn't want to go.

He arrived at Cabanatuan in the middle of January, a huge hot and dusty place, six-tenths of a mile long (roughly the length of eleven football fields end to end) and half a mile wide, all surrounded by three high barbed-wire fences that formed a no-man's-land, a kill zone for the guards. Same sawali shacks as O'Donnell, same rice slop as everywhere else, men in the same rags and loincloths.

He worked the farm, digging, planting, hoeing with homemade tools. Camotes, corn, eggplant. He thought he might steal something and smuggle it back to camp under his hat or waistband. Then he saw what happened to the skeletal men who got caught doing that, and so like everyone else, he picked pigweed for himself and choked it down with his rice. Sometimes, when he thought the guards weren't looking, he'd sneak a bite of a corn stalk near the base. The stalk was kind of tender down there, at the bottom, his nose in the dirt.

In July 1944, his name appeared on a draft of eleven hundred men listed for shipment to Japan. The draft was taken by train, boxcars, back down to Manila and put up overnight in the transient section of Bilibid, across from the hospital. That night, quite by accident, Ben Steele ran into Q. P. Devore, who was on his way to Cabanatuan from a work farm in Mindinao.

Ben Steele thought Q.P. looked good; he'd been treated well at the camp in the southern islands. Q.P., on the other hand, thought his friend looked awful—his cheekbones were showing and his eyes were sunken in his head. He'd lost so much weight (he was down to 110 pounds) his skin sagged on his bones, and his knees looked like doorknobs, his ribs like a washboard. Q.P. handed him a small mirror from a Red Cross package. Ben Steele was shocked by the image in the glass.

Still, they were delighted to be together again, if only for a night passing through prison. They shared a coconut, traded tales, wondered what was ahead.

The next day Ben Steele and the rest of the draft were assembled in the prison compound. They marched out the front gate and through the streets of Manila to the docks by Manila Bay. There they were loaded aboard an old freighter, the *Canadian Inventor*, for the long trip north, a trip into the heart of the enemy's homeland.

ELEVEN

July 2, 1944, Pier 7, Manila Bay

BEN STEELE was waiting in a long line of men queued up to board the *Canadian Inventor*. Since surrender, the Japanese had been shipping boatloads of American prisoners from the Philippines to Japan and its occupied territories as slave labor. The first groups of prisoners had left Manila in 1942 in the gloom of defeat, liberation the last thing on their minds. Now, however, in the summer of 1944, America was winning the war, and the eleven hundred men lined up to board the *Inventor* felt thwarted. The Allies were gaining ground, getting close, and the men on the dock had hoped to be free in a matter of months. Today they were getting on a ship for Japan, and they knew it might be years before America could mount an invasion of the enemy's homeland to save them.

From the end of the pier, it was possible to look out on the bay, and that grand sweep of scene must have been a bitter vista to Ben Steele and his comrades. To the southwest, they could see the spit of land called Cavite—from there in December 1941, Admiral Thomas Hart's Asiatic Fleet had fled south to save itself. And looking due west across the bay through the haze hanging over the water, the prisoners could make out a dark silhouette of mountains, the ghostly promontories where they had fought for ninety-nine days, the peninsula of Bataan.

The *Inventor* was empty, riding high in the water, and every so often Ben Steele glanced up at the dark hull and grimy white superstructure. The ship looked like she'd been steaming constantly with no time to put in for refitting or repairs. A real rust bucket.

The line of men began to file slowly up the gangway to the main deck. As Ben Steele passed a forward bulkhead, he spotted a brass plaque with the name of the ship, then passed across the deck to an open hatch and ladderway leading down to a hold. Wafting up from the hold was the scent of hay and the stale smell of horses and manure. Okay, he thought, pausing at the open hatch, if horses had survived this old tub, so could he.[1]

As he started to descend the ladder, he could see that the space below was already so crowded with anxious and perspiring prisoners, he would barely have enough room to squat or sit, even with his legs drawn up tight against his chest. The only light was from the open hatch, and back in the far reaches of the hold, it was dark, choking dark.

AMERICAN PRISONERS of war were carried back to the Japanese homeland in the same spaces, the same airless holds, the Imperial Army used to transport its own troops. Japanese generals stuffed these troop ships so full of *hohei* that headquarters (in a 1941 handbook passed out prior to sailing) warned the average soldier he would be "sleeping side by side on the mess decks [with his comrades] like sardines in a tin." By "mess decks" they meant the wooden or steel shelves that had been built into the ship's storage holds between decks, sleeping platforms to double or triple the number of troops that could be carried in the spaces belowdecks. The shelves and tiers were stacked so tightly there was barely three feet between them, just enough room to squirm in and wriggle out. "Silkworm shelves," the *hohei* dubbed them. A level down, meanwhile, in poorly ventilated bottom decks, horses and their hostlers sweated out the journey. Life at every level belowdecks was so miserable (in tropical waters the holds reached temperatures of 130°) the Japanese troops complained bitterly among themselves, and headquarters, apparently getting wind of the grousing, tried to put the troops' predicament into perspective. In the 1941 handbook ("Read This Alone and the War Can Be Won"), the *hohei* were told, "Never forget that in the dark and steaming lowest decks of the ship, with no murmur of complaint at the unfairness of their treatment, the Army horses are suffering in patience . . . Remember that however exhausted you yourselves may feel, the horses will have reached a stage of exhaustion even more distressing."[2]

Among its many miscalculations in going to war with the West, Japan, a maritime nation, grossly underestimated the number of merchant ships it would need—ships to ferry troops and supplies to far-flung battlefields, ships to carry raw materials back to the homeland, ships to import enough

Going aboard freighter to Japan

food to feed Japan's people. By the end of 1942, Allied aircraft and submarines plying the southwest Pacific had sunk more than a million tons of Japanese shipping, one-fifth of its already inadequate fleet, and by the beginning of 1944 the Japanese had lost at least another fifth.[3]

As these merchant losses mounted, the remaining ships were forced to carry more and more cargo, which included consignments of prisoners of war, thousands of men jammed and stuffed into the tiers, racks, platforms, and shelves belowdecks. Under normal conditions, steaming night and day, a Japanese merchant ship, turning an average of 13 knots, could make the 1,276 nautical miles between Manila and Moji, Japan's main port of arrival for POWs, in fifteen days or less. But by the middle of 1944, harassed by Allied aircraft and roving submarine packs or slowed by aging boilers and engines, Japanese cargo ships frequently had to stop and hide or put into a friendly port for repairs, and a journey of fifteen days could easily turn into a month or more belowdecks.

THE *CANADIAN INVENTOR* sat at the dock for a day and a half, her two holds packed with American prisoners of war, then, on the morning of July 4, the ship finally set sail. Less than twenty-four hours later, she was back at anchor with boiler trouble, and she sat in Manila Bay awaiting repairs. The air temperature was near 90°, the humidity about 75 percent. The rainy season with its cooling overcast was late that year, so a bright sun beat down on the metal hull and deck.[4]

The ship's holds were not ventilated, and during the day the Japanese refused to remove the hatch covers, lest some of their human cargo escape. After a few hours sitting in the sun, the holds became like bake ovens.

"This is damn near unbearable," Ben Steele thought.

The men tried to settle down, but wherever they sat, squatted, or lay in the hold, either on the side tiers or on the bare deck in the middle of the hold, they were wedged arm to arm, belly to back. The press of men was so intense they started pouring sweat. Within an hour they were beginning to dehydrate, and by the afternoon they were clammy and light-headed, the first symptoms of men failing from thirst.

Many worried they might faint and never wake, and that sense of doom left them anxious, panting. The faster they tried to breathe, the more their hearts raced, and it wasn't long before they could feel their pulse pounding in their heads and chests. They needed air, they needed water, they needed to get out of that damn baking box.

That night, the Japanese finally peeled back the hatches and lowered buckets of water and rice. Not enough, of course. Never enough. (What was it the war minister had said? "There is no need to pamper the POWs.") At sea, it seemed, their short rations would be shorter—a couple of handfuls of rice and less than a canteen of water (sixteen ounces) per man per day.[5]

The first day a large number of men went without any food or drink at all. No one, no officer or senior sergeant, stepped forward to organize them, and the men standing directly under the hatch openings grabbed what they could while the sick and the weak and those crammed into the back reaches of the holds got nothing at all.

Here and there in the hold were five-gallon latrine buckets, which in the crowding and dark often got kicked over, spilling the contents on the men lying and sitting nearby. At some point after dark, the Japanese allowed groups of prisoners to come topside for a few moments of air, then it was back down into the stink and heat until the next night.

And so it went for eleven days, broiling in the airless hold, until the afternoon of July 16, when the *Canadian Inventor*, her boiler finally fixed, joined a small convoy of ships sailing out of Manila Bay.

Once under way, the Japanese removed the hatch covers, which allowed a bit of air to find its way down into the holds. The fresh air seemed to calm the men who were delirious and screaming and yelling. Someone stepped forward to organize the chow detail, and every man got a bite of food and a sip of water. Just enough to keep them starving and so thirsty they could think of little else.

Twenty-four hours out of port the seas became heavy and the ship ran into huge swells and squall-like winds, a Pacific typhoon. Still riding high in the water with a light cargo, the *Canadian Inventor* bobbed and tossed in the stormy seas, pitching and rolling so severely her yards and braces sometimes seemed to touch the surface of the water.

Ben Steele knew about bad weather, but he had never been through a storm at sea with swirling clouds, seventy-mile-an-hour winds, and torrents of rain. From his position in the forward hold just below the open hatch, he could see the tops of thirty-foot waves crashing across the deck, and when the ship pitched forward in a trough between giant swells, he thought, "The whole damn front end is going under the water," and he was afraid.

Men thrown off their feet went flying across the hold, bouncing off one another and tumbling and rolling from bulkhead to bulkhead. Soon the hold was a tangle of limbs and bodies sliding around in pools of vomit and excreta from the latrine buckets. In all that sliding, Air Corps Private John Crago of Huntington, Indiana, noticed that the skin on his legs, buttocks, and lower back had been scraped raw, and he tried to wedge himself in a corner of the hold and grab a beam to steady himself against the storm.

At first the Japanese left the hatches open, and the men, thirsty and filthy, welcomed the sheets of rain coming into the open holds. Then the waves started sweeping the deck, the holds took on seawater, and the Japanese slammed the hatch covers shut, leaving the prisoners rolling in the reeking dark.

When the winds finally calmed and the waves flattened, the crew discovered more boiler trouble, and the *Canadian Inventor* left her small convoy and made for Formosa. The prisoners were allowed to rotate up on deck now for a breath of air or to use one of the five *benjo* (latrine seats the Japanese also called "birdcages") that hung over the rail on ropes. A few days later, July 23, the *Inventor* tied up at the docks at Takao.

After twenty-one days in the holds, her bearded human cargo looked begrimed and smelled worse, and the Japanese ran them all up on deck and washed them down with fire hoses, then sprayed water into the holds and pumped the vile bilge into the harbor.

One day passed, two. The ship took on a large load of salt in its lower holds, then she just sat there day after day. At the end of the month she was still waiting for repairs. (*Matte-Matte Maru*, the men nicknamed the old bucket, "the Waiting-Waiting Ship.") At last, on August 4, twelve days after the ship had put into Takao, she sortied again, but after a few hours' steaming, she turned toward shore, this time putting in at the port of Keelung. More boiler trouble. More waiting for the *Matte-Matte Maru*.

In the close and crowded spaces belowdecks, tempers were growing short. The vermin (fleas, lice, rats), the starvation rations, the filth (men with dysentery and diarrhea had trouble getting through the crowd in time to use a *benjo* topside or a latrine bucket in the hold), the thick suffocating air—all of it was wearing on everyone.

Fistfights broke out over nothing, feeble men flailing at one other. (Any man suspected of stealing food or water became a whipping boy for those around him.) Some men lost control of themselves and began to scream and yell and thrash around in the reeking gloom.

"Grab him," his shipmates would yell. "Keep him fucking quiet."

All the yelling and fighting filled the hold with a din. "I'm going mad," Gene Jacobsen thought, "stark raving mad." From his sleeping shelf, Jacobsen watched a party of goons go after a hysterical man in the bottom of the forward hold. Jacobsen couldn't see clearly, but he could hear a lot of grumbling and commotion down there, then the body of the man who had been "quieted" by his bunkmates was hauled up through the hatch cover to the top deck and tossed into the sea.

After twelve days at Keelung, the *Inventor* set sail again. For the next seventeen days, she crept north, nursing her sick boiler, heeding reports of enemy submarines, and hiding in coves and inlets along the way.

The weather was better, cooler, and the prisoners were allowed on deck more often now. Each time the ship anchored offshore, they begged the guards to let them jump in the water and wash off the muck from the holds, but the nervous sentries refused.

The last ten days of the journey were among the worst. Most of the time the prisoners just sat and stared at one another or busied themselves picking off fleas and killing bedbugs. Finally on September 1, sixty-two days after boarding the ship in Manila, the American prisoners of war—beards long, hair matted, skin covered with ulcers and open sores—came stumbling down the gangway of the *Matte-Matte Maru* at Moji, Japan.

At the bottom of the gangway, a line of Japanese soldiers stood with hoses and canisters. They sprayed the prisoners down with seawater and doused them with a white powder that smelled like disinfectant, then they issued them light cotton clothing and marched them through the streets to a warehouse where the men were fed bean soup and bread, food that tasted like a feast. The detail was then separated into groups, and it was obvious to the men that they were being sent to different places.

Ben Steele was in a group of 255 men who were marched to a ferry. The ferry carried them across the narrow strait between Moji and Shimonoseki. There they boarded a train with seats. Seats! Ben Steele thought. "A real luxury." Then he remembered where he was. And what he was.

"HELLSHIPS," the prisoners of war came to call them. Between January 1942 and July 1945, the Japanese transported 156 shiploads of Allied POWs from battlefields and camps in the southwest Pacific to slave labor sites in their territories and home islands. Although they packed the prisoners in the same spaces they used for their own troops, they stuffed those spaces as if they were shipping livestock, then, out of expediency, spite, or both, denied them adequate air, food, and water. More than 126,000 Allied prisoners of war and native laborers made these journeys, and more than 21,000 died en route or went down with the ships. The prisoners on the *Canadian Inventor* fared better than most; during their passage only a handful of bodies were hauled topside and tossed into the sea. Later voyages were much crueler, and a lot more deadly.[6]

On October 11, 1944, the freighter *Arisan Maru* left Manila for Japan with some eighteen hundred prisoners of war in her main hold. The fall of 1944 was a dangerous time for Japanese merchant ships plying the waters of the South China Sea. The United States had assembled a massive armada to invade the southern Philippine island of Leyte (about four hundred miles south of Manila), the key stepping-stone, as MacArthur saw it, to taking the Philippine islands back from Japan. As a prelude to the Leyte invasion, the U.S. Navy positioned a task force of aircraft carriers near the islands, and carrier-based fighter planes and bombers began to attack Japanese targets on land and in the South China and East China seas. The Navy also dispatched submarine packs in those waters— "Convoy College," the skippers called the area, because they were going to school on any Japanese ships that sailed there. In just ninety days, September through November 1944, American air and naval forces sank 347 Japanese merchantmen (an astonishing 1,382,516 tons of shipping).

Since the hellships were never marked as prisoner of war transports (they often carried war matériel as well), American pilots and submarine skippers had no way of knowing they were shooting at fellow Americans. When they looked in their sights and lined up their targets, all they saw was the enemy.[7]

Boarding the *Arisan Maru*, Sergeant Calvin R. Graef, a coast artilleryman from Silver City, New Mexico, had been pressed into service as a deckhand and ordered to help remove the tarpaulins from the largest of the *Arisan*'s holds. When he pulled back the hatch cover and looked down, he guessed the hold could accommodate some 200 men. The Japanese jammed 1,805 into that space.[8]

After two days at sea, days of boiling heat, thick noxious air, vermin, short rations, and little water, five men were dead, likely from heat stroke and heart failure. At last, heeding the prisoners' incessant pleas, the Japanese moved six hundred men from the most crowded bays belowdecks into the ship's coal bin, a large storage space reached only by rope ladders. Six hundred men sitting and sleeping on a mound of hard black rocks.

Graef, meanwhile, and a few others who'd worked as camp cooks ashore, were selected to make the twice-daily rice ration for the cargo of captives. They did their cooking on deck, and Graef was grateful for the assignment, a couple of hours of fresh air every day. Life belowdecks had become intolerable. Men were yelling and moaning and keeling over; most had developed heat blisters (to Graef, their skin looked like "raw hamburger").

Around 5:00 p.m. on October 24, thirteen days out of port, Graef was topside cooking rice. Half the company of prisoners had been fed; the deck was rolling in a rough sea and the cooks must have had a hard time with their steam pots. All at once Japanese guards and deckhands started running wildly toward the bow, and when Graef looked back to see what had scared them, he saw a torpedo in the water astern pass within feet of the fantail. Then the gaggle of deckhands reversed itself and dashed back toward him—another torpedo, this one across the bow.

"What gives?" yelled one of the prisoners from below.

"Submarines, school of fish!" one of the cooks shouted back.

"Please, God, don't let them miss!"[9]

Seconds later three torpedoes hit the hull. The Japanese shoved the cooks belowdecks, covered the hatches, then cut the rope ladders to the coal bin and raced for the lifeboats, leaving the prisoners trapped.

In the coal hole, a few boys managed to shimmy up a pole and reattach the ropes, and in the main holds the strongest of them mounted ladders and pushed off the hatch covers.

When Graef finally got up on deck, the Japanese were gone, and the stern of the ship was already underwater. Then the boilers exploded, the ship started to slip under, and Graef was in the water.

No one could say how many men were killed belowdecks and how many made it topside into the sea—two hundred, three hundred, more. About twenty-five men, Graef among them, started swimming toward a Japanese destroyer that had come to the *Arisan*'s aid, but when they reached the destroyer's side, Japanese sailors standing along her rail grabbed grappling poles, leaned over the side, and began to push the Americans underwater.

Graef swam off and joined a group of survivors clinging to some wreckage floating nearby. At dusk he spotted two bamboo poles in the water and swam out to fetch them, but when he turned around in the gloaming to swim back, he couldn't find the wreckage and his companions. Using the poles as a makeshift raft, he drifted for what seemed like a long time, through the day and night and into the next day, when he looked up and saw a lifeboat drifting nearby.

"Hey, boat, anybody there?"

Four heads popped up. Prisoners from the ship!

The five survivors rigged a sail and decided to head west toward China, hoping to encounter friendly faces. Three days later they happened upon some Chinese junks, and with the aid of their crews, the Americans made it to the Chinese coast and, finally, into American hands.

Some eighteen hundred military and civilian prisoners of war had been belowdecks on the *Arisan Maru* when she broke in half and started to slip beneath the waves. Nine survived.

Among those who did not was Sergeant Dalton Russell, the man who had helped keep Ben Steele alive on the rocks at Tayabas Road.

BY THE FALL OF 1944, the Allies had retaken the Pacific island of Guam and were moving their air bases closer and closer to Japan. MacArthur was on the southern Philippine island of Leyte with 200,000 combat troops, and his force had pushed north to the island of Mindoro. The Japanese were rapidly losing ground, and they began to salvage and ship home what they could from the colonies they had left.

The *Oryoku Maru*, a passenger liner designed to haul cargo as well, was part of this anxious falling back under fire. On the day she was scheduled to leave Manila, the cabins and bays of her white superstructure were occupied by seven hundred Japanese civilians, women and children mostly, and a thousand Japanese sailors off sunken Japanese ships. In the middle and bottom decks of her deep cargo holds was loot from the Japanese occupation of the Philippines, including some 1,600 American prisoners of war, more than two-thirds of them officers, including Tom Hayes and most of the Navy doctors and corpsmen who had run the prison hospital at Bilibid.[10]

Japan had recently lost 122 merchant ships in the same shipping lanes the *Oryoku* planned to ply. With such losses, and with MacArthur poised to invade the big island of Luzon, the Japanese must have known that the *Oryoku Maru* would be among the last vessels able to leave Manila. And they packed her holds tight.

The crowding belowdecks was criminal. Prisoners were stuffed into the side shelves and sleeping platforms. In the open area in the middle of the holds, men were made to stand so tightly bunched that, looking down from the hatch above, the Japanese guards could see only heads and shoulders, like the tops of pickles jammed into a jar.

During the loading of Hold 3, one of the American officers, counting some 450 men already belly to back, told the guards the space was full. The Japanese ignored him and kept pushing more and more men down the ladder on top of the others. Three hundred more.

On Wednesday, December 13, around 8:00 p.m., the ship cast off and moved down to the mouth of Manila Bay, where it stopped and waited for its escorts. The hatch covers had been left askew, but the hatch openings on this particular ship were small, some fourteen feet square, much too small to ventilate the tightly packed forward and aft holds. Conditions in Hold 3 were particularly brutal; its hatch was between bulkheads that blocked the wind. Only the men directly under the opening were getting any air at all, and even there, the atmosphere was beginning to grow toxic.

The men in Holds 1 and 3 felt as if they'd been trapped in a crowded elevator, shut in an airless closet, locked in an automobile baking in the sun with the windows rolled tight. In that thick, superheated air, a man simply couldn't catch his breath, no matter how hard he tried.

THE PHYSICS OF SUFFOCATION are simple enough: put too many men into an unventilated space and they will soon start to use up the oxygen. Survival in such a milieu is a question of percentages. Everyday air is 21 percent oxygen and .04 percent carbon dioxide; decrease the former and increase the latter and a man will slowly suffocate, choking from the lack of oxygen and at the same time strangling on his own gases (carbon dioxide). At 19.5 percent oxygen, he starts to feel fuzzy headed, flustered; at 16 percent, he loses his judgment, his sense of time and place.

All this was happening in a sweating press of men deep in the disorienting dark. No wonder so many on the *Oryoku Maru* imagined themselves drowning. (Army medic Sidney Stewart saw himself being "sucked under, sucked down," as if he were struggling to reach the surface from the black depths of a "mossy pool.")

As oxygen levels fall below 16 percent, nerve cells in the brain and neck and heart, triggered by the buildup of carbon dioxide, signal the body to breathe faster, and it wasn't long before the holds became a mass of heaving chests and shoulders, mouths agape, men gasping for air. At 14 percent oxygen, the men in the aft and forward holds began to drop. Soon the deck in the middle of the aft hold had a floor mat of flesh, men standing on other men.[11]

At that point everyone had figured out that the only breathable air was directly under the open hatches, and the more those in the back of the hold tried to shove and push their way forward, the more those around the hatch started to push back. And it did not take long for all this pushing to turn to panic.

Men started screaming and yelling for air, then they began to beat one another with their fists, canteens, mess kits. All that exertion used up even more oxygen, and in the sections of the holds where the oxygen level dropped to 10 percent or less, men stopped breathing. Three in this bay, two in that, five over there by the bulkhead, sitting naked, hugging their knees to their chests, stiff and cold to the touch.[12]

On top of the suffocating heat and asphyxiating air was the torment of thirst. Their tongues were swollen and they felt a lump in their burning throats. They swallowed, swallowed again, but could get no relief. And that made them all the more irritable, all the more crazy.

Navy Commander Frank Bridget, a tough bantam of an officer in the aft hold, and Marine Corps colonel Curtis Beecher, senior officer in the forward hold, mounted the ladders and tried to quell the panic, quiet the men, but the bedlam belowdecks only grew louder and louder.

Beecher climbed to the top of the ladder now and shouted for Shunusuke Wada, the Japanese interpreter assigned to the detail. More water, the colonel demanded, they were desperate for more water. Wada looked down into the din of the hold. There was no water for the prisoners, he told Beecher. "And you are disturbing the Japanese women and the Japanese children. If you do not remain quiet, I will close the hatch."[13]

A while later, screams and yells still issuing from the dark pits forward and aft, Wada was back. He kept his word and shut the hatches. "Unless you are quiet," he told Beecher, "I shall give the guards the order to fire down into the hold."

(Beecher hated the "little rat" of an interpreter. Wada had a deformed spine, a "gnomelike" humpback, as Beecher saw him, who walked stooped and spoke in a "screeching, high-pitched voice." On the pier during loading, Beecher had tried to reason with the interpreter, got a "snarly, arrogant" reply and, knowing that it was the interpreter, not the officer in charge, in this case Lieutenant Junsaburo Toshino, who determined the fate of most details, guessed that the voyage was going to be a "miserable" one.)

A few hours before daybreak on Thursday morning, December 14, the *Oryoku Maru* got under way again and moved slowly out of the mouth of Manila Bay then eventually north up the west coast of Bataan, putting herself between her escorts and the shore. In the early morning dark, the men in the holds noticed they had more wiggle room now, and a while later when the hatches were partially opened and sunlight illuminated the dark reaches, they saw why. The bays belowdecks were littered with dead, dozens in each hold.

SOMETIME after their handful of morning rice and water (only half a canteen cup per man in the forward hold, no water at all for the prisoners aft), the men heard the sound of airplane engines overhead. In the forward hold, Colonel Beecher worked himself into a position below the open hatch where he could see some sky. American fighter planes in formation above the convoy were peeling off and diving toward the water.

The first bombs must have hit nearby because the ship rocked back and forth from the concussions. Beecher wished for the worst.

"I hope we get hit," he thought. "Better to take our chances" in the water "than continue in this hell-ship."[14]

On the next pass, a bomb landed so close it ruptured the ship's hull plates, and the metal rubbing against metal filled the black reaches of the aft hold with blue sparks, an eerie light that illuminated the faces of the men and the recumbent forms of the dead.

On their third, fourth, and fifth runs, the fighters and dive-bombers raked the convoy with 50-caliber machine gun fire. The bombing and strafing quieted the men in the holds. In the sweltering gloom, they listened as the bullets and shrapnel slammed into the deck and sliced through the superstructure, the cabins and bays where the Japanese civilians were trying to take cover.

By late afternoon December 15, many prisoners had been without water for more than twenty-four hours and they started to yell again, louder and more urgently than before. On the whole, things were "worse off than ever," Colonel Beecher thought. More and more men were dying from dehydration, their faces a ghostly gray, blood oozing from the shriveled and cracked membranes in their mouths and noses.

In the aft hold, Commander Bridget made a desperate attempt to calm the company (he tried to show them how to fan the air with a shirt or pair of shorts), but it did no good. In the forward hold, Colonel Beecher pleaded with the men to get control of themselves, but the sweating, feverish mass, crazed with thirst, just kept screaming.[15]

Sometime after dark they felt the ship getting under way, then it abruptly stopped, and the prisoners heard the sounds of hoists and winches working on deck. They guessed the *Oryoku Maru* had maneuvered toward shore and the Japanese were taking off their wounded in advance of abandoning ship.

Beecher yelled for Wada. The interpreter told him the prisoners would be taken off as well, but hours passed and nothing happened. Nothing except the heat, the thick, toxic air, the din of hundreds of men howling.

It was now, during their second night in the dark holds of the *Oryoku Maru*, that men who had endured two and a half years of hard labor, starvation rations, deadly disease, daily beatings, and random murder reached their limit.

EVEN AT THE WORST of the prison camps and work details, American POWs had managed to maintain some small sense of human kinship. Beecher had built on that base morality at Camp Cabanatuan, as had Tom Hayes and Pappy Sartin at Bilibid Prison. Now, in the desperate struggle for survival in those dark holds, some men lost the last shred of themselves, whatever humanity they had left. They became sociopaths, stealing what they wanted from the weak and settling scores with old antagonists. (One man was found strangled, another with his gut slit open with a pocket knife.) Here was the English philosopher Thomas Hobbes's worst dream, "where every man is enemy to every man," a mob of "poor, nasty, brutish" beings bent on destroying one another.[16]

The holds were madhouses now. In the murky infernos, the hysterics were screaming and the sociopaths were on the prowl. Even Beecher, battle hardened at forty-seven, was unnerved by "the moaning of the crazed and dying and the shouts of men fighting and killing one another." And then it got worse.[17]

Some men, so deranged by their thirst (their shriveled neurons misfiring and going haywire), drank blood. Sometimes they slit themselves to suck the serum, and sometimes they set upon others. (The practice, which has been historically exercised on both the living and the dead, is called "hemoposia," and is well documented in A. V. Wolf's classic study on thirst. Castaways have consumed the blood of seabirds, cavalrymen of their horses. Wolf also relates the case of a prospector who, "seeing dimly a luscious-looking arm nearby . . . seized it and mumbled it with his mouth, and greedily sought to suck the blood; he had a vague sense of protest by the owner of the arm, who seemed a long way off, and was astounded two days later to find that the wounds were inflicted on himself.")[18]

AS THE FIRST RAYS OF LIGHT FILTERED through openings in the hatch cover, Beecher took stock "of the terrible carnage in the hold"—the contorted corpses, the heaps of the unconscious, the crazed, the wounded. Even those who'd survived the night "looked like demons," filthy and drawn.[19]

The colonel called for the interpreter. He knew they were abandoning ship, he told Wada. When, he asked, were the Japanese going to get the prisoners off? And just then the American dive-bombers came back, dropping their loads and firing air-to-ground rockets.

One bomb landed by the fantail. The men in the aft hold saw a flash of yellow, felt a blast of heat, and were showered with shrapnel, timbers, and slivers of wood. Scores were killed and wounded.

From all three holds now, the prisoners started shimmying up poles and ladders into the light. The ship, listing hard to port, looked like it had run aground, and some of the men recognized where they were, just off the cliffs of Olongapo Point, a former American Navy base on Subic Bay at the Bataan-Pampanga border. From the starboard side of the *Oryoku Maru*, looking east, the beaches and concrete landings of Subic Bay were roughly eight hundred yards away. The top deck was aswarm with prisoners now, scuttling around clumps of bodies, American and Japanese, piled on deck. Meanwhile, hundreds of men had gone into the water and were making for shore.

Beecher, topside now, found a piece of life preserver and stripped off his filthy rags and jumped into the bay. Water! Cool water.

Then the planes came back for another pass. How many of his men would be killed this time? Beecher wondered. Would bombs blowing up underwater kill them outright, or would they be left unconscious and drown within sight of shore?

Around him hundreds of swimmers were frantically waving their arms and shirts at the sky, and the American pilots, apparently realizing that the lily-white bodies in the bay might not be enemy, broke off their approach.

Beecher wasn't so thirsty anymore; maybe the bay water was restoring him, he thought. Meanwhile, he could see that ashore Japanese soldiers and Naval Infantry had manned a number of gun posts along the shoreline and seawall, and now those machine guns were being trained on the prisoners paddling in the water.

One Japanese gunner was swinging the barrel of his machine gun back and forth at the swimmers, as if to warn them to swim directly to shore and not down the coast. Beecher, his feet touching bottom now, stood up in the water, directly in front of the menacing Japanese gunner, and began to direct the swimmers to the seawall steps and landing points.

Weak and exhausted from two days and nights belowdecks, some of the swimmers started to drown, but instead of letting them go to their deaths, their stronger comrades grabbed them and hauled them into shallow water. And as Beecher looked back, he also saw men near him paddling back out to the ship on bits of wreckage or in damaged lifeboats to pick up the weak, the wounded, the unconscious abandoned on deck. Their sense of society, it seemed, had been restored, even if only for the moment. Three, four times they went back to rescue their comrades. What grit, Beecher thought.[20]

JAPANESE SOLDIERS ashore herded the prisoners up a path to a cluster of trees, where Tom Hayes and other doctors set up a temporary infirmary. The medicos had only the scant supplies they'd carried aboard ship and had managed to save swimming ashore. For bandages they tore up the rags they were wearing and went naked.

That night, with Wada the interpreter and Lieutenant Toshino back in charge (they'd somehow escaped the ship), the Japanese confined the prisoners outdoors on two side-by-side concrete tennis courts surrounded by a twelve-foot-high chicken-wire fence. Then they ordered a roll call.

Beecher climbed the referee's chair and started yelling out names. The count continued for hours. By dusk, they knew that some 250 of the 1,619 men who had boarded the *Oryoku Maru* two days earlier were dead, and at least a score of the survivors were in such bad shape they were not expected to survive.[21]

On December 20, Japanese guards moved the detail north to San Fernando, La Union, then some days after that to Lingayen Gulf, where, on December 27, the prisoners were loaded aboard two freighters— about eleven hundred on the *Enoura Maru*, the remainder on the *Brazil Maru*—bound for Takao, Formosa.

Since there were fewer of them to jam into the holds, the space belowdecks was not as tight, but the *Enoura Maru* and *Brazil Maru* were no less hellships. Dark, smothering spaces, with scant water and rations. The wounded, the critically sick, the addled and enfeebled—all were at the end of their endurance, and every day two or three of them died.

On New Year's Eve the two ships made port at Takao, and the prisoners from the *Brazil Maru* were transferred to the *Enoura Maru*. Beecher watched as the weak men crossed the top deck to the hatches leading below. "Walking skeletons," he thought.[22]

The harbor was crowded with ships, and the *Enoura Maru* tied up at a buoy alongside a tanker. For several days the men in the holds heard antiaircraft fire, and the prisoners who'd been allowed on deck to cook the detail's rice reported seeing high-flying planes. Beecher reckoned the crowded harbor was "an ideal target," and he "felt sure" that if the *Enoura Maru* stayed in port much longer, the detail would be bombed. Again.

On Tuesday, January 9, at first light the guards called for the chow detail to come on deck. A while later buckets of rice, water, and soup were lowered into the hold. Beecher got his handful and sat down against a bulkhead to eat. He dipped his spoon into his mess cup, lifted the spoon to his mouth, and just then the space around him exploded.

The shock wave from the bomb hit Beecher hard. He shook his head, shook it again, trying to get his wits back. He saw holes in the hull, flames licking at the bulkheads. He looked at his legs, checked his body. No puncture wounds, no blood. Around him, however, the hold was havoc.

Dozens of men had been killed instantly, their contorted and mutilated bodies scattered across the deck and against the bulkheads. Scores more lay nearby with gaping wounds, the life bleeding out of them. Many of Beecher's friends were dead. Gunner Farrell, one of the colonel's battalion officers, was holding his head in his hands, one of his eyes blown out.

The prisoners guessed the ship had taken several hits. One bomb had fallen on the edge of the most forward hold, killing more than half the five hundred men there. When the doctors were done doing what they could, they tried to take stock: overall some three hundred men had been killed, they thought, and as many wounded.

Beecher asked for permission to remove the corpses from the holds, but for three days Wada and Toshino refused. (More punishment, the colonel figured, for the American bombings.) Finally the Japanese lowered cargo nets, hauled the bodies up, and dropped them onto a barge to be cremated in a common grave ashore.

THE *ENOURA MARU* was too badly damaged to continue, and on Saturday, January 13, the surviving prisoners were transferred back to the *Brazil Maru*. That night, after the ship had gotten under way, Wada demanded a roll call. Beecher, exhausted, tried to get a count. Nine hundred and seventy-five, he reported, more than six hundred men gone from the original detail.

For the next seventeen days the *Brazil Maru* sailed slowly up the China coast, steaming by day, putting into coves and inlets at night. Not long out of port, it became clear there was something wrong with the ship's water supply and fresh-water condensers. The water tasted brackish and the prisoners were getting less and less with their rice. Now, from wounds that would not heal, from dysentery, disease, and declines of thirst and hunger that were irreversible, men died twelve to fifteen a day. Wada ordered Beecher to take daily roll calls. Sometimes a man would answer "here," then die before the count was finished.

They arrived at Moji, Japan, on January 30. There was snow on the ground. The survivors, in Japanese cotton issue, stood shivering on deck—only 425 of them, one-quarter of the 1,619 men who had started the journey on December 13 at Pier 7.

Frank Bridget, the indefatigable leader of the aft hold on the *Oryoku Maru*, was dead. So was Tom Hayes (who had buried his secret diaries in the dirt of Bilibid Prison before he shoved off). In all, eighty-four doctors, dentists, pharmacists, and corpsmen from the prison died on the December 13 draft, including Gordon Lambert, the doctor who had saved Ben Steele's life.

In the weeks that followed, as the survivors finally came to their senses, they began to count their great good luck. For every one of them, three had died. What but luck could explain that?

There was no accounting for the sadness, of course, the emptiness that always follows the euphoria of luck. Almost every man had lost a buddy, a friend for the road. And they could not shake the feeling that their lives, their great good luck, had somehow been purchased at someone else's expense.

To a man, they also remembered a voice. When the bedlam was at its height, when men were screaming and moaning and begging for their lives, Father William T. Cummings, the Maryknoll priest who in Bilibid had read Ben Steele the last rites, would make his way to the middle of the hold and shout to be heard.

"Listen to me," he would yell. "You must listen to me!"

Then, in a clear but calming voice, he would recite a prayer.[23]

> Our Father, who art in heaven . . .
> Give us this day our daily bread.
> And forgive us our trespasses,
> As we forgive those who trespass against us . . .

He recited that same evensong every night, a prayer for the living, a prayer of thanks, a prayer for the dead.

The priest ministered to anyone who needed him, and almost everyone did. In a month he recited more last rites than most padres offer in a year of combat, then berated himself openly for not being able to hold the hand and ease the dying angst of every man in the ship who needed him.

"Father, please, pray for me," they begged, or, "Baptize me, Father. I don't want to die without being baptized."

He was a short, thin man, forty-one years old, in constant pain from an old back injury that had required spinal fusion. He had chronic asthma as well, and the close air in the holds must have been torture for him. Nothing, however, seemed to slow his ministrations. He played medic as well as priest, crawling over and across men to get to the worst of the wretches in the back of the holds. To some men, Cummings's soft incantations—"humming whispers," Sidney Stewart called them—sounded like the voice of God; to others it was the voice of faith, or a friend.[24]

Each night he tried to take his rice with a different circle of men. One night he talked of his days in Manila before the war. He liked working with indigents, street children, he said, and if he survived, he planned to continue the same kind of missionary work in Tokyo.

"The bastards are hopeless," one of the men said.

"Son," Cummings came back, "no one is hopeless."[25]

Bill Cummings died on a Sunday in the hold of the *Brazil Maru*, two days short of making port at Moji.

TWELVE

September 1, 1944, Shimonoseki, Japan

A S THE TRAIN carrying Ben Steele and some 250 other Americans headed east from Shimonoseki, the men sat quietly and stared out the windows at the stops along the way—Chōfu, Ozuki, Habu. At the Asagawa River, the tracks turned sharply north into the highlands, one sylvan valley after another hemmed by hillsides draped with evergreens and stands of jade bamboo.

At length they came to the city of Mine (pronounced *Min-ay*) in Yamaguchi Prefecture, some twenty-four linear miles from Shimonoseki. They disembarked and walked for what seemed a long way, all of it uphill, until they reached Mugikawa. On a flat of land across from the village was a large compound surrounded by a high wooden fence. Inside the compound were rows of two-story wood buildings connected by well-groomed walkways. This, they were told, was to be their new camp. "Omine-machi," the guards called it, "big mountain town," mountains that had been a rich source of anthracite coal for almost seventy years.

During his time as a prisoner of war, Ben Steele had worked as a road builder, a stevedore, a farm hand. Soon he would add coal miner to his wartime résumé.

THE BARRACKS were the best the prisoners had seen, but the work they were forced to perform was grueling, especially for men so malnourished. They worked underground, twelve-hour shifts around the clock, ten days at a stretch with one day off. They were convict labor, picking and shoveling and hauling and loading in a labyrinth of damp laterals, long diagonals, and cramped coal drifts a half mile underground. They worked sick, they worked hungry, they worked hurt.

They worked and waited. That was the worst of it, the waiting, marking time, the days since surrender (871 . . . 906 . . . 1,002). Rescue, liberation, freedom—they could think of little else. Often they'd look up and see flights of American bombers overhead, and a short time later they would hear the faint report of explosions, like far-off thunder. Surely their deliverance was at hand. Just stay alive, they told one another, and be careful. Like all the places where they had been penned, Omine-machi had its share of thugs and sadists, civilian and ex-military guards who carried a *kombō*, a short, curved, hardwood club that could break a man's bones or crack a man's skull. A prisoner might not recover from a beating like that. All this way to end as ashes.

THE BARRACKS compound was a mile from the colliery and mine heads. Four men lived in a ten-by-ten room, eight rooms on each floor. The floors were covered with tatami, woven straw mats on which the men slept. The doors, windows, and sliding walls were rice paper and wood decorated with pieces of seashell. The barracks had electric lights but no heat, and winter in Mine, roughly the same latitude as Oklahoma City, was cold. (The men were issued cotton bed quilts, but these "little old comforters," as one of the boys referred to them, were too small to cover the large *gaijin*, foreigners.) Each barracks had its own privy, but they shared a communal bath, two large concrete tubs under an outdoor pavilion.

Breakfast and supper, the beginning-of-shift and end-of-shift meals, were served in a mess hall; their midshift meal they carried to work in wooden boxes (*bentō*) tied with a piece of string. Breakfast was rice-barley gruel, often laced with weevils; lunch was cooked rice with a sprinkling of vegetables, various greens, and tubers; dinner, more rice with vegetables and perhaps fish, always stinking or spoiled. The fish was usually mackerel or tuna, but there was never enough for individual portions, and it was served as a condiment on rice or in soup. At each meal the men also got soybean buns, a wartime staple in Japan, as tough to chew as hardtack.

The overall individual ration was small, an average of twenty-two ounces of food a day. The Japanese said their own people were starving, and the prisoners should expect to suffer along with everyone else, and by and large that was true. Cold weather had hurt the fall harvest of 1944, and by early 1945 the United States had control of the sea-lanes around Japan, in effect blockading the country and preventing vital shipments of foodstuffs from the south. Often the only place a Japanese *shufu*, housewife, could buy food was on the black market, where rice sold for seventy times the normal price. In short, the Nipponjin were hungry, but not nearly as hungry as the skeletons in prison drag who watched their Japanese overseers wolf down meals that seemed a lot more substantial and appetizing than the pathetic rations put in front of the prisoners.[1]

The first week in camp each prisoner was issued two sets of clothes (plain army uniforms), a pair of zori (sandals), cloth work boots, and a wool overcoat (captured swag) for the winter. The day the prisoners got their issue, the Japanese shaved their heads, a prophylactic against parasites, then they gave each man a prisoner number. Ben Steele was *sanbyaku gojū kyū*, 359. The numbers were afixed to their uniforms, then the prisoners were told to sit on a bench and face a camera. These mug shots were pasted on individual cards, the man's number on top, his name below. 291, Private, Woodrow Smith . . . 326, Private, Gerald Greenman . . . 435, Private, Dan Pinkston. Different men with the same face—tight lips, insolent jaw, smoldering eyes—sending their captives the same message.

WHEN THE AMERICANS ARRIVED in camp, they joined 180 British prisoners of war captured in the Dutch East Indies and already working there. The British, who occupied five of the eleven barracks in the compound, apparently felt that their tenure gave them certain privileges. In the mess hall, for example, they liked to cut ahead of the Americans on the chow line. The Americans, naturally, refused to step aside (they figured their ancestors had long since settled the issue of superiority with the British) and there followed what Army Private Dan Pinkston of Naples, Florida, called, some "downright knock-'em-down, drag-'em-out fistfights." It took more than "a few whippings," Pinkston noted, to get the British "educated to the fact that the line formed in the rear."[2]

The Japanese were happy with their British prisoners. The Englishmen were neat and well mannered. Most of the time they followed orders and worked cooperatively to meet their production quotas. The *Americajin*, by contrast, were unruly malingerers, always complaining.

Those Americans! the Japanese supervisors would say, *karera ni wa taku-san no ketten ga atta*, "they have many faults." So many that there was a waiting line of Americans for the compound's *dokubō*, its solitary confinement cell. After a while the Japanese got the idea that the two groups of *gaijin* didn't get along and stopped trying to mingle them. And in time the colonials and red coats reached a rapprochement: they agreed they would never understand each other.

"You know what you've done?" a Brit told Irwin Scott. "You've gone and ruined our prison camp."

"How the hell do you ruin a prison camp?" Scott said.[3]

> It's a long way to Tipperary,
> It's a long way to go.
> It's a long way to Tipperary
> To the sweetest girl I know!

From the start, they liked the same marching song, about the only thing the two groups could agree on. The British sang it every day walking to work, and the Americans, their Anglophobia tempered, picked up on the tune and often sang it coming out of the mines.

Nobuyasu Sugiyama thought the song so catchy, he learned every word of the chorus, and many of the verses, too. Sugiyama started working at the mine in the fall of 1942, a seventeen-year-old civilian supervisor assigned to shepherd the British prisoners between the compound and the mine head. They marched, he marched; they sang, he sang, too.

> Goodbye Piccadilly,
> Farewell Leicester Square!
> It's a long long way to Tipperary,
> But my heart's right there.

The Tommies must have enjoyed this subtle subversion, their Japanese overseer marching along, pumping his arms, joining them in a song intended to boost their morale. Nobuyasu Sugiyama thought nothing of it. He liked the British. They worked hard and did what they were asked to do.

He liked his job as well. At sixteen he had graduated from the mining branch of a prefecture technical school and the next year started working for the Sanyo Muen Mine at Omine-machi. He was a good-looking, agreeable boy, and his bosses were impressed that someone so young went about his work with such purpose. His father had died when he was a child, and now he was the sole support and head of his household—mother, grandfather, two younger brothers, and a cousin. He'd been at the mine only a short time in the fall of 1942 when the British prisoners arrived, but already he'd decided to make mining his career and thought of himself as a loyal company man. Company officials responded by putting him in charge of the British prisoners, whom, by all accounts, he treated well, slipping them extra food from his own stores, buying them tobacco in town.

When three hundred Americans arrived at Omine-machi in the fall of 1944, the mine bosses thought Nobuyasu Sugiyama the right man to take them over. He'd done a good job with the British; he'd do a good job with this new group of *gaijin*.

Sugiyama assumed, as would most Japanese, that there was little difference between white English-speaking foreigners, and he expected that his relationship with the Americans would be as harmonious as it was with the British. But to the hard-bitten Yanks, Sugiyama was just another Jap jailer, and a wet-behind-the-ears jailer at that. At first they dubbed him "the Boy." "Hey, Junior," they would sometimes yell, and Nobuyasu Sugiyama could tell from their tone that the term was no compliment. These American *furyo* (POWs) were different, he thought. With them, there would be no singing.[4]

SOMETIMES, walking the mile from the barracks to the colliery to begin his shift, Ben Steele would survey the countryside—the emerald green hills and mountains, the odd little homes in the village, the women coming down from the slopes with firewood in baskets on their backs. "This place is quite scenic," he'd think. Then he'd remember how tired and hungry he was or, looking himself over, scowl at the accumulated layers of soot and mine grime on his trouser legs and think about the long day he was about to spend in a dark hole under tons of rock.

The colliery—a collection of buildings and sheds on the surface connected by a lattice of pipes, chutes, conduits, and spillways—was spread out in a valley and occupied the slopes of Mount Botayama, a region that had produced a granular, oil-rich variety of coal since 1877. Here and there in the valley were a dozen mine heads, arched entranceways leading to a subterranean complex of diagonals, tunnels, laterals, and dusty coal drifts, "the sunless depths of the earth," as Stephen Crane described the nocturnal world where men spend long hours digging and shoveling in the dark.[5]

At the beginning of a shift (5:30 a.m. for the early shift, 4:30 p.m. for the late), the men gathered at the mine head and boarded a small cable-car train that carried them into the heart of the mountain. The main tunnels and most of the side laterals had electric lights, but not the coal drifts. There men wielded picks and shovels in a gloom, the beams from their hat lamps flipping this way and that like miniature searchlights.

The prisoners worked in seven-man crews. Ben Steele was assigned to *roku shotai muen*, coal crew number six. Each day his crew descended into the mountain and disembarked in one of the main tunnels, then walked a half mile to the coal drift (the side lateral) they were working. Two men with picks loosened the coal, then two others with shovels threw it onto a V-shaped metal trough that ran back down the drift to a connecting lateral and a conveyor belt that emptied into a large hopper, which, in turn, filled coal cars bound for the surface.

It was eerie down there in the stygian caverns and drifts, their headlamps throwing shadows on the cave walls. After an hour digging and shoveling, the men were covered in black dust. The dust filled their lungs, of course—the makeshift masks they fashioned from rags were poor filters—and they always finished a shift coughing and hacking and blowing their noses.

Sometimes they also came out shaken, for mine work was dangerous. The weight of the mountain was always pushing down on the timber braces that supported the ceilings, and these braces frequently collapsed, burying part of the drift and sending thick black clouds billowing out into the main tunnels. None of the Americans were killed in these cave-ins—Japanese miners had long since mapped escape routes for just such emergencies—but each collapse left everyone, including the Japanese supervisors, on edge.

WHEN THEIR SHIFT WAS DONE, the men headed for the *sentō*, the communal bath, for their group soak. The etiquette of the communal hot tub called for a dirty bather to soap up and rinse off at a faucet before slipping into the water. The Americans, naturally, just piled in. The rock crews, timber crews, and men working topside quickly learned to get to the tubs ahead of the coal crews, whose grimy members always left the water the color and consistency of ink.

On their one day off in ten, the men washed and repaired clothing, cleaned the latrines and dumped the honey pots, picked lice off one another, reread the shredded stack of letters they carried from camp to camp. Most of the time they sat around gabbing, and the talk always turned to food. Sizzling steaks and chops, plump chickens, mounds of mashed potatoes and butter, bowls of applesauce and ice cream.

When they weren't talking about food, they were trying to scrounge or steal it. They stole from the gardens of the locals and from the guards' cabbage patch but rarely from one another. In a society of hungry captives, taking another man's grub was considered a capital crime, the lowest and most craven form of behavior. In November and December 1944, every American in camp received an eleven-pound Red Cross package. And just in time. Working in the cold had left them even hungrier, if that was possible, and the packages helped the men survive into the new year. In February 1945 a much smaller shipment of Red Cross boxes arrived, one package shared among six. Ben Steele collected the cans allotted him, scratched his initials on the tops with a rock, and stowed them in his room. A few nights later returning to his barracks, he discovered his stash gone. Checking through the barracks, he met another man who'd been robbed, Sergeant Ralph Keenan of Denver. The two nosed around the compound, and it wasn't long before they had a line on the thief.

What should they do? they asked each other. No point reporting the theft to the Japanese—they wouldn't give a damn. And the two hungry prisoners were also certain that their own officers, a couple of captains who had never exerted their authority, would just shrug the matter off. If they wanted their supplies back, they concluded, they'd have to go after the stuff themselves.

They found the pilferer hiding in his room. Turned out he'd eaten almost every damn can he'd filched. They stood there for a few seconds thinking about their empty stomachs, then they took off their belts, wrapped the rough strands of hemp around their knuckles, and began to beat the robber bloody.

"Stop!" he begged them. "Please, stop."

But his assailants kept flailing away.

"We ought to kill you," Ben Steele yelled, kicking and punching the man. "Kill you, you lousy son of a bitch."

THE JAPANESE HAD CAPTURED 192,600 Allied military prisoners of war—Americans, Britons, Australians, Indians, Dutchmen. They penned their captives in 367 prisons and work camps located along what has come to be called the Pacific Rim—Japan, Manchuria, Formosa, the Philippines, China, Hong Kong, Burma, Siam, French Indochina, Malaya, and the islands of the Dutch East Indies. One hundred and sixty-five of these work camps were in Japan and Manchuria. Together they served as a source of slave labor for vital Japanese industries: tanneries, textile factories, steel and lumber mills, coal and iron and copper mines, chemical plants, dry docks, wharfs, rail yards and terminals, construction and irrigation projects, processing plants, and refineries.[6]

The Americans chafed under their chains, and in every factory and work site, they plotted rebellion, a state of mind as natural to them as conformity was to the Japanese. There was still a good bit of fight in them too, patriotism in some men, simple revenge in others. And they exercised these impulses in a thousand small acts of sabotage—breaking tools, jamming machines, botching jobs.

At Omine-machi, coal cars were always going off the tracks, slowing production, and electric blowers in the ventilation system frequently had to be shut down so Japanese repairmen could remove the rocks and debris jamming the motors. The Japanese also noticed something strange about the mine's daily yields. The Americans appeared to be working hard enough—each time a Japanese supervisor poked his nose into a drift, he'd find the crew of prisoners working away, but despite all the work, the American coal crews never seemed to meet the production quotas mine officials set for them.

The Americans were goldbricking, of course, faking it. Using lookouts and a system of signals and whistles, the prisoners alerted one another at the approach of a Japanese, and men who had been sitting around, snoozing and lollygagging, would jump up and make a great show of work.

If the Japanese caught on, they never said so. They wouldn't. To charge anyone in Japan, even a lowly prisoner of war, with nonfeasance and not have proof would make the complainant look silly, lose face. So the Japanese administered "private punishment" instead, which is to say they punched, slapped, kicked, and cudgeled the prisoners for any infraction.

The bullies meting out this punishment acquired nicknames, descriptive epithets. "Fat Boy" and "the Frog" liked to use clubs, while "the Weasel" and "the Bull" preferred to hammer men with their fists. ("When the Bull hits you," one of the men said, "you stayed hit.") Nobuyasu Sugiyama, "Junior" now, was much younger than the other supervisors and was always trying to prove himself their equal.[7]

Here was a prisoner who wasn't shoveling fast enough. Slap! And here was a man too slow pushing a coal car down a lateral. Slap, again. Sugiyama slapped Sergeant Robert E. Kay from Electra, Texas, so hard and so often, the sergeant's ears were sore for months. Sometimes Junior would beat a man for thirty minutes or more—knock him down, pull him up, scream at him to stand at attention, then knock him down again. These lazy Americans, they weren't fooling him. If he thought a crew was sloughing off or putting on a show of work, he'd come up behind a man, pull off his cap, feel his forehead for sweat and, taking dry skin as evidence of sloth, slap the hell out of him.

In April 1945 Sugiyama was hospitalized for appendicitis, and when he returned to work, he was assigned to supervise several construction and cleanup crews topside. He wasn't happy with this new assignment; the Americans were "ignoring" him, he felt, and he detected a very strong "anti-Japanese feeling" in the American straw boss, likely a sergeant, who was their ramrod.

Things came to a head one late summer day, a small problem with some string. A work crew of nineteen men had been mixing cement. With almost everything in Japan in short supply, Sugiyama had left standing orders for the topside crews to take care with the cement bags, and when he went to inspect them later in the day and found the bottoms ripped out, he told the guards to line up the men.

Indeed, the prisoners had been monkeying with the sacks, but their purpose was salvage not sabotage; they were after the short lengths of string that held the bags together bottom and top, string they needed to mend their clothing and gear, tie their shoes (if they had them), secure their *bentō* boxes.

Sugiyama was very angry. He wanted to know which of them had taken the string and damaged the sacks. In other words, who had deliberately ignored his instructions?

When no one owned up, he made the prisoners form two lines, one facing the other, then he ordered them to start slapping one another.

To the Japanese, "line slapping" was a familiar form of corporal punishment, used in schools and military training camps. To the Americans, it was just more of the malignant mauling they had endured since the day they surrendered.

Supervisors wielding clubs joined the proceedings to make sure the prisoners weren't pulling their punches. Standing at the end of the line, Private Paul A. Dobyns of Mount Vernon, Missouri, had no slapping partner, so Sugiyama stepped into the gap.

Poor Dobyns, his comrades knew he was in for it. Junior slapped Dobyns so hard so often he knocked him to the ground. Then the real punishment began. Sugiyama drew his leg back and kicked Dobyns, kicked him in the head, the face, the ribs, the back. Kicked, kicked.

The line slapping, meanwhile, continued. One of the men guessed that they had slapped and swatted one another for almost thirty minutes. Toward the end of the time, the prisoners were so exhausted they could hardly raise their hands to deliver another blow.

Dobyns was in terrible shape. Sugiyama had turned his face into chopped meat and left him half deaf. Private Dick Bilyeu, a fellow Missourian, helped carry Dobyns to the bath and put him to bed. His face was inflated, his left eye swollen shut. Sugiyama seemed to have crushed the man's spirit as well. Dobyns refused to eat, and Bilyeu and others had to force-feed him to keep him alive.[8]

THE ALLIES were closing in fast, taking back territory as they moved closer to the enemy homeland. On January 9, 1945, American forces at last returned to the big island of Luzon, coming ashore at Lingayen Gulf not far from where the Japanese had landed three years before. American forces soon reoccupied Clark Field. A special column of troops, meanwhile, drove south through Japanese lines and entered Manila on February 4, liberating the civilian internment camp at the University of Santo Tomas and the POW compound at Bilibid Prison. By early March the last pockets of resistance in the capital had been eliminated. Half the city was in rubble, but Manila at last had been liberated.[9]

That spring, American bombers were mobilized for a massive air attack on Japan. On March 10, a little after midnight, the first planes in a force of 334 B-29 bombers carrying two thousand tons of incendiaries, oil-gel and jellied gasoline bombs, appeared over Honshū. Their target was Tokyo, and their mission was to set the city ablaze. When they were finished, almost sixteen square miles of the enemy capital was in ashes. More than one hundred thousand Japanese men, women, and children were killed in the six-hour conflagration; a million more were injured; a million lost their homes. In the days that followed, the B-29s set Nagoya, Ōsaka, Kōbe, and other Japanese cities aflame.[10]

On April 1, American naval and ground forces continued their push north, invading the Japanese island of Okinawa, just 340 miles from Honshu. The fighting was savage and grim, with no quarter asked or given. As American casualties mounted, scientists at a secret location in New Mexico pushed ahead with the development of a new, experimental weapon, an atom bomb. Such a weapon, American leaders concluded, might bring the Japanese to their knees, end the war early and forestall the need to invade the Japanese home islands.

Germany formally surrendered in May, and the war in Europe was over. The next month the leaders of the United States, Britain, and Russia met at Potsdam, Germany, to talk about the economic and political shape of postwar Europe. In their final report they also defined the terms for a Japanese surrender. "We do not intend that the Japanese shall be enslaved as a race or destroyed as a nation," they wrote, "but stern justice shall be meted out to all war criminals, including those who have visited cruelties upon our prisoners."[11]

IN THE WORK and slave labor camps, American prisoners of war, reading the glum faces of their supervisors and eavesdropping on the gossip of a few friendly guards, could see that their keepers knew the war was lost. And the Americans began to worry that the Imperial Army, either out of military expediency or as an act of final revenge, might issue orders to work camp commanders to kill the seventy thousand prisoners of war being held in the home islands.[12]

At Omine-machi that spring, the mine guards ordered a group of prisoners to dig a long trench in the barracks compound and cover it with steel reinforcing rods, timbers, and mounds of dirt. The ditch was an air-raid shelter, the prisoners were told, but many of the men, especially Irwin Scott and a few of his fellow marines in camp, huddled together and imagined a more perfidious purpose. "They're going to shove

us in there and slaughter us," Scott told his comrades, a suspicion soon shared by almost everyone in camp.

That summer, as homeland shortages and suffering increased and Japanese fear of a ground invasion mounted, the guards at Omine began to taunt their charges. "If America ever invades our islands," they said, "we are going to shoot you, all of you." So the prisoners sat down and made a plan. At the first sign of trouble—if the guards, say, attempted to herd them into the long trench—they would stage a "general uprising, kill anyone we can get ahold of," then break out of the camp, head into the hills around the mine, and try to hold out until the American invaders could rescue them.[13]

WHEN THE AMERICAN B-29 *Enola Gay* dropped the atomic bomb on Hiroshima at 8:15 a.m. on August 6, the sound of the blast reached the city of Omine, fifty-five miles away. At the colliery, the men heard the rumble of the bomb and felt the vibrations for what seemed like several minutes.

About an hour later, a huge smokelike cloud seemed to block the sun. The prisoners, who had been tracking the flights of American bombers for weeks, guessed that their air force had dropped a very large conventional bomb, perhaps one of those "blockbusters" they'd heard the British were using in Europe.

In the days that followed, the Japanese civilian guards and mine supervisors seemed especially short-tempered and peevish, quick to strike. Clearly, something was up. The prisoners huddled in their barracks. What should they do? Take a chance, break out of the compound, and head for the hills? Or wait?

After breakfast on August 16, the Japanese commandant of the camp and the British major who was the senior officer in charge called an assembly of prisoners in the mess hall. The commandant announced there would be no work that day, which was strange, since the day before had been the prisoners' regular day off. Some of the men were uneasy, ready to act. Then, in a steady voice, the commandant said that Japan had surrendered to the Allies, and he, in turn, was surrendering the camp to the British major. The war was over.

At first there was quiet. Ben Steele and Irwin Scott and Dan Pinkston and John Crago and the rest of them just sat there and stared at the two officers standing in front of the room. For months the guards had been telling them, "You'll be old men with canes by the time you get out of here," and there were moments, moments without heart or hope, when they believed them. Now, the enemy had surrendered. Just like that, after breakfast.

A few men clapped, politely. A few others began to cry.

"Thank you, God," they said. "Thank you."

Ben Steele shut his eyes. He thought, "I haven't seen the family since October 1940, almost five years. I wonder if they're all still alive."

Later, their officers told them they were to stay in camp and wait for the Allies to land and find them. They should be patient; there were lots of camps to liberate. Meanwhile, American aircraft would drop food to them, the officers said. They should get ready. They'd soon have something to eat.

August 31, 1945
To any American that can read this letter
We're writing this en route to Japan where we'll attempt to find you fellows and drop these supplies. Before going into a long letter here are a few instructions:

The other day we were up over a couple of P.O.W. camps and dropped supplies. The results were tragic. The oil drums in which the supplies were packed went careening down on the P.O.W.'s and their barracks and injured several fellows. Two were killed because the chutes failed to open. The men had gathered together in a bunch and I think a barrel went right into the middle of them. This time we intend to go a little higher and give the chutes more time to open. We also have instructions not to drop the supplies right in the camp, but near it. So watch out for the stuff as it comes down and watch where it goes and get it as soon as possible because we don't want the Japs to get it any more than you do . . .

It won't be long before you all will see American troops. A few special troops have already landed in Tokyo to prepare for the occupation forces which are coming in the near future. The Pacific Fleet is in Yokohama Bay waiting for MacArthur to lead the boys ashore. Incidentally, in case any of you were in the Philippines, Gen. Wainwright has been found in a Prison Camp on Manchuria by the Russians and is now in China witnessing the surrender of the Japs there.

The damned war is all over but the signing of the papers. Hold on a bit longer, fellows and you'll be on your way home. You're top priority on the list to go back "Stateside."

The crew of V-23
Capt. Edward P. Gumphrey
322nd Air Division[14]

Pamphlets that came with the food and clothing advised the men not to gorge themselves; they should start with fruit juice and soup, give their starved systems a chance to adjust to food rich in protein, fats, complex carbohydrates. They should go slow, eat light.

They ate everything. Chocolate, crackers, canned bread, meat, vegetables. They rushed to the parachutes, dumped the drums on the ground, got down on their hands and knees, and ate until they were sick. Then they rolled over, vomited, wiped the puke off their faces and started all over again.

The drums held cigarettes too (Old Golds, Lucky Strikes, Chesterfields) and the men chain-smoked night and day. "Damn place looks like it's on fire," Ben Steele thought, puffing along with rest of them.

After two weeks of waiting, they got word to proceed to the Omine city railroad station, and on September 15 they boarded trains, along with men from four other prison camps in the area, for Wakayama City near Wakanoura Bay, where the hospital ships USS *Consolation* and USS *Sanctuary* were anchored and waiting.

At Wakanoura beach, medical crews had set up receiving centers, and each man was stripped (his clothing was burned), given a bath or shower, sprayed with DDT, issued new trousers and a shirt, and given a physical. Then they boarded launches and were carried out to the ships, where they were put in pajamas and assigned a bed.

Most had the same complaints and conditions: enlarged livers (many were jaundiced) and weakened hearts. Malnutrition had also caused their optic nerves to degenerate, and a number had eye trouble. They suffered from bronchitis and respiratory infections—all that coal dust in the dank mines. Many had roundworms, boils, skin ulcers.

Psychiatrists, curiously, found them "in excellent condition, displaying both patience and gratefulness," behavior apparently taken as a sign of stability instead of what it was, the habit of stoic acceptance that had allowed them to survive three years of torment and want. Doctors also noted that the men's "descriptions of horrible experiences were characterized by a tendency toward understatement." As if the men knew already that their stories of surrender and imprisonment might be too much for the uninitiated to hear or understand.[15]

LIFE ABOARD the *Consolation* was sweet. For the moment they had everything they could want. Hot food, ice cream, cigarettes, pitchers of steaming coffee. And sheets, clean sheets starched snow-white. It felt so good to lie on them that Ben Steele refused to shut his eyes. He was happy, as happy as he could remember, and he didn't want that feeling to pass or to waste one second of it sleeping.

The nurses aboard the hospital ships (thirty on the *Consolation*) were as curious about their charges as their charges, libidos awakening, were about them. The women were accustomed to being around men hardened by combat or rough around the edges from the rigors of war, but there was something different, something very different about these POWs.

Lieutenant Doris Schwartz, a nurse on the USS *Marigold*, noticed some of her patients wandering about the ship, touching this thing and that, "as if to assure themselves of their reality." All of them seemed awed by the smallest things, conveniences everyone else took for granted.

Showers, for instance. They would stand under the hot water so long, they "emerged glowing." Others would sit for hours flipping through magazines—*Saturday Evening Post, Collier's, Life*—didn't make any difference how old the issue was. During the years they'd been away, there had been dramatic changes at home, and now they sat up in bed wide-eyed, slowly turning the pages hour after hour trying to catch up.

Most of all, they ate. Oh, how they ate! After a while the nurses and doctors tried to shrink their portions and limit their trips to the chow line, but "stealing food to live" had made the POWs artful dodgers and the nurses found chicken legs, bread, fruit, and pie "hidden under pillows, in pajama pockets, everywhere." "The appearance of food," Lieutenant Schwartz noted, "makes animals of them again."[16]

On September 22, the *Consolation* made port at Okinawa, and the men from the Air Corps, Ben Steele among them, boarded airplanes for the long hops back to the States: first to Guam, then Hawaii, and finally, on September 30, American soil, San Francisco, where they were checked into the army's Letterman General Hospital. After they were settled, most had the same request: Could they please use a telephone?

Ben Steele had trouble connecting. Finally an operator came on the line and told him there was no such exchange. He asked for information, had to be a listing for a Ben or Elizabeth Steele somewhere in Billings, he said. But there wasn't. All right, he said, connect him to the police department. Maybe they could locate the folks. The cops commiserated but couldn't help. Never mind, he'd call his Uncle Jimmy, his father's brother. If Jimmy was home, he'd know where the folks were.

The operator put the call through. The phone rang. A girl, a young girl from the sound of her, came on the line.

"Hello?" she said brightly.

"Hello," he answered back.

"Who's this?" the girl said.

"This is Bud."

A long silence, then the sound of a telephone handset hitting the floor. Goddamn, he thought, she must have fainted.

"Hey! . . . hey!" he yelled.

Then in the background he heard shouting. "It's Bud! Everybody, it's Bud!" Chairs rattled on a wooden floor and from the footfalls and all the shouting, it sounded like people were running around in circles. "It's Bud," he heard someone yell again. "Good Lord, it's Bud."

The girl came back on the phone. She was very excited.

"Bud, this is Polly," Uncle Jimmy's daughter, she said. They hadn't heard anything about him for so long, they thought he might be dead. "Where you at, Bud?"

"I'm in San Francisco—"

"He's in San Francisco," she yelled to the others.

"Where's the folks?" he asked.

"They're livin' up to Broadview, Bud," she said. The Old Man was managing the Spiedel Ranch up there.

"Well, give me their address and I'll write 'em."

"No, Bud. Dad said we're gonna get in the car and get on up there and tell 'em you're home."

When he finally connected with his family, his mother was beside herself. Between sobs she told him how much she'd missed him, how worried she'd been, how little word they'd had. He told her about the good care he was getting, all he was eating, how he couldn't wait to get back to Montana.

"We got lots of food here, Bud," she said. "We'll have a real celebration. It'll make a great Thanksgiving."

LETTERMAN GENERAL HOSPITAL was a way station for the returnees, the first of several hospitals and convalescent centers where they were to recover. The army was keeping a close medical eye on the former prisoners of war, testing them, talking to them, cataloging their ills. At Letterman, the army was also collecting evidence. The American government was preparing the "stern justice" it had promised the Japanese at Potsdam, and in every hospital, reception depot, and repatriation center where former POWs were being processed, lawyers and legal assistants were taking thousands of statements and affidavits about war atrocities and the criminals who had committed them.

A week later, on October 6, Ben Steele was transferred to Baxter General Hospital in Spokane, Washington, the closest army hospital to Billings, some six hundred miles east across the mountains. He was assigned to Ward B-5 with nine other returnees and examined again.

During forty-one months of captivity, he had dropped more than fifty pounds, but eating his way across the day and through the night, he had gained weight steadily since his release. (He figured he weighed 110 pounds on August 15, the day the Japanese surrendered. Now he was up to his prewar weight, roughly 165.) He seemed to have recovered from the jaundice, malaria, and pneumonia that had dogged him at Omine-machi, but he still suffered the lingering effects of severe malnutrition, beriberi in particular. His ankles and feet were slightly swollen, his skin was dry with red patches, and he had a slight heart anomaly. He also had bouts of dysentery; blood tests revealed the presence of amebiasis, a parasitic infection. He was missing several teeth as well, lost to malnutrition or the rocks that came in his prison camp rice.

Doctors treated the malnutrition with high doses of vitamins, the dysentery with carbasone, an antiprotozoan medicine, and dentists built him a prosthetic appliance for the missing teeth. Every night nurses also gave him a dose of phenobarbital, a barbiturate used as a hypnotic and sedative. His chart said they were treating him for "extreme nervousness," which was to say, he couldn't sleep.

He got through the days all right, but the nights were bad. At night he was slapped and punched and kicked all over again. He had lived so long in the world of the unknowable, the unforeseen, his psyche was still on tenterhooks. Extreme nervousness—a good description for the fear that followed him to bed. But what could they do, the doctors? There was no therapy for war, no drugs or talking cure to blunt what war leaves behind in the minds of the men coming home from the battlefields and prison camps. If a man was going to bed nervous, best anyone could do was give him a pill and urge him to get over it.

(Although there were psychiatrists serving in World War II, most of their work focused on keeping men in combat, restoring their psychological balance so they could resume their place on the fighting line or in the cockpit. The only serious research on so-called war neurosis, as Freud labeled it in World War I, was done by Colonel Roy R. Grinker and Major John P. Spiegel, two Army Air Force doctors who studied the effects of war on American and British air and ground forces in the campaign in North Africa in 1943. In May 1945, while Ben Steele was still a prisoner of war, the two men published *Men Under Stress*, a rare detailed look at the impact of war on the psyche, particularly the American psyche. Grinker and Spiegel did not talk with prisoners of war, but their findings can easily be transfigured to explain the experience of the men in the camps. Their work suggests that when an American soldier exchanges his "birthright of independence" for captivity, he cannot help but feel inferior. "The shattered confidence" and "helplessness which have been the product of [a prisoner's war] experiences" linger, and when a man is repatriated, he returns home "physically and psychologically depleted." The greater the "injury" to his psyche, the more difficult the "repair." The key was "to seek a solution" that would restore his sense of independence. He would never again experience the surety he had when he marched off to war—the enemy had taken care of that—but if his personality was strong enough and if he could find work or activity that restored his sense of self-sufficiency, he might "recover" and begin to build a new life.)[17]

BEN STEELE had started drawing again.

Not long after he arrived at Baxter, he took a call from Father John Duffy, the Catholic priest at Bilibid who had secreted the young artist's charcoal and pencil drawings in his Mass kit. The priest, recovering at Walter Reed Hospital in Washington, D.C., said he had some bad news. He'd shipped out on the *Oryoku Maru*, and when the ship was bombed and went down in Olongapo Bay, he left his Mass kit, and all Ben Steele's drawings, behind. Perhaps, Duffy suggested, he could start to re-create them.

His days were busy but quiet. Medical appointments, dental appointments, passes into town. He listened to the radio and read the newspapers, trying to catch up on the country he'd left four years before. He also wrote home regularly.

> *BAXTER GENERAL HOSPITAL*
> *Spokane, Washington*
> *Oct. 16, 1945*
>
> *Dearest Mother & Family:*
> *Thought would write a few more lines to let you know I am still O.K. and expecting to [be transferred to a nearby convalescent center] any moment now . . .*
>
> *I know it must have been awful hard for you Mother. Thought about you so much and how you were worrying. Am so happy to be back can't express my feelings . . . Will close with*
>
> *Love & kisses*
> *Bud*

Since the folks had no phone out at Broadview (none of the rural ranchers did), they had to plan his homecoming by mail.

Dearest Bud,

We are waiting every day to hear you are coming home. I guess they want to be sure you are able to return home. Have you had any steak yet? I remember how you used to love steak. There have been so many times here when we had everything to eat. I could never enjoy it thinking you were hungry . . .

Yes, Joe & Jean are pretty big & I am sure you would never know them. Joe said to me, "You will have to cook a lot of grub when Bud comes home as the way he talked, he could eat the whole tablefull."

Lots of love
Mother Dad
& kids.

A few days later, the beginning of the third week in October, a reporter from the *Spokane Daily Chronicle* came wandering through Ward B-5 in search of a story about returning prisoners of war.

BATAAN SURVIVOR AT BAXTER
RECALLS JAPS' BEASTLINESS

There was nothing unusual about a man receiving the last sacrament in Bilibid, the prison where the Japanese sent men to die when they were too feeble and sick to work.

This man was very sick. Over his frame, which normally carried a weight of 175 pounds, his skin was stretched drum-tight. He weighed maybe 100 pounds. This night in Bilibid, they thought, the man was going to die. They gave him the last sacrament.

But the man didn't want to die and he lived. His name is Sgt Benjamin C. Steele Jr. and he now is a patient at . . .

The article went on to list some of the grisly details of his imprisonment ("I have been beaten so many times I couldn't count them," he told the reporter), the death march, Tayabas Road, the hellships. Next day he clipped the article out of the paper and enclosed it in a letter home. When the letter arrived in Broadview, the article was read, reread, read again. Between readings, Bess Steele made up her mind to do something she'd been thinking about for nearly a month, since the day her son first called home.

Broadview Mont
Oct 23-1945
Dear Bud,
Received your letter & clipping Bud. Dad & I both cried when we read that clipping. Can't imagine anything like that happening to you. I hope MacArthur orders every Jap killed over there. I am so bitter toward them & I know you have a bitter feeling also. And more than we could ever have . . .

Well Bud I made up my mind to go to Spokane . . . I will leave this weekend & will go by bus.

Lots of Love
Kisses from all
Mother

The bus from Billings followed old Route 10 west through Livingston and up into Butte, then through the mountains to Missoula and Coeur d'Alene, Idaho, crossing the Washington state line east of Opportunity and, around three in the afternoon, finally stopping at the Greyhound bus terminal in downtown Spokane.

Bud had gotten there early, two hours early, and wandered around the terminal. When he got bored with circling, he sat down to wait, but he couldn't sit still, so he got up, circled some more, took a seat again. Then a voice from a loudspeaker announced that the bus from Coeur d'Alene would arrive in a few minutes. His chest grew tight; he could feel his pulse throbbing in his throat.

He walked out of the terminal and into the large open garage where the buses pulled up to unload. He found a spot against a wall where he could lean and watch.

The passengers got off slowly, stepping down onto the gray concrete platform.

"Five years," he thought. "I haven't seen her in so long."

And suddenly, there she was.

In an instant, they embraced.

"God, Bud," she said, "how I missed you."

She held him tight and for a long time.

"All right," she said at last, collecting herself, never taking her eyes off him. "Now I want you to walk"—she pointed to a spot a few feet away—"walk around over there."

"I'm fine, Mother," he said, "really."

Then she hugged him again.

SHE WAS OLDER than he remembered. In October 1940 when he left home, his mother was fifty, still dark-haired and lovely. Five years later, sitting across from him in the parlor of a family friend in Spokane, she looked seventy.

Her once dark hair was light gray going to white, her face creased, eyes exhausted.

She wanted to know everything, she said, everything that had happened to him, and he knew right away that talking to that reporter had been a mistake.

He tried to stick to what he thought she already knew, what she'd read in the newspapers, but his mother kept pressing him for details. She wanted the worst of it.

Finally he told her, "Look, Mother, you just won't believe where I've been. And I can't even explain that."

ON WEDNESDAY, November 14, thousands of people filled the streets of Spokane to honor General Jonathan "Skinny" Wainwright, a native son from nearby Walla Walla who had spent the war with Ned King in prison camps in Karenko, Formosa, and Mukden, Manchuria. A thin man before the war, Wainwright looked drawn now as he sat atop the boot of the open touring car that carried him down Sprague and Riverside avenues past some fifty thousand people (the largest crowd ever to gather in the city) who had lined up five and six deep at the curb to welcome him home with confetti and hurrahs that echoed through the downtown streets.

Following the general's party was a line of automobiles carrying former prisoners of war from the Army Air Force Regional and Convalescent Hospital at nearby Fort George Wright, among them Ben Steele.

People were leaning out of windows and waving from rooftops, more people than any of the former prisoners had ever seen. In the crowds along the curb, men removed their hats in salute, and women clutching handkerchiefs daubed the tears from their eyes.

Ben Steele was overwhelmed—all those cheers, all that attention— but he could not stop himself from wondering, "How do people really feel about us?" Hadn't he and his comrades let them down by giving up, surrendering? And how could a man think himself a hero just for staying alive?

HIS DISCOMFIT had really started several days before, on a trip to the suburbs to visit the wife and parents of his friend Walter Mace, who had died at Camp O'Donnell.

He'd been with Walter at the end in Zero Ward and had promised the dying man he'd visit his wife, Peggy, who was living with her in-laws.

He expected the visit would be wrenching, and he was right.

He told them how much he had liked Walter, what a fine man he was, and how he had gotten sick, so sick there was nothing anyone could do for him.

At the end, he said, the very end, Walter was thinking of home. ("'Go see Peggy,'" he quoted Walter as saying. "'Talk to her. Tell her. You promise?'")

Peggy was inconsolable. All he could do was sit there in her grief.

When he went back for dinner a few days later—he didn't want to go, but he felt he had no choice—he reminded himself to censor what he said.

The truth was, Walter had lost heart. Lying in his own filth and a swarm of flies, he gave up. Ben Steele had seen it in his rheumy eyes, the final look of sadness and submission that filled the face of almost every man who had entered Zero Ward.

HIS FURLOUGH started the day after the parade. He was eager to get home for Thanksgiving to see his mother again and the Old Man and Jean and Joe and Gert and her family. He wondered how much Billings had changed in the five years he'd been away. And he longed to set eyes on the prairie again, the image that filled his mind whenever he thought of home.

He boarded the North Coast Limited in Spokane and settled down in a seat for the six-hundred-mile trip to Billings. Not long after the train crossed the border into western Montana, another passenger, a man in a suit and tie, approached him. Ben Steele had seen the man eyeing the decorations on his uniform, the three rows of red, green, white, and gold campaign ribbons below his silver Air Corps wings.

"Who are you?" the man asked.

"I'm Bud Steele," he said. "How ya doin'?"

"Bud Steele? Really?"

He nodded.

"My God," the man said. "The whole town's been wondering about you."

And he offered Ben Steele a drink from a bottle of whiskey. By the time the train rolled into Billings, one drink had become five and Ben Steele walked right past his youngest sister without recognizing her.

"Hey, Bud!" she yelled. "It's me, Bud, Jean!"

The whole family was there, fifty of them, everyone hugging and kissing him and patting him on the back all watery eyed and blowing their noses. He looked around, taking it all in—the city seemed untouched by the war. Same small-town feel, anyway.

On Thanksgiving they went to Aunt Jo's in Musselshell for dinner. A real crowd, even the neighbors from the old days at Hawk Creek. It was the kind of meal he'd been imaging for years—turkey, dressing, mashed and sweet potatoes, green beans, gravy, cake, and pie. He stuffed himself, and everyone got a kick out of watching him.

AT HOME a few days later, his mother pulled him aside.

She had something to give him, she said, and she slipped her engagement ring off her right hand and held it out to him.

"This is the only thing I have of any value," she said. "And I want you to have it."

He tried to refuse, but she kept pushing it at him.

"You're going to take it, Bud. I want you to have it."

He could see there was no point arguing.

"Thanks, Mother," he said and slipped the diamond carefully into his pocket.

A COOL NOVEMBER MORNING and he is up early with the folks at the ranch in Broadview the Old Man is managing. His furlough has been a good one, about a week left, and this morning he's looking forward to helping the Old Man with some chores. Stock needs tending, and after breakfast he strolls out to the barn to get a horse. He takes the bay in the second stall, slips on a bridle, then a blanket and saddle. He works slowly, enjoying the creak and smell of leather, the barn dust, the protests of the bay against unfamiliar hands.

When he's done he leads the animal into the yard, puts his foot into the left stirrup, and finds his seat. His first time ahorse in years, and he sits there for a minute, taking in the ranch, the corrals, the chickens in the yard.

He'd been staring at the same scene for days, wandering out of the house every so often and lifting his nose to the wind to catch the scent of sage, studying the magpies and sparrows wintering in the hills, listening to the sound of the wind. He couldn't get enough of it, the rolling brown prairie, the cottonwoods, the winter grass, the feeling of being free.

THIRTEEN

NOW CAME THE DEFEATED, called to accounts.

In the fourteen years between 1931 and 1945, fifty million people—soldiers and civilians, belligerents and innocents—had lost their lives to war. Much of the world was in ruin, and tens of millions were homeless and adrift. As the Allies saw it, the war had been a criminal act, an assault on civilization, and they meant to make sure that the malefactors responsible for this misery answered for their acts.

The bill of particulars against the Japanese was long and unsettling. Murder, rape, torture—Nanking, Singapore, Hong Kong. More than twenty-four million men, women, and children had died in the fighting in Asia. Filipinos, Chinese, Koreans, Malayans, Thais, Burmese, Indians, Japanese. Crimes against peace. Crimes against humanity.

The victors wanted vengeance, a coda to the killing, an epilogue to all the loss. On August 28, 1945, two weeks after Emperor Hirohito announced Japan's surrender, the War Crimes Office of the War Department cabled General MacArthur (now supreme commander of the Allied Powers and in effect the military governor of Japan) a list of suspected Japanese war criminals and invited him to add his own warrants. Officials in Washington and on MacArthur's staff in Tokyo envisioned thousands of prosecutions, but for the moment they were after forty of the most notorious malefactors.

Number one on the list was Japan's political panjandrum, Hideki Tojo, war minister and prime minister for most of the war. The next nine names were also familiar, right-wing politicians and militarists who had made total war state policy. Then came name number eleven, Lieutenant General Masaharu Homma, former commander of the 14th Imperial Army, conqueror of the Philippines.[1]

Japanese diplomats were surprised to see Homma's name on the list, and so was Homma. On September 15, as he was preparing to leave Tokyo for Yokohama to surrender himself to military authorities, he paused to talk with American reporters. The general seemed genuinely ignorant of the charges against him. What was this "march of death" the reporters were talking about? And why were they referring to him in their dispatches as "the Beast of Bataan"?

From the back benches, the arrest looked like the work of Douglas MacArthur, personal revenge for the defeat MacArthur had suffered four years earlier at Homma's hands. No doubt the new supreme commander was satisfied to see his old nemesis in custody. Homma, after all, had humiliated him in battle, forced him to flee in the night and abandon his men to the enemy's tender mercies. But MacArthur was not the author of Homma's unhappy actualities. That role, in a roundabout way, belonged to a little-known fighter pilot, a tall blond Texan named Ed Dyess.[2]

WHEN THE JAPANESE BOMBED Clark Field in December 1941, Captain William E. Dyess of Albany, Texas, was commander of the 21st Pursuit Squadron. After surrender, Dyess made the torturous death march and rode the suffocating trains to Camp O'Donnell. In early November 1942, he was sent with a large draft of prisoners to a work camp at Davao on the southern island of Mindanao. A daring man, Dyess dreamed of escape, and one day in April 1943, he slipped into the jungle with nine confederates and began a long trek that would eventually land him, along with Lieutenant Colonel S. M. Mellnick and Navy Commander Melvyn McCoy, in Australia and then, finally, home.

Passing through Sydney, the men told their stories to MacArthur and his staff, and later in Washington they repeated the grim details of their capture and confinement for the generals and admirals at the War Department. Mellnick and McCoy had been captured on Corregidor and knew nothing of the march, but Dyess had made the sixty-six-mile trek, and he had lived for months in the doleful O'Donnell.

Officials in Washington had long suspected that American prisoners of war were being treated cruelly and with wanton neglect. Now, for the first time, the American government had hard evidence of those atrocities, the testimony of Mellnick, McCoy, and Dyess.

During the fall and early winter of 1943, the Roosevelt administration ordered the three men to keep silent. The Swedish relief ship *Gripsholm*, a neutral vessel, was still plying the Pacific with repatriated nationals and Red Cross packages for Allied prisoners of war, and the War Department felt that any story of Japanese atrocities might provoke the enemy to refuse the ship and perhaps treat the thousands of men in Japanese hands with even more malice.

Washington, however, has always been a loquacious city, and a story about a "death march" was hard to keep under wraps. A number of newspapers and magazines pressed the Office of War Information and the Office of Censorship to let them pursue the story. Dyess, in fact, was eager to tell his countrymen about the plight of the comrades he'd left behind, and he had reached an agreement with the *Chicago Tribune* to serialize his story as soon as the press ban was lifted.

In December 1943, Ed Dyess was killed during a training flight in California. Now, spurred by Dyess's wife, Marajen, the *Tribune* fought the news embargo even harder. Finally, on January 27, 1944, the government lifted the ban, and the Army and War departments issued a long and detailed press release based on the accounts of the three former prisoners of war. Three days later, the *Tribune*, and one hundred of its affiliated newspapers, published the first part of the Dyess account.

"THE STORY I am about to tell is true," Dyess began. And day after day, Ed Dyess gave American newspaper readers another installment.

These tales of atrocities left Americans enraged. And their anger filled bag after bag in the White House mail room: "Every Jap man, woman and child, even unto the third and forth generation, should be forthwith exterminated" . . . "Why do the stinkin Japs do such lousy things to our boys. Why?"[3]

Congress was brimming with vitriol as well. Senator Bennett Champ Clark of Missouri wanted to "hang the Mikado [the emperor] and bomb Japan out of existence," and Senator Ernest McFarland of Arizona wanted the Japanese to be "lined up and shot and suffer the tortures of hell."[4]

Reporters, knowing his inclination to grandiloquence, went to MacArthur for comment, but the general kept largely silent about the men he'd left behind. "The stories speak for themselves" was all he would say.

At a press conference on February 1, President Roosevelt was asked whether "the individual Japanese responsible for this crime would be tracked down and ultimately punished."

"There is no question about that," he said.

[*Masaharu Homma, Prison Diary, September 17, 1945*] The country has been defeated, and I am here in prison, lamenting my situation. The loss that I could not change.

We have plumbing, as well as two restrooms. The only thing that I dislike is the fact that there is a lock on the door, and that we are constantly being guarded. Lunch was kidney beans, stewed tomatoes, potatoes, corn, and canned peaches. We also had watery pineapple juice, bread with butter, and 1 box of Camels . . .

The American army has begun writing many things down in order to record my position on the crime I am accused of committing, the "Death March." I will take full responsibility for my subordinates' actions, but I also intend to make my own role very clear . . .

Though the light of the moon shines, my room remains pitch-black. Thus, even the pine trees and the mountain seen from the prison window seem to all be enveloped in sadness.[5]

His accusers would try to make him out a monster, but his six American military lawyers and a succession of American military jailers liked him from the start. He was large for a Japanese, six feet tall by most accounts, sturdy, and imposing among his more diminutive countrymen, but there was never any swagger in his gait, never any strut. He had the analytical mind of a strategist but the inclination of an artist, the general who wrote poetry, painted flowers, loved nothing so much as a good book. He spoke English well, liked English-language novels, listened to classical Western music. These predilections, and his cosmopolitan looks and ways, gave his political enemies a lot to talk about. In an army of Anglophobes, Homma was said to be "pro-British," the most "Western"-leaning of the generals of the Imperial General Staff. He resented these aspersions, this insult to his loyalty. He was Japanese, every inch of him. If he thought of himself as anything, it was a royalist, a patrician without title or brief. He was devoted to the idea of the royal family and the emperor, embodiments, as he saw them, of everything that was Japanese. He was, without question, a romantic, a modern Lancelot clinging to old-fashioned ideals of purity, honor, nobility. Now from a cell in the Yokohama city jail, three days after he had surrendered to American authorities, those ideals must have seemed somewhat shopworn, for he was being cast as a man without virtue or mercy, a low man who held life cheap.

[*Homma, Prison Diary, September 18*] Right now, I am being charged with transporting 70,000 prisoners at Bataan for a long distance in the heat and without food or drink and the subsequent deaths that resulted . . . Additional charges that I am not aware of may come up during the trial . . .

I think I will have to be especially prepared to receive a harsh punishment compared to everyone else.

He was born in Meiji 21 (1888) in a backwater, Sado Island, fifty miles west of Niigata in the Sea of Japan, the only child of Kankichi and Matsu Homma. In aspect and personality, the boy favored his handsome father, a prosperous gentleman farmer with a taste for the good life. For his worldview, however, he turned to his mother, a devout Buddhist who counseled harmony in all human dealings.

At eighteen he was accepted into Japan's prestigious Rikugun Shikan Gakkoō, the national army military academy at Ichigaya in Tokyo and graduated in May 1907, second in a class of 1,183 cadets, a second lieutenant of infantry assigned to a line regiment. In 1912 he won appointment to the Army General Staff College, the service's elite training school for future generals and general staff officers, and quickly developed a reputation as a ferocious scholar with a talent for language, especially English, memorizing pages at a time from an English dictionary, then, so the legend goes, ripping them out and swallowing them when he was done.[6]

After army college, he met a beautiful woman, Toshiko, from a prominent Tokyo family and asked her to marry him. In two years they had two sons, Michio and Masahiko, and not long thereafter, in 1917, Homma was posted to Britain as an attaché and military observer. Either by choice or common practice, Toshiko stayed behind in Tokyo. The years of separation, however, turned out to be too much for her. She seemed to lose interest in her family and sent her children to Sado Island to live with Machi-san, Homma's widowed mother. Masaharu returned to Japan to try to settle things, but by then Toshiko was living with another man, and Homma filed for divorce.

Although the scandal stung his pride, it did not hurt his career. By 1925 he was back working at army headquarters, an urbane man well traveled, now rubbing shoulders with some of the capital's political and business elite, among them the director of the Ooji Paper Manufacturing Company, Naokitsu Takada, and his lovely twenty-one-year-old daughter, Fujiko.

At their first meeting, Fujiko, wearing a silk kimono of fine gauze with a Chinese sash, served Masaharu tea. She was a bit bewildered by this big man with large eyes, a dark tan, and a white linen suit. He sat there with his hands folded in his lap, so nervous and tongue-tied all he could think to say was, "This is the first time I've worn my lieutenant colonel's badge." They were married November 8, 1926, in the Ueno section of Tokyo. He was thirty-eight, she was twenty-three. She raised his sons as hers and later had two children of her own, Hisako and Seisako.

Meanwhile, Homma the soldier steadily gained rank and held important field and staff commands, especially in 1937 as head of the army's powerful Propaganda Corps. In the years that followed he served in China, then, on November 2, 1941, five weeks before the attack on Pearl Harbor, General Gen Sugiyama, Imperial Army chief of staff, gave Homma command of the 14th Army. His mission was to take the Philippines in fifty days. Homma won his victory, forced MacArthur to flee, but instead of fifty days, his 14th Army took five months to secure the islands, and a displeased Sugiyama, spurred no doubt by another of Homma's antagonists, Prime Minister General Hideki Tojo, relieved the general of command, put him on reserve status, and shipped him home in the summer of 1942, in effect cashiering him.

His army career was over, and he spent the war years at home with Fujiko and their two young children. (Michio, the oldest boy from his first marriage, died of a childhood illness; his second son, Masahiko, joined the army and was stationed in Manchuria, a second lieutenant.) In August 1945, after Japan surrendered, Homma learned from friends in government that his name was on an American list of war criminals, and he slipped out of Tokyo for a few days and headed north to Sado Island to say good-bye to Machi-san, then he surrendered himself to Japanese gendarmes and American intelligence officers.

[*Homma, Prison Diary, September 19*] The guards change every day, so the way things are run changes as well . . .

I can tell that I am the one most hated by the Americans after reading the article in the *Mainichi* Newspaper that has my name in the headlines. This cannot be helped.

His world was now a twenty-by-twenty-foot cell in a dank three-story city jail. He had no direct contact with Fujiko or his children, but he could pass word to them through the good offices of a former prime minister, Kantarō Suzuki, who was allowed to visit the prisoners and act as their go-between. Homma had not yet formally been charged or arraigned and had only the vaguest notion of why he'd been arrested. The newspapers were saying that he "ordered the Americans to take the infamous death march of Bataan," but he'd done no such thing, and he couldn't understand where the papers were getting that. Some days it seemed they were blaming him for the whole war, and playing the scapegoat didn't sit well with the general.[7]

"The loss of the war is the responsibility of everyone," he wrote in his diary on September 24. "We are merely the unfortunate ones who are representatively responsible and sacrificed . . . I did not personally do anything wrong . . . I do not have a guilty conscience. This is what I would like my children to understand."

EVERY DAY he thought about his fate. He'd read that the accused war criminals in Germany were going to face a court of judges from many nations. Would he too "be subject to an international trial," he wondered, or would he have to account for himself in front of an American tribunal, judged by men he had once defeated?

The more he thought about the future, the more disquieted he became. "The cold fall wind touches my skin. My dreams at dawn do not bring tranquillity."

On October 3 MacArthur's headquarters announced it was ready to bring to trial General Tomoyuki Yamashita, commander of Japanese forces in the Philippines at the end of the war. The *Nippon Times* said Yamashita would be brought before a United States Military Commission in Manila. The article also included the government's main charge. Yamashita, it said, had "unlawfully disregarded and failed to discharge his duty as commander to control the operations of the members of his command, permitting them to commit brutal atrocities and other high crimes."[8]

Reading this, Homma was sure he was looking at the basic elements of the government's case against him as well.

[*Homma, Prison Diary, October 3, 1945*] The outcome of Yamashita's trial will give us an idea of what will happen to us.

In fact, the charges against the two men, and the tribunals that passed as trials, were not only similar, they were unprecedented and would make political and legal history.

YAMASHITA had been sent to the Philippines in the fall of 1944 to lead the 275,000 Japanese troops there in a delaying action. The Japanese knew they could not hold the islands—the Americans had more men, ships, planes—but the longer they could keep the enemy fighting, the better their chances at the peace table or, if it came to it, the more time they'd have to prepare for an Allied invasion of the Japanese home islands. During the battle Yamashita lost contact with his field commanders, at least one of whom took it upon himself to wage a *gyokusai suru*, a fight to the death, in Manila. Thus disposed, Japanese troops and their officers there set about slaughtering thousands of civilians in the city and its surrounding provinces. Yamashita, at first on the run from the American Army, then holed up with a third of his command in the mountains 155 miles north of Manila and, cut off from his commanders, apparently knew nothing of the arson, rape, murder, and torture being conducted by the drunken, frenzied *hohei* holding Manila. In the weeks that followed, the rest of Yamashita's force spent their time on the run, falling back before the Americans— sick and starving Japanese troops eating grass and hiding in the mountains to stay alive. Finally at 4:00 p.m. on September 1, Yamashita walked down a path from his mountain headquarters and, under a prior arrangement, turned his command and himself over to the American Army.

He was immediately arrested and told he would be tried as a war criminal.[9]

[*Nippon Times*] MANILA, October 11.—General Tomoyuki Yamashita, so-called "Tiger of Malaya" and last Japanese commander in the Philippines, pleaded innocent today to charges of violating the laws of war in failing to stop the atrocities committed by his troops . . .

Yamashita was not charged with committing the crimes personally. His trial, scheduled to begin October 29, [will hinge] on the question of responsibility held by the Imperial general for acts of troops under his command [and] will determine the precedent for other future war criminal prosecutions.

[*Homma, Prison Diary*] [Yamashita's] sentencing will be my sentencing as well. I wonder what will happen.

He wanted to live—on that point he was clear—but if his jail cell diary was a transcript of his psyche, his thoughts turned daily on death.

October 9: "There are many people here (myself included), who feel that the death penalty is better than being imprisoned here for ten years."

October 13: "I would rather be sentenced to death than receive a long prison sentence."

October 19: "I no longer regard my life as precious."

He was clearly preparing himself, doing what every right-thinking Japanese would do in his place. The way a Japanese met death was taken by his countrymen as an emblem of the way he had lived his life. Hope for the best, embrace the worst. Life is precious—let it go, like it was nothing at all.[10]

He must have been a little afraid, though, afraid of losing what he had found in Fujiko. He wrote of her often, "ached" for her and his children. First at the Yokohama jail, then, later when he was transferred to Omori Prison in Tokyo, Fujiko would stand outside the gate and politely ask to see her husband. Each time, she was turned away. Guards would deliver her presents of food and toiletries and bed linen, but the rules did not permit visits, the Americans told her.

[*Homma, Prison Diary, October 24*] I am truly grateful for the white rice, seaweed, chestnuts, and other gifts . . . My only regret is that I cannot even see . . . the faces I long to see.

He read the newspapers daily, and the stories about all the social and political shifts taking place outside the prison walls left him alienated and estranged—stories about wage-and-price controls, Japanese women demanding suffrage, Americans planting their flag on Mount Fuji, the emperor calling on MacArthur, instead of the other way around. *Shikata ga nai*, Japan was changing and there was nothing to do but watch.

Every day he tried to prepare himself for his upcoming trial, even though no charges had been filed yet. He didn't expect much from his former enemies. He guessed they'd give him an "unfair" hearing in which he would be "pushed around by a large number of justices," then taken outside and hanged or shot. And the accounts of Yamashita's trial, which was just beginning in Manila, only confirmed these suspicions. "There is no room for optimism," he wrote.

WHEN SCORES OF NATIONS met in convention at The Hague (1907) and Geneva (1929) to discuss the consequences of armed conflict, they agreed to a set of rules that, among other things, called for the protection of civilian populations and the fair treatment of prisoners of war—limits on armed conflict that came to be called the "law of war." Implicit in the rules was the belief that those who violated them should be punished. The question was, how and by whom.[11]

President Roosevelt had stated publicly that America intended a legal punishment, full-fledged trials, but as more stories of Nazi and Nipponese villainy reached the War Department, some of the president's cabinet officers, and some of America's allies, began to talk about political rather than legal punishment. Secretary of State Cordell Hull wanted to bring "Hitler and Mussolini and Tojo and their arch accomplices . . . before a drumhead court-martial" and shoot them "at sunrise." Across the Atlantic, British Prime Minister Winston Churchill told his cabinet ministers that war criminals should be summarily "executed" as "outlaws" and wondered whether the Americans would send him an electric chair on "lend-lease."[12]

By the beginning of 1945, the War Department and America's allies had settled on a basic plan. There would be two international tribunals with civilian judges, one at Nuremberg, Germany, and the other in Tokyo, to try the war's archcriminals, the heads of state and their political henchmen who had committed omnibus crimes against humanity and peace—in other words, the men who had started and prosecuted a world war and caused the deaths of some fifty million people. Meanwhile, military men, the major field or area commanders, charged with specific war crimes (overt acts, as the law calls atrocities) would be given national trials by military commissions (boards of officers) sitting in those venues where the crimes were said to have taken place.

And so it was in the fall of 1945 that Tomoyuki Yamashita and Masaharu Homma found themselves preparing to stand trial before two military commissions in the Philippines, commissions whose procedures—particularly the all-important rules of evidence—were so "bare bones" that the trials took on the appearance of kangaroo courts. In a military commission, for example, none of the documents, reports, statements, letters, affidavits, or depositions submitted as evidence had to be verified or supported by direct testimony, which gave that evidence the quality of hearsay, accusations that were impossible for the defense to challenge or disprove.[13]

The Allies also wanted to rush this justice along. The trials were to be the epilogue of a long war, and President Harry Truman, Churchill, and the other victorious leaders knew that a war-weary world wanted the sad, painful story to end. "Proceed, without avoidable delay," Truman ordered MacArthur, who, in turn, through a surrogate, told his legal section, "speed is of the essence."[14]

[Nippon Times, *Wednesday, October 31*] In the Philippines General Tomoyuki Yamashita . . . is being tried by five American generals who will write a new chapter in international law if they hold him responsible for the reign of terror which his troops spread throughout the Philippines.[15]

MORALLY RESPONSIBLE, politically responsible, but heretofore not legally responsible. Commanders have always had to account for the behavior of their men, but that responsibility has always been fiduciary rather than criminal. If his men went astray for want of oversight, the custom was to revoke a commander's trusteeship and retire or cashier him. Only if his actions had been wanton—if, say, he'd explicitly ordered his men to sack a city or slaughter innocents, clear violations of the traditional conventions of war—was a general hauled before a tribunal.

Now, after four years of total war, a war in which belligerents killed innocents in far greater numbers than they had killed one another, the victors were determined to expand the idea of "command responsibility," at least as it applied to the men they had defeated, men, by the by, who had once defeated them.

It was new law applied retroactively, ex post facto law, the kind of law prohibited by the U.S. Constitution. And Tomoyuki Yamashita and Masaharu Homma were to be its first defendants.

Each man was charged with failing "to discharge his duty as commander to control the operations of the members of his command, permitting them to commit brutal atrocities and other high crimes."[16]

"Permitting them . . ." What did that mean? The victors had taken a doctrine of English common law, *respondeat superior* (the principal must answer for the actions of his agents), and applied it to war, this against all precedent and tradition.

IN THE NEWSPAPERS Homma was reading, and in press accounts worldwide, editors were portraying Japan's accused war criminals as atavistic butchers. One of Yamashita's lawyers was convinced that Americans "believed firmly that all Japanese army officers were 'Samurai fanatics' . . . whose hands dripped with the blood of helpless and innocent women and children." Sensibilities were particularly raw in Manila, which ranked as one of the most ruined cities of the war, a checkerboard of rubbled blocks and razed buildings. Even the structure where the trials were taking place (the former residence of the United States high commissioner to the Philippines) had been badly damaged, its façade still pockmarked with bullet and shrapnel holes. No trial could have taken place in a more charged atmosphere or in more inimical surroundings.[17]

The defense team for each man was understaffed and overworked. Yamashita's six lawyers had only a small staff of clerks to help them prepare the case. The six prosecutors, meanwhile, had all the investigative and legal machinery of the War Crimes Office in Washington, the War Crimes Branch of MacArthur's staff in Tokyo, and the Army War Crimes Investigation Detachment in Manila—scores of lawyers and investigators working six days a week to turn up volumes of evidence and churn out hundreds of charges and the legal precedents to support them.

The prosecution's strategy in both trials was the same: introduce into evidence, through long bills of particulars (123 separate allegations against

Yamashita, 47 against Homma), as many atrocities as they could get on the record, then use the weight and scope of that record—the evidence detailing acts of torture, rape, and murder by various means, among them beheading, bayoneting, bludgeoning, hanging, and incineration—as proof that the atrocities were planned and so widespread that the commanders must have known they were taking place but did nothing to stop them.[18]

Yamashita's lawyers put up a good fight. In a series of motions and objections, they challenged every aspect of the case—the validity of the charges, the loose rules of evidence, even the legitimacy of the court itself. All the arguing made MacArthur, monitoring events from his headquarters in Tokyo, impatient, and he pressured the Yamashita commission to speed up its work. The five judges on the commission in turn warned Yamashita's lawyers that henceforth all they wanted to hear were the "essential facts without a mass of non-essentials and immaterial details." Trial tactics such as "extended cross-examinations" were little more than "fishing expeditions" that served "no useful purpose . . . wasting valuable time," they said. Such tactics, they warned, "verged on contempt" and "insubordination" and were "grounds for [a] court-martial," an admonition that left Yamashita's lawyers feeling that they were fighting "the demands of the mob for vengeance," the private agendas of the judges, and the judges' superiors in Tokyo and Washington as well.[19]

[*Homma, Prison Diary, December 8*] (Saturday, cloudy) A man in full military gear brought an American newspaper and showed it to me. Yamashita was given the death sentence. This is the worst possible result. Now I have to finally prepare myself. The cold pierces my body through the concrete. I go to bed at 8:30.

[*December 9*] (Sunday, sunny) I lay awake thinking about Yamashita's death sentence . . . If Yamashita, who was a test case for me, was sentenced to death, I shall receive the same sentence. The cruel acts that were committed by Yamashita's subordinates were unspeakable . . . I'm not sure what else they will charge me with . . . From the point of view of "responsibility as a commanding officer" we are the same.

FIRST LIEUTENANT ROBERT L. PELZ was marking time, waiting for orders the army was done with him. He'd been overseas three years now, first in Europe, then since late summer here, at a dusty base near Lingayen Gulf doing his job as an adjutant, an administrative officer for a battalion that handled the logistics of the port. Not a bad billet for a twenty-seven-year-old New Yorker with a law degree from Columbia University who had done his duty and was eager to get home and start his career with some tony Manhattan law firm.[20]

The work was easy. Twice a day, midmorning and midafternoon, the lieutenant had to make sure the daily shipments of supplies, mail, and newspapers were distributed to the various commands in the islands. The rest of the time was his, and he spent it reading books, thinking about women, and counting the days till he could shed his uniform and take a ship home.

One day in late November, sitting at his desk and going through the day's mail and circulars, he noticed a directive from headquarters: "Every battalion shall report to this command the names of all officers who are lawyers."

What an odd request, he thought. What the hell did the army want with lawyers? And against all common sense and conventional army wisdom (a smart soldier kept his head down off the battlefield as well as on it), he picked up the telephone and called the adjutant at headquarters, a man he knew and who knew him.

"What do you want lawyers for?" Bob Pelz asked.

"Well, there's a high-level order we got here—" The man stopped midsentence. "Wait a minute!" he said. "Aren't you a lawyer?"

Bob Pelz knew instantly he'd screwed up.

"Well," he stammered, "no, not exactly."

"What do you mean, not exactly?"

His acquaintance sounded annoyed. "Did you pass the bar exam or not?"

"Well, yes," Bob Pelz said, "but I never practiced."

There was a pause, as if the man was scribbling something.

"I've got your name down," he said. "I'm not fooling around with this order. This came from Big Shot himself."

[*Pelz, Journal, December 4, 1945*] Major English and I have moved heaven and earth to get the [new] orders [to report to the judge advocate general's office] revoked . . . This setup [here in Lingayen] is too magnificent to leave . . . Manila doesn't sound attractive, and I'm too close to going home to want Japan. Besides, I have absolutely no spirit of adventure, I like my cozy comforts too much.

IN DECEMBER 1945, when Bob Pelz reported for duty, the judge advocate general's office at army headquarters on Quezon Boulevard in Manila was a busy place. Dozens of officers with law degrees had been reassigned to the office to prosecute and defend 215 Japanese accused of war crimes in the Philippines. The trials were run two or three a day, the defendants representing all ranks and echelons. Each accused was given an attorney or two, depending on the complexity of the case, drawn from the pool of lawyers summoned to Manila.[21]

It was interesting work for a smart New York lawyer, but Bob Pelz was still grumbling about his lot. "What the hell do I have to defend a Jap for?" he asked himself. "I mean, I hate the Japs. You read *The New York Times* and you can't help but hate the Japs. These son of a bitch defendants are keeping me from getting home."

Officially the defense attorneys were told to "fight" each case "on its merits" and keep their defendants from being "railroaded" by the military commissions. Unofficially they were reminded of the purpose of the trials—to make sure war criminals got what they deserved. "It was obvious that we are not expected to put up a gigantic defense," Bob Pelz wrote in his diary. "We are supposed to be good soldiers and go along."

He spent his first days on the job boning up on military law. ("Note: bill of particulars is a detailed informal statement of a plaintiff's case of action," he wrote.) Nights he explored what was left of exotic Manila, the "luscious tenderloin steaks" flown in from the States, the "bewilderingly attractive Filipino girls" at the new dance halls.

Then, one afternoon, waiting for his first client to show up, he learned that he was being assigned to a new case. A prominent Japanese lieutenant general, Masaharu Homma, had just been flown in from Tokyo under great security to stand trial for his life. This was more like it. "His trial will be well-publicized," Pelz wrote, "and probably exciting."

THERE WERE SIX OF THEM on the defense team. Major John Skeen, lead counsel, was a twenty-seven-year-old admiralty lawyer from Baltimore who had never argued a case in court. Captain George Ott was a corporate lawyer, and Captain Frank Coder was a field artilleryman. First Lieutenant Leonard Nataupsky, like Bob Pelz a newly minted attorney, had been working in the Quartermaster Corps. And Captain George Furness, a New Englander, was a real estate lawyer.

As a group they had only scant trial experience and no background at all in complexities of criminal law or the tactics of defending a client in a capital case. The six prosecution lawyers, meanwhile, were experienced and well prepared. They were part of a large legal machine and had been working together well in advance of the case coming to trial.

Looking at the two lineups made Bob Pelz smile. Seemed to him "they took all the good ones and made them prosecutors, and the amateurs, the dumb ones, they put on the defense."

First thing the dumb ones did was meet with their famous client.

[*Pelz, Journal, December 16*] He was obviously nervous and eager; he looked like a tired-out grandfather who has girded his loins for a last battle. Bowing graciously to each of us, he sat down and read a little speech he had written in English . . . Very intelligent, he has prepared much of his defense to those charges he had heard about . . . Basically, [he says] he knew nothing of these atrocities. As he put it, only an Oriental can understand that a Jap General does not question the actions of his subordinates.

An arraignment was scheduled for Wednesday, December 19, and the day before, the five general officers of commission took the attorneys through a dry run. Their putative purpose was to make sure all the parties understood the procedures for the trial, but Major General Leo Donovan, who had served on the Yamashita court and who was president and law member (chief judge) of the Homma court, had another agenda. He was not going to let this particular team of defense attorneys use the same trial tactics employed by Yamashita's defense team, tactics that had annoyed MacArthur.

"I'm not trying to hamstring anybody," Donovan said. "I'm perfectly willing to hear your side of it." But everything, he went on, everything was going to be done with dispatch. Any lawyers' tricks, he went on, would be considered a "perverse opposition to lawful authority." In other words, the military lawyers would be in contempt of court, or worse.

Donovan's fulminating aside, Bob Pelz thought "the arraignment went smoothly." There were a number of reporters and photographers there, and the defense team, aware of the part public opinion would play in the trial, tried hard to court them. The next day a picture of Homma surrounded by his American attorneys appeared in the *Manila Times*. "General Homma, I thought, made an excellent appearance in a quiet business suit," Bob Pelz wrote.

On December 21, the defense got some good news. Yamashita's lawyers had applied to the U.S. Supreme Court to overturn his conviction and, after a lot of wrangling behind closed doors, the Court finally agreed to hear the case. The legal questions in *In re Yamashita* would be the same for *In re Homma*.[22]

THE TRIAL began on Thursday, January 3, 1946 at 8:30 a.m. in the former high commissioner's residence, an imposing edifice that faced Manila Bay. Army engineers had worked night and day to repair and renovate the battle-damaged building, in particular the large ground-floor reception hall where Yamashita had stood trial and where Homma now sat with his defense team. To A. Frank Reel, who had been one of Yamashita's lawyers, the large room was less a court than a theater where America could stage its postwar dramas of recompense and revenge.

"Loudspeakers were suspended from the ceiling and were placed at strategic points along the walls. On either side, in the 'wings,' were spotlights, and overhead were strung six powerful klieg lights . . . In the balconies were moving-picture cameramen and radio commentators . . . On the floor were seats for three hundred spectators . . . The front of the large room was semicircular, with seven French doors that looked out onto Manila Bay. This part of the room was the stage. Before the middle window, on a slightly raised platform, was the judges' bench," and below it, to the right and left, tables for prosecution and defense and, of course, the witness box.[23]

Some of the drama took place in pretrial motions, one in particular, the matter of the trial's convening authority, Douglas A. MacArthur. As supreme commander of Allied powers in Japan, MacArthur in his headquarters in Tokyo was the provenance for everything that was taking place in the courtroom in Manila. He was empowered to pick the judges, prosecutors, defense attorneys. He had the authority to decide which defendants would be tried before military commissions and which would enjoy the more protective legalities of an international tribunal run by experienced civilian judges. He had set the rules of evidence, the court procedures, the timetables for the trials. And it was MacArthur who would certify the verdicts, which made his office alone the place of last appeal. He could set aside a sentence, save a man's life, or establish the time, place, and manner of his execution.

The Yamashita defense team had largely avoided the issue of MacArthur's overarching judicial power. Homma's lawyers, however, were determined to press the point. And at a press conference the week before the opening of the trial, they mentioned the incendiary issue.

"No man," they told reporters, "should be placed in the position of being in essence accuser, prosecutor, defense counsel, judge, jury, court of review, and court of final appeal. He should particularly not be placed in this position where he is a military commander who was defeated by the accused in a campaign out of which the charges arose."

Almost immediately their boss, Lieutenant Colonel Bernard A. Brown of Sioux City, Iowa, the head of the war crimes section of the Manila judge advocate general's office, grabbed the young lawyers and gave them a tongue lashing. They were accusing the supreme commander of conducting a kangaroo court, he said, and in referring to MacArthur as having been "*defeated* by the accused," they were poking a stick in the supreme commander's eye. Did they have any idea what the army could do to them? Brown asked. MacArthur may be "a black-hearted son of a bitch," Brown said, but he was the army, and the army "never forgets."

ALONE in his cell on the second floor of the residence, waiting for the proceedings to start, Homma felt himself unraveling.

> [*Homma, Prison Diary, December 30, 1945*] [Ichiro] Kishimoto [interpreter] came by to bring me some personal things this evening. I cried again after seeing pictures of my wife and children and after rereading their letters. Why do I do such cruel things to myself after trying so hard to not think about them?

> [*January 1, 1946*] I do not fear death, but I also do not want to die . . . I dreamt at night that all of my teeth fell out and I could not get any false teeth to replace them. This was a nightmare that got worse from last night when I dreamt that four of my teeth fell out. I guess it is natural that I do not have any good dreams.

[*January 2*] This evening, I plan on clipping my nails and cutting my hair, which I will have them take back [to Japan] in place of my remains.

THE PROSECUTION began by calling to the stand Japanese staff officers to talk about the 14th Army chain of command. Bob Pelz was on his feet during a lot of this testimony, objecting to the rules of evidence or challenging the accuracy of something a witness said. General Donovan appeared annoyed by these interruptions, and at the end of the first week, on Sunday, their first day off, the chief judge summoned Lieutenant Colonel Frank Meek, the lead prosecutor, and Major Skeen, head of the defense team, to his office. He wanted to talk about the attorney from New York.

[*Pelz, Journal, January 6, 1946*] Gen. Donovan is enraged at me . . . He as much as admitted that he would like to hold me in contempt, but can't find an excuse. Skeen and I went over the record . . . Naturally I'm paranoid, but it only enhances my basic ideas about Army brass hats who can't stand the slightest opposition.

Truth was, the first week of trial disgusted Bob Pelz. "Donovan is rushing the thing through and anything goes," he wrote in his journal. "More and more the trial looks like a farce. What else can it be when anything comes into evidence? I'll never mock common law rules of evidence again . . . The reporters can already see that Donovan plans to brook no delay. He reconvenes the commission before he hits the chair."

On Wednesday, January 9, the prosecution finally got to the core of its case and trotted out the first in what was to become a grim and relentless parade of witnesses who had been on what the press now commonly called the "death march."

The parade had been carefully assembled, a string of survivors and a thick folder of affidavits, testimony to document the atrocious behavior of the Japanese guards and the suffering of the tens of the thousands of American and Filipino prisoners of war who, beginning April 9, 1942, had struggled up the Old National Road from Mariveles or points north to the railhead at San Fernando, sixty-six miles of hunger and thirst, murder and mayhem.

The stories these witnesses told stunned the courtroom and created in many in the audience the same sense of shock and surreality suffered by the men who had made the march. All part of the prosecution's plan.

Let the living bring the dead into the courtroom—the headless shades, the bloody poltergeists, the wretched phantoms—and bury the defendant with the spectral detritus of the past.

It did not seem to matter to the judges, as Bob Pelz said in his diary, that most of the witnesses' tales were "exaggerated a little after the passage of years"—prevarication and perjury motivated by a desire for revenge, the need of the survivors to strike back at their torturers and tormentors. And it didn't matter because, as Bob Pelz wrote, their tall tales were "reasonably true." So what if only thirty men, not two hundred, had been penned together in an excrement-covered field? And what did it matter if there were only two heads alongside the road between Lamao and Limay instead of eight, ten, twenty? There was enough fact in the fictions issuing from the witness chair to give the defense trouble, enough truth in all that telling to be "very damaging" to the balding man in the business suit, the sad-faced defendant.

The defense, given only fifteen days to prepare its case, had neither the time nor the resources to vet the testimony or separate opinion and opprobrium from fact. They continued to object, pointing out inconsistencies, gaps in logic, memories that didn't seem to track. But most of the time the most they could do was listen.

Here, for example, was Master Sergeant James Baldassarre, a rear-echelon soldier who had worked in supply at one of the main food dumps on Bataan. Baldassarre was a perfect prosecution witness. Fifty-one years old and a career soldier with twenty-eight years in the service, he knew exactly what was expected of him in court.

> Q: Now, did you notice anything along the road as you were marching between Balanga and Lubao?
> A: Many Americans and Filipinos were slaughtered by the Japanese.
> Q: Did you see them slaughtered?
> A: I saw many Americans and Filipinos who were shot by the Japanese between Balanga and Lubao, many of them.
> Q: You personally saw that?
> A: Yes sir, I see it.
> Q: Did you see many bodies?
> A: Many of them. Hundreds of them. God knows how many! Filipinos, American women and Filipino women in a family way stabbed right through the belly, and children stabbed.

Baldassarre had seen it all, including atrocities no one else had seen. Then he told the court he had spotted the Japanese commander along the road.

Q: Now during this march from Bataan did you see any high ranking Japanese officers riding on the route of the march?
A: Many of them, quite a few of them. There is one right in this place now right now, that I can recognize who was riding in an official car, a Japanese official car.
Q: Who is that?
A: Lieutenant General Homma . . . He was there; he must be there, his car was there. Of course, I can't verify if it was correct, but it must be him in the car. The car was there . . . I also asked a Japanese guard. I said, "Who is that man?" He said, "That is General Homma."[24]

Other men would tell the same tale, and at the time it did not seem to strike the commission judges as curious that Japanese guards, barely literate in their own language, spoke English or that they would take the time to point out their commander to the enemy prisoners they were hurriedly pushing north off the peninsula.

After his appearance, Baldassarre paused outside court to talk to reporters and deliver what *Time* magazine called "a fierce little speech."

> They should hang the man. He is a no-good son of a bitch. I should pull the rope. This is too much of a trial. They should never give him a trial. They never trialed us. They killed people like flies. Send him to me. I'll fix him up.

"Then," *Time* went on, "Sergeant Baldassarre put a cigar in his mouth, pushed his overseas cap back off his sunburned forehead and walked out with the air of a man who has just paid an old debt."[25]

The bitter testimony of death march witnesses disconcerted the defendant, as almost everyone in court could see.

> [*Homma, Prison Diary, January 9*] We have finally entered the Bataan march stage [of the trial]. The American soldiers are all upset, and in that anger, they have put together all these lies. I am so upset by this that my eyes start to tear.

His attorneys could see his discomfort was genuine.

> [*Pelz, Journal, January 9*] [Homma] was shaken and practically in tears from emotion and fury—the last because he said there were not hundreds of dead. He seems concerned that we of the defense should believe it.

The next day, Thursday, January 10, the prosecution called thirty-two-year-old Philippine Army Captain Pedro Felix, one of the few survivors of the massacre on April 12, 1942. The captain told the court how after surrender, his unit, the 91st Infantry, had been herded along trails through the hills until it reached a ravine near the Pantingan River. He recounted how the officers and sergeants had been segregated from the rest of the men, how they were wired together in groups of twenty or more and made to stand looking down into the ravine.

Q: How many times in all were you bayonetted?

A: I was bayonetted four times sir.

Q: You say that two of these bayonet thrusts went through you. Will you kindly indicate by your hands on your body where they entered and where they came out? Stand up.

The chief judge interrupted.

Donovan: I would like to go a little further than that and have him pull his shirt off and indicate it.

Felix got to his feet, stripped to his waist, and turned his bare back toward the five generals on the bench.

Donovan: Do you count four [scars] there?

Felix: Yes, sir.

Donovan: One, two, three, four—is that correct?

Meek [chief prosecutor]: Yes, sir . . .

Donovan: Thank you very much. You can put your shirt on later.[26]

By the end of the day, the defendant was reeling.

"I saw Homma this evening," Bob Pelz wrote, "and he is becoming a broken man. I truly believe he had no idea of the things that had occurred."

[*Homma, Prison Diary, January 11*] It pains me to listen. All the strength has left my knees, and I feel as though I am going to break down.

With the recounting of each atrocity, Homma's face seemed to sag, and his shoulders rolled forward as if his body were about to fold in on itself.

On Saturday morning, January 19, Dr. Gilbert T. Cullen, a sixty-eight-year-old American physician who had been living and working for years on the island of Panay, slowly made his way to the witness stand. Cullen told how Japanese soldiers, convinced he had information about American forces, beat the old doctor, then took out ropes and strung him up, first by his thumbs and then his toes and ankles, pulled some of his nails out, burned his flesh, beat him again, and again.

Homma closed his eyes in obvious anguish and [General] Donovan noticed it, even nudging [Major General Basilio] Valdes [another judge]. Later Donovan, whom we are all getting to like better, told Skeen [head of the defense], "I really believe that old man is suffering when he hears some of these atrocities."

It was as if his officers, from the most junior subaltern to his chief of staff, had let him down. They knew how to press a fight, all right, how to get their *nikudan*, their human bullets, to throw themselves against an enemy, but either through intent or indifference they had failed in their duty to control their men. In fact in many cases, too many, it was now clear to the general, they had even encouraged the violence, incited the terrible impulse in all fighting men to keep killing and wounding even after the battle has been won.

And it was this appetite to injure, instilled in basic training, whetted by the "warrior" ethos, and inherent in every army that has ever taken the field, that led the *hohei* to turn a parade of prisoners into a death march. Homma had been accused of violating the law of war, that loose canon of traditions and conventions that presumes limits on the behavior of soldiers in battle, everyone acting according to the rules, reasonable men killing one another in reasonable ways. If the evidence proved anything, it proved that presumption false.

AFTER SIXTEEN DAYS OF TRIAL, the prosecution had called 136 people to the witness stand and had introduced into evidence 322 exhibits. Their strategy had been clear from the outset: try to show that during his tenure as commander in chief, Homma had either allowed, ignored, or tacitly encouraged (the five judges could take their pick) a broad pattern of atrocity and abuse. There was little, if any, evidence that the defendant knew of these crimes, so prosecutors tried to use the weight of accusation and inference to bury him.

On January 21 the prosecution finished its case, and the court recessed for a week to give the defense time to prepare its witnesses. The plan was to divide the defense witnesses into two groups. The first would try to answer the charges; the second would testify to the defendant's good character. People who knew him well, old friends and comrades and family too—his wife, Fukjiko.

Homma had been dead set against her appearing. He did not want her pilloried in the press or on the witness stand, but his lawyers, short on time and effective witnesses, had insisted. They needed her, they told him, and, judging from his hangdog demeanor, so did he.

FUJIKO had arrived on a Sunday in the early morning dark. The next day, Bob Pelz, Frank Coder, and George Furness paid her a courtesy call. She gave each attorney a small gift, a token of thanks for defending her husband. They were instantly enchanted. "A charming lady," Pelz wrote, "she seems to carry her load beautifully."

On Wednesday, the defense trotted her out for photographers. "She makes a wonderful impression wherever she goes," Bob Pelz thought, "so graceful and charming is she." And on Saturday, she sat for a press conference. Through an interpreter she told reporters how she'd been married for twenty years and had two children, a daughter and son, eighteen and sixteen years old, respectively. Then she answered a few questions about her husband. She described him as a quiet, almost book-ish man who enjoyed the plays of John Galsworthy and George Bernard Shaw. His favorite novel, she volunteered, was by an American named Margaret Mitchell, *Gone With the Wind*. When she was done she smiled, bowed slightly, retired with the attorneys in tow. A real "Japanese lady," *Time* magazine said.[27]

The army ensconced her in the nurses' quarters at a local hospital, a nice room with a high, Western-style bed, a dresser, makeup table, nightstand, and chair. Accustomed to rationing and shortages, she found the food "extravagant," and remembering that her family was going without rice in destitute Tokyo, she felt "suddenly . . . shameful" eating her dinner.

Skeen had promised she could visit her husband regularly, and the morning after she arrived the lawyer came to fetch her.

"I will try to let you see him as much as possible," Skeen said. "Please just follow the regulations."

"Of course," she said.

"When I say 'regulations,' they are not complicated. For example, weapons are forbidden, but since this does not seem to be within the realm of the manners of the Japanese, I suppose it won't be a problem."

She appreciated the American's sense of humor. A while later a staff car carried her to the residence of the former high commissioner. Down-stairs she was introduced to Marshall Williams, a captain of the military police who would be monitoring her meeting with her husband. Captain Williams led her upstairs and across a hallway to the door of what appeared to be an old storage room. The room had two sleeping cots against the wall. Her husband was standing there in a dark business suit, waiting. He looked spent, and when he saw her, his Fu-san, he started to cry.

They went downstairs to the library, and with Captain Williams standing off to the side they sat down and talked. Masaharu was nervous at first, his heart pounding against his chest. After a few minutes the sound of his wife's voice began to soothe and calm him, and he could feel his fear falling away.

In the days that followed, husband and wife were allowed to meet often. A member of the defense staff would drive Fujiko over to the residence, and as soon as she entered the great front hall, Captain Williams would greet her and shout up to the second floor, "Your wife is here to see you." Then she would hear footfalls on the stairs and her husband would come down with a bright expression on his face.

Each meeting lasted about thirty minutes. She wanted to stay longer, and could have; Skeen had asked Williams to give the couple more time, but the general, watching the clock, always rose to end their meeting exactly on the half hour.

"You should go now," he would say to her, rather formally. "We must not take advantage of Mr. Williams's kindness. He is taking time away from his own rest period to come here to watch over us."

Then, as he turned to go, he would always say the same thing to his jailer. "Please look after my wife."

IN ALL THEY MET EIGHT TIMES. At each meeting he wanted to talk about what should happen when he was gone—the arrangements for his funeral, the children's future, his aging mother's comfort, and the like. She did not.

"It's all right," she would say, whenever he tried to broach the subject. "We will still be able to eat meals together soon."[28]

After a while, he gave up trying to get her to talk about what would happen when he was gone and decided to put what he wanted to say on paper.

[*Homma, letter, "The State of My Mind on January 24"*] I find my mind strangely calm. It may be resignation if it had to be explained. Since I saw the face of my wife and read letters from my children, I have come to feel an extremely transcendental feeling over life and death . . . I have seen the person I wanted to see . . . In my wife's hands I can leave my mother and the future of my children with no worry.

[*"To My Wife, January 25"*] In 20 years of our married life, we've had many differences of opinion. Those quarrels have now become sweet memories . . . Twenty years feels short but it is long. I am content that we have lived a happy life together.

If there is what is called the other world, we'll be married again there. I'll go first and wait for you there, but you mustn't hurry. Live as long as you can for the children and do things I haven't been able to do, for me. You will see our grandchildren or great grandchildren and tell me all about them when we meet again in the other world. Thank you very much for everything . . . With endless regret I part with you.[29]

NONE OF HOMMA'S ATTORNEYS expected to win the case, but it was clear they were making progress with at least two of the five judges—Brigadier General Arthur G. Trudeau and Major General Basilio J. Valdes of the Philippine Army. Perhaps one or both could be swayed to spare the defendant's life.

In his opening statement on Monday, January 28, chief defense attorney John Skeen laid out his case. He began by depicting Homma as an outsider in his own army. Then he contended that the general was ill served by officers who had ignored his instructions and had not kept him informed, this while the general was preoccupied with the "bitter campaign" to finish the fight in the Philippines, a job that made it "impossible to direct his full attention" to administration or oversight, particularly of the garrison units responsible for moving the prisoners of war.[30]

The prosecution had been unable to link the defendant directly to the death march, the centerpiece horror of the government's case. It could produce no evidence whatsoever—no documents or testimony—that Homma had either ordered the bloody atrocities that took place on the Old National Road or that he had been told about the slaughter and had failed to stop it. Instead, prosecutors had relied on circumstantial evidence and the power of inference. Now the defense had to counter those inferences, and Homma's lawyers could think of only two lines of attack.

They could establish their client's ignorance—try to prove he did not know what his men were doing—or they could shift the responsibility for the crime to someone else. As it turned out, they tried both tacks. The first involved them in a conundrum; the second had them chasing a ghost.

The defense began by calling as witnesses several of Homma's staff officers, men who, presumably, could show that Homma was unaware of the events taking place on the Old National Road. Homma had suggested the names to his attorneys. He had also warned them that his men might lie.

Lieutenant General Takeji Wachi took the stand first. "A sinister-looking little man," *The New York Times* described him. Wachi said Homma had issued orders to all unit commanders to treat prisoners of war with a "friendly spirit and not to mistreat them." Then he testified that he had been on the Old National Road five times on various errands during the two weeks of the death march and had seen soldiers falling along the wayside. "What action did you take?" he was asked. The Japanese put the sick men on trucks, Wachi said, and when there were no trucks coming by, "I had the Japanese soldiers give a hand and carry these prisoners to a place such as beneath the eaves of a building and place them down there."[31]

Guards helping prisoners into the shade? Trucks pulling over to give them a ride?

> Q: Did you see any dead bodies along the road there?
> A: No, none at all, none at all.
> Q: Were you ever informed of any atrocities committed by the Japanese Army against prisoners of war during the march? . . .
> A: No, I have never heard of it . . .
> Q: Did you ever receive any report of any deaths of prisoners on that march? . . .
> A: I heard later that there were some who died.
> Q: About how many?
> A: I don't remember the number but it wasn't many.
> Q: Was any report made to you as chief of staff of the execution of prisoners?
> A: I found no cases of executions.[32]

And so it went, one incredible assertion after another. Major Moriya Wada, who had been assigned to work with the supply and transportation section, the units whose soldiers acted as guards on the death march, told the court that he had seen only five dead along the road. When his superior, a colonel in the transportation section, heard of these corpses, he ordered his staff "to inspect the dead closely and bury them."

> Wada: As a result of this order, around the 20th of April the report came in that the men who died along the road between Balanga and San Fernando died because of sickness.
>
> Q: Did the report state how many they had buried along the road?
> A: Yes.
> Q: How many?
> A: They reported that there were approximately 18 bodies between the 11th [of April] and the 18th.[33]

The pat answers and apparent fictions were obvious to almost everyone. Even the most untutored courtroom observer could see that after more than two thousand pages of prosecution testimony, there was no denying the death march, no denying the hundreds of bodies by the road or the scars being counted by the judges. So why did the witnesses lie? Because "we live in an age of terror," Homma told his attorneys in private. If his men had admitted that they had ill served their commander by insulating him from the grim actualities of the march—failing to report what they were being told about the atrocities, or misrepresenting what they had seen firsthand driving the road—they knew they would likely find themselves on trial along with their chief.

SO THE DEFENSE TRIED a second tack. It sought to show the defendant as a commander whose authority, especially his control over his troops, was undermined by the handful of interlopers from Tokyo and Saigon dispatched by headquarters to "advise" the general, in effect agents his political enemies had sent to eavesdrop and interfere in his command.

Foremost among these was a name the defense discovered during pretrial interviews: Masanobu Tsuji, a forty-year-old lieutenant colonel on the Imperial General Staff in Tokyo whose specialty was operations and intelligence, mass murder, and political chaos.

In an army of ultraconservatives, Tsuji was among the most arch, an intriguer who apparently knew no bounds. He believed his country was fighting a race war, and he hated whites (save Germans and Italians, Japan's Axis partners) and any Asians allied with them. "We must, at the very least, beat these Westerners into submission . . . with no thought of leniency," he wrote in a monograph widely circulated in the Imperial Army. In early April 1942, several days before Homma launched his second offensive on Bataan, Masanobu Tsuji appeared unannounced in Manila. He told Homma's staff that he had been sent as a "liaison" from Tokyo. Then he got into a car and set out for various field headquarters on Bataan, collaring division and regimental commanders and issuing strange and frightening orders.[34]

Wachi testified that Tsuji had tried to bully division commanders in the field into following his suggestion to "mete out . . . severe treatment" to prisoners of war.

Q: What did you mean by "severe treatment"?
A: It means to kill.[35]

Here was the villain the defense had been looking for, a real war criminal, Tokyo's agent provocateur urging Homma's field commanders to order their troops to molest and murder unarmed American prisoners of war, those *keto*, hairy white beasts.

The problem was, Tsuji was nowhere to be found, no record of his death, no reports of his person. Just the testimony of Homma's staff officers, witnesses whose credibility was obviously in question. (Years later, other staff officers would come forward to talk about the homicidal colonel, among them Lieutenant General Takeo Imai, at the time commander of the 141st Infantry Regiment on Bataan. Imai said Tsuji told him, "Kill all your prisoners," but Imai refused to act without written orders, and a few days later, the enigmatic Colonel Tsuji was gone.)[36]

DESPITE THE REALITIES of the trial and the weaknesses in the defense case, Bob Pelz still hoped his client might escape the rope. "Maj. Gen. Valdes [one of the five judges] . . . has been tremendously impressed by Homma's obviously sincere emotions during this trial," the attorney wrote in his diary. "Valdes says he has not slept for three nights because of the trial. Despite the killings of some in his family by Japs, despite everything, he does not want to hang a man who could not control these troops in their actions . . . I wonder if any American generals have this sensitivity."

On February 5, the day Homma was scheduled to testify, word reached the Philippines that the U.S. Supreme Court had denied General Yamashita's appeal, rejecting all the legal arguments Homma's defense team had hoped to use in its case as well.

In the majority (6-2) opinion written by Chief Justice Harlan F. Stone, the court ruled that the defendant could be tried by a military commission, a wartime court, because (absent a peace treaty) America and Japan technically were still at war. Since such a commission was legal, and since the Supreme Court lacked jurisdiction to review the findings of military commissions, the defendant in effect had no claim to protection under the Fifth Amendment. In plain terms, as an enemy combatant, he had no legal right to a "fair trial," at least as that term was understood by most Americans and spelled out in the Constitution of the United States.

At the heart of the case, of course, was the issue of command responsibility. The majority held that the law of war "plainly imposed on petitioner . . . an affirmative duty to take such measures as were within his power and appropriate in the circumstances" to protect civilians and prisoners of war from harm. Thus, the court concluded, the defendant's "responsibility" was clear.[37]

Not to the two dissenting justices, however. Wiley B. Rutledge and Frank Murphy thought the majority's reasoning was rife with pettifoggery.

To Rutledge, the great issue, as he called it, was the Fifth Amendment with its "safeguards" for a fair trial, safeguards Yamashita had been denied. His trial, the justice wrote, was filled with "broad departures from the fundamentals of fair play," fundamentals at the heart of American culture and society.

"I cannot believe in the face of this record that the petitioner has had the fair trial our Constitution and laws command." Using italics to add emphasis, Rutledge wrote, "*no* person shall be deprived of life, liberty or property without due process of law."[38]

Justice Murphy, a civil libertarian and former high commissioner in the Philippines, was even more pointed. Yamashita, he wrote, had been "rushed to trial under an improper charge, given insufficient time to prepare an adequate defense, deprived of the benefits of some of the most elementary rules of evidence and summarily sentenced to be hanged."

The trial had thus undermined the very values so many Americans had given their lives to defend. At its heart, he said, was "an uncurbed spirit of revenge and retribution, masked in formal legal procedure for purposes of dealing with a fallen enemy commander."

Such a spirit, he went on, was "unworthy of the traditions of our people" and "to conclude otherwise, is to admit that the enemy has lost the battle but has destroyed our ideals."[39]

IF HOMMA STILL HOPED for a reprieve, he did not say. But learning of the Court's decision the same day he was to take the witness stand likely deepened his dread.

At midmorning on Tuesday, February 5, lead defense counsel John Skeen started the direct examination of his client.

Q: How long did you serve in the Japanese Army?
A: I was with the Japanese Army about 38 years.

Then Skeen took him through that career, trying to turn his liabilities as a general into evidence to support the defense case—his affinity for Anglos, his liberal ideas, his disagreements with Tojo and the high command.

Skeen's next job was more difficult—to show the commission how a Japanese commander in chief could be isolated in the middle of his own army.

Q: Did you choose your own staff officers?
A: No, I did not choose my staff officers. I was almost the last [member of the 14th Army staff assigned to the Philippine invasion force].
Q: From where did the order come regarding appointments of staff officers in the Japanese Army?
A: From Imperial GHQ.
Q: Could you remove any staff officers or senior commander on your own authority?
A: No, I cannot.[40]

So he was surrounded by subordinates who owed their political loyalty, and army careers, to others, and those subordinates had an unusual amount of power and autonomy. They could keep him informed or not, and in doing so they could, in effect, manipulate his orders, a practice so common in the Imperial Army it even had a name, *gekokujo*, "the rule of the higher by the lower," a reflection of the power of the junior officer corps, whose ranks were rife with political incendiaries, cunning zealots in key posts.[41]

AFTER LUNCH, Skeen prepared to take his client through the most difficult part of his testimony.

Skeen asked him if he'd had occasion to be on the Old National Road during the movement of prisoners north.

Yes, Homma said, he had been on the roads of Bataan three times during that period.

Q: Did you see any signs of mistreatment of prisoners?
A: Oh, no, I did not.
Q: Did any one of your staff officers make an inspection of the march of prisoners from Bataan to San Fernando?
A: Yes, I think they did, on their own initiative . . . General Wachi, Colonel Takatsu, and Major Wada, they did.
Q: . . . Did you receive any reports from these officers as to mistreatment of prisoners on the march?
A: I did not receive any such report.
Q: Now, had they seen occurrences, would they have been reported to you?
A: Certainly they would.
Q: Did you receive reports from any officers, or anyone, as to mistreatment of prisoners on the march?
A: I did not receive any such reports.
Q: . . . What was the apparent physical condition of the prisoners [that you'd seen]?
A: They looked rather tired and haggard.
Q: . . . In your trip[s] did you see any bodies, dead bodies, along the road?
A: No, I did not see. From the testimony I heard in court it appeared

to me that there were many dead bodies lying along the roadside, but I do not see how it could be so, why I did not see any bodies lying on the road on my whole trip. However, I was not looking for them particularly, to find them.[42]

It was a risky strategy, born more of desperation than design. Skeen, Pelz, and company were pinning their case on their client's credibility. Homma was telling the court that he'd seen nothing untoward along the route of the march, a general in a staff car with his mind so fixed on finishing a battle that he could look out the window without noticing the trees. Maybe the judges, all generals themselves, men who also had experienced the myopia of command, would believe him.

ON CROSS-EXAMINATION, Frank Meek, the chief prosecutor, tore away at each of the defendant's assertions.

Q: . . . You were reported to have said [in a newspaper interview in Tokyo after arrest] "I saw the death march, and it wasn't very bad."

A: . . . I meant that I saw the march, which I related here.

Q: And what you did see of it, you didn't think it was very bad?

A: I stated here yesterday that I saw a few columns of the march, and nothing—I saw nothing extraordinary happen.

Q: . . . While you were in command in the Philippines, no report was ever made to you of any deaths in that march?

A: It may have been made, but I cannot state with any amount of certainty.

Q: . . . There were many atrocities . . . Prisoners were beaten, bayonetted and shot . . . Does that indicate to you that the plan for the kind of treatment of prisoners of war that you had issued prior to the invasion was being followed out?

A: I came to know for the first time in the court of such atrocities, and I am ashamed of myself should these atrocities have happened.[43]

At the end of his cross-examination, Meek focused on the main charge: Homma's overarching responsibility as commander in chief.

Q: You knew that your responsibility was to treat prisoners of war according to the terms of international law and the Geneva Convention?

A: I shouldn't call it a responsibility, but I knew that prisoners of war should be treated according to international law.

Q: You knew that was your responsibility, to see that was done, didn't you?

A: It should be observed.

Q: Is that the best answer you can give?

A: I have responsibility in the moral sense about everything that happened under my command.

Q: That includes the care, feeding, the furnishing of medicine to civilian internees, as well?

A: Everything what happened under my command, I said.[44]

THE LAST WITNESS for the defense took the stand on the afternoon of February 7. As Bob Pelz described the scene, the witness was "completely undaunted" by the bright lights, the whirring gears of the movie cameras, the popping of flash bulbs."

Q: What is your name?

A: Fujiko Homma.

She was dressed in a dark kimono with a white obi and wooden sandals, and her hair was pulled back in a bun. "We will probably never see a more dramatic spectacle in court," Bob Pelz wrote that night. "Mrs. Homma almost gaily took the stand in defense of her husband."

She had worked with defense lawyers for several days preparing her testimony. Skeen had tried to warn her to accept the "misfortune that awaits," but she still hoped for a good result.[45]

Captain Frank Coder handled her questioning for the defense. As they had rehearsed, she told the court about her husband's political attitudes, his views on the war, his ostracism by the Imperial Army elite—a reprise of the defense's main themes.

Then Coder came at her with a question the two had not rehearsed.

Q: Can you tell us generally what kind of a man General Homma is?

She paused for a moment ("I have not really thought about this," she told herself), then spoke into the microphone in front of her.

A: I have come from Tokyo to here, and I am proud of the fact that I am the wife of General Homma. I have one daughter, and my wish for her is that some day I wish that she will marry a man like my husband, Masaharu Homma. He is that kind of man.[46]

The gallery was quiet, the defendant wet eyed.

[*Pelz, Journal, February 7*] No one could help but feel a lump in their throat as this lovely woman quietly talked of her husband . . . I believe [judges] Valdes and Trudeau were most affected of the commission. Bowing as she walked out, Mrs. Homma received a slight bow and smile from Trudeau. Even Major Tisdelle [General King's aide, a former POW and a witness for the prosecution] said to me, "She is a lovely woman, but she does not really know her husband. I kept seeing the tortured bodies of my friends as she spoke."

That day, Masaharu and Fujiko saw each other for the last time.

He was locked in his room on the second floor of the residence. She was allowed to speak to him through a small wire-mesh screen in the door. His voice, she thought, "has the calm of a man who has already settled himself to his fate."

As the half hour approached, they waited for Captain Williams to appear and take her away, but the officer was nowhere in sight. After more than an hour, Williams finally arrived—drunk. (Fujiko later found out that her proctor had gone on a bender so she and her husband could be together, in her words, "for as long as possible for the last time on earth.")[47]

Later, back at the nurses' quarters, Skeen came to see her.

"Missus, your part is over," the defense attorney said. "It is best that you go home."

"I would like to stay as long as I can," she pleaded.

"No," the attorney said. "Your husband does not want you to have to see him receive the verdict."

She would be leaving in forty-eight hours, he told her. Lieutenant Pelz would fly to Tokyo with her and escort her home.

THE NEXT DAY, Saturday, February 9, Pelz joined George Ott, Frank Coder, and John Skeen to deliver the closing arguments for the defense.

"In order to find the accused guilty under the charge," Skeen began, "the prosecution must prove beyond all reasonable doubt that he is connected with the atrocities which have been alleged."[48]

Skeen went on to summarize Homma's troubles as a commander—the shortages of food and medicine, poorly trained troops, his lack of control over his staff. "In judging whether he 'did unlawfully disregard and fail to control the operations of the members of his command,'" Skeen continued, "you must base your decision not on the control he should have had, not on the control he would have had as the commander of an army of the United States, but on the control he actually has as a lieutenant general of the Japanese Imperial Army . . . I cannot stress this point too strongly."[49]

Then Skeen reviewed the shaky testimony of Homma's staff officers, evidence that had to be answered. "In no case did a staff officer testify that he had ever reported to the accused any case of an atrocity or laxity on the part of subordinate officers," Skeen said. "Why were they not reported? In some cases because they did not believe maltreatment existed and in others because they did not want him to know about it. It should be obvious to the Commission after listening to the testimony of staff officers of the accused that they did not honestly inform him as to the actual conditions."[50]

Then, all arguments exhausted, the defense attorney made a simple appeal.

> Finally it should be pointed out that all of the evidence is not to be found within the printed pages of the record. In the short space of six weeks all members of his counsel have become thoroughly convinced of the sincerity and integrity of General Homma and are proud to have represented him . . . You have observed his manner on the witness stand . . . Can you say after talking with him that he is a cruel and heartless man that would have permitted his troops to commit atrocities had he known about them? . . . We therefore submit that after a careful analysis of all the evidence in the light of American justice this Commission should render a verdict of not guilty under the Charge.[51]

In his closing argument for the prosecution, Meek reviewed the list of atrocities—the bombing of Manila, rapes and murders of civilians, the conditions at O'Donnell and Cabanatuan, finally the death march.

Never will there be a blot in human history to compare in my estimation with the Death March. Someone is to blame for these marches, and that someone is the accused . . . What do we have? We have the testimony here of the dead and the dying. We have heard testimony that they didn't have food. We [heard] that they did not have water . . . These things, gentlemen of the commission, cannot be denied. They cannot be overlooked. Someone had to be responsible. That someone is this accused . . . He is not the fine humanitarian soul [the defense] would have you believe . . . General Homma, as he has said, is morally responsible. I submit he is responsible in every sense of the word . . . Hard as it is for anyone to pass judgment on his fellow man, there is but one plain, clear duty for the members of this commission, and that is to find this accused guilty as charged, and in doing that the prosecution in this case expects and requests the death penalty.[52]

General Donovan adjourned the session and announced that the commission would reconvene in two days, February 11, "at which time the finding of this case will be announced." That night, Bob Pelz went to see his client.

"I paid what must be my last visit to the General," he wrote afterward. "It touched me deeply and when I told him that it has meant much to me to have known him, he bowed his head and said, 'I am honored that you should say so.' Then I bid him au revoir although we both knew, in our hearts, that it was not au revoir . . . I shall never forget the General. I believe he is a good man who was placed by fate in an impossible situation. Truly he will die for the sins of others."

Sometime before 1:00 a.m. Sunday, Bob Pelz and Fujiko boarded a four-engine C-54 Skymaster at Clark Field for the long flight north to Tokyo. "Mrs. Homma cried a little as she saw the lights of Manila fade," Pelz noted in his diary.

The next afternoon in Manila, General Donovan called the commission into session and read the charges against the accused. Then he told the defendant, dressed in a white linen suit and dark tie, to rise, come forward, and stand before the bar with his lead attorney, Major Skeen.

Donovan: Upon secret written ballot, two-thirds or more of the members concurring, the commission finds you, of the charge, guilty . . . Has the accused or his counsel anything further to offer before sentence is announced? Do you wish to make a statement?

Homma: I wish to thank the gentlemen on the commission for the courteous ways which I have been treated all through and during my trial. I thank you very much.

Donovan: Sentence. Upon secret written ballot, two-thirds or more of the members concurring, the commission sentences you to be shot to death with musketry. The accused will be escorted from the courtroom.[53]

The same day, in Washington, D.C., the U.S. Supreme Court officially refused to hear Homma's writ of habeas corpus. Justices Rutledge and Murphy again dissented. The trials, Murphy suggested, had been nothing more than "pretense," no better than "blood purges."[54]

In the weeks that followed, the Homma verdict worked its way up the chain of command, reviewed and certified at each step, until it reached the desk of the final authority in the case, Douglas MacArthur.

On Monday, March 11, the supreme commander announced that he was beginning a "conclusive" review of the case, a review that began with a visit from the condemned man's wife, Fujiko. Accompanied by George Furness, who was handling all the posttrial legal matters, Fujiko met with MacArthur for some forty minutes. She stressed that she had not come to beg for mercy; "My husband would be very angry with me if I did," she told reporters. Rather she asked the supreme commander to take special care reviewing the facts in the case, in effect a plea for clemency. Furness said MacArthur "understood and sympathized" with the aggrieved woman's request.[55]

Nine days later, none of that empathy was apparent. Declaring, "If this defendant does not deserve his judicial fate, none in jurisdictional history ever did," MacArthur ordered his surrogates in the Philippines to carry out the death sentence. He also decided to use the occasion to respond to Rutledge and Murphy.

"No trial could have been fairer than this one," he insisted. "The trial was conducted in the unshaded light of truth, the whole truth and nothing but the truth."[56]

HOMMA WAITED in a prisoner of war camp near Los Baños for the army to set the date of his execution. He spent the hours, days, weeks praying, reading, and writing.

He wrote a last letter to his mother, Machi-san.

Dear Mother,
I don't know how to express to you the depth of my gratitude for raising and caring for me all these years. Since I left for the academy to become an army officer at 18, I haven't lived with you and have not returned your kindness. I went my own way, and made you worry constantly. Now, at the end, instead of taking care of you, I will die before you do. What an impiety for a son. No matter how much I apologize, it will never be enough . . . Please forgive me.[57]

And a last letter to his children.

Dear Masahiko, Hisako, Seisako,
It is the greatest of sorrows to die without seeing you, however this is my destiny and nothing can be done . . . No matter how much I write, I still miss you . . . Please take good care of your mother. She will be the greatest legacy I leave to you, and you will be the greatest asset I can leave to her.[58]

Not knowing the date he was to die, he wrote several "final" letters to Fujiko.

[*March 10, 1946, letter from the "condemned cell"*] I always write my letter thinking this would be the last one for me to write . . . Prison life makes me like a living corpse . . . It is unbearable to wait for the day of my execution wondering if a call for me may come today or tonight.

Now [that] I've been reduced to being a carp on the chopping board, there's nothing that can be done . . . I will resign myself to my fate and stand before the muzzles of the American soldiers' rifles . . .

At last, goodbye.[59]

Another week passed with no word.

"Everyday I picture you, mother, Hisako and Seisaku in my mind's eye," he wrote on March 19. "I always think to myself, 'Today might be the last day.'"

He wanted to prepare himself for his final moments and decide what he might say. Perhaps recite something from the sutras? Offer his family a final good-bye?

"I will die," he finally resolved, "giving cheers [banzais] to the Emperor."[60]

He passed those last days reading books and Buddhist scriptures. He was still hoping for enlightenment, some spiritual release. At the end of every day, however, he found himself earthbound, still behind bars, waiting.

"My nerves," he wrote Fujiko, "have become as sharp and thin as a needle . . . I often have dreams of the family . . . My agony is great."[61]

At last he was handed notice of his execution, the sentence to be carried out April 3. He sat down and scribbled his "very last letter," assuring his family that "it will be better to be shot to death" like a soldier on the battlefield than spend the rest of his life "in such a cage." Then, following Buddhist tradition, he wrote his death poem, his last attempt to find a moment of peace in the life he was about to leave.

. . . With a smile I'll give the life I offered long ago, as I have now found a place to die.

It will be good to become the earth of Manila, looking at the mountains of Bataan, where my comrades sleep.[62]

IN THE LATE WINTER of 1946, when Captain Ivan J. Birrer of Kansas arrived at the Philippine Detention and Rehabilitation Center, an army jail near Los Baños that doubled as the place of execution for condemned war criminals, the officer in charge, an aging colonel named John Fonvielle, took one look at the young officer's sterling record—psychology major in college, certificate from the Army's Command and Staff College at Fort Leavenworth, Kansas—and made him his adjutant. It became Birrer's job to relay instructions and assignments to the center's staff, and in late March, when orders arrived to prepare for the execution of Masaharu Homma, Fonvielle called Birrer into his office.

"Okay," the colonel said, "you're the adjutant, you take care of whatever has to be done."[63]

The center had two execution sites. One was a wooden scaffold with tin skirting that stood in the shade of a mango tree, thirteen steps leading up to a platform with a trapdoor. Nearby on a patch of bare ground flanked by woods was a tall, thick wooden plank planted in the ground as a backstop for a firing squad.[64]

At roughly 1:00 a.m. on Wednesday, April 3, 1946, Masaharu Homma arrived at the execution center from the nearby prisoner of war camp and was put inside a small concrete blockhouse that sat in the middle of the compound and was surrounded by barbed wire. A lieutenant colonel who had escorted the condemned man from Los Baños sought out the center's young adjutant.

"Here," the colonel said, handing Ivan Birrer a two-page single-spaced legal document. "You will read this to the general."

Birrer made his way across the compound, two brawny military police sergeants with flashlights leading the way to the blockhouse where the condemned man was waiting. The room was bare except for a cot on which Homma sat.

Ivan Birrer started to read. He had recited death warrants to other prisoners, but never one this long, this detailed. It began with an outline of the charges, then came a list of the specifications followed by the findings of the court. Birrer tried to read slowly, carefully. Since there had been no time to look it over, he didn't want to make a mistake, louse up the drill. From time to time, he tried to catch a glimpse of the general out of the corner of his eye to see if he was listening.

Homma sat in silence, looking at no one or nothing in particular. After he had finished the first page, Birrer flipped to the second and kept reading. Then, all at once, he became aware of what he was reading.

The warrant included a summary of Homma's military career, a paragraph, in Birrer's opinion, of "blistering" insult, the kind of thing MacArthur had included in his final review of the verdict: "The proceedings show the defendant lacked the basic firmness of character and moral fortitude essential to officers charged with the high command of military forces in the field."[65]

Homma was standing now, angry and staring at the young American officer. His execution had nothing to do with character or morality. "I'm being shot tonight because we lost the war," he told Birrer dryly. Then he sat down again.

Birrer, stunned, stopped for a moment, then, not knowing what to say, picked up where he'd left off.

"General it is my duty to tell you that the sentence will be carried out at zero-two-hundred today," some thirty to forty minutes hence. And with that, Birrer left the condemned man in the company of the burly sergeants, crossed the yard again, and stopped near the mango tree to wait.

The execution site was lit with floodlights, but the aging generator that drove them was cranky, and the yellow lights would dim, go bright again, then dim once more. Beyond the circle of pulsing lights, the compound sat in the pale silver of a full moon, a place of silhouettes and shadows and warm night breezes.

Shortly before 2:00 a.m., the condemned man came out of the blockhouse, flanked by the two guards. He walked slowly, deliberately across the yard to the spot where the wooden plank had been set in the ground.

A doctor had pinned a six-inch square of white cloth on the general's shirt over his heart. The executioner, Lieutenant Charles R. Rexroad, had set his six riflemen in a line twenty-five yards away. Now he moved the condemned man into position in front of the plank.

"General," Rexroad asked him, "do you have any last words?"

Masaharu Homma seemed to lean forward, then turn, Birrer guessed, in the direction of Tokyo, home of the Imperial Palace.

"Banzai!" Homma yelled. "Banzai! Banzai!"

Rexroad took his position.

Ready, he said, aim, fire!

IMAGINE, AFTER EVERYTHING, THIS

H E SPOTTED HER right away. Beautiful smile, gorgeous hair. And the way she moved, out there on the dance floor, every guy in Elmo Club watching her.[1]

She was sitting with her girlfriend now at a nearby table. That's Bobbie Mellis, Ben Steele told Porky Dillon. All grown up from the girl he once knew. Must be eighteen, nineteen, "kind of a knockout." They should go over, he said, introduce themselves, buy the girls a drink.

She remembered him from before the war, working with her father out at the Clark ranch. So Bud Steele was back. No worse for the wear, apparently. He still had that shock of dark hair, those deep brown eyes.

The four of them ordered steaks and rounds of whiskey and beer. They talked, they danced. When the Elmo closed at 4:00 a.m., they drove down from the heights to a diner on Montana Avenue for breakfast.

BEN STEELE was twenty-eight, Roberta Mellis twenty, a bookkeeper at the Billings Gas Company. They dated almost every night for two weeks. At the end of his leave, sitting in the Elmo Club again, he said he had a question. He took a pencil out of his pocket and wrote something on a cocktail napkin.

"Marry me?" it said.

"Yes," she answered.

Back at the convalescent center in Spokane, his doctors told him he wasn't ready for marriage. He wasn't "normal" yet. "Take it easy," they said. "Get back on your feet first. Don't fall in love with the first girl that comes along." His family was against it, too. "She isn't a Catholic," his mother said.

In Spokane he bought Bobbie a wedding dress. A few weeks later, on February 16, 1946, at the Little Flower Catholic Church in Billings, they were married. She was in white, he was in uniform. Bobbie and Bud.

They honeymooned in Miami at the Embassy Hotel, a fancy art deco hostelry on the beach that served as an army rest and recuperation center for former prisoners of war. Then during the spring and summer they lived in a bungalow on the grounds of Fort George Wright in Spokane while he finished his treatment. On December 12, 1946, Bobbie gave birth to a daughter, Rosemarie.

They returned to Montana and set up housekeeping in a bedroom in his in-laws' house east of town near Shepherd, not far from the old Clark ranch. He was home, married to a Montana girl, living on the land he knew. He sketched, saw friends, thought about his future. In the fall he planned a trip to New London, Ohio, to spend time with an old comrade, Father John E. Duffy.

THE PRIEST had come west to see him that summer. He'd driven out from New London in his brand-new Pontiac, met the folks at the ranch the Old Man was managing in Broadview, said hello to Bobbie and the baby.

They traded war stories for a while, then Duffy asked about his plans, and when the priest discovered that Ben Steele was at loose ends—thinking about this, thinking about that—he suggested he come to Ohio. They could work together on a book. He'd been thinking about a book since Bilibid Prison, a book that would include the kind of sketches that went down on the *Oryoku Maru*. Duffy would write the text, he said, and Ben would create the drawings.

Bobbie did not want him to go. Neither did his parents. Something about that priest, they said, the way he kept complaining about how Montana's gravel roads were ruining the tires on his new car. Besides, Duffy hadn't written anything yet. He'd been thinking about it, he said, working on the book in his head. Would Ben like to hear the title? "We Met Them at the Beaches."

That spring, to spur him along, the priest sent him carfare, and Ben Steele sat down to sort things out. He wanted to draw, of that he was sure, and here was a man who supported his work, a man with a little influence. He knew that in Cleveland, just sixty miles from New London, there was an excellent institute of art. He might matriculate, if they'd have him.

AT FIRST he got along well with the priest. He liked New London, a town that looked like a village—sleepy squares and greenswards, maples, oaks, and buckeyes. Duffy's old stone church, Our Lady of Lourdes, was on Park Street, across from some schools and a block from the town center. There in a room in the rectory, Ben Steele sat down to draw.

He drew from memory, drew all day every day and into the night. In the evening, when Duffy's clerical duties were done, the priest would return to the rectory to inspect the work of his protégé. He liked what he saw, he said, but he had a few suggestions. They should do a scene about this, they should do a scene about that, battle scenes mostly, keeping up the good fight.

Ben Steele had something else in mind, the other side of war, tableaux from the death march, O'Donnell, Tayabas Road. After several weeks of this back-and-forth, he began to wonder about the book and asked the priest to see some pages.

"Oh, there's lots of time," Duffy said. "Time isn't an element here."

"It is for me," Ben Steele said.

IN AUGUST that year, 1947, he bought a small place in New London with his back pay from the army, took a part-time job as a housepainter, and brought Bobbie and the baby out to live with him.

She was lonely right from the start. Her husband was always working, and she was pregnant again. She liked New London well enough, a picture-book place with small-town manners and ways, but she had never really lived outside Montana, and she missed the West, missed her friends and family. The locals tried to welcome her, invited her to garden parties and the like, but with a baby on her hip and another on the way, she had little time for soirees. And she found no society in the church, either. She'd converted to Catholicism to marry Bud, but she never took to her new religion, and now Duffy was nagging her about skipping confession and missing Mass.

Early that fall, at the urging of an alumnus who'd seen his work, Ben Steele applied to the Cleveland Institute of Art, a well-regarded four-year studio program. The freshman class was full, the registrar said, but he was welcome to come by with his portfolio and a professor would take a look and tell him if he had any talent.

He gathered up his drawings and charcoals, got in his 1939 black Ford

Victoria, and headed east along Lake Shore Drive into downtown Cleveland. Carl Gaertner, a well-known painter, happened to be at school that day. Ben Steele opened his portfolio. There was the water line at O'Donnell, the bars of Bilibid, a guard bayoneting a marcher on the Old National Road. A few hours later, he was admitted to the freshman class.

More than a third of the class that year were veterans, but, as far as he could tell, he was the only prisoner of war. In the company of other vets, he kept silent about his service. If someone sought his particulars, he'd say something like, "I just was ground crew in the Air Corps," or change the subject, rush off to class.

"What's this I hear about you?" his design teacher said one day.

"What are you talking about?" he said.

"I'm talking about being a POW and all that."

"I don't know," Ben Steele said. "I just was."

He didn't want to talk about it. Those other guys on campus, they'd won the war, but he'd surrendered, and the stain of that sometimes left him uncertain, shamefaced.

HE LIKED HIS CLASSES A LOT. One semester the great German caricaturist George Grosz held a workshop at the school. Ben Steele was dazzled by his war work, especially the artist's haunting pen-and-ink *Survivor*. His favorite class was with John Teyral, a master draftsman who could suggest a world with just a few well-placed lines. As artists say, he knew how to get the thing right, something his new student, Ben Steele, had been struggling with.

He was up every day at 6:00 a.m. Made himself a brown-bag lunch, filled a thermos with coffee, and left immediately for school, often arriving at the old redbrick building on Juniper Road before eight, ahead of everyone else. He spent all day in class, often staying late for extra instruction. Back in New London, he'd grab a bit of dinner and sit at a drawing board half the night.

Bobbie was miserable. Bud always seemed someplace else, and the loneliness was consuming her. He knew there was trouble and ignored it. Art was his religion now, and school was his sanctuary. The way he saw it, he'd been a long time getting here. All the way from Bilibid Prison, those first charcoal scratches on the concrete floor. How could Bobbie understand that? How could he explain it to her?

In November they had another baby, Julie Margaret. He was a sophomore now, busier than ever. Through the winter and into the early spring, Bobbie, brooding, started to lose weight and write home about her troubles. In the fall of 1948, her parents drove east for a visit, took one look at her—she'd lost twenty-five pounds—and told her to pack. "I thought maybe we had a future together," she told them.

He was determined to finish school and didn't try to stop her. He thought, she'll be back. She just needs time home. He'd stay in school, make bus trips back to Billings, rebuild the marriage.

He sold their house to save money and sent her the furniture. A few months later, he received an envelope from a law firm in Billings. "Mental cruelty," the divorce papers said.

He phoned her that night. Why was she doing this?

"That's what I want," she said.

He didn't believe it. He was going to come west during break week, he said. They could talk, sort the mess out. She said nothing.

After that, the letters started to arrive, letters from his friends and family in Billings. They had seen Bobbie around town, they said, seen her with other men.

His work and grades started to slip. He suffered from dyspepsia, woke up from pillow-tearing war dreams. In the late spring of 1949, he got on a bus for the long ride home.

He went to her folks' house in Shepherd to talk to her and see the girls. She hardly looked at him. A few days later he asked her to lunch.

Bobbie was back working as a bookkeeper in Billings, her folks helping to raise the girls. He met her at a restaurant downtown. She seemed in a hurry, ate quickly. She had to get back to work, she said, then left.

He finished his lunch and wandered out into the sunlight, and as he looked back toward her office, he spotted her crossing the street and entering another restaurant.

The cuckold in him couldn't resist. When he came through the door he saw her at a table, cooing with a local celebrity, a singing cowboy. The man spotted him before she did and almost knocked her over running out the back door.

"Oh," she said, "I just—"

"Goddamn you!" he said. "That's just about your speed, by God."

———

THE NEXT DAY he got on a bus back to Ohio. Past prairie, past farmland, one tiny town after another. An endless ride, alone.

He thought about the war, about coming home, about the beautiful girl he'd married. He remembered telling himself back then, "I've already been through hell, so everything's going to be easy from now on."

He'd made a mess of it, he could see that now. And then he realized, "I still love her. I don't know why, but I still do."

He loved his girls too and never imagined he would miss them so much, ache for them. His eyes started to water.

"Goddamn it," he thought. "Goddamn it."

Then, for the first time in his life, he started to feel sorry for himself. He'd never been so low. Imagine, after everything, this.

"I should end it all," he told himself. "Get a gun. Blow my brains out."

IN THE SPRING of 1950 he got ready to receive his diploma. His mother alone came out to cheer for him.

"I never thought I'd see you graduate from college," Bess Steele said, a big smile on her face.

He enrolled right away at Kent State University to earn education credits and by the fall of 1951 was certified to teach art. He was living in a rooming house in New London now, dating a bit, teaching art at the junior high and high school, drawing and painting on the side.

That November he attended the high school's annual Thanksgiving alumni dance, a big event in New London. He was wandering around the gym, drinking punch, when he spotted a woman he'd met in passing several times in town, Shirley Anne Emerson.

He knew a bit about her from her aunt Nonie, his landlady. She had graduated from Ohio Wesleyan University, a journalism major and art minor. She had worked as a buyer in a department store in Mansfield for a while, then had moved home to help her ailing grandfather. She was in the accounting department at a local factory now and was writing freelance articles for the Cleveland *Plain Dealer*. All in all an interesting gal, twenty-six years old, easy to look at.

She was sitting with friends, talking, when he wandered over.

"Would you like to dance?" he said.

She looked up, recognized him.

They danced a lot that night. He was like no one she'd ever known, this cowboy turned artist, this former prisoner of war.

They started to have dinner regularly, sometimes at Aunt Nonie's, sometimes at her mother's. When the town of Wakeman invited him to show some of his war art and give a talk about his experience, she went with him and was impressed.

Truth was, she'd liked him from the first, and it wasn't long before she was telling herself, "This is the one," this nice-looking man with a wonderful laugh and dark piercing eyes. She wondered how such a man could suffer so much and still have such "boyish appeal."

In May he said to her, "We better talk about getting married." She didn't know the difference between a steer and a cow, but he didn't care.

"Yes," she said, "we should."

She told him she might not be able to bear children, a consequence of an old operation.

"Well, that's all right," he said. "We have two girls."

AFTER THE WEDDING they went to Denver, where he got his master's degree, then he took a job with the Department of the Army setting up craft shops on army bases and posts in Kansas, Washington, D.C., Georgia. Finally, in 1959, he told Shirley he wanted to move back home to Montana, and he applied for a job as an assistant professor of art at Eastern Montana College in Billings. The next year they built a trim little split-level about a mile and a half down the road from the college. The house sat in an enclave of small streets tucked up against the long wall of rimrocks that frames the city's north side and separates it from the vast prairie beyond.

He was a natural teacher, popular with the students. Then on the first day of his second semester, he walked into his classroom and saw a ghost, a Japanese.

The student's name was Harry Koyama, the son of beet farmers from out Hardin way, the first Japanese that Ben Steele had encountered since the war. He looked at those dark, almond-shaped eyes, and his heart hardened and filled with hate. And when he found out that the boy's family had been locked up in an internment camp during the war, he assumed the boy hated him as well.

"This is awful," Ben Steele thought. "What am I going to do?" After class he went back to his small office to think.

He told himself, okay, the war is over. He wasn't a prisoner any-more and this wasn't Japan. It was America, and "this kid's an American, too." That being the case, "I have to treat him like everybody else, no different."

For a while it worked. He seemed okay with Harry, and Harry seemed okay with him. Then the student discovered that his professor had been a prisoner of the Japanese, and Ben Steele could feel the boy pulling away, withdrawing.

That troubled the teacher in him, and he sat the student down for a talk. By the end of the semester, Harry Koyama was among the best stu-dents in the class. And Ben Steele was beginning to wonder what had happened to all that hate he'd brought home.

IN 1999, THE MORNING after his eighty-second birthday, Ben Steele, long retired from the classroom, awoke early, after six. Shirley would not stir for another hour but he was up before the sun, an old man long off the range holding to the habits of a young Montana cowboy.

He sat on the side of the bed for a moment, shaking off the numb-ness of the night, then he pushed himself to his feet, performed his morning ablutions, and made his way down the darkened hall and around a corner into the kitchen. The morning light was just beginning to fill the room, and he stood at the glass doors to the back patio, watch-ing the first rays of sun play on the towers of rimrock that rose up be-hind the well-ordered neighborhood of ranch houses and split-level homes in suburban Billings where they lived.

Since he was a man of habit, it is easy to guess what was going through his mind that cool November morning as he watched the rim-rocks change color from gray to light brown, the color, he once re-marked, of the young antelope that come down from the mountains in the spring to romp among the sage by the highway and feed on the first green shoots of prairie grass. He was happy to be free. Every morning for fifty-four years he'd had the same first thought:

"I can go where I want to go, I can do what I want to do, it's wonderful."

And this notion, this simple sense of emancipation that came to him as he cleaned his teeth and combed his hair and pulled on his blue jeans and plaid shirt, made him a most agreeable man, a man with a warm handshake and an irresistible smile.

He had errands to run that morning, and after cereal and toast he set-tled himself behind the wheel of his pickup, a new gray Dodge Dakota with a camper top. He was not an acquisitive man—the salary of an art professor had never allowed for luxury, and what's more he was cheap, so "tightfisted," his grown daughters liked to joke, he could make the face on an Indian-head nickel cry out in pain—but he had to have that new truck.

His first stop was the ophthamologist to prepare for cataract surgery a week hence. Old men, he liked to joke, were like old cars—some damn part or other was always wearing out. Overall he was healthy enough, a bit overweight perhaps (Shirley fed him sensibly but he had a sweet tooth and kept candy hidden in the cab of the truck) and a little slow of foot (poor circulation often left him leg weary), but he could still climb into a canoe to fish the Big Horn or wade out into the icy cur-rents of the Stillwater to chase the trout in the eddies. He even planned to get on a horse again. A friend from the East was due that night, a ten-derfoot eager to understand the open range and ride side by side with an old cowboy, a man who believed in the boundless.

After the eye doctor, he headed east on Broadwater Avenue to a branch post office to mail something to his adopted son, Sean, then he turned the truck back up toward the rimrocks, looking for KEMC, Billings's public radio station, where he was scheduled to give an inter-view on his life and work.

Artist and educator Ben Steele was born November 17, 1917, in Roundup Montana to Benjamin Cardwell Steele and . . .

It was just before 10:50 a.m. and Elizabeth McNamer was taping her show *Speakers Corner* in studio B at KEMC radio. McNamer was some-thing of a personality in Billings. An Irishwoman educated in England, she had lived long in the American West but had held hard to her An-glican intonations. An odd voice for cowboy country, but then Billings was a town where the word "character" seemed to apply to a lot of folks.

Ben grew up on the family homestead south of Musselshell on Hawk Creek. He attended school . . .

McNamer had known Ben Steele for years, which is to say that like most who claimed his acquaintance, she really knew his work.

In forty years of days, Professor Steele had trained hundreds of painters and draftsmen, a handful of whom enjoyed some renown: Clyde Aspevig, Jim Reineking, Elliott Eaton, Kevin Red Star. Outside the classroom, their teacher had developed something of a reputation as well. In forty years of nights and weekends, Ben Steele had holed up in the studio behind his house in the lee of the rims producing his own work, art that reflected his life.

Ben volunteered for the United States Army Air Corps and served from 1940 to 1946. Present at the bombing of Clark Field in the Philippines . . .

He painted the West and he painted the war. And though his "war stuff," as he liked to call it, was in every sense art, almost everyone tended to look at it as testimony, an affidavit of the suffering of those days.

Elizabeth McNamer described that work for her listeners, then asked her interviewee what it had been like to make the infamous death march. Ben Steele leaned forward.

We were so thirsty on the death march that we would . . .

Seven or eight minutes into the interview, Elizabeth McNamer noticed that her guest seemed suddenly unsettled. The bright brown eyes, usually so relaxed, looked distressed.

"What's the matter, Ben?"

He sat very still for a moment.

"I've got this pain in my back," he said.

McNamer reckoned he was getting stiff from leaning forward at the microphone.

"Why don't you stand up for a minute," she suggested. But he could not raise himself, and the pain was getting worse.

"Lois," said Elizabeth, "can you get Ben a glass of water? He's not feeling very well. And maybe someone should call an ambulance."

Lois Bent, the producer, was sitting on the other side of the glass window that separated studio B and the control room. When she came around the corner into the studio, she found Ben Steele slumped forward in his chair.

"Mm–my back . . . ," he mumbled.

"Ben! Ben!" Lois was bending over him, yelling.

"Oh my God!" said Elizabeth.

She was just about to make a second call for an ambulance when two paramedics, Michelle Motherway and Julia Johnson, rushed into the room.

To Motherway the man looked ashen, "like the color of the wall." And his blood pressure was low, "eighty over sixty," she told Johnson, dangerously low. His symptoms suggested a ruptured aortic aneurysm. He had "that look," as paramedics say, that "impending sense of doom."

They picked him up in his chair and hustled him into the ambulance.

"We're fighting time," Motherwell told the emergency room doctor, Ron Winters, on the radio, then, turning to the driver, Alicia Kraft, she said, "Get going . . . and go as fast as you can."

The ambulance raced down Twenty-seventh Street to Deaconess Hospital. Dr. Winters was waiting at the emergency room door. Motherway had been right, it was an aneurysm. This guy is in trouble, Winters thought, and he grabbed for a phone and summoned a surgeon.

Meanwhile, in the shadow of the rimrocks, in their gray clapboard house on Cascade Avenue, Shirley Steele had just returned from her own errands and was standing at the ironing board in the laundry room downstairs when the phone rang.

"Shirley, it's Elizabeth McNamer. We're taking Ben to the hospital. He's very ill."

When Shirley Steele arrived at the emergency room, she found her husband in cubicle 13, lying on a gurney surrounded by doctors and nurses. His face and head were swollen out of all proportion. He was screaming and moaning. She should leave, a nurse said, ushering her to a small waiting room.

A few minutes later a doctor appeared in the doorway.

"Excuse me, are you Mrs. Steele?"

"Yes?"

"I'm Scott Millikan."

"Yes?"

"He's bleeding badly and we have to stop it," the doctor said.

The rent in his aorta was pouring blood into his viscera, drowning his organs and driving his blood pressure down to forty and sending his body into a deep and dangerous state of shock.

"If I do nothing," Millikan continued, "he will be dead in ten minutes, and if I do something he may still be dead in ten minutes."

"Go ahead," Shirley Steele said.

The surgeon sprinted for the operating room. He had an hour—"the golden hour of trauma," clinicians call it—sixty minutes from the onset of bleeding to arrest the flow or lose the patient.

Studying the ambulance log, Millikan calculated that the aneurysm had ruptured around 10:55 a.m.; Motherway was at the patient's side by 11:02; Winters received him at 11:18; Millikan was attending by 11:32; and at 11:45 Ben Steele was on an operating table, saline solution dripping into one arm, plasma in the other, and an oxygen tube down his throat. Scott Millikan was leaning over the patient, a scalpel in his hand and ten minutes left.

He cut the patient lengthwise from the sternum to the pubis. Five minutes to find the fissure. They saw the aneurysm almost immediately, a balloon in the aortic wall three and a half inches wide, the largest the surgeon had seen. And there was the rent with blood pouring out of it.

It was speed work, a kind of medical sprint, and after they had clamped the aorta and cut off the bleeding, the surgical team paused before beginning their distance run, the hours it would take to remove the aneurysm and try to repair the damage.

"All right," said the anesthesiologist, taking a breather, "who is this guy? What's the story here?"

A nurse said, "This is Ben Steele."

"Wait a minute," Millikan said. "I know that name."

"He was an art professor," the nurse said, "and he was in that death march of Bataan."

The surgeon turned to his assistant. "This is great, 'cause now I know this son of a bitch is tough. He's already proved he's a survivor."

Five hours later Millikan wandered into the waiting room and flopped into a chair in front of the family—Shirley, Rosemarie, and Julie. The doctor had changed into clean green scrubs and was wearing hospital slippers but no socks.

"Sorry about the bare feet," he said wearily. "It got a little deep in there."

Then he gave them the news: the patient had lost a lot of blood; they had given him thirteen units during the operation. His main worry now was Ben's blood pressure: a sudden or sustained drop would likely cause a brain hemorrhage, and if that happened, it was unlikely the patient would survive.

And there was more: Ben's kidneys or heart might fail; his lungs might fill with fluid and he might drown; a blood clot might form and shoot to the brain; his internal organs, which had been swimming in blood, might have been damaged and could shut down.

Adding it all up, Millikan said, the patient's prognosis was no better than "minute to minute."

Julie asked a few questions, Rosemarie was too frightened to speak, and Shirley shut her eyes and took several deep breaths.

"Hold it together," she said to herself. "You have to hold it together."

The next day, Friday, Millikan revised his prognosis. Now it was "hour to hour." By Saturday Ben had improved to "day to day." He could manage a few words at that point, and early Saturday morning Shirley was able to speak with him.

She stood by his bed in the intensive care unit, her left hand on the bed rail, her right hand wrapped around two of his fingers.

"How ya doin', kid?" she said and touched his cheek. "Hey! You need a shave."

He looked at her and blinked.

"I thought—" He blinked again. "I thought they had killed me," he said.

Then he turned his head and smiled.

NOTES

All Japanese names are presented given name family name.

GHOSTS

1. *Hohei*, literally translated, is "foot soldier." The Japanese used the word to refer to infantry. All soldiers, including infantry, artillery, armor, communications, and so forth, were called *heiti*, "soldier" or, in modern translation, "serviceman." We use *hohei* throughout to mean both infantryman and common soldier in all branches of the Japanese military.

CHAPTER ONE

1. Schlesinger, *Almanac of American History*, 481-82. Roosevelt signed the Selective Training and Service Act on September 16, 1940. The first draft took place on October 29.
2. Gallup, *Gallup Poll*, vol. 1, "December 23—Threat to America's Future," 312.
3. "May 14, 1939—Most Important Problem," ibid., 154; "May 10, 1940—Neutrality," ibid., 222; "July 7, 1940—European War," ibid., 231; "October 14, 1940—European War," ibid., 245.
4. Roosevelt, "For a Declaration of War Against Japan," in Copeland, *World's Great Speeches*, 531. Morton, *Fall of the Philippines*, and Watson, *Chief of Staff*, go into great detail on the meetings of the various war plans boards and committees in the War Department. These boards gathered regularly throughout the 1920s and 1930s to draft military plans and policies based on the periodic shifts in American foreign policy. The planners tried to anticipate potential enemies and attacks and plan a defense, both on American soil and American possessions overseas.
5. Interviews with Q. P. Devore and Ben Steele. All conversations are as the principals remember and report them, sometimes in whole, sometimes in fragments. In either case, nothing in quotation has been either reconstituted or imagined.
6. Gleeck, *Over Seventy-five Years*, 22-37, for poem, preceding details, and quotations.
7. Miller, *Bataan Uncensored*, 59.
8. Ibid., 63.

9. From the accounts of many officers and from Sayre, *Glad Adventure*, 221, who says MacArthur held to this fiction as late as November 27, ten days before the attack on Pearl Harbor and the same day Washington sent him a "war warning" that "hostile action" was "possible at any moment"; also Watson, *Chief of Staff*, 507. A number of officers on the command staff had read the same intelligence reports and worried that the Japanese were marshaling troops for a move on the Philippines. The strike would surely come in December or January, not April, the incendiary prelude to the rainy season and, as even the most insouciant second lieutenant knew, the worst month to launch an attack. Hersey, *Men on Bataan*, 19.

10. "Monkey men . . . ," Lee, *They Call It Pacific*, 10; the "eyeball" quotations come from an interview with Zoeth Skinner, 2002, but the subject is a familiar one, explained fully and well in Dower, *War Without Mercy*, 94–180. See also Johnson, *Japanese Through American Eyes*, 19, 145–54; "We'll knock . . . ," Zoeth Skinner, interview, 2002.

11. Rogers, *The Good Years*, 93.

12. Miller, *Bataan Uncensored*, 63.

13. Frank Tremaine (UP correspondent in Honolulu), interview, 2000.

14. Frank Bigelow, interview, 1999.

15. Rita Palmer, Army Nurse Corps, interview, 1984.

16. Zoeth Skinner, interview, 1999.

17. Ind, *Bataan*, 64.

18. Here too there is controversy. Ind, ibid., 101, an air intelligence officer, said he had photos showing some planes "lined up neatly" on the runway; Shimada, "Opening Air Offensive Against the Philippines," 93, writes that Japanese pilots found their targets "lined up on the target fields."

19. For the Shinto myth of creation, see Sansom, *Japan*, 22ff; Storry, *History of Modern Japan*, 25ff. For the Japanese view, see Sakamaki Shunzo, "Shinto: Japanese Ethnocentrism," in Moore, *The Japanese Mind*, 24–26. For a wider view, see Holtom, *Modern Japan and Shinto Nationalism*. Embree, *The Japanese Nation*, 165–75, provides the best context in Western terms. Ballou, *Shinto*, is the single best source for Shinto as a basis for nationalism and war, and all quotations, unless otherwise noted, are taken from this text, 19–25ff.

20. Holtom, *National Faith of Japan*, 15, 23. The Zero was a new and revolutionary fighter plane. Formally it was designated the A6M2. Zero—*Reisen* or "Zero fighter"—quickly became its nickname, which was intended to commemorate the year 1940, when its trials were finished and it went into full production.

21. All the quotations that follow are from Sakai, Caidin, and Saito, *Samurai!* Sakai, now deceased, is the only Japanese character in our book we did not interview or for whom we did not have primary sources—notes, letters, transcripts of interviews with other writers, and so forth. Saito gave Caidin Sakai's notes and transcripts of his interviews with Sakai. Caidin's papers, from his many books, are archived at the University of Wyoming. A search of that archive failed to turn up Saito's transcripts. There are letters referring to the work, but not the vital transcripts themselves. Nor were these documents in other archives, private or public. Permission to

quote at length from the memoir was given by DeeDee Caidin, executor of Caidin's estate. A subsequent book on Sakai claims to have found errors in the memoir, but these turn on one or two combat incidents. Sakai became a public figure after his memoir, *Samurai!* was published in 1957, and he was interviewed many times. We could find no interview in which Sakai challenged or disputed Caidin's account of his life or the details of his part in the attack on Clark Field.

22. A British Officer "Literature of the Russo-Japanese War," 509.

23. McClain, *Japan*, 407.

24. Erfurth, "Surprise," 355, 367; Musashi, *Book of Five Rings*, 48; Allied Translator and Interpreter Section (ATIS), *Japan's Decision to Fight*, 10.

25. Erfurth, "Surprise," 361.

26. Sakai, Caidin, and Saito, *Samurai!* 48–52. Sakai's times are at variance with the most authoritative Japanese account in English on the attack: Shimada, "Opening Air Offensive Against the Philippines," 90–91, and Morton, *Fall of the Philippines*, 79–90. We have followed Shimada and Morton.

27. Morton, *Fall of the Philippines*, 79–90.

28. Sakai, Caidin, and Saito, *Samurai!* 51.

29. ATIS, *Japan's Decision to Fight*, 31.

30. There are many conflicting accounts of the circumstances that led to destruction of the Far East Air Force at Clark Field. Various historians, biographers, and writers hold, or at least suggest, that the principals are accountable. Some point the finger at MacArthur or Sutherland or Brereton or certain subalterns at FEAF (Air Corps) headquarters at Nielson Field or on the communications staff at Clark Field. Taking a wider or more historical view, others cite the actions of the army and navy chiefs in Washington, indeed, even President Roosevelt, who waited so long to reinforce a protectorate then so clearly in harm's way. The wider view from within the War Department, where admirals and generals regularly changed their war plans to reflect the constant shifts in national and foreign policy, can be seen, in careful detail, in Watson, *Chief of Staff*; and, in much broader context, in Kennedy, *Freedom From Fear*; Morton, *Strategy and Command*; Dumond, *America in Our Time*; and Kennedy, Cohen, and Bailey, *American Pagent*. The most balanced and likely most accurate view of what led to the calamity at Clark, which includes the colloquy between commanders, is Watson, "Pearl Harbor and Clark Field." He concludes that "general confusion and bad luck" were responsible for the debacle (209). Edmonds, *They Fought with What They Had*, a smoothly crafted and moving book that adds extensive interviews to the few logs and records that survived that day, seems to suggest the same thing. This much is clear: news of the attack on Pearl Harbor reached Manila sometime after 2:30 a.m.; the Japanese bombed small bases in the northern and southern Philippines around dawn; the enemy hit Baguio, 105 miles north of Clark Field, at 9:30 a.m. and Clark sometime between 12:15 and 12:40 p.m., a full ten hours after the attack on Pearl Harbor.

31. Fifty-three bombers attacked the field, 27 Mitsubishi G3M "Nells" and 26 G4M "Bettys." Their combined payload was 636 sixty-kilogram bombs. Figures supplied by Ricardo Trota Jose, correspondence March 12, 2002, who cites Osamu Tagaya,

Mitsubishi Type 1 Rikko "Betty" Units of World War 2 (Botley, Oxford: Osprey Publishing, 2001), 22.

32. Bartsch, "Was MacArthur Ill-Served," 72-117, mentions many of the these details, which were confirmed by the authors in interviews with veterans.

33. Helen Cassiani Nestor, interview, 2002.

34. Ibid.

35. Steele and Devore see one another regularly and have replayed that conversation in the barracks many times across the years. This part of the colloquy is drawn from multiple interviews with both men.

36. No reliable figures exist in extant medical records. This estimate is based on calculations made from figures in Morton, *Fall of the Philippines*, and Edmonds, *They Fought with What They Had*.

37. Some interviewees report the base "nearly abandoned," though that seems an exaggeration. Edmonds, *They Fought with What They Had*, 111-12, and Watson, *Chief of Staff*, 212, suggest that the force "disintegrated" and that a "substantial portion . . . took off" during and after the attack.

CHAPTER TWO

1. Ryotaro Nishimura, interviews with authors, 2000–2002.

2. Smaller landings had taken place earlier on Luzon, and two days after the main force secured the beach at Lingayen, some 7,000 troops of the 16th Division landed south of Manila on Luzon's east coast at Lamon Bay. Morton, *Fall of the Philippines*, 125, lists 14th Army total strength at the time of the invasion (combat, support, and air force troops) at 43,110.

3. Morton, *Fall of the Philippines*, 50.

4. Historical Section, *Japanese Studies in World War II*, Monograph 1, 13.

5. Ardant du Picq, "Battle Studies," 157; Stouffer et al., *The American Soldier*, 54-81.

6. Historical Section, *Japanese Studies in World War II*, Monograph 1, 13.

7. Watson, *Chief of Staff*, 432-33.

8. Jose, *The Philippine Army*, 102.

9. Wainwright, *General Wainwright's Story*, 7; Philippine Department Plan Orange, 1940 Revision 1, RG 165, NARA, quoted in Jose, *The Philippine Army*, 185.

10. Hersey, *Men on Bataan*, 289; Linn, *Guardians of the Empire*, 229, 236.

11. Watson, *Chief of Staff*, 415.

12. Leeb, "Defense," 13-14.

13. Linn, *Guardians of the Empire*, 171-78. Watson, *Chief of Staff*, has many of the key documents that detail the changing strategies in Washington and tactics in Manila, but Linn, particularly in chapter 9, "Orange to Rainbow, 1919-1940," puts together the disparate pieces of evidence and offers a coherent narrative of the confusion, interservice rivalries, personal ambitions of military leaders, and an air of unreality that, eventually, led to disaster.

14. From a 1941 memo to the army chief of staff, quoted in Watson, *Chief of Staff*, 389.

15. Linn, *Guardians of the Empire*, 240-45; Jose, *The Philippine Army*, 175; Watson, *Chief of Staff*, 420-21.

16. Watson, *Chief of Staff*, 432; MacArthur, Memorandum: "Defense of the Philippines."
17. Poweleit, *USAFFE*, 18-20.
18. Mallonée, *Naked Flagpole*, 30.
19. Ibid., 32-35.
20. Blesse, "The Filipino Fighting Man," 6; Mallonée, *Naked Flagpole*, 31.
21. Brougher, "Battle of Bataan," 1.
22. William H. Gentry, interview, 1998.
23. Miller, *Bataan Uncensored*, 94.
24. There are no official records to confirm that Lieutenant Ben Morin was the first POW in the islands in World War II. He was captured sometime in the early or midafternoon of December 22, 1941. It is possible that other Americans serving as advisers to the Philippine Army were taken prisoner when their units collapsed the same day or that an American pilot might earlier have gone down behind enemy lines. From his conversations with the authors, Morin believes his unit was the first to be taken captive, a distinction he does not value.
25. All the preceding comes from a 2000 interview with Ben Morin. Father Morin— he took his vows in 1948 and spent much of his tenure as a priest working with the poor in Latin America—says that during the war he prayed almost exclusively to the Blessed Mother and is more than likely to have done so on the road to Lingayen Gulf.
26. MacArthur, Radio Message to AGWAR, December 22, 1941, uses the 40,000 figure. Morton, *Fall of the Philippines*, 162, calculates that, in fact, MacArthur had some 80,000 men on the main island, roughly 20,000 Americans and Philippine Scouts in American ranks, and the rest Philippine Army reservists and regulars. MacArthur likely offered the fiction to support his contention that he was suffering an "enormous tactical discrepancy." Although he outnumbered the Japanese some two to one, using Wainwright's ratio of the number of troops actually prepared for combat, he likely had no more than 8,000 men who, at that point, could put up a fight.

CHAPTER THREE

1. This account is based on Swinson, *Four Samurai*, 34-36; Tsunoda, *Once There Was a Dream*, 205-15; Okada, "The Tragic General."
2. Tsunoda, *Once There Was a Dream*, 212-15.
3. Ibid, 222-23.
4. *USA v. Homma*, 3047-56.
5. Homma, "Statement on the Charge," 2; Thompson, Doud, and Scofield, *How the Japanese Army Fights*, 14; Tsunoda, *Once There Was a Dream*, 230.
6. Tasuku Yamanari, Kozo Watanabe, Isao Shinohara, Yoshiaki Nagai, interviews, 2000.
7. Whitman, *Bataan*, 1-9, pulls together details from many sources, including Mallonée, Collier, Toland, and others. For this section we also draw on Duckworth, "Official History"; Jackson, *Diary*; and Lee, *They Call It Pacific*.
8. Volckmann, *We Remained*, 24; Whitman, *Bataan*, 3-4.

9. Wainwright, *General Wainwright's Story*, 46.

10. Lee, *They Call It Pacific*, 135.

11. Dooley, "Personal Record," 51; Wainwright, *General Wainwright's Story*, 45.

12. Whitman, *Bataan*, 24-25, 76.

13. Ibid., 115ff, 134.

14. Tsunoda, *Once There Was a Dream*, 228.

15. Ibid., 227-28.

16. MacArthur, *Reports*, vol. 2, part 1, 81.

17. Tsunoda, *Once There Was a Dream*, 240.

18. "The Fall of Manila," *New York Times*, January 3, 1942.

19. Tsunoda, *Once There Was a Dream*, 239-42.

20. Arhutick, "Diary," 2; Ind, *Bataan*, 189.

CHAPTER FOUR

1. Material in this section is drawn from Committee on History, *Bataan*; Paguio, *Bataan*; Merrill, *Plant Life*, 75; Allied Geographic Section, *Terrain Handbook 42*.

2. Tsunoda, *Once There Was a Dream*, 237-38.

3. U.S. Army General Headquarters, Statement by Masami Maeda, March 7, 1950, 3.

4. U.S. Army General Headquarters, Interrogation of Tokutaro Sato, April 18, 1947.

5. Tsunoda, *Once There Was a Dream*, 252.

6. ATIS, *Combat in the Mt. Natib Area*, 2.

7. U.S. Army General Headquarters, Interrogation of Akira Nara; Toland, interview with Akira Nara.

8. Toland, interview with Akira Nara.

9. Slim, *Defeat into Victory*, 537.

10. Tsunoda, *Once There Was a Dream*, 243-44.

11. Imai, "Tragedy of Fukuyama Regiment," 2.

12. Tsunoda, *Once There Was a Dream*, 243; Imai, "Tragedy of Fukuyama Regiment," 1.

13. Imperial Japanese Forces in the Philippines, "New Order," 80, 100-102, 193.

14. Coox, *Unfought War*, 29; Tolischus, *Through Japanese Eyes*, 112.

15. ATIS, *Luzon Campaign 16th Division*, 72-74; ATIS, *Combat in the Mt. Natib Area*, 2.

16. This scene is drawn from Toland, interview with Akira Nara, and U.S. Army General Headquarters, Interrogation of Akira Nara, June 14, 1949, 2.

17. Hideo Sekihara, interview, 2000.

18. "Banzai" has many meanings. In its simplest form, it is a way of saying "hurrah," an unadulterated cheer, but it is also shorthand for "Long live the emperor" (*Tenno Heika banzai!*) and suggests a swelling of patriotic sentiment.

19. Details are drawn from Lory, *Japan's Military Masters*; Nihon Senbotsu Gakusei Kinen-Kai, *Listen to the Voices*; Office of Strategic Services, *Morale in the Japanese Military Services*; Tasaki, *Long the Imperial Way*; Noma, *Zone of Emptiness*. On this or any subject about the training and practice of the Imperial Army, Drea's *In the Service of the Emperor* should be required reading.

20. Tasaki, *Long the Imperial Way*, 16.

21. Saxe, "Reveries," 245–46; Tanaka, *Hidden Horrors*, 202–203; Noma, *Zone of Emptiness*, 153–54, 228.

22. Tsurumi, *Social Change*, 116–17.

23. Details in this section are drawn from Gibney, *Sensō*, and Nihon Senbotsu Gakusei Kinen-Kai, *Listen to the Voices.*

24. The figure 2,287,000 represents the number of men under arms in December 1941.

25. Friday, *Samurai*, 18, 137–38, and throughout. Karl Friday and Thomas Conlan are among a new generation of scholars who have cut through the hoary myths of samurai loyalty and fidelity that until recently dominated this field of scholarship. The elegant and lyrical work of Ivan Morris, to cite just one example, offers a misleading view of samurai ethics and life. Until recently that view, largely romantic, was drawn mostly from literary texts. Instead Friday and Conlan went back to original documents from the early eras of Japanese warfare and offer a new, clear-eyed portrait of the samurai.

26. Jansen, "Samurai," 528.

27. Ikegami, *Taming of the Samurai*, 285, 281. We combined two sections of the *Hagakure* here. *Hagakure* translates as "in the shadow of the leaves," and Ikegami (290) suggests that the title reflects the samurai ethic of "service without recognition," or selfless service. There are several English translations of selected portions of the *Hagakure*. Yamamoto (Wilson trans.) and the lines Ikegami uses in her study of the samurai fall most easily, and clearly, on the English-speaking ear. The most complete version, with index, numbered sections, and an excellent introduction, is Yamamoto (Mukoh trans.). Forsaking consistency for clarity and style, we made use of all three sources.

28. Ikegami translates Bushido as "culture of honor" (*Taming of the Samurai*, 281–82) and it reflects a style of scholarship that tended to ennoble ancient Japanese warriors. Conlan and Friday largely redefined honor in terms of self-interest, but there are excellent examples of the classic historiography—extrapolating history from literature rather than primary sources—in Singer, *Mirror, Sword and Jewel*, and Morris, *Nobility of Failure*. The provenance of Bushido suggested here is explained well and concisely in Sansom, *Japan*, 498–507.

29. From the Imperial Rescript to Soldiers and Sailors issued in 1882 to the newly formed armed forces. Lory, *Japan's Military Masters*, 239–45. In an appendix, Lory includes a complete translation of the rescript.

30. Ashmead-Bartlett, *Port Arthur*, 480–82.

31. All this is another way to think of *Yamato-damashi*, "Japanese spirit." A good definition of the term is offered in a footnote to Sakurai, *Human Bullets*, 10.

32. Humphreys, *Way of the Heavenly Sword*, 12.

33. Ibid.; Collected Imperial Edicts: Battlefield Practices, 3.

34. ATIS, *Combat in the Mt. Natib Area*, 15.

35. Imai, "Tragedy of Fukuyama Regiment," 3; Tsunoda, *Once There Was a Dream*, 245; ATIS, *Combat in the Mt. Natib Area*, 10.

36. ATIS, *Combat in the Mt. Natib Area*, 16.

37. Nakamura, Diary, 8.

38. ATIS, *Combat in the Mt. Natib Area*, 17-18.

39. Nakamura, Diary, 8.

40. Imai, "Tragedy of Fukuyama Regiment," 11-14.

41. Nakamura, Diary, 8.

42. Homma, *Hito Hakengun*, 5. Although Homma is listed as the author, the actual editor is Watari Shudan Hōdōbu or the Department of Information, Watari Group (Watari the code name for the 14th Army).

43. Tsunoda, *Once There Was a Dream*, 245.

44. ATIS, *65th Brigade Combat Report*, 99-100.

45. Ibid.

46. Nakamura, Diary, 8.

47. Hideo Sekihara, interview, 2000.

48. ATIS, *Combat in the Mt. Natib Area*, 29.

49. Nakamura, Diary, 9.

50. Ibid. The last entry in the diary is January 23, 1942. Nakamura's diary was one of several recovered by USAFFE soldiers from dead Japanese and sent to MacArthur's intelligence section on Corregidor for translation.

51. Hideo Sekihara, interview, 2000.

52. Minobu Kawaguchi, interview, 2000.

53. Stanton, "Bataan."

54. The story of the landing and battle at Quinauan Point is drawn from Morton, *Fall of the Philippines*, 296-324; Whitman, *Bataan*, 269-93; interview with Kiyoshi Kinoshita; Tsuneoka, *Gyokusai*.

55. Tsuneoka, *Gyokusai*, 5, 48. This message was never delivered. After the Americans surrendered in April 1942, Imperial Japanese Army officer Noboru Tsuneoka was sent to search for Tsunehiro's missing battalion on the west coast of Bataan. The search party found the colonel's body. Tsuneoka wrote: "When I examined the pockets in the uniform, I discovered a piece of paper. This was the report that Tsunehiro had written to Division leader Kimura."

56. Hearn, *Japan*, 245; Gauntlett, *Cardinal Principles*, 83.

57. Gauntlett, *Cardinal Principles*, 83; Hearn, *Japan*, 245; Tsunoda et al., *Sources of Japanese Tradition*, 1: 99. The Yasukuni Shrine was established in 1869 to honor the 3,588 souls of those who died fighting to create what was to become Japan's constitutional monarchy. Soon the names of all those who died for their country were enshrined there. The history of the Yasukuni Shrine was taught often in school, usually after a dramatic tale of death and glory. And in the decades leading up to World War II, the role of the shrine was included in the daily catechism of training camp.

58. Lory, *Japan's Military Masters*, 81.

59. Kishimoto, "Some Japanese Cultural Traits," 119; Lory, *Japan's Military Masters*, 45; Hearn, *Kokoro*, 283-85, 291; Collected Imperial Edicts: Battlefield Practices, 4, 6.

60. Hearn, *Kokoro*, 290-91.

61. All the details of Kiyoshi Kinoshita's story are drawn from two interviews (one with the authors and a follow-up interview with an associate) and from several pieces of correspondence.

62. Dyess, *Dyess Story*, 43.

63. The ideas on shame in this section are more fully explained in Edwards, "Honour, Shame, Humiliation"; Benedict, *Chrysanthemum and the Sword*; Doi, *Anatomy of Dependence*. Doi and Benedict represent, in effect, the two sides in the debate over *Nipponjinron*. We found both positions reflected in the interviews we conducted.

CHAPTER FIVE

1. The details of this important meeting were first reported by John Toland in *But Not in Shame*. We drew on Toland's original interviews, preserved in handwritten notes, and on two interviews we conducted with junior staff officers who were in attendance at the time—Tokutaro Sato and Moriya Wada. We also relied on Homma's diary as it appears in Tsunoda, *Once There Was a Dream*.

2. Tsunoda, *Once There Was a Dream*, 252-53.

3. Ibid.

4. Toland, interview with Kumao Imoto; Hewlett, Original Cable.

5. These figures represent an attempt to reconcile several sources: Whitman, *Bataan*; Morton, *Fall of the Philippines*; Toland, *But Not in Shame*; *USA v. Homma* (especially Exhibit Y, February 9, 1946, Prosecution Exhibits 401-25, vol. 5); ATIS, *Combat in the Mt. Natib Area*; ATIS, *65th Brigade Combat Report*; U.S. Department of the Army, "Information Regarding Strength and Composition."

6. Tokutaro Sato, interview, 2000.

7. This and all from Homma that follows in this section, including the incident on the train, are drawn from Tsunoda, *Once There Was a Dream*, 252-58.

8. MacArthur, Cable Nos. 258, 371, 382.

9. Dooley, "Personal Record," 84.

10. MacArthur, Cable No. 438.

11. This section is drawn from Stauffer, *Quartermaster Corps*, chap. 1; Ancheta, *Wainwright Papers*, vol. 4, chap. II; James, *Years of MacArthur*, vol. 2, part I; Miller, *Bataan Uncensored*, 75-76.

12. MacArthur, "Message from General MacArthur," January 15, 1942.

13. Hewlett, "Quartermasters on Bataan," 64.

14. Hill, "Lessons of Bataan," 14-15.

15. Ibid.; Dominick Pellegrino, correspondence with authors.

16. Schedler, "Bombs in Manila Bay," 4.

17. Jackson, *Diary*, 44.

18. Ind, *Bataan*, 336.

19. Ibid., 296.

20. Cooper, "Army Medical Department Activities," 37; Chunn, *Of Rice and Men*, 1.

21. Cooper, "Memorandum to AC of S G-4."

22. Bumgarner, *Parade of the Dead*, 71.

23. Cooper, "Army Medical Department Activities," Appendix 3; Hibbs, "Beriberi," 275; Keys, *Biology of Human Starvation*, 783-818.

24. Keys, *Biology of Human Starvation*, 790; Wilson, "Address to Congress," 430.

25. Brawner G-4, Memorandum to Dept A.G.

26. Gillespie, "Malaria," 506; Wainwright, *General Wainwright's Story*, 63; Funk, "Medical Supply Situation."

27. Dooley, "Personal Record," 114–16.

28. Miller, *Bataan Uncensored*, 193.

29. Beck, *MacArthur and Wainwright*, 66.

30. Ibid., 67–68; Dooley, "Personal Record," 45.

31. Beck, *MacArthur and Wainwright*, 40; Marshall, "Strategic Policy."

32. Roosevelt, Fireside Chats "On the Progress of the War," February 23, 1942.

33. James, *Years of MacArthur*, 2: 125–41; Considine, "MacArthur the Magnificent," February 23 and 24, 1942.

34. Miller, *Bataan Uncensored*, 193; Morton, interview with Sutherland.

35. Waldrop, *MacArthur on War*, 353–66; Considine, "MacArthur the Magnificent," March 14, 1942.

36. MacArthur, Radio Message to AGWAR, January 23, 1942; Lee, *They Call It Pacific*, 252; Willoughby and Chamberlain, *MacArthur*, 49; Huff, *My Fifteen Years with General MacArthur*, 8.

37. Beck, *MacArthur and Wainwright*, 108; Huff, *My Fifteen Years with General MacArthur*, 52–32; Wainwright, *General Wainwright's Story*, 4. There are many versions of the story surrounding MacArthur's decision to abandon his command. The earliest versions come from the journalists Frazier Hunt and Clark Lee, fashioned from interviews with MacArthur. In his *Reminiscences* (140), MacArthur says he planned to resign his commission and join the troops in the trenches on Bataan. In fact there are no truly independent accounts of what the general said or was thinking after he received the order.

38. MacArthur, *Reminiscences*, 142–43; Huff, *My Fifteen Years with General MacArthur*, 56.

39. Chunn, *Of Rice and Men*, ii. The wallpaper paste simile was common in the interviews.

40. We were unable to find either the first publication or provenance of this bit of doggerel, so popular on Bataan and later in literature about the battle. Most historians rely on Wainwright, *General Wainwright's Story*, 54, for the lyrics. He states unequivocally that United Press correspondent Frank Hewlett wrote them, but Hewlett's daughter, Jean Hewlett, told us in an interview, "I have clear memories of my father saying that he did *not* create" the ditty. She reckoned he heard it in the field and "improved it a bit when he wrote it down."

WHISKEY, WAGES, AND THE KINDNESS OF STRANGERS

1. Judgment Roll 5516, *The United States of America v. Ben Steele*, March 17, 1934, indictment.

CHAPTER 6

1. Toland, interview with Takushiro Hattori, one of the planners of the second offensive. Hattori says there were 16,000 troops in the 16th Division, 8,000 in the 65th Brigade, and 15,000 in the 4th Division.

2. Takesada Shigeta, interviews and correspondence, 2000–2001.

3. Hirohisa Murata, interview, 2000.

4. *Handbook on Japanese Military Forces*, 65; Hirohisa Murata, interview.

5. Details about the experience of the Provisional Air Corps unit in Sector B March 29 through April 7, 1942, are drawn from interviews with Ben Steele and Q. P. Devore, and from Coleman, *Bataan and Beyond*, 41–57.

6. Brougher, "Battle of Bataan," 4–5.

7. Material on the second offensive is drawn from Chunn, *Of Rice and Men*; Babcock, "Philippine Campaign," parts I and II; Mallonée, *Naked Flagpole*; Morton, *Fall of the Philippines*; Tisdelle, "Story of Bataan Collapse"; and Whitman, *Bataan*. The figure of fourteen rounds per minute comes from Toland, interview with Jesse Traywick.

8. Profiles of the American Generals on Bataan; Whitman, *Bataan*, 30–31, 169–71.

9. Holt, "King of Bataan," 3.

10. Snow, *Signposts of Experience*, 36.

11. Jones, interview with Brigadier General Jones.

12. Morton, *Fall of the Philippines*, 405.

13. Chunn, *Of Rice and Men*, 1–3.

14. Mallonée, *Naked Flagpole*, 120.

15. Morton, *Fall of the Philippines*, 384, 431–32; Whitman, *Bataan*, 491–92.

16. Dooley, "Personal Record," 133.

17. Whitman, *Bataan*, 512–13.

18. Mallonée, *Naked Flagpole*, 128.

19. The account of the action in Sector B and the events involving the Provisional Air Corps Regiment from April 7 through April 9 are drawn from Coleman, *Bataan and Beyond*, 41–57; Whitman, *Bataan*, 528–31; and interviews with Q. P. Devore and Ben Steele.

20. Wainwright, *General Wainright's Story*, 79, 82.

21. Judge Advocate General, *Basic Field Manual*, 67.

22. Toland, interview with James R. N. Weaver.

23. Collier, Notebooks, book 4, 2.

24. The scene, including King's speech, ibid., 2–6.

25. King, "General King's Own Story," 6.

26. Ryotaro Nishimura, interview, 2000.

27. There are many versions of the meeting at the agricultural station in Lamao, all based on the observations of King's aide, Major Achille C. Tisdelle. Major Tisdelle's handwritten diary offers none of the detail found in Louis Morton's two versions of the event, one in his official U.S. Army history, *Fall of the Philippines*, and the other, "Bataan Diary of Major Achille C. Tisdelle." Morton cites the "diary" as his source for both but says "the original" was in Tisdelle's possession. It is possible that Morton was given a composite account or that Tisdelle used his handwritten diary to reconstitute the scenes in a memoirlike diary immediately after the war. Files at the army's Military History Institute in Carlisle, Pennsylvania, contained typed accounts of Tisdelle's experience and these accounts support Morton's version,

though their provenance is unclear. Since there was no reconciling the obvious dis-crepancies, we used those portions of the story that were either verified or tangen-tially supported by King's and Tisdelle's testimony in *USA v. Homma*, as well as John Toland's handwritten notes of his interviews with the two men. King's final thoughts in the section come from "General King's Own Story," 6.

CHAPTER SEVEN

1. Durdin, "All Captives Slain," 1.
2. Brown Davidson, interview, 2000.
3. Humphrey O'Leary, interview, 2000.
4. Comments that follow are from interviews with Jinzaburo Chaki, Tozo Takeuchi, and Tasuku Yamanari, 2000.
5. John Emerick, interviews, 1998–1999.
6. FitzPatrick, *Hike into the Sun*, 56.
7. Dyess, *Dyess Story*, 68.
8. Ibid., 70. Dyess gets this story from someone else, whom he does not identify. Other accounts, those less detailed, confirm the incident.
9. Coox, "Effectiveness of the Japanese Military," 39.
10. Richard Gordon, interview, 1999.
11. Stewart, *Give Us This Day*, 68–70.
12. Hunt, *Behind Japanese Lines*, 29.
13. Goldblith, *Appetite for Life*, 54.
14. Gordon, interview, 1999.
15. Gautier, *I Came Back from Bataan*, 72.
16. Levering, *Horror Trek*, 63.
17. O'Leary, interview, 1999.
18. Tenney, *My Hitch in Hell*, 48. Other men mentioned this incident in interviews and had a slightly different version of the quotation offered by Tenney.
19. Dyess, *Dyess Story*, 75.
20. Zoeth Skinner, interviews, 1999, 2005.
21. Dyess, *Dyess Story*, 76.
22. Mallonée, *Naked Flagpole*, 149.
23. Tenney, *My Hitch in Hell*, 53–58.
24. Thomas, *As I Remember*, 151.
25. Aquino, Statement to John Toland, 3.
26. Smith, Affidavit/Statement.
27. Dyess, *Dyess Story*, 79; Cave, *Beyond Courage*, 173; Gordon, interview.
28. Levering, *Horror Trek*, 65.
29. Gordon, interview, 1999.
30. Stewart, *Give Us This Day*, 72.
31. John Olson, interview, 1999.
32. Stewart, *Give Us This Day*, 73.
33. Thomas, *As I Remember*, 147.

34. FitzPatrick, *Hike into the Sun*, 62.

35. Sneddon, *Zero Ward*, 25.

36. Davidson, interview, 2000; Irwin Scott, interview, 2005; Coleman, *Bataan and Beyond*, 72; Hunt, *Behind Japanese Lines*, 52.

37. Hunt, *Behind Japanese Lines*, 32.

38. Gautier, *I Came Back from Bataan*, 76.

39. Grashio, *Return to Freedom*, 39.

40. Cave, *Beyond Courage*, 172.

41. Dyess, *Dyess Story*, 77; Ashton, *And Somebody Gives a Damn!* 201.

42. Davidson, interview, 2000.

43. Monaghan, *Under the Red Sun*, 109.

44. A. C. Drake, Affidavit/Statement, 95; Alabado, *Bataan*, 54; Agoncillo, *Fateful Years*, 212.

45. Skinner, interview, 2005.

46. J. Baldassarre, Affidavit/Statement, 37.

47. In late March 1942, five Imperial Army officers met to draw up a plan to deal with POWs. From intelligence reports, they expected some 40,000 captives, and since the army's plan of attack anticipated a three-week campaign on Bataan, the five planners thought they would have until April 20 to get everything ready to receive the prisoners. When the plan was done, the officers—Major General Yoshikata Kawane, commander of the Luzon Line of Communication Unit (transportation and supply); Colonel Toshimitsu Takatsu, Kawane's chief of staff; Major Moriya Wada, a staff officer; Major Hisashi Sekiguchi from the Medical Department; and an officer from a well-digging unit—reviewed the details with Major General Takeji Wachi, the 14th Army chief of staff. Wachi, in turn, took the scheme to Lieutenant General Masaharu Homma for final approval. The plan was simple: Filipino and American soldiers would be collected together at various spots between Mariveles and Cabcaben at the tip of the peninsula, assembled in marching formations on the Old National Road, then walked north to the railhead at San Fernando—from the town of Mariveles, a hike of exactly sixty-six miles. At the San Fernando train station, the prisoners would be put in boxcars and hauled north twenty-five miles to the town of Capas. At Capas they would detrain and march another seven miles to Camp O'Donnell, a former Philippine Army training base in Pampanga Province that would be converted to hold prisoners of war. On the first part of the march—from Mariveles to Balanga—the prisoners would be guarded by soldiers from the various units that had taken part in the final offensive, combat and support troops from frontline units. At Balanga, rear-echelon troops under the command of General Kawane, men from the 61st Line of Communication Dispatch Unit (service), would take over as guards for the rest of the trek. Kawane was told he could carry the prisoners in trucks—if he could find them. The Imperial Army had some 240 trucks in its inventory. It also had captured an unknown number of vehicles from the American Army. (Perhaps a thousand to fifteen hundred allied vehicles were in running condition at the time of surrender; it

is anyone's guess.) The Imperial Army used all available transport to move its own men and supplies south on Bataan to stage for the upcoming invasion of Corregidor. The plan also called for the army's Sanitation Unit to set up field hospitals in Balanga. The army's chief of administration was ordered to dispatch cooks and trucks with food and cooking supplies to Bataan and to set up feeding stations. The first station would be at Balanga, then, moving north, at Orani, Lubao, and, finally, San Fernando. The prisoners would eat what Imperial troops ate: rice and whatever else happened to be available at the time. On April 2, seven days before surrender, staff aides told Colonel Takatsu and Major Wada that the preparations to receive, quarter, and feed the prisoners were still incomplete. The two officers told their subordinates to "put in their best effort and further their preparation." On April 9, the day General King sent a white flag forward, Major Wada asked for an update on the preparations and was told little had changed since April 2. Meanwhile, Wada and the others discovered that they would have to move and feed some 76,000 POWs, almost twice the number they had expected. What is more, there were some 25,000 Filipino refugees in the battle zone as well, and they too would have to be relocated. The officers quickly concluded that motor transport would be impossible. General Kawane decided to move them on foot and assigned a unit of some 300 men from the 61st Line of Communication Unit, under the command of First Lieutenant Toshio Omura, to guide the prisoners as they marched north from Balanga to the railhead at San Fernando. The formations would cover some twelve to fifteen miles a day. The only surety was water; there were plenty of artesian wells along the route of the march so the prisoners would be able to slake their thirst. *USA v. Homma*, 2463-64, 2581-82, 2666-74, 2686-89, 3076-79; Wada, Affidavit/Statement, 1-6; Wada, interview, 2000; Yoshikata Kawane, Affidavit/Statement, 1-5; Falk, *Bataan*, 35-42; Falk, "Bataan Death March," 28-46; Homma, "Statement on the Charge," 1-11; Bateman, interview with Achille Tisdelle, 12; Uji, Affidavit/Statement, 1-3.

48. Simmons, *Hell Revisited*, 19-20.
49. Gordon, *Horyo*, 96; Gordon, interview, 1999.
50. We interviewed more than 100 men who made the death march. More than 70 said they got something—rice, tea, salt, hard biscuits, water—at Balanga or Orani.
51. FitzPatrick, *Hike into the Sun*, 66.
52. Locke, *Kobe House P.O.W.*, 32.
53. Miller, *Bataan Uncensored*, 223.
54. Sneddon, *Zero Ward*, 28.
55. Poweleit, *USAFFE*, 54.
56. FitzPatrick, *Hike into the Sun*, 67; Hunt, *Behind Japanese Lines*, 31.
57. Tenney, *My Hitch in Hell*, 56.
58. Gordon, *Horyo*, 96.
59. Dyess, *Dyess Story*, 85-86.
60. Bank, *Back from the Living Dead*, 20; Levering, *Horror Trek*, 73; FitzPatrick, *Hike into the Sun*, 71; Sneddon, *Zero Ward*, 27; Tenney, *My Hitch in Hell*, 57.
61. Sneddon, *Zero Ward*, 24.
62. Ibid., 26.

63. Miller, *Bataan Uncensored*, 233, 220; Tenney, *My Hitch in Hell*, 47, 56–57; Levering, *Horror Trek*, 69; Connor, *Japanese Extermination Camps*, 40.

64. What follows is drawn from interviews with Guillermo Almario, Natividad Almario, Lorenzo Capistrano, Juanita Caraguy, Milagros Cortez, Juana Diaz, Jaluria Galina, Candido Gallardo, Bartolome Gana, Amado Guevarra, Ismael Guzon, Migel Layug, Ciriaco Manahan, Faustino Perez, Edilberto Sadural, and Marcelo Tuazon, 2000.

65. In Philippine society, no shame was greater than to be known as *walang-habag*, someone "without pity."

66. FitzPatrick, *Hike into the Sun*, 68–72.

67. Richard Gordon's story is drawn from an extensive interview with the authors and his memoir, *Horyo*.

68. Zoeth Skinner's story is drawn from interviews and correspondence, 1999–2005.

69. Poweleit, *USAFFE*, 56.

70. Felix, "Massacre of the 91st Division"; Ramirez, interview with Felix; *USA v. Homma*, 1010–57; Ongpauco, *They Refused to Die*, 90–102.

71. Nagai, interview, 2000.

72. There is no confirmed figure on the number of men who were executed at the Pantingan River on April 12 and 13. The incident is mentioned in passing in the proceedings of the Tokyo War Crimes Tribunals, but no one was ever prosecuted for it. The incident seems to have been considered just another part of the death march.

73. Isamu Murakami, interview, 2000.

74. Takesada Shigeta, interview and correspondence, 2000–2004.

CHAPTER EIGHT

1. Collier, Notebooks, 52–53.

2. Olson, *O'Donnell*, 44. In late April 1942, John Olson was named camp adjutant, and he kept an official diary, as well as filling out the daily strength reports. No other individual is likely to have such an overview. We used his monograph liberally throughout this chapter, vetting, where possible, his facts and figures.

3. Ibid., 41–46.

4. King delivered such remarks often in O'Donnell whenever a group of men gathered around him. In their memoirs, journals, and diaries, scores of men quoted and paraphrased him. Each account is slightly different. We have tried to verify the most oft-repeated phrases and have ordered them for coherence.

5. King, Affidavit/Statement, 1–2.

6. Determining the number of Americans and Filipinos living and dead on Bataan, then later in O'Donnell and the other prisoner venues, is at best to make an estimate. Records either were not kept or were lost or reconstructed long after the war. The figures we used are from Ned King's 1946 "Report of Operations," which he compiled in prison camp and assembled from the recollections of his senior staff; Collier's Notebooks (written in 1943 in prison camp); Jonathan Wainwright's Diaries and *General Wainwright's Story*; Colonel Nicoll Galbraith's "Diaries" (also writ-

ten in prison camp); and material from the judge advocate general's office. In January 1942 at the start of the battle, there were approximately 12,000 Americans on Bataan. At surrender on April 9, there were approximately 9,700 Americans; 2,300 had been killed or were wounded and missing. The overall strength of the American-Filipino force on Bataan on April 2 was 78,100; at the tip of the peninsula, 26,000 Filipino civilians were in refugee camps. Sometime before surrender, roughly 2,000 men (300 Americans, the rest Filipinos) and a handful of American nurses found their way across the bay to Corregidor. That left some 76,000 military personnel on Bataan—the number at surrender and the number that, in theory, started the death march. Approximately 500 Americans and perhaps as many as 2,500 Filipinos were killed or died on the death march or in the boxcars from San Fernando. In the end, O'Donnell held 9,270 Americans and either 45,000 (King, Affidavit/Statement, 7) or 47,000 Filipinos (IMTFE, "JAG Report No. 75," 12,597). No one can say for sure what happened to the 15,000 to 17,000 Filipinos who were on Bataan but not in O'Donnell. Some were killed on the field of battle, some deserted during the fighting, and a large number are believed to have slipped into the bush at surrender and passed themselves off as civilians.

7. Poweleit, *USAFFE*, 63–66.
8. Collier, Notebooks, 47.
9. Stewart, *Give Us This Day*, 63.
10. Scott, interview, 2000.
11. Poweleit, *USAFFE*, 65–68.
12. John Aldrich, interview, 1999.
13. Browe, "O'Donnell," 53.
14. Poweleit, *USAFFE*, 67–70.
15. Brain, *Soldier of Bataan*, 35–36.
16. Gene Jacobsen, interview, 2000.
17. Skinner, interview, 1999.
18. Des Pres, *Survivor*, 6–9; Darwin, *Descent of Man*, 619.
19. Gordon, interview, 1999.
20. "No ideas but in things" is borrowed from William Carlos Williams, "A Sort of Song," *The Collected Poems*, vol. 2, 55. Williams, of course, was talking about metaphor rather than staying in the moment.
21. Poweleit, *USAFFE*, 69–70.
22. Morton, *Fall of the Philippines*, 546.
23. Wainwright, *General Wainwright's Story*, 122–23.
24. MacArthur, *Reminiscences*, 146.
25. Cooper, "Army Medicine Department Activities," 108.
26. Musselman, Affidavit/Statement, 3–4.
27. O'Leary, interview, 1999.
28. Olson, *O'Donnell*, 186–87.
29. Here we expand and amplify the notions that Terrence Des Pres puts forward in *The Survivor*, 5–16, namely, that "in ordinary times, to protect the living, aid the sick

and bury the dead" are the most "elementary . . . of human" activities. And survival, Des Pres discovered, "depends on staying human."

30. Stewart, *Give Us This Day*, 62–64.
31. Scott, interview, 2000.
32. Aldrich, interview, 1999.

"A FINAL DETERMINATION"

1. "April was . . ." is a nod to the beginning of T. S. Eliot's "The Waste Land"; All headlines taken from the *Billings Gazette*, April 4–11, 1942.

CHAPTER NINE

1. Louis Kolger, interview, 2000.
2. Conrad, "Heart of Darkness," in *The Complete Short Fiction of Joseph Conrad*, vol. 3, 12.
3. Preston Hubbard, interview, 2000. See Hubbard, *Apocalypse Undone*, for additional details.
4. Ken Calvit, interview, 1999.
5. Scott, interviews, 1999–2001.
6. All quotations from Ashton here and following in this section come from his account of his experiences at Tayabas Road in *Bataan Diary*, 215–221. His hand-drawn map on page 221 is remarkably accurate. Using that crude chart, we were able to eliminate one river after another along the old Route 1G until we finally found the site, later confirmed by former Filipino guerrillas still living near the Basiad.
7. Steve Kramerich, interview, 1999.
8. Ashton, *Bataan Diary*, 219. Parts of his account of giving lethal injections—the only parts we used—were supported by at least two men who were among the final group of 108 prisoners leaving Tayabas Road on July 28, 1942.
9. Hayes, "Notebook," book I, 42.
10. Shearer, "Shearer's Journal," 22.

CHAPTER TEN

1. Sartin, "Report of Activities," 22.
2. Hayes, "Notebook," book I, 5.
3. Patton, "Account of Captivity," 99–101.
4. Hayes, "Notebook," book I, 42.
5. Smith, *Prisoner of the Emperor*, 61.
6. Hayes, "Notebook," book I, 45–46.
7. Ibid., book II, 38.
8. Kramerich, interview, 1999.
9. Hayes, "Notebook," book II, 39.
10. Ibid., book I, 7.
11. Richard Beck, interview, 1999.
12. Fowler, *Recipes out of Bilibid*, 23, 30, 44.

13. Hayes, "Notebook," book I, 14–15.

14. Ibid., book II, 30.

15. Des Pres, *Survivor*, 186.

16. Hayes, "Notebook," book II, 24, 75, 67, 96.

17. Ibid., book III, 61–62.

18. Dostoevsky, *Memoirs from the House of the Dead*, 200.

19. Scott, interview, 2000.

20. Kramerich, interview, 1999.

21. The details of Robinson's life were supplied by Zoeth Skinner.

22. Hayes, "Notebook," book III, 20–24.

23. American National Red Cross, *Prisoners of War Bulletin*, 9.

24. Hayes, "Notebook," book II, 8.

25. Ibid.

26. Schloat's story is drawn from Schloat, *Freedom!*, and from a day-long 1999 interview at his home in California.

27. Hayes, "Notebook," book III, 100.

28. Ibid., 106.

29. John Dower's *War Without Mercy* details the raw enmity of the Pacific War; Hayes, "Notebook," book II, 83, 101.

30. IMTFE, "Line of Communication and Treatment of POWs," 14,287; see Waterford, *Prisoners of the Japanese*, in general for figures on Allied POWs in the Pacific.

31. IMTFE, "Instructions of War Minister Hideki Tojo," 14,428–430.

32. IMTFE, "Report on POW Labor Conditions," 14,493–496.

CHAPTER ELEVEN

1. The *Canadian Inventor* was part of a merchant fleet Canada built after World War I. At 8,100 dead weight tons, she was among the largest of that fleet, 400 feet long and 52 feet wide, with a depth of 28.5 feet and a top speed of 13 knots. Between the world wars, Canada realized it could not compete for business in the world shipping market and began to sell off many of its merchant vessels. Japan, meanwhile, had been acquiring merchant ships on the open market.

2. Tsuji, *Japan's Greatest Victory*, 246–49.

3. For a concise explanation of Japanese losses, see Calvocoressi, Wint, and Pritchard, *Total War*, 1092–93, 1150–57.

4. The July 1944 voyage of the *Canadian Inventor* is drawn from interviews with John Crago, Dan Irwin, Gene Jacobsen, and Ben Steele. Also see Nordin, *We Were Next to Nothing*; Gautier, *I Came Back from Bataan*; Jacobsen, *Who Refused to Die*; Hoover, Affidavit/Statement, 1.

5. Hata, "From Consideration to Contempt," 266.

6. Hellship figures vary widely among the many accounts of these voyages. There were no official postwar lists or totals. We cite Michno, *Death on the Hellships*, 317. Also see Waterford, *Prisoners of the Japanese*, 167–68. Waterford lists 56 transports carrying some 68,000 passengers. Michno's figures are likely much higher because, as his notes indicate, he built on the work of others, including Waterford. The two

authors agree roughly on the number of prisoners of war and captives lost at sea, some 22,000 men.

7. Figures come from Keegan, *Times Atlas of the Second World War*, 164-65, 194-95. Also see Morison, *Two-Ocean War*, 504. Morison (511-12) also reports that during four years of war, American forces sank 2,117 Japanese merchant vessels (8 million tons). In July 1944 alone, the month the *Canadian Inventor* sailed from Manila, 40 were sunk.

8. For the story of the *Arisan Maru*, we rely heavily on Graef, "We Prayed to Die."

9. Ibid., 178.

10. The story of the *Oryoku Maru* is summarized in many books about World War II in the Pacific and in accounts from and about prisoners of war. The most dramatic and detailed is George Weller's "Horror of Jap Prison Ship Told," an eighteen-part series syndicated by the *Chicago Daily News Foreign Press Service* and appearing in several American newspapers in 1945. It is the first full account and stands still as the most dramatic of the secondary sources. Among primary sources, the most clear-eyed and accurate are Curtis Beecher, "A Survivor's Account," and Carey Smith, "Memoir." The secondary sources are often in conflict on many points in the story. Even in the primary accounts, it is well nigh impossible to reconcile the disparities in numbers, names, and the sequence of events. We relied on Smith, a physician, and Colonel Beecher, the man who really led the detail. To help establish the sequence of events, we also used "Outline of Trip," Roy Bodine's day-by-day record of the journeys.

11. Stewart, "Give Us This Day," 120.

12. Ibid.

13. Espy, "Cruise of Death," 6.

14. Beecher, "A Survivor's Account," 72.

15. Espy, "Cruise of Death," 8.

16. Hobbes, *Leviathan*, 70.

17. Beecher, "A Survivor's Account," 73.

18. The accounts of drinking blood on the *Oryoku Maru* come from, among others, Beecher, "A Survivor's Account"; O. Wilson, "After Bataan"; Smith, "Memoir"; an interview with Ernie Bale; and Wolf, *Thirst*, 250, 340, 378, 402, 406.

19. Beecher, "A Survivor's Account," 72.

20. Ibid., 73-74.

21. Ibid., 77.

22. Ibid., 87.

23. The most detailed account of Father Cummings's work on the *Oryoku Maru* comes from Stewart, *Give Us This Day*, 120-71. He is also mentioned in Beecher, "A Survivor's Account." Roper, *Brothers of Paul*, 87-94, pulls together material from a number of sources, including Louis Kolger, whom we interviewed. It was our general impression from scores of interviews that every man who'd met "Father Bill" remembered him.

24. Stewart, *Give Us This Day*, 152.

25. Ibid., 150.

CHAPTER TWELVE

1. Interviews with Ben Steele; Gibbs, "Omine"; McClain, *Japan*, 507; ATIS, *Interrogation Report No. 0447*, 25-26.

2. We take our Omine-machi numbers from Gibbs, "Omine," and from interviews with Dan Pinkston Irwin, who supplied valuable data and documents, including a detailed roster of Americans at the camp and a number of mug shots of the prisoners.

3. Scott, interview, 1999.

4. Nobuyasu Sugiyama, interview, 2000; Military Commission, "Trial and Appeal of . . . Nobuyasu Sugiyama," 1, 31-32, 36, 41, 46-47, 49, 52, 69.

5. Crane, "In the Depths of a Coal Mine."

6. Waterford, *Prisoners of the Japanese*, 144.

7. Military Commission, "Trial and Appeal of . . . Nobuyasu Sugiyama," 1-3; Sugiyama, interview, 2000.

8. In 1947, Nobuyasu Sugiyama was tried as a Class-C war criminal (crimes against humanity) by the International Military Tribunal for the Far East, the Allied war crimes court, meeting in Yokohama. He was charged with violating the laws and customs of war and convicted of seven counts of mistreating prisoners of war. In November 1948, after appeals, he began a sentence of twenty years at hard labor. He served six years and eleven months of that sentence at Sugamo Prison in Tokyo before his sentence was reduced, a common practice for many of those convicted of war crimes.

9. No one can say how much war news reached the prisoners of war working in the slave labor camps. Likely very little, unless they had hidden radios. The Japanese people knew the war was going badly, but their news was heavily censored. Most men had no idea that the Philippines, and the former places of confinement, had been liberated.

10. Rhodes, *Making of the Atomic Bomb*, 598-600.

11. The Berlin (Potsdam) Conference, "Project, Protocol of the Proceedings of the Potsdam Conference."

12. A number of writers have attempted discover whether Imperial Army Headquarters issued so-called Kill-All orders—directives to exterminate all POWs—in the late spring or early summer of 1945. No such orders were found. However, as United Press correspondent Arnold Brackman points out in *The Other Nuremberg*, 40, in the weeks between the emperor's announcement of surrender and the appearance of American forces in the streets of Tokyo, "bonfires glowed day and night" at the War Ministry offices of Ichigaya Hill "as tons of records were burned." Fragments of orders issued by field commanders in the territories outside Japan, as well as war crimes testimony and diaries and other documents introduced into evidence at the Tokyo war crimes trials, suggest that at least some prison camp commanders, and perhaps some high-ranking officers at headquarters in Tokyo, either acting on their own or perhaps on what they thought were the wishes of superiors, made preparations for a "final disposition" of the prisoner problem, as one order put it (IMTFE, "Prosecution Exhibit 2701"). The International Military Tribunal for the Far East

(*Judgment*, chap. 8, 1001) concluded that across the course of the war there were a "vast" number of such "atrocities" and that the pattern of butchery was so common "in all theaters" of the Pacific war, it was clear that such acts "were either secretly ordered or willfully permitted by the Japanese Government or individual members thereof and by the leaders of the armed forces."

13. Rhodes, *Making of the Atomic Bomb*, 685.
14. Courtesy of Ben Steele.
15. Ship's log, USS *Consolation*.
16. Schwartz, "My Three Months," 84–85.
17. Grinker and Spiegel, *Men Under Stress*, 184–88, 443–57.

CHAPTER THIRTEEN

1. Lael, *Yamashita Precedent*, 56–60; "MacArthur 'Wanted' List," 1; "Atrocities?" 5.
2. The material on Ed Dyess and the release of the death march material that follows is drawn from Dyess, *Dyess Story*; Dyess, "Tells Jap Torture"; Leahy, Memorandum for the President; Dyess's "Statement"; Leavelle, "Tribune's Fight"; Marshall, Memorandum for the President: (Gripsholm); Marshall, Memorandum for the President: Major Dyess's Report; Dyess, Statement of Maj. William E. Dyess; "The Story Behind the Story," 3, 6.
3. Letters to FDR.
4. Trohan, "Call For New Blows," 1–2.
5. All of Masaharu Homma's diary entries and poems are from General Homma's Prison Diary; Sugamo Isho Hensankai, *Last Letters of the Century*; Tsunoda, *Once There Was a Dream*. All other material on Homma is from Okada, "The Tragic General"; Imamura, *Memoirs*; Swinson, *Four Samurai*; Tatsumi, "About General Homma"; interview and correspondence with Masahiko Homma, as well as photographs and family documents supplied by Mr. Homma; interviews with Robert Pelz, 1999, as well as trial notes, documents, and correspondence supplied by Pelz.
6. Tsunoda, *Once There Was a Dream*, 52.
7. "Homma, Kuroda Placed in Prison at Yokohama," 1.
8. "Yamashita to Face Trial," 1.
9. Material on the life, career, and trial of General Tomoyuki Yamashita is from Kenworthy, *Tiger of Malaya*; Lael, *Yamashita Precedent*; Piccigallo, *Japanese on Trial*; Stratton, "Tiger of Malaya"; Swinson, *Four Samurai*.
10. Kishimoto, "Some Japanese Cultural Traits," 119.
11. Drummond, "Britain and the United States," 1.
12. Hull quoted in Lael, *Yamashita Precedent*, 45; Brook, "Cabinet Secretaries' Notebooks," December 14, 1942.
13. Fitch, "Regulations," 4.
14. Truman quoted in Lael, *Yamashita Precedent*, 67.
15. "Yamashita Trial Starts," 2.
16. Lael, *Yamashita Precedent*, 80; United Nations War Crimes Commission, *Law Reports*, vol. 4, 3.

17. Guy, "In Defense of Yamashita," 158.

18. For the particulars of the Yamashita proceedings, see United Nations War Crimes Commission, *Law Reports*, vol. 4, case 21.

19. Lael, *Yamashita Precedent*, 90-91, 138-39; Reel, *Case of General Yamashita*, 39, 85-86, 241; United Nations War Crimes Commission, *Law Reports*, vol. 4, 17.

20. The material on Robert Pelz is from Pelz, correspondence; Pelz, Journal, vol. 4; Pelz, Scrapbook; Robert L. Pelz, interviews; Mary Jane Pelz, interview, 1999; photographs, trial notes, and private memoranda supplied by Mr. Pelz.

21. Piccigallo, *Japanese on Trial*, 67.

22. Lael, *Yamashita Precedent*, 101-102.

23. Reel, *Case of General Yamashita*, 27-28.

24. *USA v. Homma*, 844, 876-78.

25. "The Last Word."

26. *USA v. Homma*, 1016-18.

27. "The Wives."

28. Fujiko Homma, "Why Did Homma Masaharu Die?" See also Homma, Prison Diary, January 24, 1946.

29. Homma, Letters. Additional letters in Sugamo Isho Hensankai, *Last Letters of the Century*.

30. *USA v. Homma*, 2439-43.

31. Trumball, "Lines of Defense," 10; *USA v. Homma*, 2464, 2484.

32. *USA v. Homma*, 2509-11.

33. Ibid., 2737.

34. The information on Tsuji and on his activities on Bataan comes from Tsuji, *Underground Escape* and *Japan's Greatest Victory*; Ward, *Killer They Called a God*; Toland, *Rising Sun*; Toland, interview with Nobuhiko Jimbo; Yamamoto, "Information on Lt. Col Tsuji." In November 2000, attempting to verify some of the information about Tsuji, we received the following from G. L. Moulton, executive secretary, Agency Release Panel, Central Intelligence Agency, Washington, D.C.: "In response to your . . . request for information pertaining to 'Masanobu Tsuji, former officer in the Imperial Japanese Army during World War II' . . . we are neither confirming nor denying that such documents exist. It has been determined that such information—that is, whether or not any responsive records exist—would be classified for reasons of national security."

35. *USA v. Homma*, 2478-80, 2548.

36. Imai, "A Strange Order."

37. *In re Yamashita*, 327 U.S. 16.

38. Ibid., 42, 45, 79, 80.

39. Ibid., 27-29, 41.

40. *USA v. Homma*, 3029-32, 3036-37.

41. Coox, *Year of the Tiger*, 40.

42. *USA v. Homma*, 3072-80.

43. Ibid., 3166-68, 3199-200.

44. Ibid., 3210-11.

45. F. Homma, "Why Did Homma Masaharu Die?"

46. *USA v. Homma*, 3281–82.

47. F. Homma, "Why Did Homma Masaharu Die?"

48. *USA v. Homma*, 3330–63.

49. Ibid., 3333.

50. Ibid., 3334.

51. Ibid., 3342.

52. Ibid., 3352–56.

53. Ibid., 3364–65.

54. *In re Yamashita*, 327 U.S. 759.

55. "Homma's Wife Makes Appeal"; F. Homma, correspondence to MacArthur; "MacArthur Begins Final Review," 2; "Mrs. Homma Today."

56. MacArthur, *Reminiscences*, 296–98.

57. Sugamo Isho Hensankai, *Last Letters of the Century*, 579.

58. Ibid., 580.

59. Homma, Letters.

60. Ibid.

61. Ibid.

62. Sugamo Isho Hensankai, *Last Letters of the Century*, 578–80.

63. Ivan Birrer, interview, 2000.

64. Fonvielle, "Payment."

65. MacArthur, *Reminiscences*, 296–97.

IMAGINE, AFTER EVERYTHING, THIS

1. This chapter is drawn from interviews with Ben Steele, Shirley Steele, Bobbie (Mellis) Miller, Rosemarie Steele, Julie (Steele) Jorgenson, Lois Bent, Elizabeth McNamer, Scott Millikan, Michelle Motherway, and Julia Johnson; Ben Steele's medical records; as well as various reports and emergency department medical/ nursing records, Deaconess Hospital, Billings, Montana, 1999. Bess Steele died in 1972; the Old Man followed her six years later.

SELECTED BIBLIOGRAPHY

These citations represent only those sources in the Notes.

ARCHIVES

BUMED   U.S. Navy Bureau of Medicine and Surgery, Washington, D.C.
DCM   Douglas County Museum, Roseburg, Oregon
FDR   Franklin Delano Roosevelt Library, New Hyde Park, New York
GCM   George C. Marshall Research Foundation, Lexington, Virginia
MAC   MacArthur Memorial Library and Archives, Norfolk, Virginia
NARA   National Archives and Records Administration, College Park, Maryland
USMA   United States Military Academy Library, West Point, New York
USMHI   United States Military History Institute, Carlisle, Pennsylvania

Agoncillo, Teodoro A. *The Fateful Years*. 2 vols. Quezon City, Philippines: R. P. Garcia, 1965.
Alabado, Corban. *Bataan, Death March, Capas: A Tale of Japanese Cruelty and American Injustice*. San Francisco: Sulu Books, 1995.
Allied Geographic Section Southwest Pacific Area. *Terrain Handbook 42 (Central Luzon) Philippine Series*. 1944.
———. *Terrain Handbook 49 (Camarines) Philippine Series*. 3/3/1945.
Allied Translator and Interpreter Section (ATIS). *Combat in the Mt. Natib Area, Bataan*. No. 151, no. 10-EP-151. Microform. 7/13/1944.
———. *Interrogation Report No. 0447*. No. 21-M-1. Microform. 5/7/1945.
———. *Japan's Decision to Fight*. No. 131, no. 10-RR-31. Microform. 12/1/1945.
———. *Luzon Campaign of 16th Division 24 December 1941–3 January 1942*. No. 355, no. 10-EP-355. Microform. 1946.
———. *65th Combat Brigade Report on Philippines Operation*. January 19, 1945.
American National Red Cross. *Prisoners of War Bulletin* 1, no. 1 (1943): 9.
Ancheta, Celedonio, ed. *The Wainwright Papers*. Vol. 4. Detroit: New Day, 1980-.

Aquino, A. Statement to John Toland: "The Death March April 9, 1942." FDR, Toland Collection, Series 1, "Rising Sun," box 1, folder "Bataan."

Ardant du Picq, Charles. "Battle Studies: Ancient and Modern Battle." In *Roots of Strategy*, book 2, 292.

Arhutick, L. "Diary of Cpl. L. Arhutick." USMHI, Morton Collection, box 10.

Ashmead-Bartlett, Ellis. *Port Arthur: The Siege and Capitulation.* 2d ed. London: William Blackwood, 1906.

Ashton, Paul. *And Somebody Gives a Damn!* Santa Barbara: Ashton Publications, 1990.

———. *Bataan Diary.* Santa Barbara: Ashton Publications, 1984.

"Atrocities? Why Homma Never Heard of Them!—Says Yanks Got Food on Death March." *The Chicago Daily Tribune*, September 16, 1945.

Babcock, Stanton. "The Philippine Campaign," Parts I and II. *Cavalry Journal* 52 (March–April 1943): 7-11; 52 (May–June 1943): 28-35.

Baldassarre, J. Affidavit/Statement for the War Crimes Office, 1945. NARA, SCAP, RG 331.

Ballou, Robert O. *Shinto, the Unconquered Enemy: Japan's Doctrine of Racial Superiority and World Conquest.* New York: Viking, 1945.

Bank, Bert. *Back from the Living Dead: The Infamous Death March and 33 Months in a Japanese Prison.* Tuscaloosa, AL: Major Bert Bank, 1945.

Bartsch, William. "Was MacArthur Ill-Served by His Air Force Commanders in the Philippines?" *Air Power History* 44, no. 2 (Summer 1997): 44-63.

Batemen, J. C. Interview with Major Achille Carlisle Tisdelle, January 22, 1946. USMHI, Morton Collection, box 5.

Beck, John Jacob. *MacArthur and Wainwright: Sacrifice of the Philippines.* Albuquerque: University of New Mexico Press, 1974.

Beecher, Curtis. "A Survivor's Account of Americans Who Were Prisoners of the Japanese in the Philippine Islands April, May 1942–December 1944." DCM, Curtis Beecher Collection.

Benedict, Ruth. *The Chrysanthemum and the Sword: Patterns of Japanese Culture.* Boston: Houghton Mifflin, 1989.

Berlin (Potsdam) Conference, July 17–August 2, 1945. Protocol of the Proceedings August 1, 1945. www.yale.edu/lawweb/avalon/decade/decade17.htm.

Blesse, F. A. "The Filipino Fighting Man: An Appraisal of the Men Charged With Defending the Philippine Commonwealth." *Philippines* 1, no. 8 (1941): 6-7.

Bodine, Roy L. Jr. "Outline of Trip Manila P.I. to Fukuoka, Japan." DCM, Curtis Beecher Collection.

Brackman, Arnold C. *The Other Nuremberg: The Untold Story of the Tokyo War Crimes Trials.* New York: Morrow, 1987.

Brain, Philip S. Jr. *Soldier of Bataan.* Minneapolis: Rotary Club of Minneapolis, 1990.

Brawner G-4. Memorandum to Dept A.G., 14 January 1942. USMHI, Morton Collection, box 9.

British Officer, A. "The Literature of the Russo-Japanese War." *American Historical Review* 16, no. 3 (April 1911): 508-28.

Brook, Norman. "Cabinet Secretaries' Notebooks from World War Two: War Crimes and War Criminals." 2006. www.nationalarchives.gov.uk/releases/2006/january/january1/default.htm.

Brougher, W. "The Battle of Bataan." USMHI, Morton Collection, box 3.

Browe, J. H. "O'Donnell." John Olson personal collection.

Bumgarner, John R. *Parade of the Dead: A U.S. Army Physician's Memoir of Imprisonment by the Japanese, 1942–1945.* Jefferson, NC: McFarland, 1995.

Calvocoressi, Peter, Guy Wint, and John Pritchard. *Total War: Causes and Courses of the Second World War.* 2d ed. New York: Pantheon, 1989.

Cave, Dorothy. *Beyond Courage: One Regiment Against Japan 1941–1945.* Las Cruces, NM: Yucca Tree Press, 1992.

Chunn, Calvin Ellsworth. *Of Rice and Men: The Story of Americans Under the Rising Sun.* Los Angeles: Veterans' Publishing Company, 1946.

Clausewitz, Carl von, *On War.* Edited by Michael Howard and Peter Paret. Princeton: Princeton University Press, 1976.

Coleman, John S. *Bataan and Beyond: Memories of an American P.O.W.* College Station, TX: Texas A&M University Press, 1978.

Collected Imperial Edicts: Appendix—Battlefield Practices. MAC, RG 2, box 5, folder 2 "G2 Journals, Annexes 1–5, Misc. Japanese Papers."

Collier, J. V. Notebooks, book 4, 1943. USMHI, Morton Collection, box 3.

Committee on History, Department of Education Culture Sports Bataan. *Bataan: Isang Balik—Tanaw Hanggang 1941 (Bataan up to 1941: A Retrospect).* Quezon City, Philippines: APO Production Unit, 1989.

Connor, J. *The Japanese Extermination Camps.* Langley Park, MD: J. Connor, 1987.

Conrad, Joseph. "Heart of Darkness." In *The Complete Short Fiction of Joseph Conrad.* Hopewell, NJ: Ecco Press, 1992.

Considine, Bob. "MacArthur the Magnificent." *The Washington Post*, February 23 and 24, March 14, 1942.

Cooper, Wibb E. "Army Medical Department Activities in the Philippines from 1941 to 6 May 1942, and including medical activities in Japanese Prisoner of War Camps." 1945. USMA, Nininger Collection.

———. "Memorandum to AC of S G-4 USFIP." April 2, 1942. NARA, Morton Collection, RG 319, box 270.

Coox, Alvin D. *The Unfought War: Japan, 1941–1942.* San Diego: San Diego State University Press, 1992.

———. *Year of the Tiger.* Tokyo: Orient/West, 1964.

———. "The Effectiveness of the Japanese Military Establishment in the Second World War." In *Military Effectiveness.* Edited by Allan R. Millett and Williamson Murray, vol. 3. 1–44. Boston: Allen & Unwin, 1988.

Copeland, Lewis, ed. *The World's Great Speeches.* Garden City, NY: Garden City Publishing, 1973.

Crane, Stephen, "In The Depths of A Coal Mine." In *Stephen Crane: Prose and Poetry.* Edited by J. Levenson. New York: Library of America, 1984.

————. *The Red Badge of Courage*. Edited by Sculley Bradley et al. New York: W. W. Norton, 1976.

Darwin, Charles, *Descent of Man and Selection in Relation to Sex*. New York: D. Appleton and Co., 1880.

Des Pres, Terrence. *The Survivor: An Anatomy of Life in the Death Camps*. New York: Oxford University Press, 1976.

Doi, Takeo. *The Anatomy of Dependence*. Translated by John Bester. New York: Kodansha, 1973.

Dooley, Thomas. "Personal Record of Thomas Dooley." Received from author.

Dower, John W. *War Without Mercy*. New York: Pantheon Books, 1986.

Drake, A. C. Affidavit/Statement for the War Crimes Office, September 12, 1945. NARA, SCAP, RG 331.

Drea, Edward J. *In the Service of the Emperor: Essays on the Imperial Japanese Army*. Lincoln: University of Nebraska Press, 1998.

Drummond, Roscoe. "Britain and the United States to Force Their Surrender at End of War." *Christian Science Monitor*, October 7, 1942.

Duckworth, James W. "Official History of General Hospital No. 1, USAFFE, at Camp Limay, Bataan; Little Bagvio, Bataan; and Camp O'Donnell, Tarlac, Philippine Islands." NARA, Philippine Archive Collection, RG 407, box 12.

Dumond, Dwight Lowell. *America in Our Time, 1896–1946*. New York: Henry Holt, 1947.

Durdin, F. Tillman. "All Captives Slain: Civilians Also Killed as the Japanese Spread Terror in Nanking." *The New York Times*, December 13, 1937.

Dyess, William. *The Dyess Story: The Eye-Witness Account of the Death March from Bataan and the Narrative of Experiences in Japanese Prison Camps and of Eventual Escape*. New York: Putnam, 1944.

————. Statement of Maj. William E. Dyess, Air Corps, Concerning Experiences and Observations as Prisoner of War in the Philippines—April 9, 1942, to April 4, 1943. August 21, 1943. NARA, RG 18, AAG DECIMAL FILE 1946-1947, box 644.

Dyess, William, and Charles Leavelle. "Tells Jap Torture on Bataan Death March." *The Chicago Daily Tribune*, January 30, 1944.

Edmonds, Walter D. *They Fought with What They Had*. Boston: Little, Brown, 1951.

Edwards, Peter. "Honour, Shame, Humiliation and Modern Japan." In *Friendship East & West: Philosophical Perspectives*. Edited by Oliver Leaman. London: RoutledgeCurzon, 1996.

Embree, John F. *The Japanese Nation: A Social Survey*. Westport, CT: Greenwood Press, 1975.

Erfurth, Waldemar. "Surprise." In *Roots of Strategy*, book 4.

Espy, John. "Cruise of Death: The Weller Articles." Received from author.

Falk, Stanley. *Bataan: The March of Death*. New York: W. W. Norton, 1962.

————. "The Bataan Death March." Master's thesis, Georgetown University, 1952.

"Fall of Manila, The." *The New York Times*, January 3, 1942.

Felix, Pedro. "The Massacre of the 91st Division in Bataan, 12 April 1942." NARA, SCAP, RG 331.

Fitch, B. M. "Regulations Governing the Trials of War Criminals." September 24, 1945. Received from Robert Pelz.

FitzPatrick, Bernard. *The Hike into the Sun*. Jefferson, NC: McFarland, 1993.

Fonvielle, John. "Payment." 1946. Received from Ivan Birrer.

Fowler, Halstead. *Recipes out of Bilibid*. New York: George W. Stewart, 1946.

Friday, Karl. *Samurai, Warfare and the State of Early Medieval Japan*. New York: Routledge, 2004.

Funk, A. J. "Medical Supply Situation Is Serious." Handwritten note to General Beebe, March 31, 1942. NARA, Morton Collection RG 319, box 270.

Galbraith, Nicoll. "Diaries of Colonel Nicoll F. Galbraith, Assistant Chief of Staff G4." Received from the Galbraith family.

Gallup, George H. *The Gallup Poll*, vol. 1, 1935-1948. New York: Random House, 1972.

Gauntlett, John Owen, trans. *Kokutai No Hongi: Cardinal Principles of the National Entity of Japan*. Cambridge: Harvard University Press, 1949.

Gautier, James Jr. *I Came Back from Bataan*. Greenville, SC: Emerald House Group, 1997.

Gibbs, John M. "Omine, A Divisional Camp of the Hiroshima Group on the Island of Honshu." Washington, D.C.: Liaison and Research Branch, American Prisoner of War Information Bureau, July 31, 1946.

Gibney, Frank. *Sensō: The Japanese Remember the Pacific War*. Armonk, NY: M. E. Sharpe, 1995.

Gillespie, James. "Malaria and the Defense of Bataan." In *Communicable Disease*. Edited by John Boyd Coates and Leonard Heaton, vol. 6. Washington, D.C.: Office of the Surgeon General, Department of the Army, 1963.

Gleeck, Lewis E., Jr. *Over Seventy-five Years of Philippine-American History*. Manila: Carmelo and Bauermann, 1976.

Goldblith, Samuel. *Appetite for Life: An Autobiography*. Trumbull, CT: Food & Nutrition Press, 1996.

Gordon, Richard. *Horyo: Memoirs of an American POW*. St. Paul, MN: Paragon House, 1999.

Graef, Calvin Robert. "We Prayed to Die." *Cosmopolitan*, April 1945, 52-55, 177-80.

Grashio, Samuel C. *Return to Freedom*. Tulsa: MCN Press, 1982.

Grinker, Roy R., and John P. Spiegel. *Men Under Stress*. Philadelphia: Blakiston, 1945.

Guy, George. "In Defense of Yamashita." *Wyoming Law Review* (1950): 153-80.

Handbook on Japanese Military Forces. War Department Technical Manual. Washington, D.C.: Government Printing Office, 1944.

Hata, Ikuhiko. "From Consideration to Contempt: The Changing Nature of Japanese Military and Popular Perceptions of Prisoners of War Through the Ages." In *Prisoners of War and Their Captors in World War II*. Edited by Bob Moore and Kent Fedorowich, 253-76. Washington, D.C.: Berg, 1996.

Hayes, Thomas H. "Bilibid Notebook." Books 1-4. BUMED.

Hearn, Lafcadio. *Japan: An Attempt at Interpretation*. New York: Macmillan, 1904.

———. *Kokoro: Hints and Echoes of Japanese Inner Life*. Rutland, VT: Charles E. Tuttle, 1972.

Hersey, John. *Men on Bataan*, New York: Knopf, 1942.

Hewlett, Frank. Hewlett Original Cable HX20. United Press, February 13, 1942. Received from the Hewlett family.

———. "Quartermasters on Bataan Performed Heroic Feats." *Quartermaster Review* 21 (May–June 1942): 64, 92.

Hibbs, Ralph. "Beriberi in Japanese Prison Camps." *Internal Medicine* 25 (1946): 270-82.

Hill, Milton. "Lessons of Bataan." *Infantry Journal* 52 (1942): 8-21.

Historical Section, G-2 GHQ FEC. *Japanese Studies in World War II.* Monograph 1: *Philippines Operations Record 6 November 1941–30 June 1942*; Monograph 2: *Philippines Operations Record 1 December 1941–10 April 1942*. Microfilm. Washington, D.C.: Library of Congress Photo Duplication Service, 1963.

Hobbes, Thomas, *Leviathan.* Edited by Richard E. Flathman and David Johnston. New York: W. W. Norton, 1997.

Holt, Thaddeus. "King of Bataan." Manuscript. Received from Thaddeus Holt, 2000.

Holtom, D. C. *Modern Japan and Shinto Nationalism: A Study of Present-Day Trends in Japanese Religions.* Chicago: University of Chicago Press, 1943.

———. *The National Faith of Japan: A Study in Modern Shinto.* London: Kegan Paul, Trench, Trubner & Co, 1938.

"Homma, Kuroda Placed in Prison at Yokohama." *Nippon Times*, October 5, 1945.

Homma, Fujiko. Correspondence to General Douglas MacArthur, March 11, 1946. MAC, RG 5.

———. "Mrs. Homma Pleads to MacArthur on Behalf of Her Husband." Press release. MAC, RG 5, box 28.

———. "Why Did Homma Masaharu Die?" *Maru Magazine* (1954): 24-31.

Homma, Masaharu. General Homma's Prison Diary. FDR, Toland Collection, Series 1, "Rising Sun," box 5, file H.

———. *Hito Hakengun (Philippine Expeditionary Force).* 2d ed. Tokyo: Watari Group Information Department Publication.

———. Letters of Masaharu Homma. 1946. FDR, Toland Collection, Series 1, "Rising Sun," box 5, file H.

———. "Materials for Defence." FDR, Toland Collection, Series 1, "Rising Sun," box 5, file H.

———. Scrapbooks of Masaharu Homma. Received from Masahiko Homma.

———. "Statement on the Charge of So Called 'Death March of Bataan.'" FDR, Toland Collection, Series 1, "Rising Sun," box 5, file H.

"Homma's Wife Makes Appeal to MacArthur." Associated Press, March 11, 1946.

Hoover, Hobert Hadley. Affidavit/Statement for the War Crimes Office, October 15, 1945. NARA, SCAP, RG 331.

Hubbard, Preston John. *Apocalypse Undone.* Nashville: Vanderbilt University Press, 1990.

Huff, Sidney L. *My Fifteen Years With General MacArthur: A First-hand Account of America's Greatest Soldier.* New York: Paperback Library, 1964.

Humphreys, Leonard A. *The Way of the Heavenly Sword: The Japanese Army in the 1920's.* Stanford: Stanford University Press, 1995.

Hunt, Ray C. *Behind Japanese Lines: An American Guerrilla in the Philippines.* Lexington: University Press of Kentucky, 1986.

Ikegami, Eiko. *The Taming of the Samurai: Honorific Individualism and the Making of Modern Japan*. Cambridge, MA: Harvard University Press, 1995.

Imai, Takeo. "A Strange Order Received at Bataan Battle Front." FDR, Toland Collection, Series 1, "Rising Sun," box 1, "Bataan" File.

———. "Tragedy of Fukuyama Regiment: Was It Imperial Headquarters' Mistake?" FDR, Toland Collection, Series 1, "Rising Sun," box 1, "Bataan" File.

Imamura, Hitoshi. *Memoirs of General Imamura Hitoshi*. Tokyo: Free Asia Press, 1960.

Imperial Japanese Forces in the Philippines. "New Order, Short Essays." Parts I–II. MAC, RG 2, box 5, folder 2.

In re Yamashita, 327 U.S.

Ind, Allison. *Bataan: The Judgement Seat: The Saga of the Philippine Command of the United States Army Air Force, May 1941 to May 1942*. New York: Macmillan, 1944.

International Military Tribunal for the Far East (IMTFE). *Judgment*. Chap. 8, 1001. 11/1/1948. www.ibiblio.org/hyperwar/PTO/IMTFE/IMTFE-8.html.

———. "Instructions of War Minister Hideki Tojo to the Newly Appointed Commanders of the Prisoner of War Camps." *Record of Proceedings* 29, 14,428-430. Tokyo.

———. "JAG Report No. 75 on Deaths, Mistreatment of Prisoners and Living Conditions at Camp O'Donnell." *Record of Proceedings* 26, 12,597-601. Tokyo.

———. "Line of Communication and Treatment of POWs including Forced Labor." *Record of Proceedings* 29, 14,287-290. Tokyo.

———. "Prosecution Exhibit 2701: Journal of the Taiwan POW Camp H.Q. in Taihoku, Extreme Measures for POWs." *Record of Proceedings* 30, 14,724-727. Tokyo.

———. "Report on POW Labor Conditions, September 1942." *Record of Proceedings* 29, 14,493-496. Tokyo.

Jackson, Calvin G. *Diary of Col. Calvin G. Jackson, M.D.* Ada, OH: Ohio Northern University, 1992.

Jacobsen, Gene S. *Who Refused to Die*. Self-published, 1995.

James, D. Clayton. *The Years of MacArthur. Vol. 2: 1941–1945*. Boston: Houghton Mifflin, 1975.

Jansen, Marius B. "Samurai." In *The Cambridge History of Japan*, vol. 5, 528-33. New York: Cambridge University Press, 1999.

Johnson, Sheila K. *The Japanese Through American Eyes*. Stanford: Stanford University Press, 1988.

Jones, Thomas. Interview with Brigadier General Jones, June 1964. MAC, RG 32.

Jose, Ricardo Trota. *The Philippine Army, 1935–1942*. Manila: Ateneo de Manila University Press, 1992.

Judge Advocate General. *Basic Field Manual, Rules of Land Warfare, FM 27–10*. Washington, D.C.: Government Printing Office, 1940.

Kawane, Yoshikata. Affidavit/Statement, March 5, 1948. NARA, SCAP, RG 331.

Keegan, John, ed. *The Times Atlas of the Second World War*. New York: Harper, 1989.

Kennedy, David M. *Freedom From Fear: The American People in Depression and War, 1929–1945*. New York: Oxford University Press, 1999.

Kennedy, David M., Lizabeth Cohen, and Thomas A. Bailey. *The American Pageant*. 12th ed. Boston: Houghton Mifflin, 2002.

Kenworthy, Aubrey. *The Tiger of Malaya: The Story of General Tomoyuki Yamashita and "Death March" General Masaharu Homma*. New York: Exposition Press, 1953.

Keys, Ancel et al. *The Biology of Human Starvation*. Vol. 2. Minneapolis: University of Minnesota Press, 1950.

King, Edward P. Affidavit/Statement for the War Crimes Office, January 14, 1946. NARA, SCAP, RG 331.

———. "General King's Own Story: Exhausted Yanks Buried Alive by Japan on Bataan Death March." *Atlanta Constitution*, September 26, 1945.

———. "Report of Operations of the Luzon Force 22 March–9 April 1942," January 29, 1946. USMHI, Morton Collection, box 11.

Kishimoto, Hideo. "Some Japanese Cultural Traits and Religions." In Moore, *The Japanese Mind*.

Lael, Richard. *The Yamashita Precedent: War Crimes and Command Responsibility*. Wilmington, DE: Scholarly Resources, 1982.

"Last Word, The." *Time*, January 21, 1946.

Leahy, William. Memorandum for the President: Major Dyess' Report on Japanese Atrocities, September 5, 1943. NARA, RG 218, box 20.

Leavelle, C. "Tribune's Fight to Tell Dyess Atrocity Facts." *The Chicago Daily Tribune*, February 23, 1944.

Lee, Clark. *They Call It Pacific: An Eye-Witness Story of Our War Against Japan From Bataan to the Solomons*. New York: Viking, 1943.

Leeb, Ritter von. "Defense." In *Roots of Strategy*, book 3, 69.

Letters to FDR from Americans about the Bataan Death March, 1944. FDR, Official WWII File 4675.

Levering, Robert W. *Horror Trek: A True Story of Bataan, the Death March and Three and One-half Years in Japanese Prison Camps*. Dayton: Horstman, 1948.

Linn, Brian McAllister. *Guardians of the Empire: The U.S. Army and the Pacific, 1902–1940*. Chapel Hill: University of North Carolina Press, 1997.

Locke, A. J. *Kobe House P.O.W. No. 13*. Self-published, 1998.

Lory, Hillis. *Japan's Military Masters: The Army in Japanese Life*. New York: Viking, 1943.

"MacArthur Begins Final Review of Homma's Sentence." *The Washington Post*, March 11, 1946.

"MacArthur 'Wanted' List Hints Purge in Cabinet." *The Washington Post*, September 15, 1945.

MacArthur, Douglas. Cable No. 258, February 12, 1942. MAC.

———. Cable No. 371, February 26, 1942. MAC.

———. Cable No. 382, February 28, 1942. MAC.

———. Cable No. 438, March 7, 1942. MAC.

———. Memorandum: "Defense of the Philippines." December 3, 1941. MAC.

———. "Message from General MacArthur." January 15, 1942. MAC, RG 2, box 2, folder 3.

———. Radio Message to AGWAR. December 22, 1941. MAC, RG 2, box 2, folder 2.

———. Radio Message to AGWAR. January 23, 1942. MAC, RG 2, box 2, folder 4.

———. *Reminiscences*. New York: McGraw-Hill, 1964.

—————. *Reports of General MacArthur: Japanese Operations in the Southwest Pacific Area.* Vol. 2, parts 1–2. Washington, D.C.: Government Printing Office, 1966.

Mallonée, Richard C., ed. *The Naked Flagpole: Battle for Bataan from the Diary of Richard C. Mallonée.* San Rafael, CA: Presidio Press, 1980.

Marshall, George. Memorandum for the President: (Gripsholm), July 14, 1943. NARA, RG 218, box 20.

—————. Memorandum for the President: Major Dyess's Report on Japanese Atrocities, September 5, 1943. NARA, RG 218, box 20.

—————. Memorandum: "Strategic Policy, Far Eastern Theater," January 2, 1942. GCM.

McClain, James L. *Japan: A Modern History.* New York: W. W. Norton, 2002.

Merrill, Elmer D. *Plant Life of the Pacific World.* Rutland, VT: Charles E. Tuttle, 1981.

Michno, Gregory. *Death on the Hellships: Prisoners at Sea in the Pacific War.* Annapolis: Naval Institute Press, 2001.

Military Commission, 8th Army. "Trial and Appeal of Sakujiro Aramaki, Akiyoshi Koga, Nobuyasu Sugiyama, Kukuma Yamaguichi, Takenosuke Fujisaki, Tomoe Nishimura, Toraichi Takashita." Case Docket No. 199, Yokohama, Japan, July 29, 1947, to August 15, 1947. NARA, SCAP, RG 153.

Miller, E. B. *Bataan Uncensored.* 2d ed. Little Falls: Military Historical Society of Minnesota, 1991.

Monaghan, Forbes J. *Under the Red Sun: A Letter from Manila.* New York: Declan X. McMullen, 1946.

Moore, Charles A., ed. *The Japanese Mind: Essentials of Japanese Philosophy and Culture.* Honolulu: University of Hawaii Press, 1968.

Morison, Samuel Eliot. *The Two-Ocean War: A Short History of the United States Navy in the Second World War.* Boston: Little, Brown, 1963.

Morris, Ivan. *The Nobility of Failure: Tragic Heroes in the History of Japan.* London: Secker and Warburg, 1975.

Morton, Louis. "Bataan Diary of Major Achille C. Tisdelle." *Military Affairs* 11, no. 3 (1947): 130–48.

—————. *The Fall of the Philippines.* Washington, D.C.: Center of Military History, 1953.

—————. Interview with Lt. General Richard K. Sutherland, November 12, 1946. USMHI, Morton Collection.

—————. *Strategy and Command: The First Two Years.* Washington, D.C.: Center of Military History, 1962.

"Mrs. Homma Today Personally Presented Her Plea." Press release. MAC, RG 5, box 28, folder O.M.S. Correspondence, HOG–HON.

Musashi, Miyamoto. *A Book of Five Rings.* Translated by Victor Harris. Woodstock, NY: Overlook Press, 1974.

Musselman, Merle M. Affidavit/Statement for the War Crimes Office, July 25, 1945. NARA, SCAP, RG 331.

Nakamura. Diary of Sergeant Nakamura, November 14, 1941–January 23, 1942. MAC, RG 2, box 5, folder 3 G2 Journals, Annexes 16-31.

Nihon Senbotsu Gakusei Kinen-Kai, ed., *Listen to the Voices from the Sea: Writings of the Fallen Japanese Students.* Scranton, PA: University of Scranton Press, 2000.

Noma, Hiroshi. *Zone of Emptiness*. Cleveland: World, 1956.

Nordin, Carl S. *We Were Next to Nothing*. Jefferson, NC: McFarland Publishers, 1997.

Office of Strategic Services. *Morale in the Japanese Military Services*. Report No. 26. Microfilm. In *State Department and Intelligence Research Reports: I, Japan and Its Occupied Territories During World War II*. Washington, D.C.: University Publications of America, 1977.

Okada, Masukichi. "The Tragic General: Homma Masaharu." *Maru Magazine* (1957): 152–59.

Olson, John E. *O'Donnell: Andersonville of the Pacific*. Lake Quivra, KS: J. E. Olson, 1985.

Ongpauco, Fidel L. *They Refused to Die: True Stories About World War II Heroes in the Philippines 1941–1945*. Quebec: Lèvesque Publications, 1982.

Paguio, Fr. Wilfredo. *Bataan, Land of Valor, People of Peace*. Manila: Jardi Press, 1997.

Patton, W. Kenneth. "Account of the Captivity at Manila PI 1942–1945." BUMED.

Pelz, Robert L. Correspondence and Miscellaneous Documents. Received from Robert Pelz.

———. Journal. Vol. 4, November 10, 1945–May 25, 1946.

———. Scrapbook of Robert Pelz.

Pettit, A. and H. Linn, *A Guide to Safety in Confined Spaces*, Report no. 87-113, (1987). Washington, D.C.: Government Printing Office.

Piccigallo, Philip R. *The Japanese on Trial*. Austin: University of Texas Press, 1979.

Poweleit, Alvin C. *USAFFE: Loyal Americans and Faithful Filipinos*. Self-published, 1975.

Profiles of the American Generals on Bataan. USMHI, Morton Collection, box 8.

Ramirez, Primitivo. Interview with Pedro L. Felix, November 7, 1945. NARA, SCAP, RG 331.

Reel, A. Frank. *The Case of General Yamashita*. Chicago: University of Chicago Press, 1949.

Remarque, Erich Maria, *All Quiet on the Western Front*. New York: Fawcett Columbine, 1996.

Rhodes, Richard. *The Making of the Atomic Bomb*. New York: Simon & Schuster, 1986.

Rogers, Paul P. *The Good Years: MacArthur and Sutherland*. New York: Praeger, 1990.

Roots of Strategy. Books 1–4. Mechanicsburg, PA: Stackpole, 1985–1999.

Roper, Richard. *Brothers of Paul: Activities of Prisoner of War Chaplains in the Philippines During World War II*. Odenton, MD: Revere Printing, 2003.

Sakai, Saburō, Martin Caidin, and Fred Saito. *Samurai!* New York: Dutton, 1957.

Sakurai, Tadayoshi. *Human Bullets: A Soldier's Story of Port Arthur*. Translated by Masujiro Honda. Lincoln: University of Nebraska Press, 1999.

Sansom, G. B. *Japan: A Short Cultural History*. Stanford, CA: Stanford University Press, 1978.

Sartin, L. B. "Report of Activities of the United States Naval Hospital in the Philippines from December 8, 1941 to January 30, 1945." BUMED.

Saxe, Marshal Maurice de. "My Reveries Upon the Art of War." In *Roots of Strategy*, book 1.

Sayre, Frances Bowes. *Glad Adventure*. New York: Macmillan, 1957.

Schedler, Dean. "Bombs in Manila Bay Spell Fresh Fish for Bataan." *Chicago Daily News*, March 31, 1942.

Schlesinger, Arthur M., Jr., ed. *The Almanac of American History*. New York: Putnam, 1983.

Schloat, Don. *Freedom! Bataan-POW-PVT*. Self-published, 1995.

Schwartz, Doris. "My Three Months in Yokohama Harbor." *Yankee Magazine* 46 (1981): 83–87, 101–03.

Shearer, Clarence. "Shearer's Journal," 1945. BUMED.

Shimada, Koichi. "The Opening Air Offensive Against the Philippines." In *The Japanese Navy in World War II: In the Words of Former Japanese Naval Officers*. Edited by David C. Evans, 2d ed., 71–104. Annapolis: Naval Institute Press, 1986.

Ship's log, USS *Consolation*, 2007. www.ussconsolation.homestead.com/ships_log.html.

Simmons, William R. *Hell Revisited*. Self-published, 1972.

Singer, Kurt. *Mirror, Sword and Jewel: The Geometry of Japanese Life*. New York: Kodansha, 1981.

Slim, William. *Defeat into Victory*. New York: Cooper Square Press, 2000.

Smith, Carey. "Memoir of Dr. Carey Smith USN, MC." Received from family.

Smith, Joseph S. Affidavit/Statement for the War Crimes Office, August 1945. NARA, SCAP, RG 331.

Smith, Stanley W. *Prisoner of the Emperor: An American POW in World War II*. Niwot, CO: University Press of Colorado, 1991.

Sneddon, Murray M. *Zero Ward: A Survivor's Nightmare*. San Jose, CA: Writers Club Press, 2000.

Snow, William J. *Signposts of Experience*. Washington, D.C.: United States Field Artillery Association, 1941.

Stanton, Martin. "Bataan: Failed Japanese Amphibious Envelopment." *Marine Corps Gazette* 81 (March 1997): 64–69.

Stauffer, Alvin. *The Quartermaster Corps: Operations in the War Against Japan*. Army Historical Series. Washington, D.C.: Office of the Chief of Military History, Department of the Army, 1956.

Stewart, Sidney. *Give Us This Day*. London: Pan Books, 1958.

Storry, Richard. *A History of Modern Japan*. New York: Penguin, 1990.

"Story Behind the Story of the Dyess Epic, The." *The Trib* (*Chicago Daily Tribune* in-house newsletter), February 1944.

Stouffer, Samuel A. et al. *The American Soldier: Adjustment During Army Life*. Vol. 1. Princeton: Princeton University Press, 1949.

Stratton, Samuel. "Tiger of Malaya." *U.S. Naval Institute Proceedings* 136 (1954): 137–43.

Sugamo Isho Hensankai (Sugamo Last Letters Editing Group). *Seiki no Isho (Last Letters of the Century)*. Tokyo: Sugamo Isho Hensankai, 1953.

Swinson, Arthur. *Four Samurai: A Quartet of Japanese Army Commanders in the Second World War*. London: Hutchinson, 1968.

Tanaka, Yuki. *Hidden Horrors: Japanese War Crimes in World War II*. Boulder, CO: Westview Press, 1996.

Tasaki, Hanama. *Long the Imperial Way*. Boston: Houghton Mifflin, 1950.

Tatsumi, Eiichi. "About General Homma." FDR, Toland Collection, Series 1, "Rising Sun," box 5, file H.

Tatsuzo, Ishikawa. *Soldiers Alive*. Honolulu: University of Hawaii Press, 2003.

Tenney, Lester I. *My Hitch in Hell: The Bataan Death March*. Washington, D.C.: Brassey's, 1995.

Thomas, Ed "Tommie." *As I Remember: The Death March of Bataan*. Sonoita, AZ: Edward E. Thomas, 1990.

Thompson, Paul W., Harold Doud, and John Scofield. *How the Japanese Army Fights*. New York: Penguin, 1942.

Tisdelle, Achille. "Journal Artillery Section USAFFE Diary." USMHI, Morton Collection, box 5.

———. "Story of Bataan Collapse," 1947. USMHI, Morton Collection, box 5.

Toland, John. *But Not in Shame: The Six Months After Pearl Harbor*. New York: Random House, 1961.

———. Interviews 1 and 2 with Major Kumao Imoto. FDR, Toland Collection, Series 1, "Rising Sun," box 6, file I.

———. Interview #2 with Colonel Takushiro Hattori. FDR, Toland Collection, Series 1, "Rising Sun," box 15.

———. Interview with Colonel Nobuhiko Jimbo. FDR, Toland Collection, Series 1, "Rising Sun," box 6, file J.

———. Interview with Lt. General Akira Nara. FDR, Toland Collection, Series 1, "Rising Sun," box 13.

———. Interview with Colonel Jesse Traywick. Library of Congress, Manuscript Division, Toland Collection.

———. Interview with Brig. Gen. James R. N. Weaver. FDR, Toland Collection, Series 1, "Rising Sun," box 6, file 1.

———. *The Rising Sun: The Decline and Fall of the Japanese Empire, 1936–1945*. New York: Random House, 1970.

Tolischus, Otto D. *Through Japanese Eyes*. New York: Reynal & Hitchcock, 1945.

Trohan, W. "Call for New Blows Against Pacific Enemy." *The Chicago Daily Tribune*, January 29, 1944.

Trumball, Robert. "Lines of Defense for Homma Shown." *The New York Times*, January 30, 1946.

Tsuji, Masanobu. *Japan's Greatest Victory, Britain's Greatest Defeat*. New York: Sarpedon, 1997.

———. *Underground Escape*. Tokyo: Robert Booth and Taro Fukuda, 1952.

Tsuneoka, Noboru, *Gyokusai: Tsunchiro Daitai No Senscki Jikiroku*. Tokyo: Human Socument-sha, 1991.

Tsunoda, Fukiko. *Issai Yume ni Gozasōrō (Once There Was a Dream): The Biography of Lieutenant General Homma Masaharu*. Tokyo: Chūō Kōronsha, 1985.

Tsunoda, Ryūsaku, Wm. Theodore de Bary, and Donald Keene, *Sources of Japanese Tradition*. New York: Columbia University Press, 1958.

Tsurumi, Kazuko. *Social Change and the Individual: Japan Before and After Defeat in World War II*. Princeton: Princeton University Press, 1970.

Uji, Shigeyoshi. Affidavit/Statement, May 27, 1948. NARA, SCAP, RG 331.

United Nations War Crimes Commission. *Law Reports of Trials of War Criminals*, vol. 4. London: His Majesty's Stationery Office, 1948.

U.S. Army General Headquarters, Far East Command, Military Intelligence Section Historical Division. Interrogation of Lt. Col. Tokutaro Sato, April 18, 1947. In *Statements of Japanese Officials on World War II*, vol. 2. 184-90. Microfilm.

———. Interrogation of Former Lt. Gen. Akira Nara 65th Brigade, June 14, 1949. Doc. No. 62638. In *Statements of Japanese Officials on World War II*, vol. 2. Microfilm.

———. Statement by Former Chief of Staff of the 14th Army Masami Maeda, March 2, 1950. Doc. No. 56234. In *Statements of Japanese Officials on World War II*, vol. 2. Microfilm.

U.S. Department of the Army, Historical Division. "Information Regarding Strength and Composition of Japanese Forces, Philippine Islands, Dec. 41–May 42." August 15, 1949. USMHI, Morton Collection, box 8.

USA v. Homma, proceedings of the trial. Microfilm. Office of the Judge Advocate General, War Crimes Division, 1946.

Volckmann, R. W. *We Remained: Three Years Behind the Enemy Lines in the Philippines*. New York: W. W. Norton, 1954.

Wada, Moriya. Affidavit/Statement, May 26, 1948. NARA, SCAP, RG 331.

Wainwright, Jonathan. Diaries: January 1, 1941–October 22, 1945. USMHI, Holt Collection.

Wainwright, Jonathan, and Bob Considine. *General Wainwright's Story: The Account of Four Years of Humiliating Defeat, Surrender and Captivity*. Garden City, NY: Doubleday, 1946.

Waldrop, Frank C. *MacArthur on War*. New York: Duell, Sloan and Pearce, 1942.

Ward, Ian. *The Killer They Called a God*. Singapore: Media Masters, 1992.

Waterford, Van. *Prisoners of the Japanese in World War II*. Jefferson, NC: McFarland, 1994.

Watson, Mark Skinner. *Chief of Staff: Prewar Plans and Preparations*. Washington, D.C.: Department of the Army, 1950.

Watson, Richard L. "Pearl Harbor and Clark Field." In *The Army Air Forces in World War II: Plans and Early Operations January 1939 to August 1942*. Edited by Wesley F. Cate and James L. Craven, vol. 1, 194-233. Chicago: University of Chicago Press, 1948.

Weller, George. "Horror of Jap Prison Ship Told." *Chicago Daily News Foreign Press Service*, 1945.

Whitman, John W. *Bataan: Our Last Ditch*. New York: Hippocrene, 1990.

Williams, William Carlos. *The Collected Poems of William Carlos Williams*. Edited by Christopher MacGowan. New York: New Directions, 1988.

Willoughby, Charles A., and John Chamberlain, *MacArthur, 1941–1951*. New York: McGraw-Hill, 1954.

Wilson, O. "After Bataan." FDR, Toland Collection, Series A, "Rising Sun," box 18.

Wilson, Woodrow. "Address to Congress after Announcing the Armistice." In *Source Records of The Great War*. Edited by Charles F. Horne and Walter F. Austin, vol. 6. New York: National Alumni, 1923.

"Wives, The." *Time*, April 1, 1946.

Wolf, A. V. *Thirst: Physiology of the Urge to Drink and the Problems of Water Lack*. Springfield, IL: Charles C. Thomas, 1958.

Yamamoto, A. "Information on Lt. Col. Tsuji from Liaison Committee for the Imperial Japanese Army and Navy to G-2," November 21, 1945. NARA, RG 331, S357.

Yamamoto, Tsunetomo. *The Hagakure: A Code to the Way of the Samurai.* Translated by Mulkoh Takao. Tokyo: Hokuseido Press, 1980.

———. *The Hagakure: The Book of the Samurai.* Translated by William Scott Wilson. New York: Kodansha, 1979.

"Yamashita, on Trial, Pleads 'Not Guilty.'" *Nippon Times*, October 11, 1945.

"Yamashita to Face Trial in the Philippines." *Nippon Times*, October 5, 1945.

"Yamashita Trial Starts in Capital of Philippines." *Nippon Times*, October 31, 1945.

ACKNOWLEDGMENTS

This book would not have been possible without the generous support of the following organizations and individuals: The Earhart Foundation (David Kennedy); The Freedom Forum, Pacific Coast Center; Novartis Pharmaceuticals (Mildred Kowalski, John Seaman). At New York University: Research Challenge Fund, Steinhardt School (Charles Sprague); Research Challenge Fund, New York University; Faculty of Arts and Science, Research Fund (Jess Benhabib, George Downs); Steinhardt Faculty Development Fund (Mary Brabeck).

We have no doubt that the following lists are incomplete and that, despite our best attempts to keep an account, we have forgotten several kind and generous sources and associates. This book represents ten years of research and writing across three countries. We made three trips to the Philippines, crisscrossed the United States at least six times, interviewed subjects in more than a dozen Japanese towns and cities, collected material from repositories and archives around the world. We estimate that we spoke at length with more than four hundred sources, nearly half of them recorded. Somewhere across the last ten years, along the way from the first interview and archive to the last, we have certainly lost a few names, and we apologize sincerely for the oversight. And although several fine readers and scholars vetted the book in manuscript, all errors of fact, emphasis, and interpretation are ours alone.

THE STEELES

Our debt to the Steele family is incalculable. Ben Steele sat for hundreds of interviews across nine years of visits to Montana, nine years of telephone calls (sometimes weekly), and nine years of follow-up correspondence. He served as our central character, our Montana guide, our model of an ordinary man caught up in extraordinary circumstances. His singular destiny is what drives the story of Bataan and its long aftermath. He withheld nothing and asked nothing be withheld. His memories (vetted in every instance possible) turned out to be remarkably accurate. He never guessed, never speculated during his answers to our questions. When he was unsure of something, he said so.

In short, he gave us his life and asked nothing in return. We have never enjoyed such trust, and we hope these pages justify his faith in us.

Across the years we also conducted scores of interviews with members of his family: his wife, Shirley Emerson Steele; his children, Sean Steele, Rosemarie Steele, and Julie Steele Jorgenson; and their mother, Bobbie Steele Miller; his aunt, Jo Boyle; his brother, Warren Steele; his sister, Gert Steele Dunham; his son-in-law, Jim Jorgenson. We thank them for their candor, their logistical support, their inexhaustible patience.

THE PHILIPPINES

Ricardo Trota Jose (University of the Philippines) and his wife, Lydia Yu-Jose (Ateno de Manila University) generously shared a lifetime of scholarship with us. Both study the history of World War II in the Philippines, both have written widely on the subject, both speak Japanese. They provided us with bibliographies, interview subjects, names of repositories, suggested skeins of research. Rico Jose supervised the translations of our interviews with Filipinos. He also went into the field with us on Bataan on several occasions and shared invaluable material from his private library and collection of World War II Philippine militaria. More than once with Filipino interviewees we traded on Rico's good name and reputation.

Divina Paredes, a well-known Filipina journalist, and her bother, Joel Paredes, formerly director of communications for the Philippine government, also helped open the country to us. Divina and her associates, Wilma and Billy Lacaba, introduced us to Philippine culture and customs and also went into the field with us, serving as translators and facilitators. Through them we met Rhett Daza, son of the onetime guerrilla leader Johnny Daza. Rhett, once a history major at UP, gave us entrée to the Filipino veterans' community. He took us north and south into the rural provinces to find old guerrillas and veterans. He also scouted battle sites for us, helped verify the original route of the death march, and across one long twenty-hour day of travel through Camarines Norte Province helped locate the rock bar bivouac at Tayabas Road on the Basiad River, a key scene in the book.

Arvin Quintos of Bataan and his extended family made it possible for us to walk the sixty-six-mile route of the death march across five days. We could not have covered that ground without the Qunitos' logistical support and goodwill. Also on Bataan, Flor T. Caragay and Rafael Viray of the Philippine Information Agency helped us locate a number of Filipino witnesses to the death march. Flor accompanied us on many of those interviews and acted as a first-line translator.

We also thank Glenn Ang, Dan and Edna Binkowski, DeRenato Dilig, Donato Edralin, Lewis Gleeck, James Halsema, Bram Hartendorp, James Litton, former Quezon City mayor Ismael Mathay, Artemio G. Matibag Jr., Leslie Murray, Dennis O'Leary and Leonore O'Leary, Lee Paredes, Gary Whatley, and Chonette Zagala for assistance with the research.

We thank the staff at the following archives: American Historical Collection at Ateneo de Manila University, University of the Philippines Library, Filipinas Heritage Library, and the Ayala Museum. Michael Anderson, formerly of the American embassy in Manila, went beyond the call of duty for a consular official, providing us with invaluable contacts and letters of transit that carried us across six provinces on three visits to the country.

Finally, we thank the following Philippine Army veterans, Philippine Scouts, Filipino guerrillas, and civilians for their stories and memories: Nonoy Acosta, Guillermo Almario, Natividad Almario, Juan Arroyo, Miguel Banco, Manuel Banzon Jr., Pedro C. Bersola, Lorenzo Capistrano, Artemio Caragay, Juanita Caraguy, Juanito Caraguy, Felipe Cataluna, Luis Conde, Milagros Cortez, Rosalina Almario Cruz, Emanuel de Ocampo, Bernade Rosas de Leon, Juana Diaz, Honorio Dizon, Monico Dominguez, Rafael Estrada, Jaluria Galina, Candido Gallardo, Bartolome Gana, Crescencia P. Garcia, Antonio Gonzales, Amado Guevarra, Ismael Guzon, Miguel Layug, Ciriaco Manahan, Elias Manlapas, Moises Montes, Armando N. Pabustan, Ireneo Pamilaran, Demitrio C. Paz, Faustino Perez, Rosario Quesada, Edilberto Sadural, Marcelo Tuazon, Gerry Valdecanas, and Basiad River veterans Luis G. VillaReal, Rafael G. Zagala, Ernesto Zulueta.

JAPAN

Kyoko Onoki, most recently of the London *Times*, became our colleague. Her tact, tenacity, and courage led to interviews with twenty-two former Imperial Army *hohei* and a prison guard. Working off long lists of questions sent to her in advance, she tracked down our sources at veterans' meetings and over the phone, then provided nearly flawless simultaneous translations during eighteen days with us of constant interviewing in cities and towns across the country. We say "flawless" because we had every page of those translations vetted by Wendy Matsumura, a doctoral candidate and instructor of Japanese at New York University, who worked with us for several years translating books and documents. Without the diligence and care of these two fine professionals, we could never have gotten the Japanese material that makes this book what it is.

We also owe a debt to NYU doctoral scholars Miho Suzuki and Mia Kobayaski. After Wendy had gone her way and Kyoko took on a new assignment, Miho and Mia acted as consultants on many matters Japanese, as did Yuko Friedman. On this score we also thank Edward Drea of the U.S. Department of Defense. A scholar of the Imperial Army and author of the fine *In the Service of the Emperor*, Ed Drea patiently fielded a number of our inquiries. Authors and scholars Thomas Conlan, Karl Friday, Frank Gibney, and Ikuhiko Hata also shared their time and research with us.

Most of all we are grateful to the veterans of the Imperial Army who fought on Bataan and sat down with us to be interviewed at length: Tatsuzo Arakawa, Jinzaburo Chaki, Junsuke Hitomi, Masahiko Homma (the general's son, who fought in Russia), Soichiro Inulkai, Minobu Kawaguchi, Kiyoshi Kinoshita, Yoshio Kunori, Toraichi Masuda, Isamu Murakami, Hirohisa Murata, Yoshiaki Nagai, Ryotaro Nishimura, Tadashi Ozaki, Tokutaro Sato, Hideo Sekihara, Takesada Shigeta, Isao Shinohara, Nobuyasu Sugiyama (civilian Omine-machi guard), Tozo Takeuchi, Moriya Wada, Kozo Watanabe, Tasuku Yamanari.

(Several of the men we are about to mention will be named again below in the list of veterans we interviewed. They are singled out here for special thanks because of their generosity and their significant contributions to this book.) We began our search for American veterans of the Philippines campaign (1941-1942) by contacting five veterans' organizations: the American Defenders of Bataan and Corregidor (ADBC), the Battling Bastards of Bataan (BBB), the 4th Marines Organization (now a chapter of the ADBC), the Philippine Scouts Heritage Society (PSHS), the American Ex–Prisoners of War (AEPW).

From the ADBC, John "the Sweede" Emerick, John Crago, Joe Poster, Paul Reuter, Andy Miller, Ralph Levenberg, Don Schloat, and Joe Vater were our constants across nine years. They helped us understand the politics of their organization and they helped us find the kind of men we were looking for—men like themselves, who had put aside their hate and bitterness and could look on history and journalism as vehicles to the meaning of what had happened to them. In the end we found dozens of such men, but we would never have met them without our eight good and constant shepherds. They believed in our project, even though it embraced their former enemies, and they believed in us. We have Joe Vater to thank for meeting Ben Steele. As the editor of the ADBC newsletter *The Quan*, Joe had copies of almost all the memoirs, articles, and published works by and about the men in his organization, including a catalog of Ben Steele's artwork. "Here," he said one day in his motel room at a regional meeting of the Atlantic Chapter of the ADBC, "you should look at this, and you should talk to this guy." We called Ben Steele the next day.

From the BBB, Richard Gordon also led us to a number of sources. One of those was the indomitable Zoeth Skinner, who frequently sent us material from his extensive private library and was always happy to field yet another inquiry, double-check yet another fact.

Across the years a number of students and associates at New York University became involved in the book. Libby Estell and Bojana Stoparic served as research assistants, and Lisa Sandberg did field research. We spent many hours in NYU's libraries and got a lot of help from their fine staffs, including Paul Baker, Lucinda Covert-Vail, Michael Hannon, Gerald Heverly, Susan Jacobs, Dave McGuire, Radu Popa, and James Terry.

We drew material from the Atlanta History Center; Canada Science and Technology Museum; Carlisle Barracks; Cleveland Institute of Art; Columbia University Library; Cowboy Artists of America Museum; Douglas County Museum; Enid/Garfield Public Library; First Division Museum at Cantigny, Robert R. McCormick Research Center; the Franklin D. Roosevelt Presidential Library; the George C. Marshall Research Foundation; Hoover Institution; Kentucky Historical Society; the MacArthur Memorial Library and Archives; Maryknoll Mission Archives; Mississippi State University Library; Montana Historical Society; National Archives and Records Administration; Princeton University Library; New York Public Library; New York University's Bobst Library and NYU Law Library; Rutgers University Library; Sioux City Public Museum; University of Wyoming American Heritage Center; United States Marine

Corps, Museum Division; United States Navy BUMED Archives; West Point Military Academy Library.

A nonfiction work of this scope would surely have failed without the guidance of skilled archivists. We were lucky to have found four of the best: Alan Aimone (USMA), Jan K. Herman (USN BUMED), James Zobel (MacArthur), and Kenneth Schlesinger (NARA). We could not have completed the manuscript without their assiduity and careful scholarship.

As with the Japanese and Filipinos, the core of the book rests on interviews with the men who fought. We interviewed, corresponded with, and received material from the following American veterans: Francis Agnes, John Aldrich, Joe Alexander, Charles Balaza, Ernie Bales, Arthur Beale, Richard Beck, Frank Bigelow, Ivan Birrer, Robert G. Bjoring, James T. Boyce, Philip Brain, John Browe, John Bumgarner, Crayton Burns, Kenneth Calvit, Wayne Carringer, Thomas Caswell, Norman Christ, John Crago, Brown Davidson, Q. P. Devore, Tom Dooley, Robert Dow, John Emerick, Dan Emery, William Evans, Harold Finer, Dick Francies, Dale Frantz, Glen Frazier, Duke Fullerton, Thomas Gage, William H. Gentry, Dominick Giantonio, Michael Gilewitch, Paul C. Gilmore, Murray Glusman, Samuel Goldblith, Richard Gordon, Weldon C. Hamilton, Neal Harrington, Thomas Harrison, William Hauser, Ralph Hibbs, W. Pat Hitchcock, Preston Hubbard, Don Ingle, George Idlett, Dan (Pinkston) Irwin, Edward Jackfert, Eugene Jacobsen, Warren G. Jorgenson, Clemens Kathman, Otis King, Louis Kolger, Stephen Kramerich, Bill Lambert, Walter Lamm, Merrill Lee, Urban Lembeck, Ralph Levenberg, Norman Matthews, Henry Merritt, Joseph Merritt, Glenn W. McKassan, Andy Miller, Sally Blaine Millett, Carmen Morelli, Sam Moody, Ben Morin, John J. Morrett, Helen Cassiani Nestor, Humphrey O'Leary, John Olson, Cletis Overton, Jay Pardue, William Parks, Dominic Pellegrino, Robert Pelz, Robert Phillips, Glen Pilkington, Thomas Pollack, Joe Poster, Harry Rosenberry, Paul Reuter, Melvin Routt, Ben Saccone, Donald Schloat, Irvin C. Scott, Winston Shillito, Zoeth Skinner, Harry Stempin, Milton Strouse, Lester Tenney, Joe Vater, Harold Vick, Kenneth Vick, Sam Vlahon, John Walker, Joseph Ward, Edgar Whitcomb, George Wonneman, Milton Young.

We spoke with the veterans' families, whose tales, for the most part, were heartbreaking. This book does not begin to document the terrible aftereffects of war, what Dixon Wecter called the "warp in the wood." We easily could have written a second volume, and we apologize to the families for not being able to include much of the material they lavished on us. We thank them nonetheless for their many diaries, memoirs, photographs, official records, and interviews. Among the many who helped us were Evonne Ashton, Frederico Baldassarre, Barry Beutell, Eleanor Crowder Bjoring, Rose Bridges, Shawnee Brittan, Spenser Coleman, Florence Crago, Lora Cummins, Barbara Davidson, Minter Dial, Theresa Emerick, Bobbie Emken, John Espy, Nicoll F. Galbraith Jr., Jannis Robb Garred, Damon Gause, Laurie Giantonio, Kathleen Hastings, Dwayne Heisinger, Betty Huxtable, Henrietta Jackfert, Georgia Jordan, Mark Kelso, Catherine Lancaster, Virginia Lee, Cathie Levenberg, John Littig, Daphne Parks Major, Allison Robb Marks, Jessie Mann Mastin, Donnie Russell Mathis, Lorna Murray, Wanda Newkirk, Dennis O'Leary, Leonora O'Leary, Geraldine O'Neil, John Patterson, Mary Jane Pelz, Audrey Phillips, Gregory Rodriguez, Nancy Rosenberry, Kate Sheets, Anne

Shubin, Bobbie Simmons, Joan Keech Spann, Ann Lancaster Stevens, Shirley C. Temple, Jeanne Greeley Thayer, Jan Thompson, Carolyn Arnold Torrence, Helen Vater, Z. Taylor Vinson, Barbara Whittinghill, Irene Wonneman.

In our general research, we had the help of a number of unstinting supernumeraries—talented scholars and authors, experts in various fields, hardworking librarians and staff archivists, assorted professionals, part-time historians, and people from various walks of life who helped us collect and verify data or answered the hundreds of arcane questions that arose during a decade of research.

Deserving special mention are Thaddeus Holt, who supplied most of the material on Ned King; Stephen Craig, whose counsel allowed us to understand the dark side of human behavior (what some call "evil"); Sue Hart and Richard S. Wheeler, writers of the West who made sure we kept myth separated from reality; Cliff Roen, a twenty-first-century cowboy who works the old homestead at Hawk Creek and took us riding there; and Stanley Falk, whose seminal work on the death march stands still as the authoritative text.

Others who assisted in our inquiries are Kathy Aldrich, Dale Alger, Frances S. Anderson, Robert Bateman, Lois Bent, Gordon Berger, Alice Booher, Peter Brand, Karen Bratten, John and Betty Brookes, Charles Bryce, DeeDee Caidin, Clarence E. Campbell, Clarence Carnahan, Andrew Carroll, Eric Chase, Ken Cleerdin, Diana Cormer, Lou D'Andrea, Dorothy Riley Dempsey, Earl Dudley, Keith Edgerton, Eugene Eisenberg, Michael Engelberg, Ann Fadiman, Bob Fauth, John Fitzgerald, William Freeman, Joe Galloway, Dodds Giagonia, Eric Gillespie, Susan Hall, Ned Harrison, Sue Hart, Carl Hedin, Philip Heineman, Jean Hewlett, Will Howorth, Pat Hoy, Rick Huston, Jim Jeffries, Frank Jenista, Erin Johnson, Gordon Jones, Mervin R. Jones, Ruth Jones, Dave Karnos, Jerry D. Kelly, Jeanne Gingles, Thomas Leonard, Grace Linden, Brian Linn, Richard Long, Sarah Loria, Greg Michno, David and Linda and Andy Maraniss, Anne Matthews, Frank McGlothlin, Elizabeth McNamer, Scott Millikan, John Mitchell, Tom Murphy, Mike Murray, Charles Perle, Richard Pyle, Cliff Roen, Cristine Rom, Richard Rongstad, Richard Roper, Don Ross, Robert Ruby, Jeffrey L. Russell, Pam Ryder, Mary Sarnecky, Mattie Sink, W. C. Smith, David Scott Smith, Sheree Smith, Seth Solomonow, Richard Sommers, Roger J. Spiller, Kamiko Spodofora, Marion Squire, Kenneth Swan, Frank Tremaine, Leo Tuason, John Waggener, John Wallace, Michael Walsh, Steven Weingartner, Linda Wheeler, Thomas M. White, Richard Willstater, Garth Wilson, Fred Wolf, Laurel Wycoff. We also thank Ken Heller, who served with the occupation forces in Japan in 1945.

We appreciate the support of our colleagues at New York University. NYU has been good to our family. The university generously supported our research and provided an education for our two sons. It has been both our sponsor and our sanctuary. We offer special thanks to our students. We hope they see their lessons in these pages.

Our agent, Esther Newberg, has stood by us through decades of failure and a few, brief moments of success. John Glusman, our initial editor, helped shape the book in its early stages before moving on. Ann King was our first and most faithful reader. Senior editor Paul Elie of Farrar, Straus and Giroux took the completed manuscript and applied to it his considerable skill and craftsmanship for a final draft and polish. Georgia Cool shepherded the manuscript through to print.

We wrote this book for our sons, who are mentioned in the dedication, and for our late fathers, Jack Dempsey and Bernie Goldman, both combat veterans of World War II in Europe. We come from large extended families, ranks and files of brothers and sisters and cousins and in-laws, and we thank all of them (notably the newest, our daughter-in-law, Rachel Cahn Norman) for their loyalty, patience, and love.

INDEX

Abo-Abo River, 214

Abucay, 195–97

"active defense" strategy, 42

Agoo, 48

agriculture, 294, 296, 320

Aguinaldo, Emilio, 40

Alangan River, 145, 146–47, 149

Aldrich, Johnny, 229, 238, 240

Amaterasu, 22

amebiasis, 335

ammunition, 46, 66, 77, 84, 96, 100, 151; Japanese shortages of, 85, 89, 99

amnesia, 262, 273

Anaconda, Mont., 132, 133

Angeles, 76

Aoya, 77

Aquino, Tony, 175, 176

Araki, Sadao, 101

Arisan Maru, 305–308

Army, Japanese, *see* Japanese Imperial Army

Army, Philippine, *see* Philippine Commonwealth Army

Army, U.S., 9, 41, 42, 345, 350; enlistee report of, 39; *esprit de corps* vs. *esprit étroit* in, 39; Japanese invasion and, 43–51; MacArthur made commander of Far East forces of, 17; Philippines withdrawal of, 3, 42, 49–51, 58–60; in POW plan, 411n; in Quinauan

Point battle, 98–105; in second battle for Bataan, 136–50; *see also* 31st Infantry, U.S.

Army Air Corps, U.S., 63, 252, 333, 389; basic training in, 10–11; Filipino expectations of, 46–47; in MacArthur's plan, 43; mechanics of, 246–47; Philippine headquarters of, 21; Steele's enlisting in, 5, 9, 218; withdrawal and, 49–50; *see also* Clark Field; 19th Bombardment Group; Provisional Air Corps Infantry

Army Air Force Regional and Convalescent Hospital, 339

Army and Navy Club, 15

Army Department, U.S., 392

Army General Staff College, Japanese, 347

Army War Crimes Investigation Detachment, 354

Arnold, Henry H., 21

art, artists, 159–60; Steele as professor of, 6, 392–93, 395; Steele's education in, 387–91

Ashmead-Bartlett, Ellis, 82

Ashton, Paul, 182, 258–65; as fighting man, 258–59; at Tayabas Road site, 259–65, 415n

Asiatic Fleet, U.S., 19, 44, 298

Aspevig, Clyde, 395

Philippines, Filipinos, 3–6, 14–32, 36–51, 55–67, 266; "active defense" vs. "defense in depth" in, 42; as backwater, 3, 14; in Camp O'Donnell, 224–25, 229, 240–41; defense problem of, 41–42; guerrilla force in, 40–41, 162, 255, 415n; independence of, 39; Japan's bombing of, 3, 25–32, 44, 45; Japan's invasion of, 3, 32, 34–39, 44–51, 348, 402n; liberation of, 418n; MacArthur's views on likelihood of Japanese attack on, 17, 18, 400n; as potential target, 12, 44; as refugees, 193–95, 205, 412n; strategic value of, 3; surrender of, 233, 244; U.S. feeling of assurance in, 17–18; U.S. invasion of, 293, 305–306, 327; War Plan Orange for, 42, 49; Yamashita's failure in, 350

Philippine Scouts, 17, 41, 43, 60, 104, 179, 199, 403n; in Bataan Death March, 185; in Bataan defense, 85, 98; 57th Infantry of, 61–62; 12th Medical Regiment of, 258–59; in 26th Cavalry, 47

photographs, 169–70, 173, 192, 290–91, 295

Pierce, Henry, 260

Pilar, 205

Pinkston, Dan, 320, 330

"Plains, The," 83

pneumonia, 229, 260, 271, 335

Port Arthur, 24, 25, 82

Port Darwin, 125

Potsdam conference (1945), 328, 334

Poweleit, Alvin C., 44–45, 190, 202; at Camp O'Donnell, 225, 228, 230–31, 233

prison camps, 200, 268, 331, 332; see also Camp Cabanatuan; Camp O'Donnell; Omine-machi

prisoner exchange, 293

Prisoner of War Information Bureau, Japanese, 293

prisoners of war, 6, 129, 154–58, 161–214, 219–42, 244, 246–331, 389, 393; beating of, 158, 164, 166–67, 170–71, 175, 177, 182, 185, 193, 197, 376; in Bilibid Prison, see Bilibid Prison; British, 163, 293, 320–21, 322, 325; camps for, see Camp Cabanatuan; Camp O'Donnell; Omine-machi; in death march, see Bataan Death March; evacuation plan for, 162–63; Imperial Army plan for, 411n–12n; international law and, 161, 207, 244, 293, 352, 377; Japanese headquarters' call for, 92; Kinoshita as, 105–106, 107; Morin as, 48, 403n; number of, 162, 325, 411n, 412n; pack carrying of, 156, 158, 164, 169; Pantingan River massacre and, 202–14, 364–65, 413n; searching and looting of, 155, 156, 164–66, 169–70; in transport ships, 297–99, 301–305, 305–17; in work details, 241–42, 246–65, 262–63, 274, 293–94; see also Tayabas Road

Prohibition, 131

Provisional Air Corps Infantry (Flying Infantry), 66–67, 104, 127–29; in Bataan Death March, 171, 172–73, 177, 182; in second battle for Bataan, 139–40, 145, 147–49

Prussians, 23, 64

Pryor Mountains, 217

psychiatrists, 332, 335

Puerto Princesa, 287

Quezon, Manuel, 39

Quinauan Point, 93, 95; battle for, 98–105, 113

quinine, 205, 228, 232, 235, 257, 271, 273, 278–79

Quinn, Michael, 222

racism, race, 18, 292, 372

radios, 19, 57, 116, 394–96, 418n; rumors and, 279; shortwave, 13, 123

surrender (*cont.*)

    Corregidor, 233–34, 244, 268, 280; of Germany, 328; of Homma, 344, 347, 349; as impermissible to Japanese, 101, 104–105; of Japan, 328, 330–31, 334, 348, 418*n*; King's views of, 146, 147, 149–54, 162, 223; of Philippines, 233, 244; of Steele, 155–56, 340, 389; Wainwright's rejection of, 147

survival of the fittest, 193, 231

Survivor (Grosz), 389

Sutherland, Richard K., 21, 123, 125, 401*n*

Suzuki, Kantarō, 349

swords, 154, 166, 179, 208, 222, 286, 289

Takada, Naokitsu, 348

Takao, 20, 303, 314–15

Takatsu, Toshimitsu, 375, 411*n*, 412*n*

Takeuchi (regimental commander), 86

Takeuchi, Tozo, 164

tanks: Japanese, 46, 48, 155–56, 160, 234; in Quinauan Point battle, 103, 104; U.S., 47–48, 103, 104

tao (local people), 193–97; as kith and kin, 195–97; as refugees, 193–95

Tarawa, 291

Tarlac Province, 163, 221–22; *see also* Camp O'Donnell; Capas

Tayabas Road, 250–65, 268, 270, 291, 295, 308, 337; Ashton at, 259–65, 415*n*; beatings at, 254, 256, 257; bets of guards at, 256; burials at, 254–55, 265; comradeship at, 252; disease at, 253–57, 259–65; escape from, 255, 265; food at, 253, 254, 256, 257; God's Own Medicine at, 264–65; guards' expressions of pity at, 257–58; rocky encampment at, 250–51, 259, 263

Teikai Maru, 57

telephones, 333–34, 336

Tenney, Laura, 173, 192

Tenney, Lester, 173, 191–92

Teyral, John, 389

Thanksgiving, 334, 340, 341

thiamine (vitamin B_1), 272, 275

31st Infantry, U.S., 15, 61, 143, 144, 162, 282

Thomas, Ed, 175, 180

Tiawir River, 90, 135, 138, 140

Time, 364, 367

Times, The (London), 82

Tisdelle, Achille C., 378, 409–10*n*

Tojo, Hideki, 55, 112, 293, 343, 348, 352, 374

Tokyo, 23, 41, 280, 343, 344, 347–48, 367, 378; bombing of, 328; Imperial General Staff in, 64–65; MacArthur in, 354, 355, 359–60; prisons in, 351–52, 418*n*; U.S. troops in, 331, 418*n*; War Ministry in, 292–93; Yasukuni Shrine in, 101, 406*n*

Tokyo Rose, 116

Tokyo War Crimes Tribunals, 353, 413*n*, 418*n*

Toland, John, 407*n*, 410*n*

Toolen, Yvonne, 258

torpedoes, 307

Toshino, Junsaburo, 310, 314, 315–16

Trail 8, 202–203

trains, 163, 200, 219, 221, 247, 249, 344; in Japan, 305, 318, 331–32; in United States, 218, 340–41

transport ships, 297–99, 301–17, 336, 417*n*; as hellships, 305, 306, 337, 416*n*; number of, 305, 416*n*

Trivel, Fred, 110

trucks, 150, 166; Japanese, 74, 85, 163, 170–73, 181, 224, 242, 246, 247, 268, 411*n*–12*n*

Trudeau, Arthur G., 369, 378

Truman, Harry, 353

Tsuchihashi, Yuichi, 66, 74

Tsuji, Masanobu, 371–72, 420*n*

Tsunehiro, Nariyoshi, 92–96, 98–101, 103, 104; Kimura's message from, 98–99; recovery of body of, 406*n*